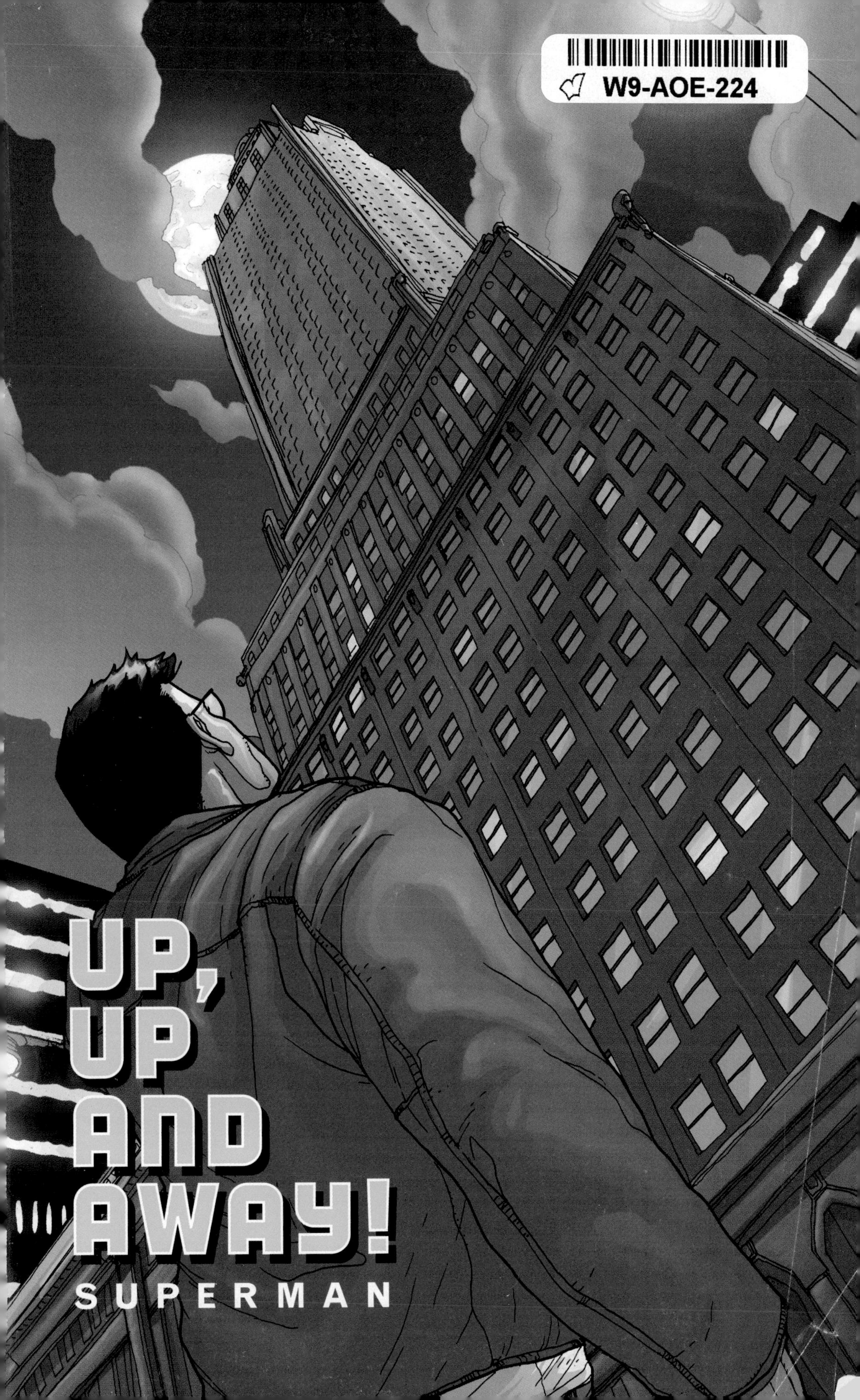
UP,
UP
AND
AWAY!
SUPERMAN

SUPER

Kurt Busiek
Geoff Johns
WRITERS

Pete Woods
Renato Guedes
ARTISTS

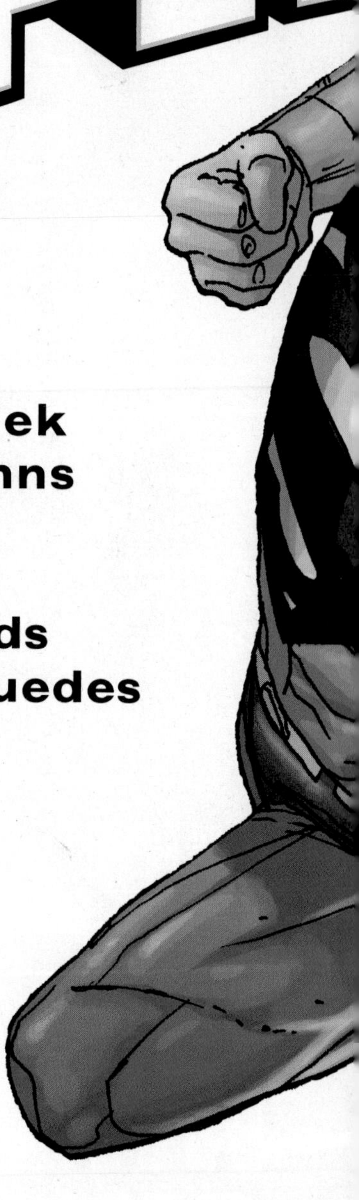

UP, UP AND AWAY!

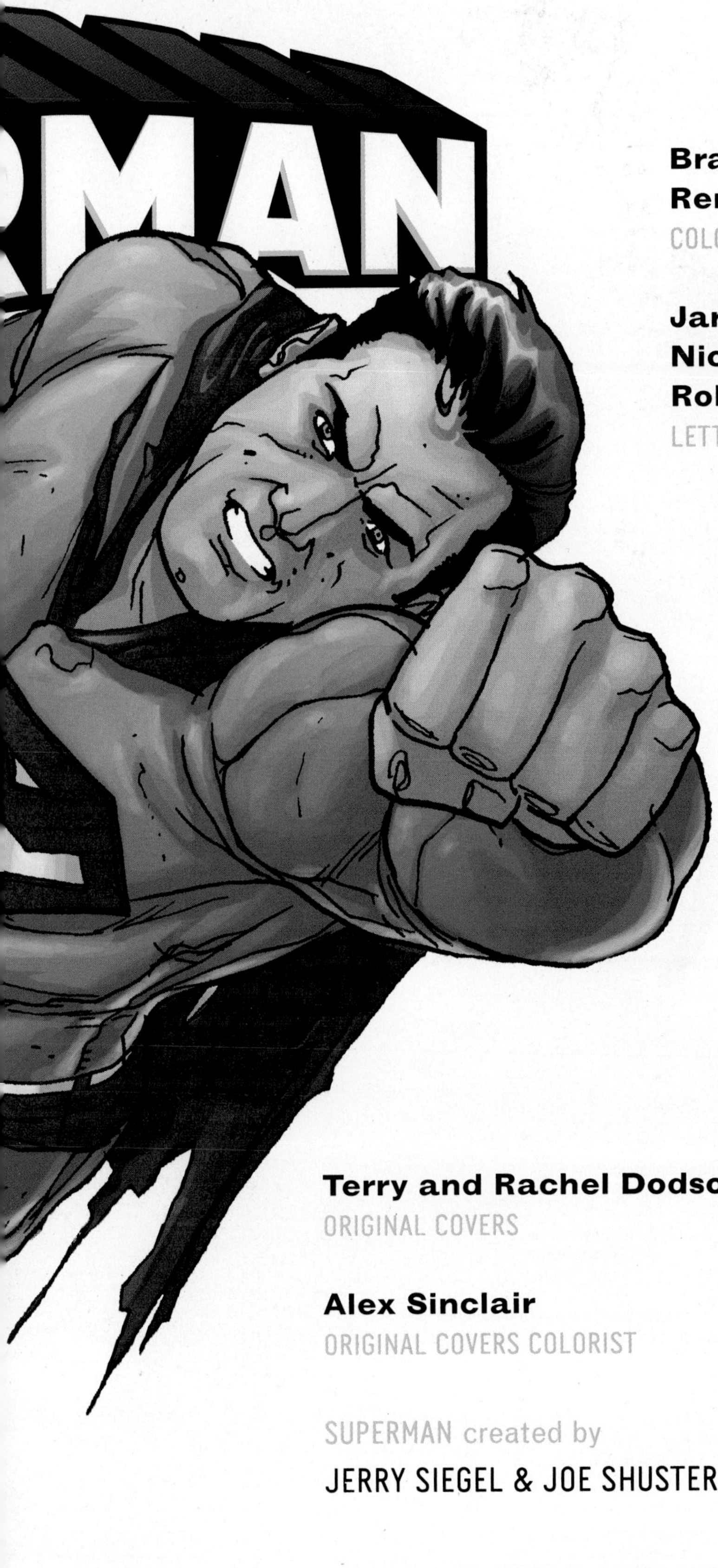

Brad Anderson
Renato Guedes
COLORISTS

Jared K. Fletcher
Nick J. Napolitano
Rob Leigh
LETTERERS

Terry and Rachel Dodson
ORIGINAL COVERS

Alex Sinclair
ORIGINAL COVERS COLORIST

SUPERMAN created by
JERRY SIEGEL & JOE SHUSTER

SUPERMAN: UP, UP AND AWAY!
Published by DC Comics. Cover, introduction, and compilation copyright
© 2006 DC Comics. All Rights Reserved.

Originally published in single magazine form in SUPERMAN 650-653 and
ACTION COMICS 837-840. Copyright © 2006 DC Comics. All Rights Reserved.
All characters, their distinctive likenesses and related elements featured
in this publication are trademarks of DC Comics.
The stories, characters and incidents featured in this publication are entirely fictional.
DC Comics does not read or accept unsolicited submissions of ideas, stories or artwork.

DC Comics, 1700 Broadway, New York, NY 10019
A Warner Bros. Entertainment Company
Printed in Canada. First Printing.
ISBN: 1-4012-0954-8. ISBN 13: 978-1-4012-0954-4.
Cover illustration by Terry and Rachel Dodson. Cover color by Alex Sinclair.
Publication design by Amelia Grohman.

Following the world-shattering event known as the Infinite Crisis,
the stories of the DC Universe catapulted ahead one year when
the World's Greatest Super-Heroes continue their adventures
in new settings and situations!

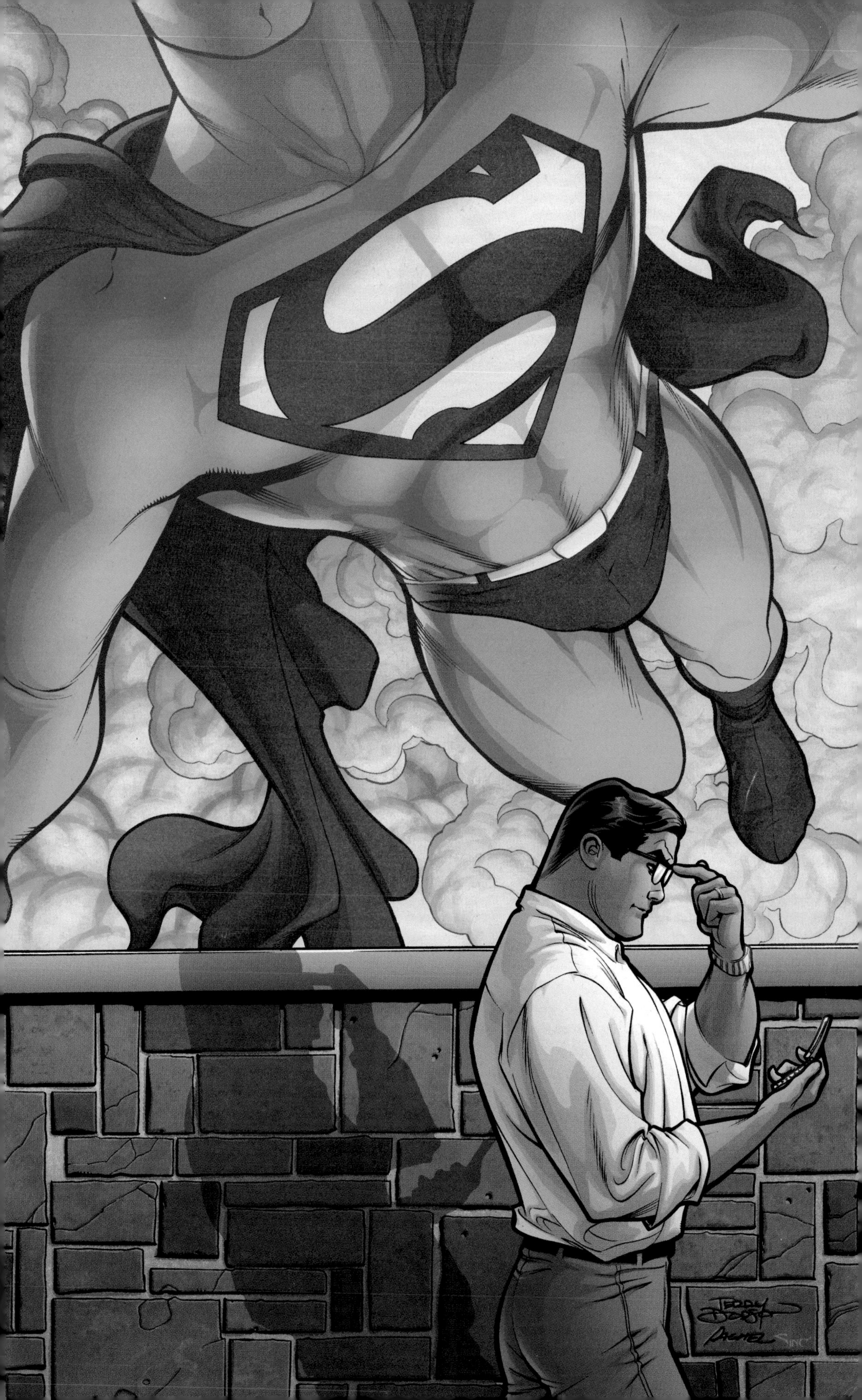

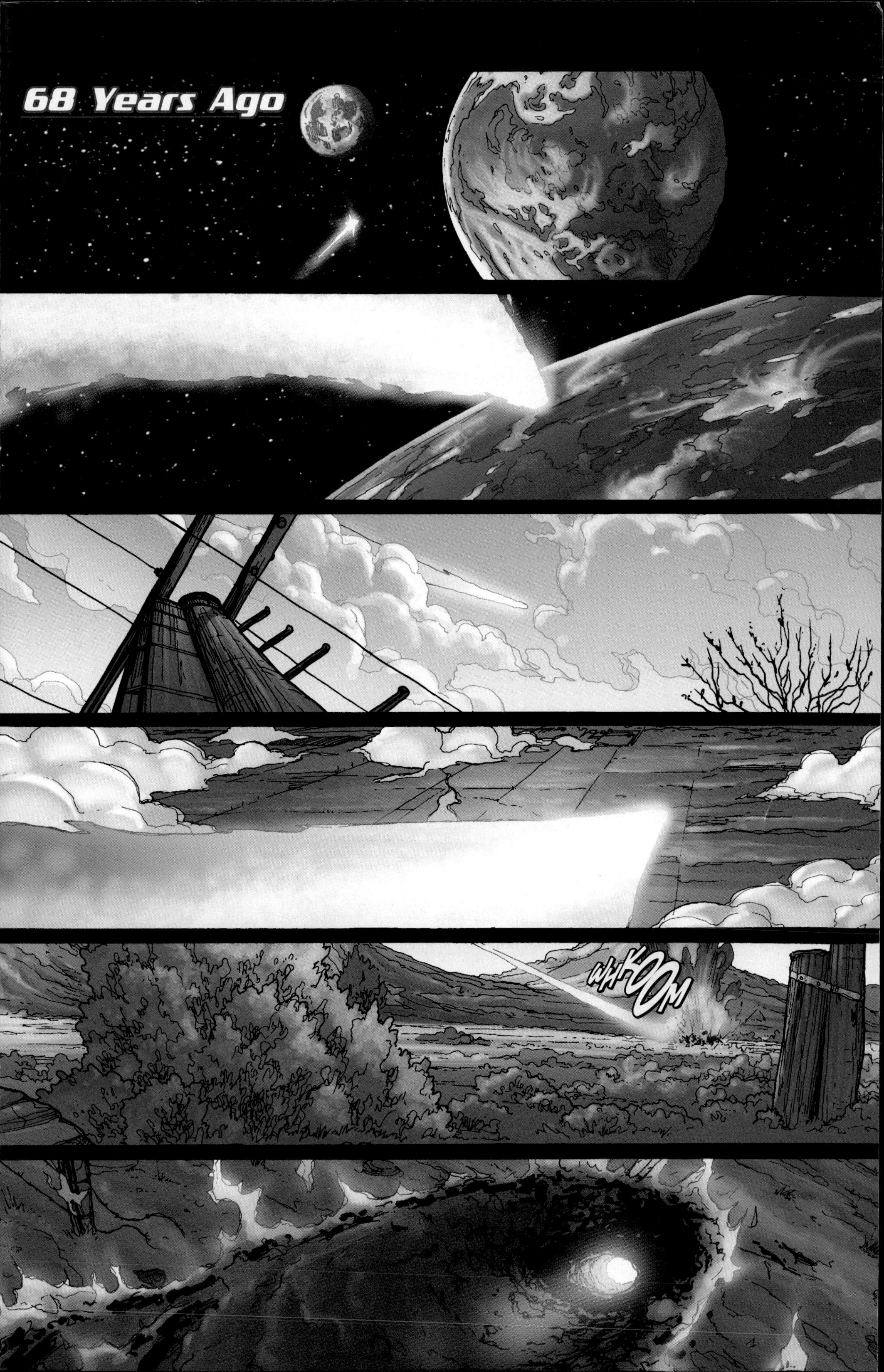
68 Years Ago
WHHKOOM

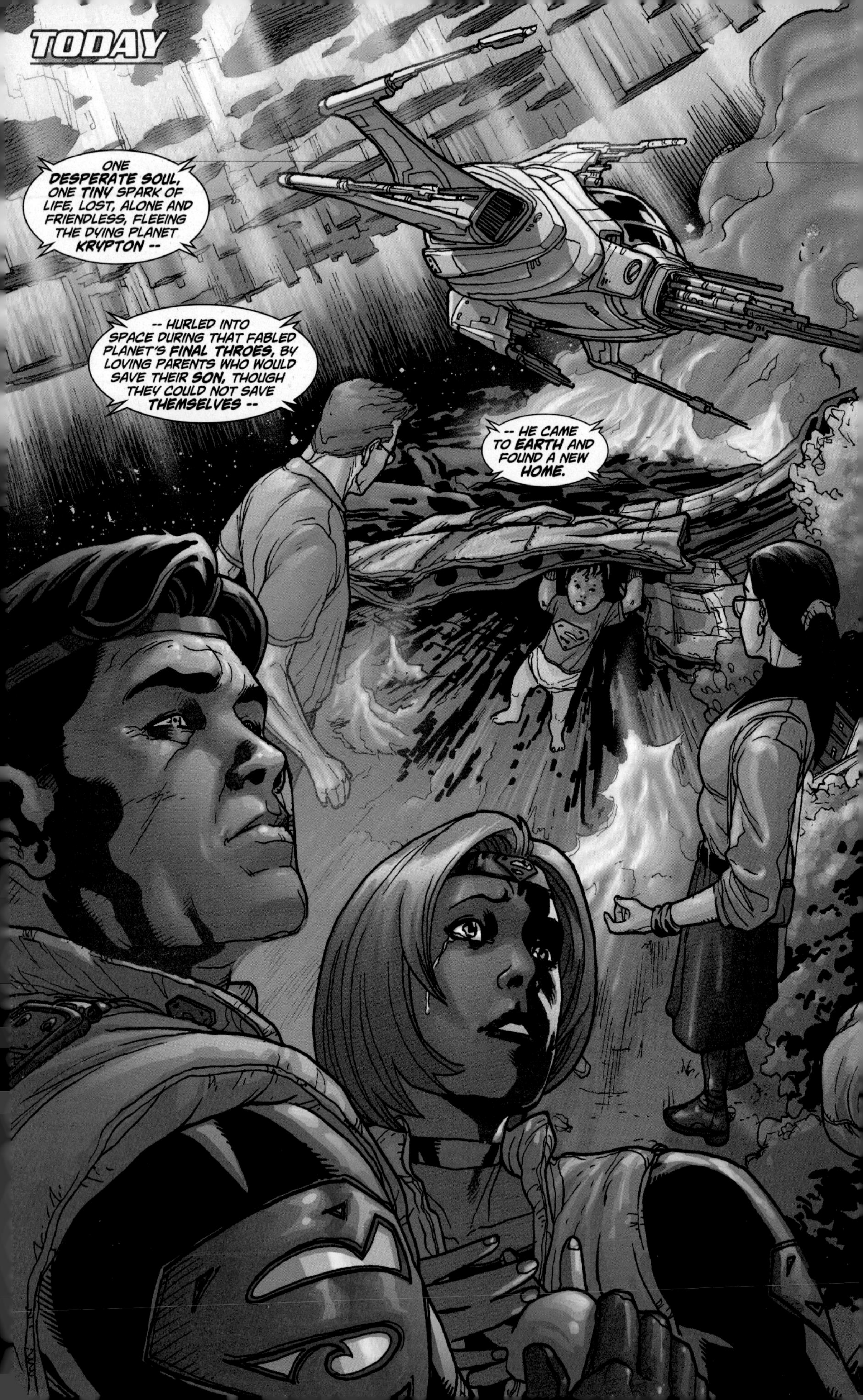
TODAY
ONE DESPERATE SOUL, ONE TINY SPARK OF LIFE, LOST, ALONE AND FRIENDLESS, FLEEING THE DYING PLANET KRYPTON --
-- HURLED INTO SPACE DURING THAT FABLED PLANET'S FINAL THROES, BY LOVING PARENTS WHO WOULD SAVE THEIR SON, THOUGH THEY COULD NOT SAVE THEMSELVES --
-- HE CAME TO EARTH AND FOUND A NEW HOME.

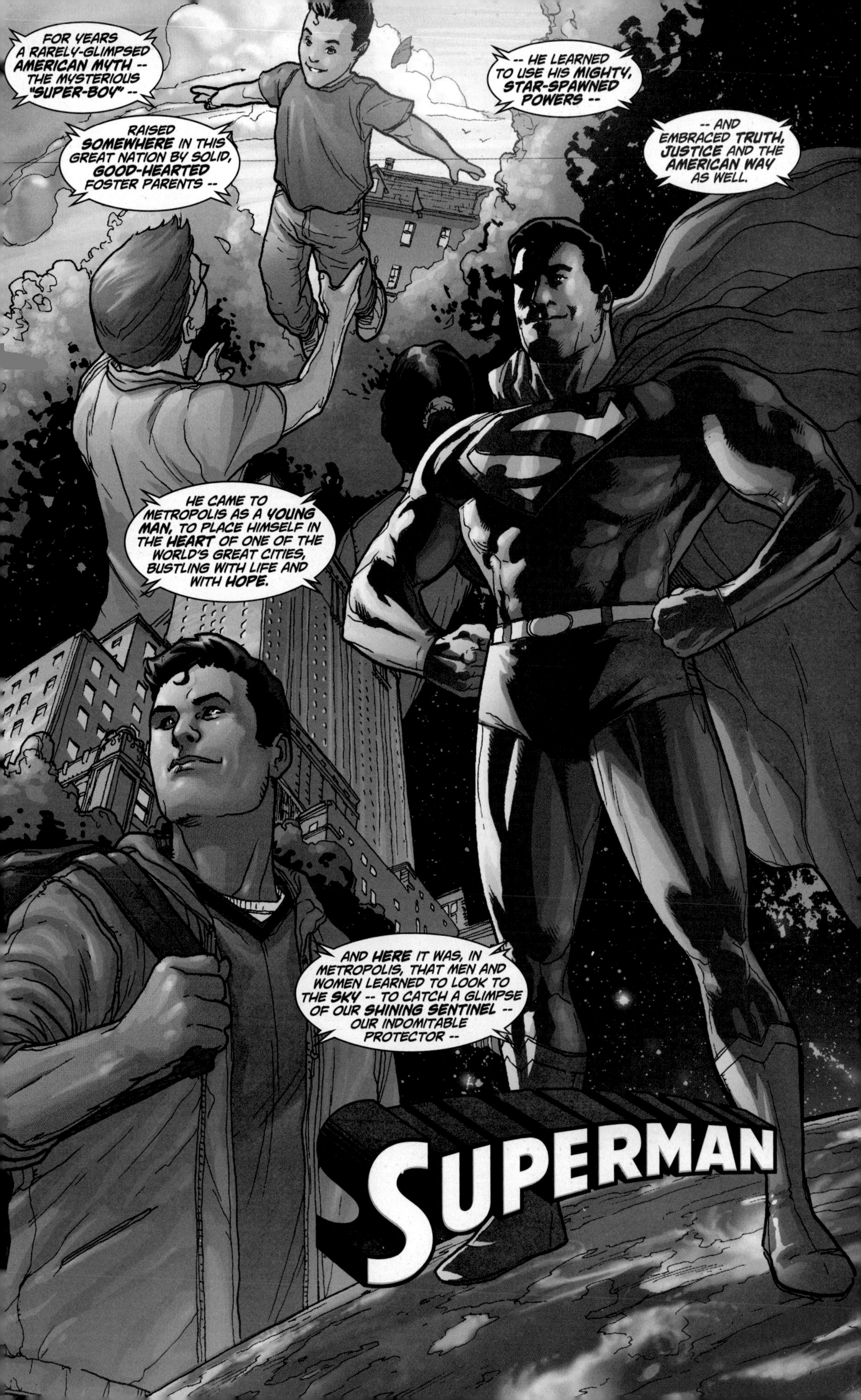
FOR YEARS A RARELY-GLIMPSED AMERICAN MYTH -- THE MYSTERIOUS "SUPER-BOY" --
RAISED SOMEWHERE IN THIS GREAT NATION BY SOLID, GOOD-HEARTED FOSTER PARENTS --
-- HE LEARNED TO USE HIS MIGHTY, STAR-SPAWNED POWERS --
-- AND EMBRACED TRUTH, JUSTICE AND THE AMERICAN WAY AS WELL.
HE CAME TO METROPOLIS AS A YOUNG MAN, TO PLACE HIMSELF IN THE HEART OF ONE OF THE WORLD'S GREAT CITIES, BUSTLING WITH LIFE AND WITH HOPE.
AND HERE IT WAS, IN METROPOLIS, THAT MEN AND WOMEN LEARNED TO LOOK TO THE SKY -- TO CATCH A GLIMPSE OF OUR SHINING SENTINEL -- OUR INDOMITABLE PROTECTOR --
SUPERMAN

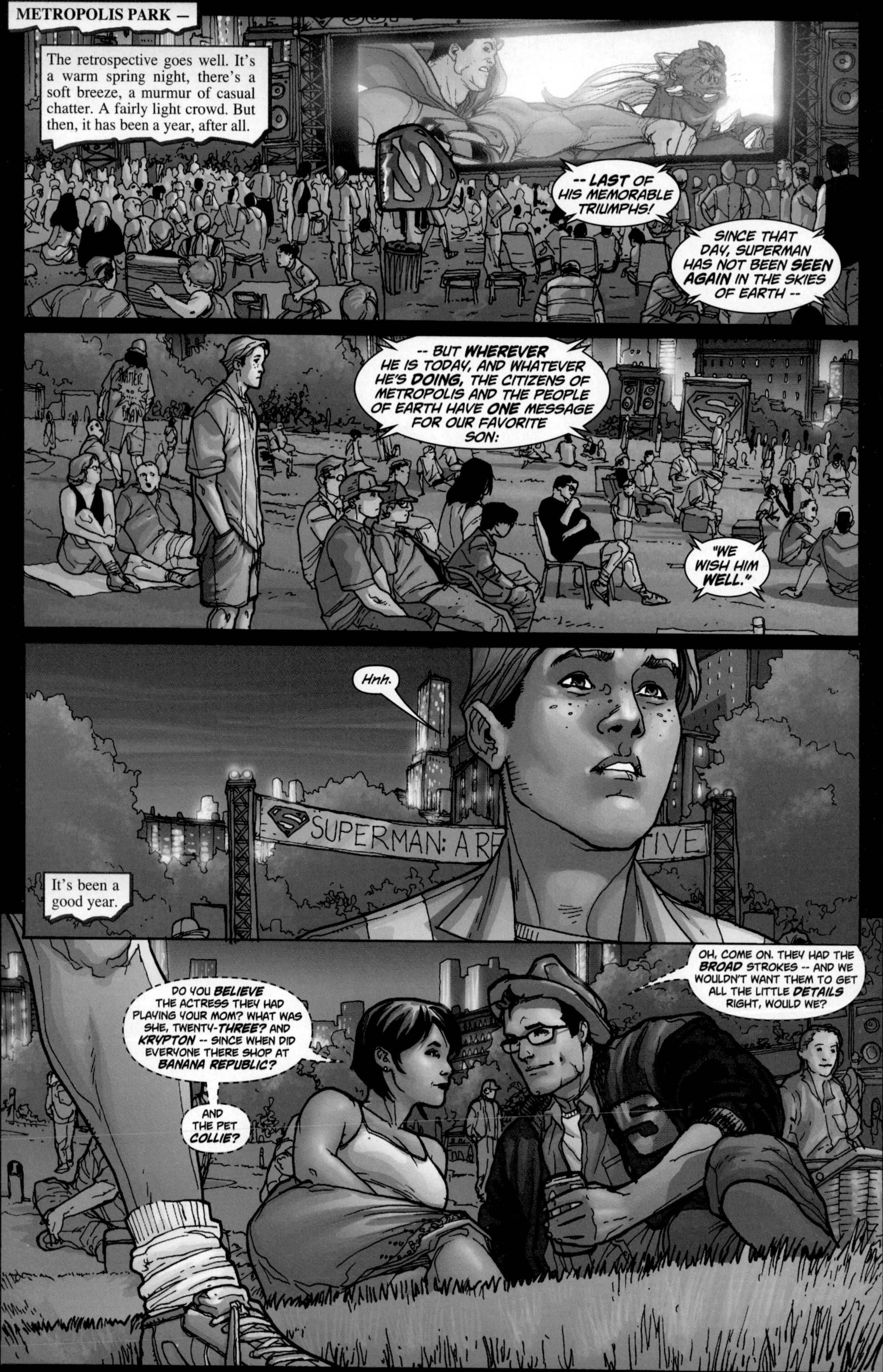
METROPOLIS PARK —
The retrospective goes well. It's a warm spring night, there's a soft breeze, a murmur of casual chatter. A fairly light crowd. But then, it has been a year, after all.
-- LAST OF HIS MEMORABLE TRIUMPHS!
SINCE THAT DAY, SUPERMAN HAS NOT BEEN SEEN AGAIN IN THE SKIES OF EARTH --
-- BUT WHEREVER HE IS TODAY, AND WHATEVER HE'S DOING, THE CITIZENS OF METROPOLIS AND THE PEOPLE OF EARTH HAVE ONE MESSAGE FOR OUR FAVORITE SON:
"WE WISH HIM WELL."
Hnh.
SUPERMAN: A R
TIVE
It's been a good year.
DO YOU BELIEVE THE ACTRESS THEY HAD PLAYING YOUR MOM? WHAT WAS SHE, TWENTY-THREE? AND KRYPTON -- SINCE WHEN DID EVERYONE THERE SHOP AT BANANA REPUBLIC?
AND THE PET COLLIE?
OH, COME ON. THEY HAD THE BROAD STROKES -- AND WE WOULDN'T WANT THEM TO GET ALL THE LITTLE DETAILS RIGHT, WOULD WE?

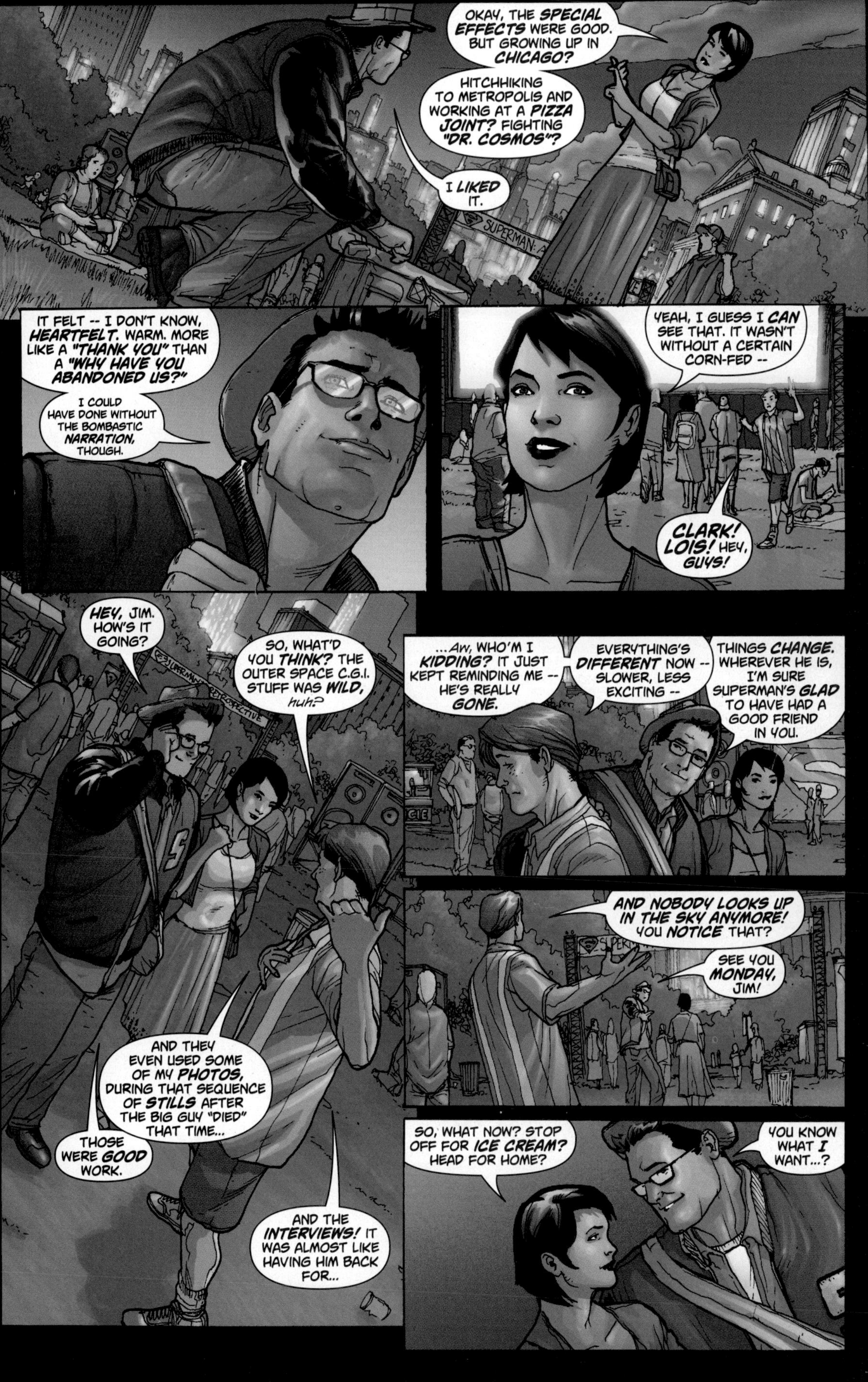
OKAY, THE SPECIAL EFFECTS WERE GOOD. BUT GROWING UP IN CHICAGO?
HITCHHIKING TO METROPOLIS AND WORKING AT A PIZZA JOINT? FIGHTING "DR. COSMOS"?
I LIKED IT.
SUPERMAN:
IT FELT -- I DON'T KNOW, HEARTFELT. WARM. MORE LIKE A "THANK YOU" THAN A "WHY HAVE YOU ABANDONED US?"
I COULD HAVE DONE WITHOUT THE BOMBASTIC NARRATION, THOUGH.
YEAH, I GUESS I CAN SEE THAT. IT WASN'T WITHOUT A CERTAIN CORN-FED --
CLARK! LOIS! HEY, GUYS!
HEY, JIM. HOW'S IT GOING?
SO, WHAT'D YOU THINK? THE OUTER SPACE C.G.I. STUFF WAS WILD, huh?
AND THEY EVEN USED SOME OF MY PHOTOS, DURING THAT SEQUENCE OF STILLS AFTER THE BIG GUY "DIED" THAT TIME...
THOSE WERE GOOD WORK.
AND THE INTERVIEWS! IT WAS ALMOST LIKE HAVING HIM BACK FOR...
...Aw, WHO'M I KIDDING? IT JUST KEPT REMINDING ME -- HE'S REALLY GONE.
EVERYTHING'S DIFFERENT NOW -- SLOWER, LESS EXCITING --
THINGS CHANGE. WHEREVER HE IS, I'M SURE SUPERMAN'S GLAD TO HAVE HAD A GOOD FRIEND IN YOU.
AND NOBODY LOOKS UP IN THE SKY ANYMORE! YOU NOTICE THAT?
SEE YOU MONDAY, JIM!
SO, WHAT NOW? STOP OFF FOR ICE CREAM? HEAD FOR HOME?
YOU KNOW WHAT I WANT...?

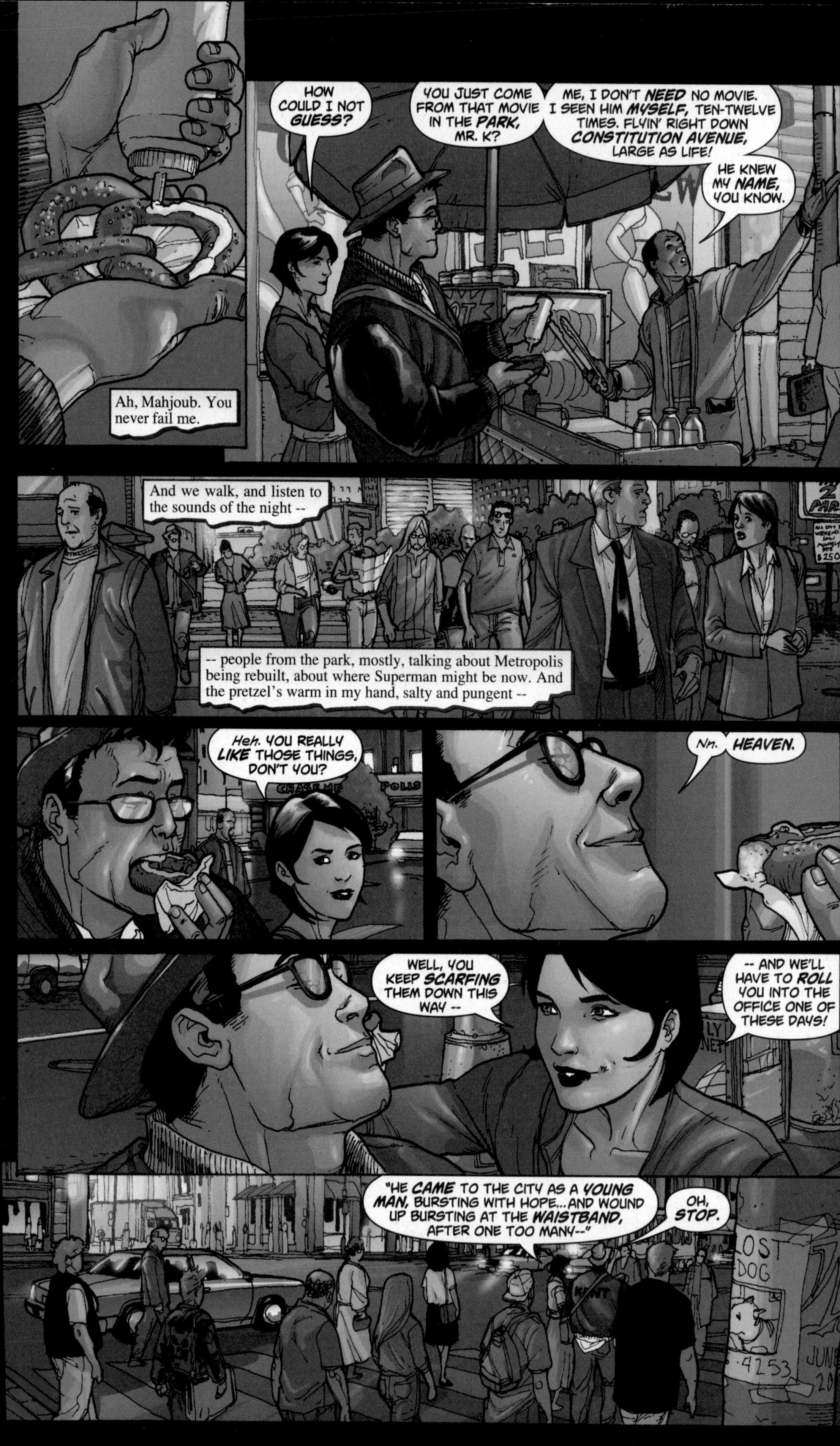
Ah, Mahjoub. You never fail me.
HOW COULD I NOT GUESS?
YOU JUST COME FROM THAT MOVIE IN THE PARK, MR. K?
ME, I DON'T NEED NO MOVIE. I SEEN HIM MYSELF, TEN-TWELVE TIMES. FLYIN' RIGHT DOWN CONSTITUTION AVENUE, LARGE AS LIFE!
HE KNEW MY NAME, YOU KNOW.
And we walk, and listen to the sounds of the night --
-- people from the park, mostly, talking about Metropolis being rebuilt, about where Superman might be now. And the pretzel's warm in my hand, salty and pungent --
Heh. YOU REALLY LIKE THOSE THINGS, DON'T YOU?
Nn. HEAVEN.
WELL, YOU KEEP SCARFING THEM DOWN THIS WAY --
-- AND WE'LL HAVE TO ROLL YOU INTO THE OFFICE ONE OF THESE DAYS!
"HE CAME TO THE CITY AS A YOUNG MAN, BURSTING WITH HOPE...AND WOUND UP BURSTING AT THE WAISTBAND, AFTER ONE TOO MANY--"
OH, STOP.
LOST DOG

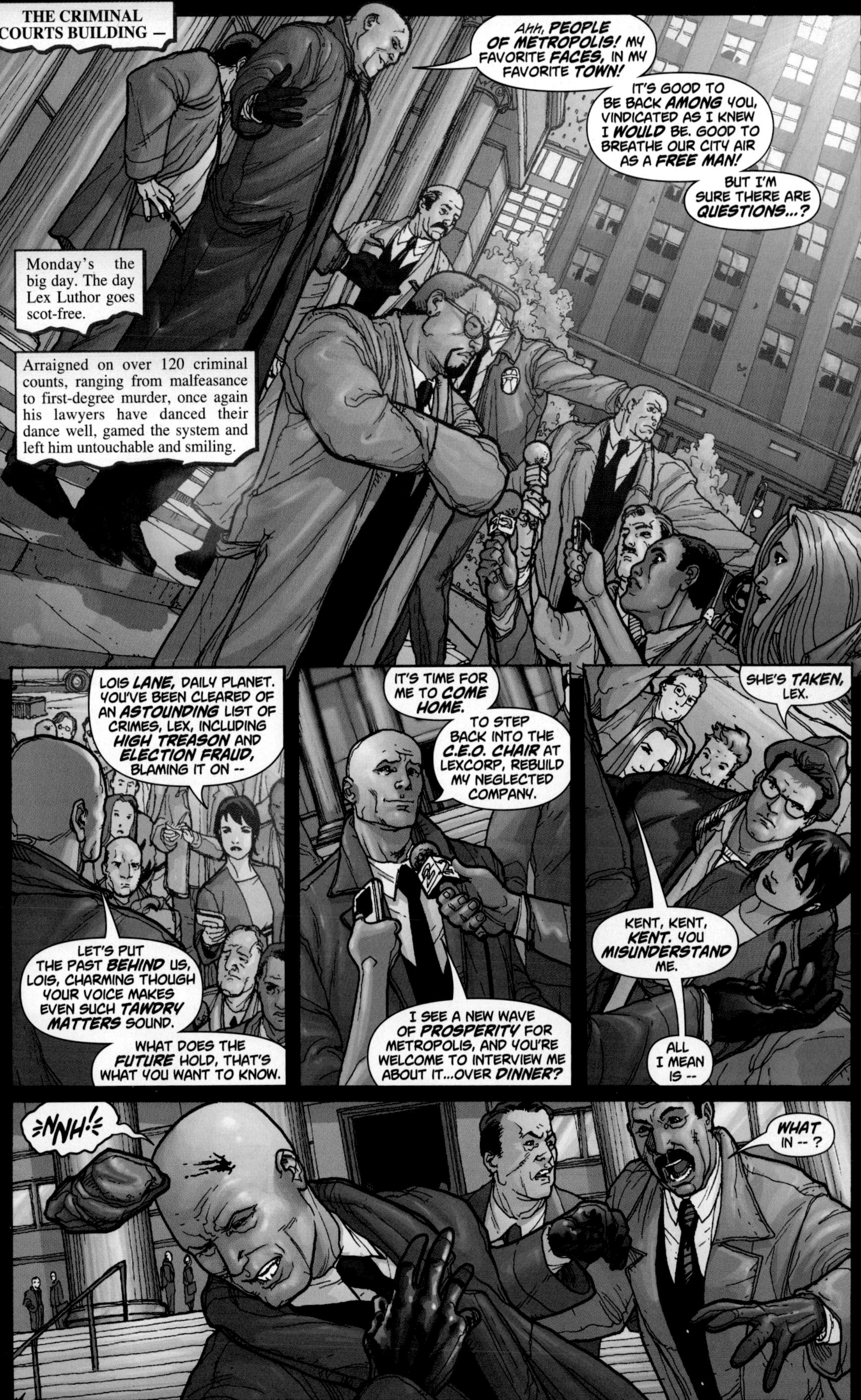
THE CRIMINAL COURTS BUILDING —
Ahh, PEOPLE OF METROPOLIS! MY FAVORITE FACES, IN MY FAVORITE TOWN!
IT'S GOOD TO BE BACK AMONG YOU, VINDICATED AS I KNEW I WOULD BE. GOOD TO BREATHE OUR CITY AIR AS A FREE MAN!
BUT I'M SURE THERE ARE QUESTIONS...?
Monday's the big day. The day Lex Luthor goes scot-free.
Arraigned on over 120 criminal counts, ranging from malfeasance to first-degree murder, once again his lawyers have danced their dance well, gamed the system and left him untouchable and smiling.
LOIS LANE, DAILY PLANET. YOU'VE BEEN CLEARED OF AN ASTOUNDING LIST OF CRIMES, LEX, INCLUDING HIGH TREASON AND ELECTION FRAUD, BLAMING IT ON --
LET'S PUT THE PAST BEHIND US, LOIS, CHARMING THOUGH YOUR VOICE MAKES EVEN SUCH TAWDRY MATTERS SOUND.
WHAT DOES THE FUTURE HOLD, THAT'S WHAT YOU WANT TO KNOW.
IT'S TIME FOR ME TO COME HOME.
TO STEP BACK INTO THE C.E.O. CHAIR AT LEXCORP, REBUILD MY NEGLECTED COMPANY.
I SEE A NEW WAVE OF PROSPERITY FOR METROPOLIS, AND YOU'RE WELCOME TO INTERVIEW ME ABOUT IT...OVER DINNER?
SHE'S TAKEN, LEX.
KENT, KENT, KENT. YOU MISUNDERSTAND ME.
ALL I MEAN IS --
NNH!
WHAT IN -- ?

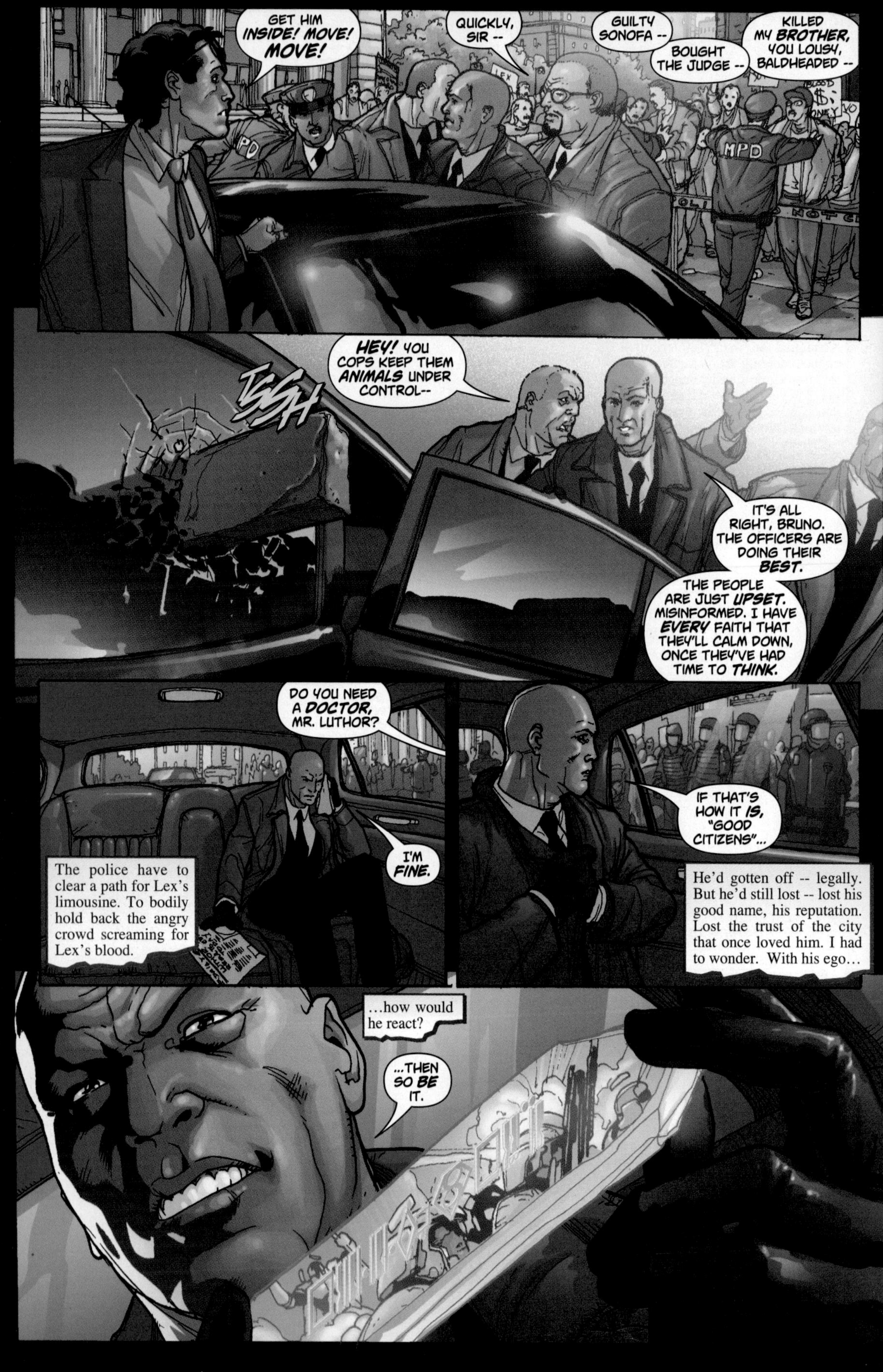
GET HIM INSIDE! MOVE! MOVE!
QUICKLY, SIR --
GUILTY SONOFA --
BOUGHT THE JUDGE --
KILLED MY BROTHER, YOU LOUSY, BALDHEADED --
MPD
HEY! YOU COPS KEEP THEM ANIMALS UNDER CONTROL--
IT'S ALL RIGHT, BRUNO. THE OFFICERS ARE DOING THEIR BEST.
THE PEOPLE ARE JUST UPSET. MISINFORMED. I HAVE EVERY FAITH THAT THEY'LL CALM DOWN, ONCE THEY'VE HAD TIME TO THINK.
DO YOU NEED A DOCTOR, MR. LUTHOR?
I'M FINE.
The police have to clear a path for Lex's limousine. To bodily hold back the angry crowd screaming for Lex's blood.
IF THAT'S HOW IT IS, "GOOD CITIZENS"...
He'd gotten off -- legally. But he'd still lost -- lost his good name, his reputation. Lost the trust of the city that once loved him. I had to wonder. With his ego…
…how would he react?
...THEN SO BE IT.

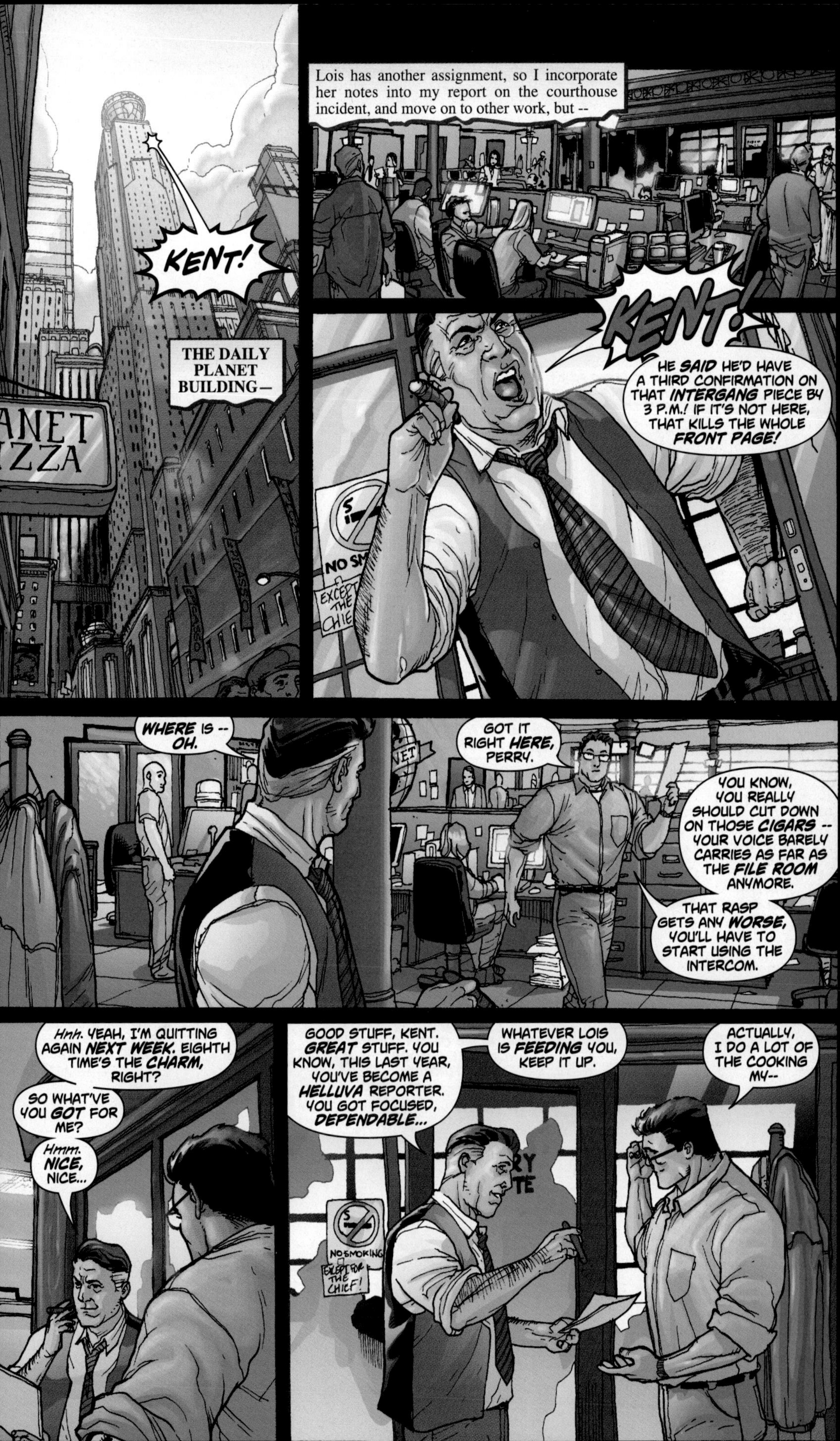
KENT!
THE DAILY PLANET BUILDING—
ANET
IZZA
Lois has another assignment, so I incorporate her notes into my report on the courthouse incident, and move on to other work, but --
KENT!
HE SAID HE'D HAVE A THIRD CONFIRMATION ON THAT INTERGANG PIECE BY 3 P.M.! IF IT'S NOT HERE, THAT KILLS THE WHOLE FRONT PAGE!
NO SM
EXCEPT THE CHIE
WHERE IS -- OH.
GOT IT RIGHT HERE, PERRY.
YOU KNOW, YOU REALLY SHOULD CUT DOWN ON THOSE CIGARS -- YOUR VOICE BARELY CARRIES AS FAR AS THE FILE ROOM ANYMORE.
THAT RASP GETS ANY WORSE, YOU'LL HAVE TO START USING THE INTERCOM.
Hnh. YEAH, I'M QUITTING AGAIN NEXT WEEK. EIGHTH TIME'S THE CHARM, RIGHT?
SO WHAT'VE YOU GOT FOR ME?
Hmm. NICE, NICE...
GOOD STUFF, KENT. GREAT STUFF. YOU KNOW, THIS LAST YEAR, YOU'VE BECOME A HELLUVA REPORTER. YOU GOT FOCUSED, DEPENDABLE...
WHATEVER LOIS IS FEEDING YOU, KEEP IT UP.
ACTUALLY, I DO A LOT OF THE COOKING MY--
NO SMOKING
EXCEPT FOR THE CHIEF!

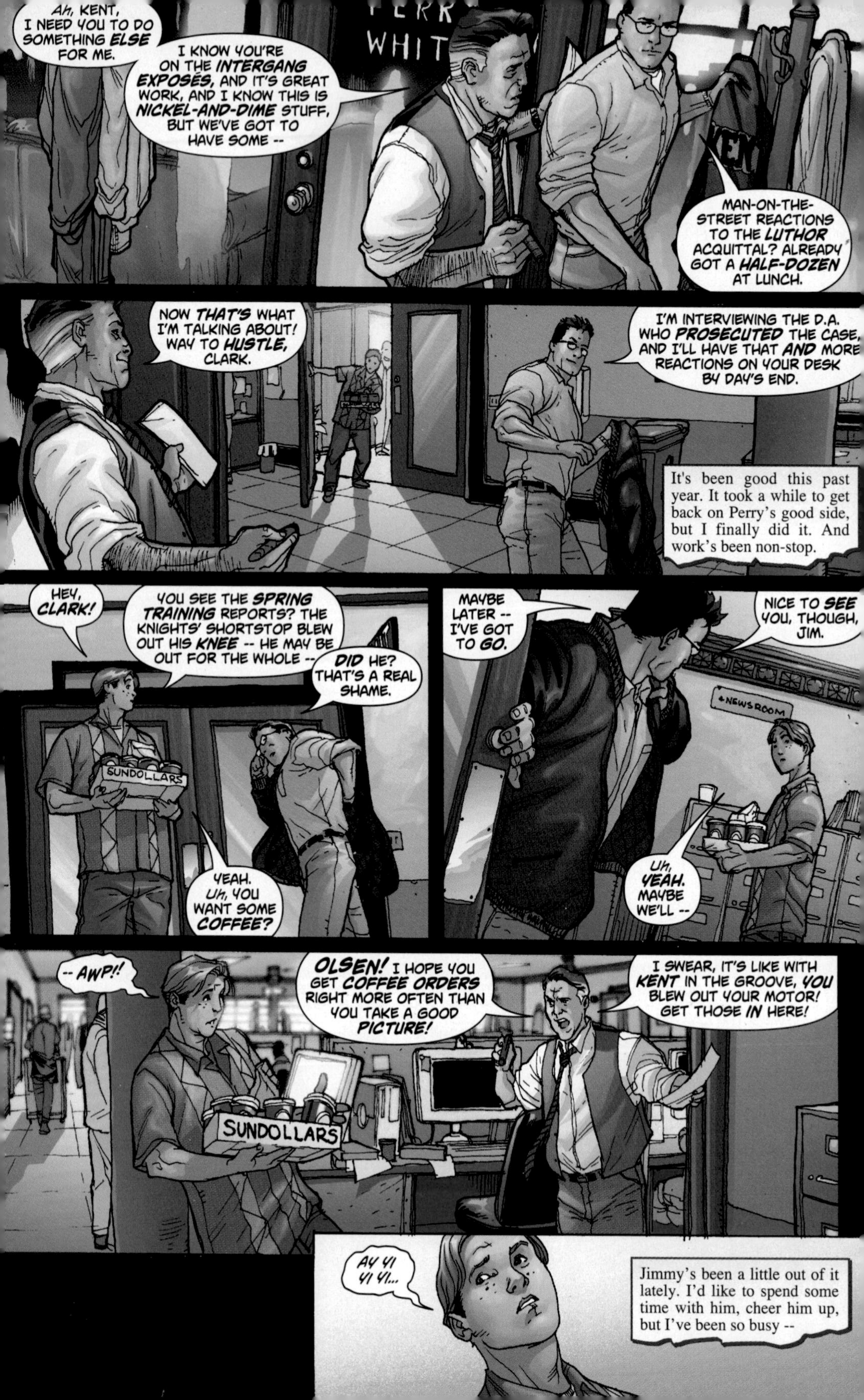

PERRY WHITE
AH, KENT, I NEED YOU TO DO SOMETHING ELSE FOR ME.
I KNOW YOU'RE ON THE INTERGANG EXPOSÉS, AND IT'S GREAT WORK, AND I KNOW THIS IS NICKEL-AND-DIME STUFF, BUT WE'VE GOT TO HAVE SOME --
KENT
MAN-ON-THE-STREET REACTIONS TO THE LUTHOR ACQUITTAL? ALREADY GOT A HALF-DOZEN AT LUNCH.
NOW THAT'S WHAT I'M TALKING ABOUT! WAY TO HUSTLE, CLARK.
I'M INTERVIEWING THE D.A. WHO PROSECUTED THE CASE, AND I'LL HAVE THAT AND MORE REACTIONS ON YOUR DESK BY DAY'S END.
It's been good this past year. It took a while to get back on Perry's good side, but I finally did it. And work's been non-stop.
HEY, CLARK!
YOU SEE THE SPRING TRAINING REPORTS? THE KNIGHTS' SHORTSTOP BLEW OUT HIS KNEE -- HE MAY BE OUT FOR THE WHOLE --
DID HE? THAT'S A REAL SHAME.
SUNDOLLARS
YEAH. UH, YOU WANT SOME COFFEE?
MAYBE LATER -- I'VE GOT TO GO.
NICE TO SEE YOU, THOUGH, JIM.
←NEWSROOM
UH, YEAH. MAYBE WE'LL --
-- AWP!!
OLSEN! I HOPE YOU GET COFFEE ORDERS RIGHT MORE OFTEN THAN YOU TAKE A GOOD PICTURE!
I SWEAR, IT'S LIKE WITH KENT IN THE GROOVE, YOU BLEW OUT YOUR MOTOR! GET THOSE IN HERE!
SUNDOLLARS
AY YI YI YI...
Jimmy's been a little out of it lately. I'd like to spend some time with him, cheer him up, but I've been so busy --

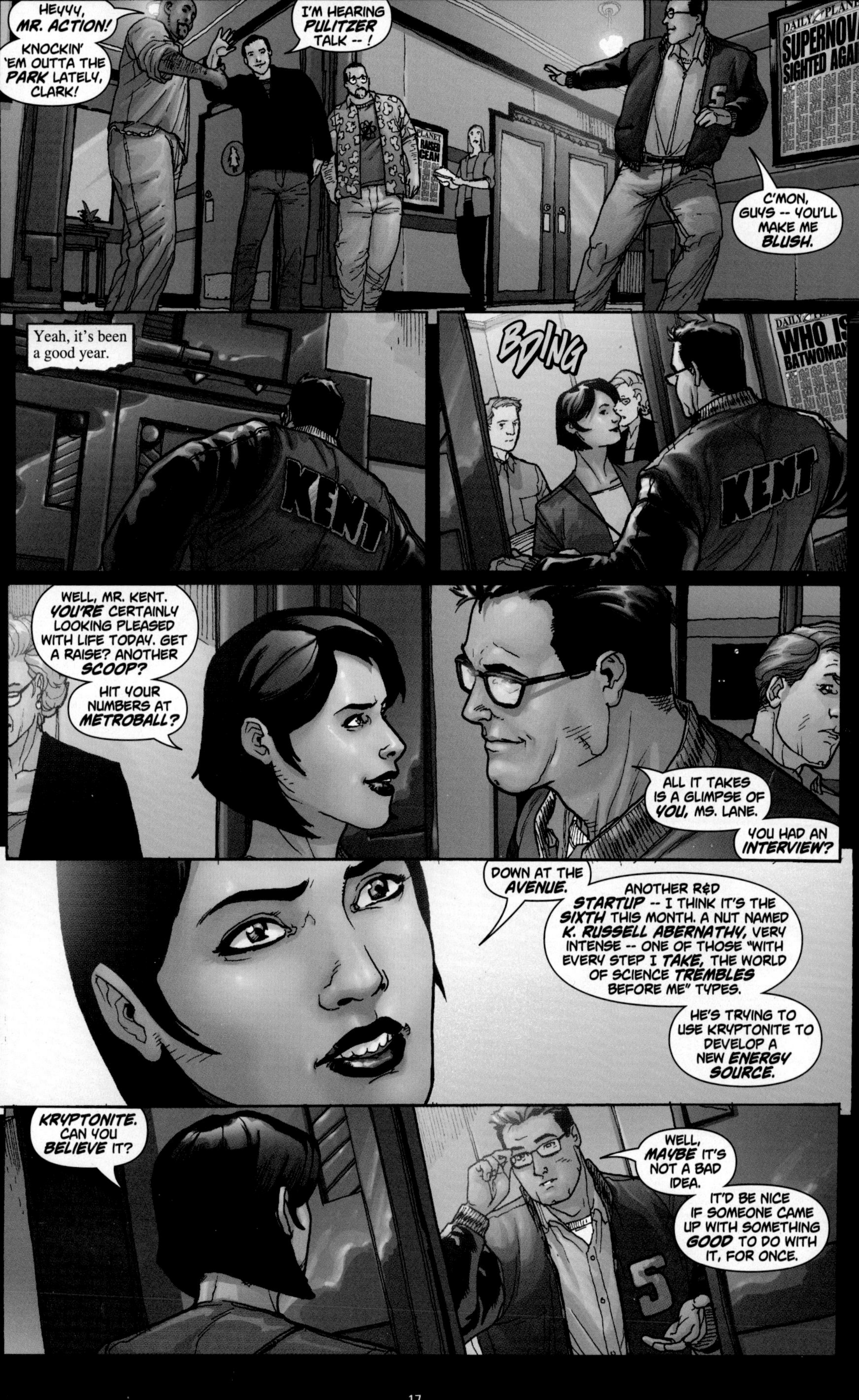
HEYYY, MR. ACTION!
KNOCKIN' 'EM OUTTA THE PARK LATELY, CLARK!
I'M HEARING PULITZER TALK -- !
C'MON, GUYS -- YOU'LL MAKE ME BLUSH.
Yeah, it's been a good year.
KENT
BDING
KENT
WELL, MR. KENT. YOU'RE CERTAINLY LOOKING PLEASED WITH LIFE TODAY. GET A RAISE? ANOTHER SCOOP?
HIT YOUR NUMBERS AT METROBALL?
ALL IT TAKES IS A GLIMPSE OF YOU, MS. LANE.
YOU HAD AN INTERVIEW?
DOWN AT THE AVENUE.
ANOTHER R&D STARTUP -- I THINK IT'S THE SIXTH THIS MONTH. A NUT NAMED K. RUSSELL ABERNATHY, VERY INTENSE -- ONE OF THOSE "WITH EVERY STEP I TAKE, THE WORLD OF SCIENCE TREMBLES BEFORE ME" TYPES.
HE'S TRYING TO USE KRYPTONITE TO DEVELOP A NEW ENERGY SOURCE.
KRYPTONITE. CAN YOU BELIEVE IT?
WELL, MAYBE IT'S NOT A BAD IDEA.
IT'D BE NICE IF SOMEONE CAME UP WITH SOMETHING GOOD TO DO WITH IT, FOR ONCE.

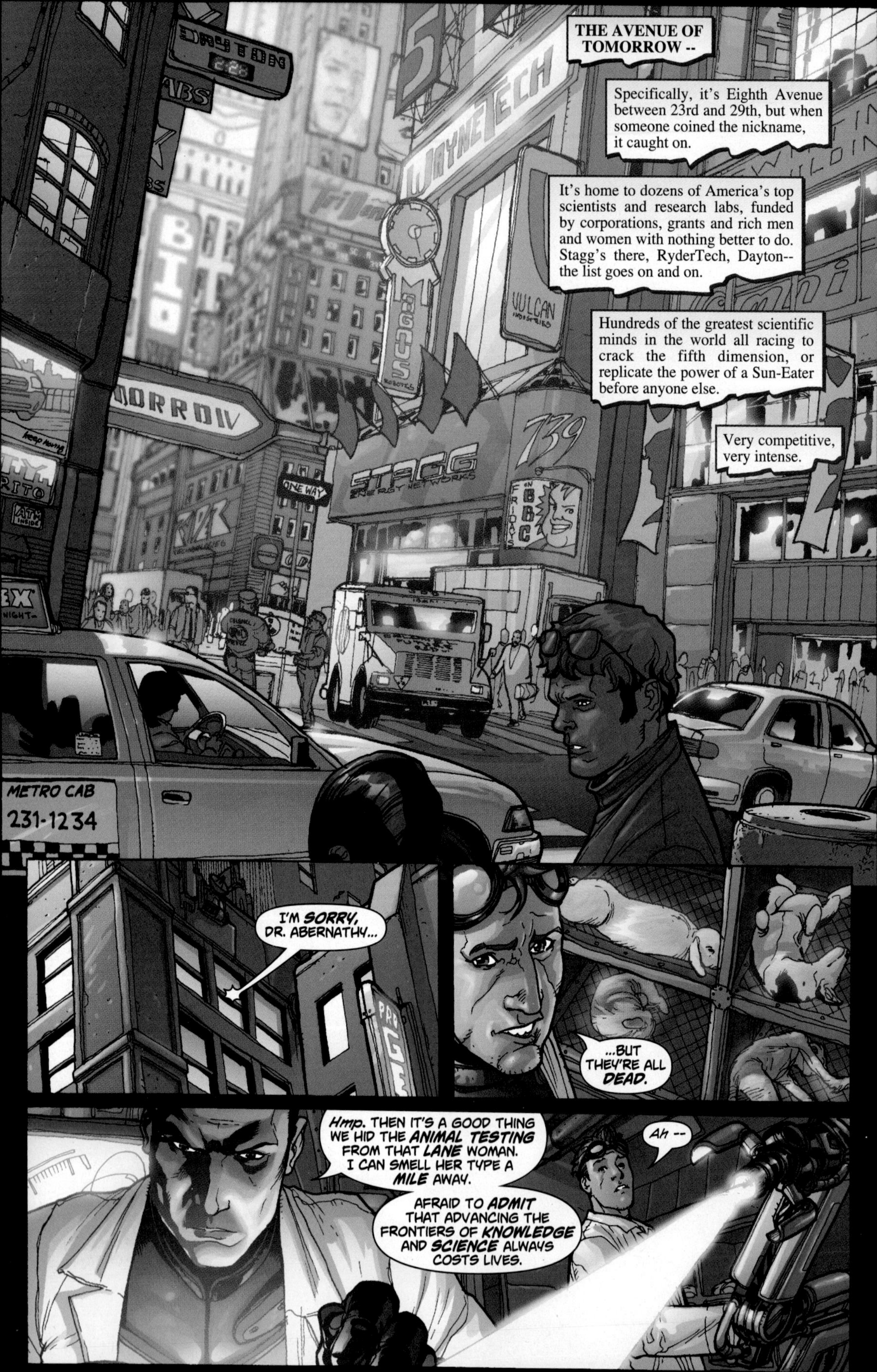

THE AVENUE OF TOMORROW --
Specifically, it's Eighth Avenue between 23rd and 29th, but when someone coined the nickname, it caught on.
It's home to dozens of America's top scientists and research labs, funded by corporations, grants and rich men and women with nothing better to do. Stagg's there, RyderTech, Dayton-- the list goes on and on.
Hundreds of the greatest scientific minds in the world all racing to crack the fifth dimension, or replicate the power of a Sun-Eater before anyone else.
Very competitive, very intense.
DAYTON
WAYNETECH
TOMORROW
ARGOUS
VULCAN
STAGG ENERGY NETWORKS
739
ONE WAY
METRO CAB
231-1234
I'M SORRY, DR. ABERNATHY...
...BUT THEY'RE ALL DEAD.
Hmp. THEN IT'S A GOOD THING WE HID THE ANIMAL TESTING FROM THAT LANE WOMAN. I CAN SMELL HER TYPE A MILE AWAY.
AFRAID TO ADMIT THAT ADVANCING THE FRONTIERS OF KNOWLEDGE AND SCIENCE ALWAYS COSTS LIVES.
Ah --

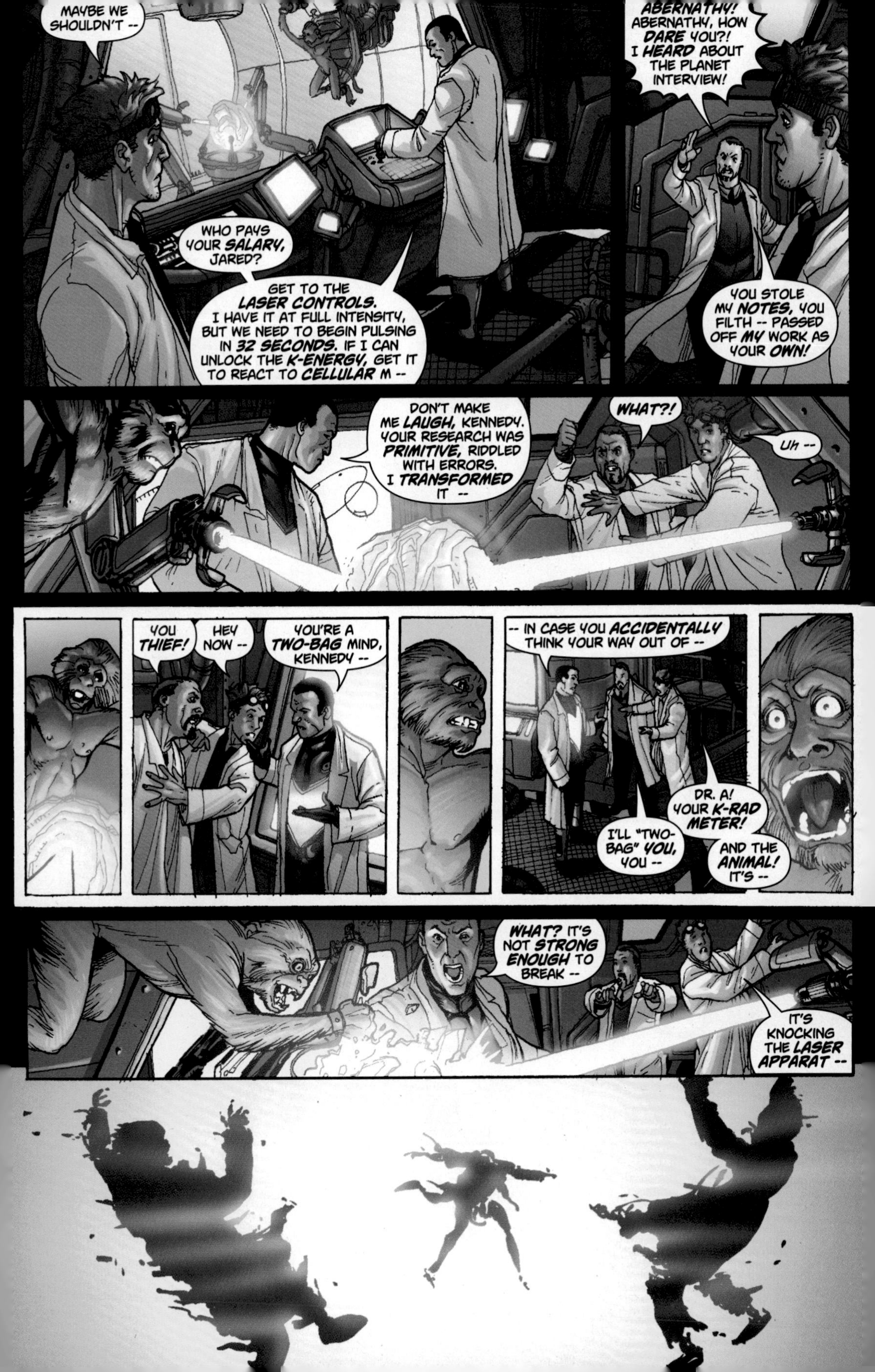
MAYBE WE SHOULDN'T --
WHO PAYS YOUR SALARY, JARED?
GET TO THE LASER CONTROLS. I HAVE IT AT FULL INTENSITY, BUT WE NEED TO BEGIN PULSING IN 32 SECONDS. IF I CAN UNLOCK THE K-ENERGY, GET IT TO REACT TO CELLULAR M --
ABERNATHY! ABERNATHY, HOW DARE YOU?! I HEARD ABOUT THE PLANET INTERVIEW!
YOU STOLE MY NOTES, YOU FILTH -- PASSED OFF MY WORK AS YOUR OWN!
DON'T MAKE ME LAUGH, KENNEDY. YOUR RESEARCH WAS PRIMITIVE, RIDDLED WITH ERRORS. I TRANSFORMED IT --
WHAT?!
Uh --
YOU THIEF!
HEY NOW --
YOU'RE A TWO-BAG MIND, KENNEDY --
-- IN CASE YOU ACCIDENTALLY THINK YOUR WAY OUT OF --
I'LL "TWO-BAG" YOU, YOU --
DR. A! YOUR K-RAD METER!
AND THE ANIMAL! IT'S --
WHAT? IT'S NOT STRONG ENOUGH TO BREAK --
IT'S KNOCKING THE LASER APPARAT --

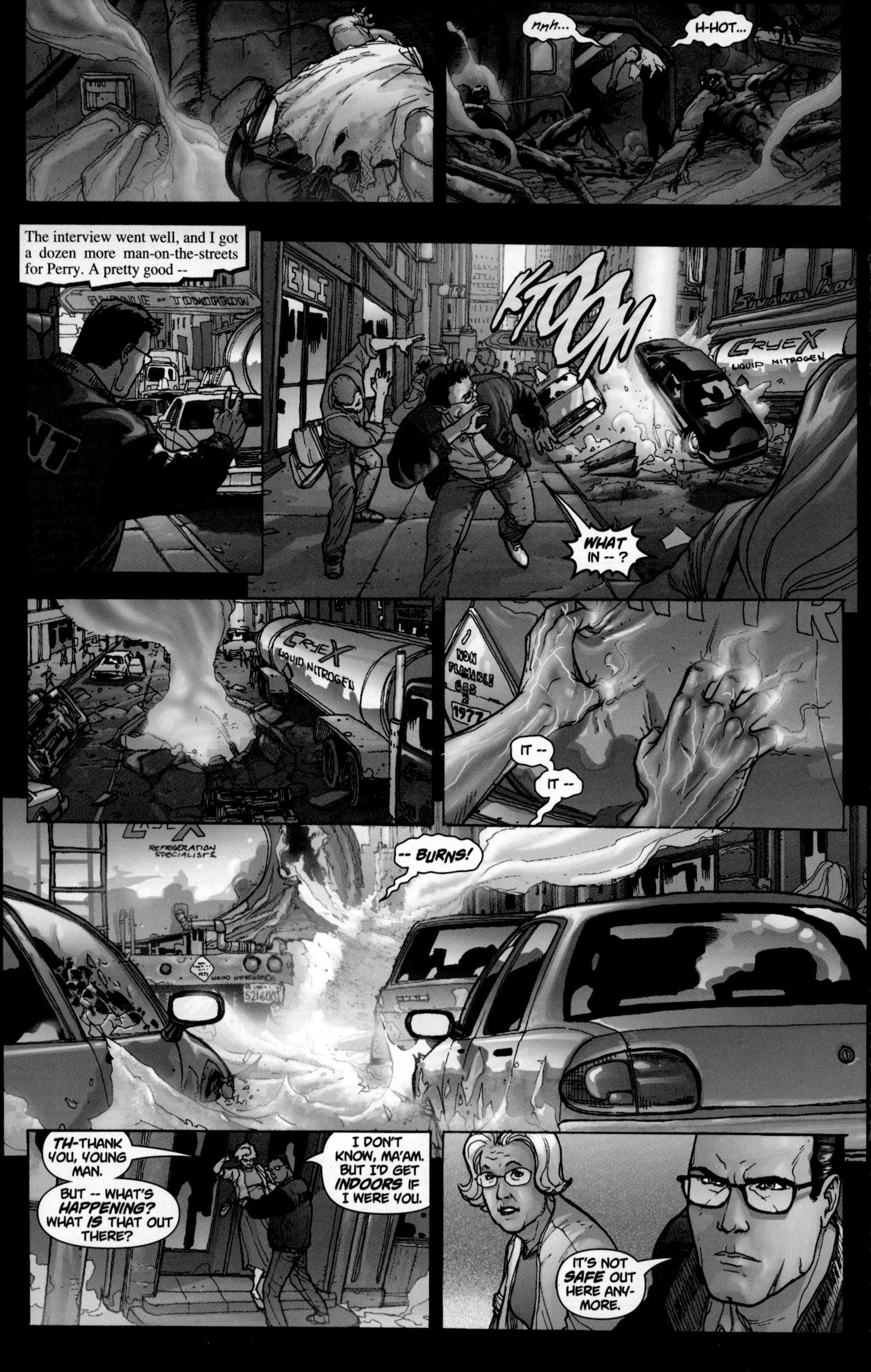
nnh...
H-HOT...
The interview went well, and I got a dozen more man-on-the-streets for Perry. A pretty good --
KTOOM
WHAT IN -- ?
CRYEX
LIQUID NITROGEN
NON FLAMMABLE GAS 2
1977
IT --
IT --
REFRIGERATION SPECIALISTS
-- BURNS!
TH-THANK YOU, YOUNG MAN.
BUT -- WHAT'S HAPPENING? WHAT IS THAT OUT THERE?
I DON'T KNOW, MA'AM. BUT I'D GET INDOORS IF I WERE YOU.
IT'S NOT SAFE OUT HERE ANY-MORE.

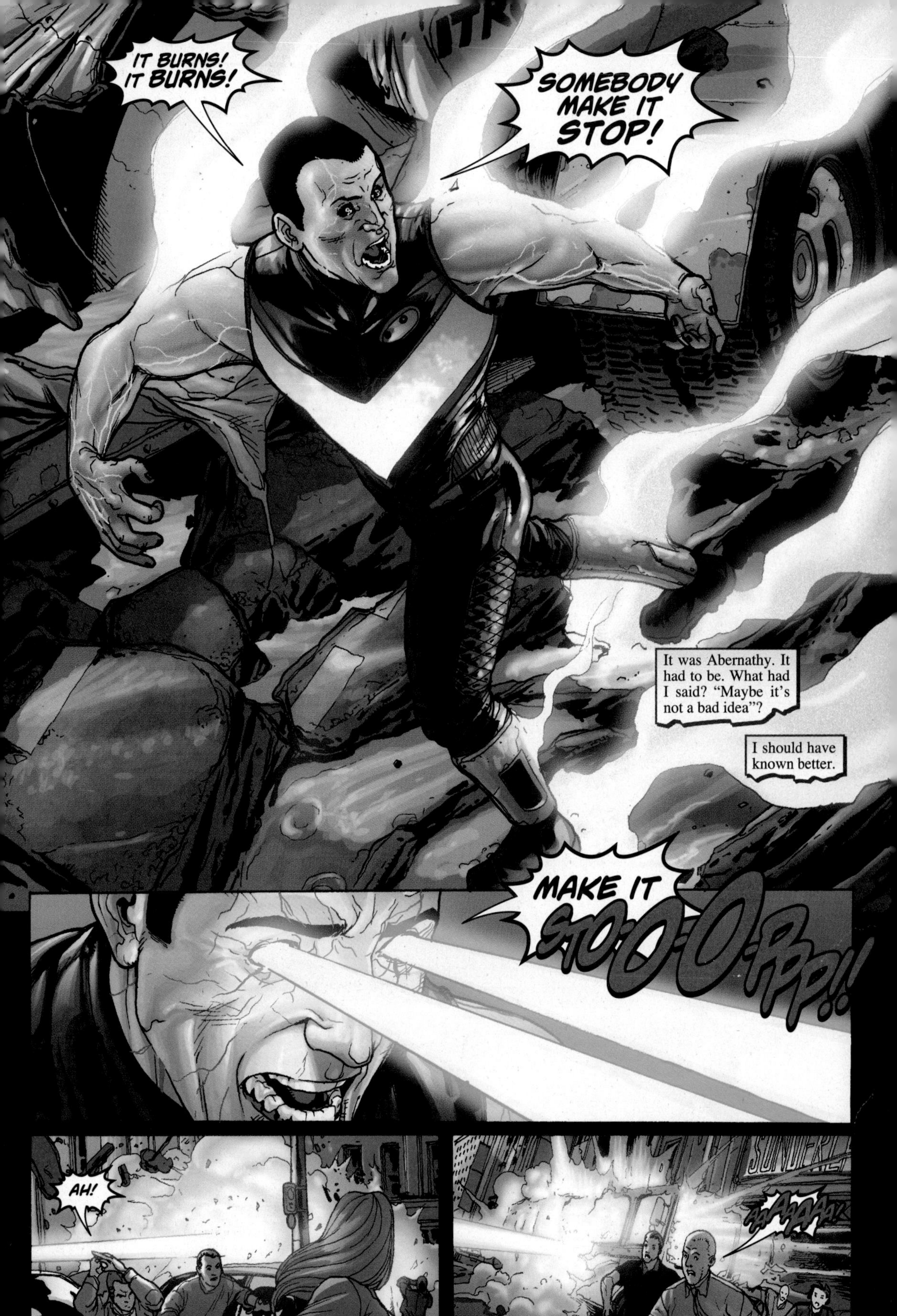
IT BURNS! IT BURNS!
SOMEBODY MAKE IT STOP!
It was Abernathy. It had to be. What had I said? "Maybe it's not a bad idea"?
I should have known better.
MAKE IT STO-O-O-PPP!!
AH!

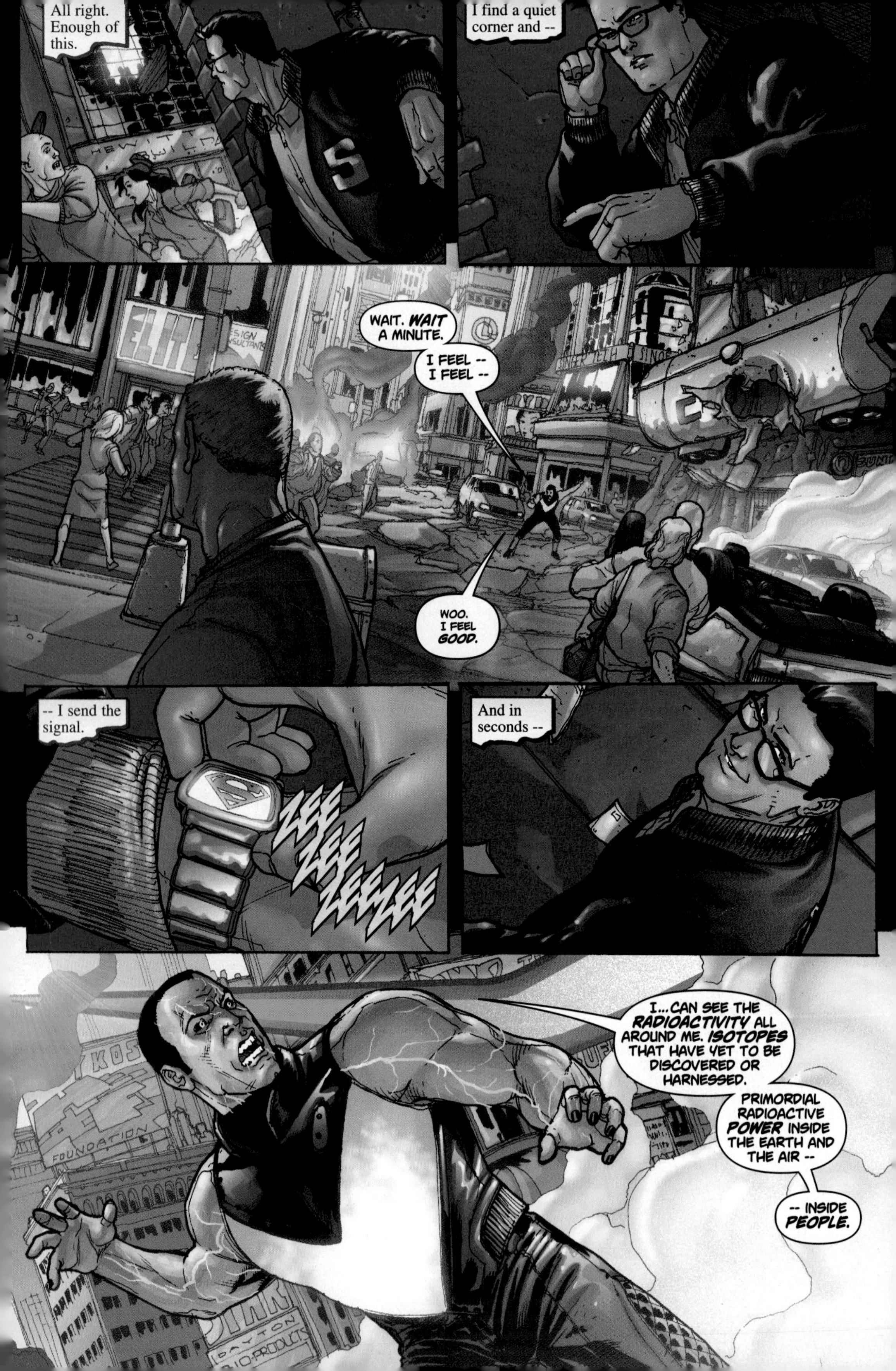
All right. Enough of this.
I find a quiet corner and --
WAIT. WAIT A MINUTE.
I FEEL -- I FEEL --
WOO. I FEEL GOOD.
-- I send the signal.
ZEE ZEE ZEE ZEE ZEE
And in seconds --
I...CAN SEE THE RADIOACTIVITY ALL AROUND ME. ISOTOPES THAT HAVE YET TO BE DISCOVERED OR HARNESSED.
PRIMORDIAL RADIOACTIVE POWER INSIDE THE EARTH AND THE AIR --
-- INSIDE PEOPLE.

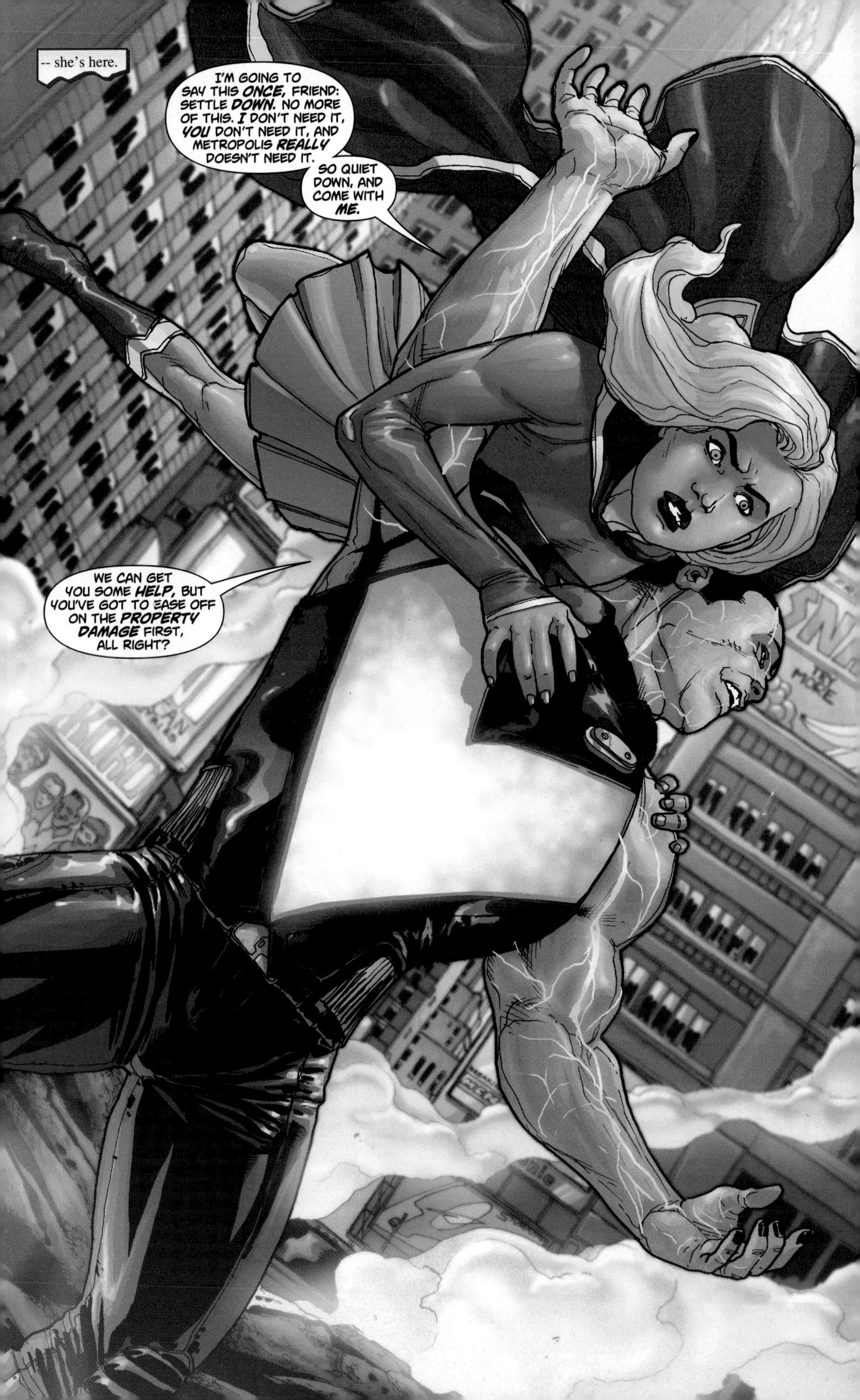
-- she's here.
I'M GOING TO SAY THIS ONCE, FRIEND: SETTLE DOWN. NO MORE OF THIS. I DON'T NEED IT, YOU DON'T NEED IT, AND METROPOLIS REALLY DOESN'T NEED IT.
SO QUIET DOWN, AND COME WITH ME.
WE CAN GET YOU SOME HELP, BUT YOU'VE GOT TO EASE OFF ON THE PROPERTY DAMAGE FIRST, ALL RIGHT?

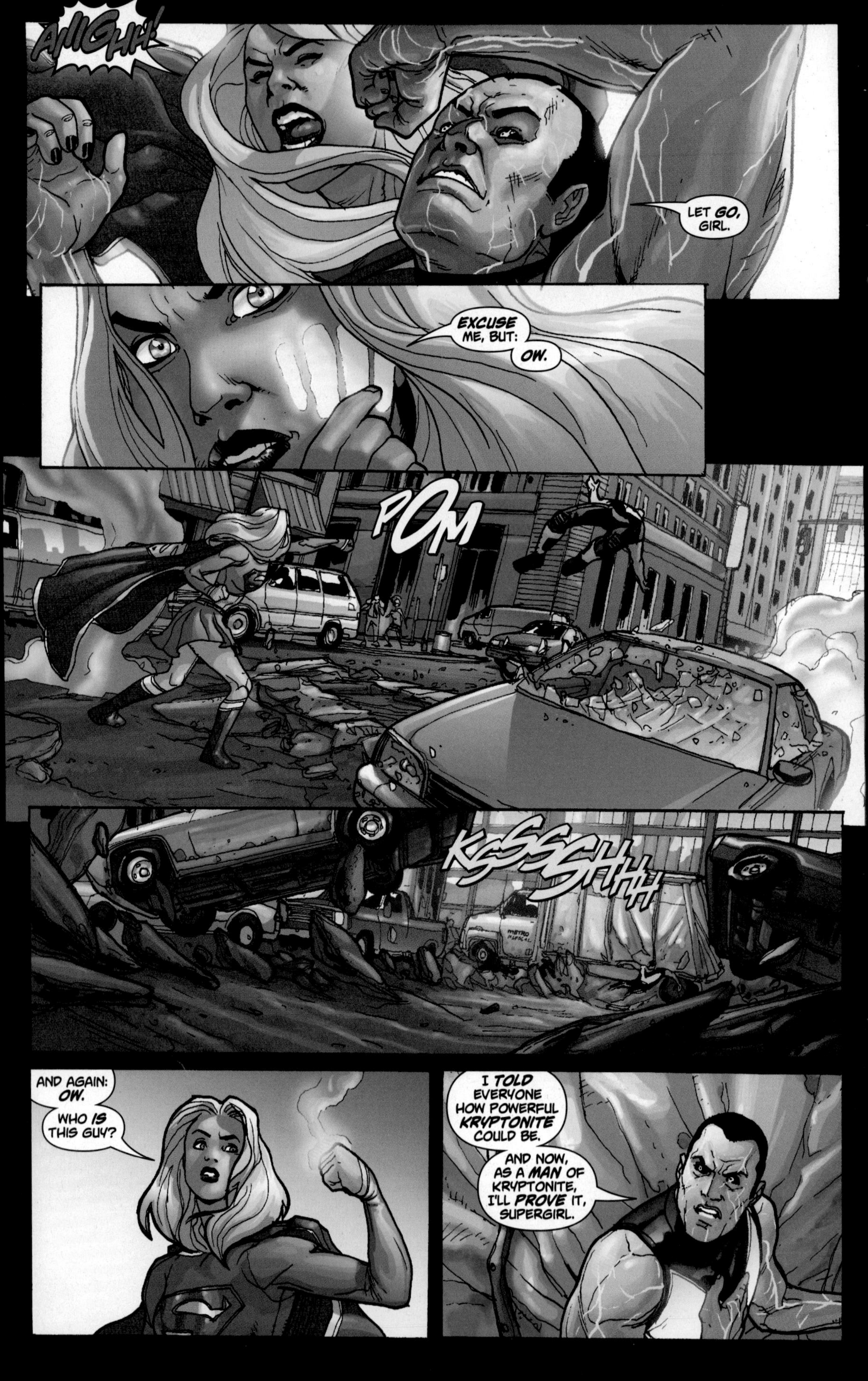
AIIIGHH!
LET GO, GIRL.
EXCUSE ME, BUT: OW.
POM
KSSSSHHH
AND AGAIN: OW.
WHO IS THIS GUY?
I TOLD EVERYONE HOW POWERFUL KRYPTONITE COULD BE.
AND NOW, AS A MAN OF KRYPTONITE, I'LL PROVE IT, SUPERGIRL.

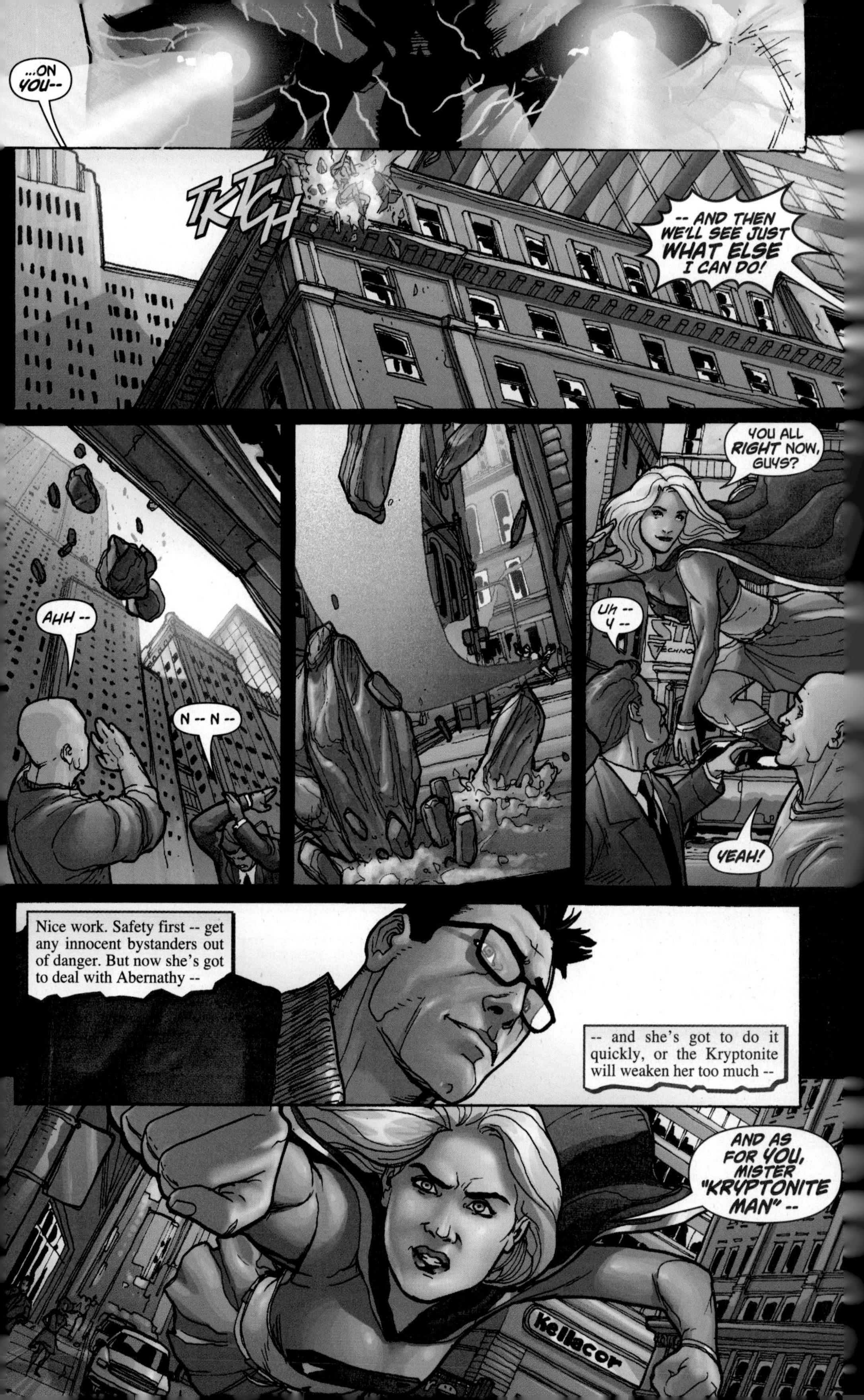
...ON YOU--
TKTCH
-- AND THEN WE'LL SEE JUST WHAT ELSE I CAN DO!
AHH --
N -- N --
YOU ALL RIGHT NOW, GUYS?
Uh -- Y --
YEAH!
Nice work. Safety first -- get any innocent bystanders out of danger. But now she's got to deal with Abernathy --
-- and she's got to do it quickly, or the Kryptonite will weaken her too much --
AND AS FOR YOU, MISTER "KRYPTONITE MAN" --
Kellacor

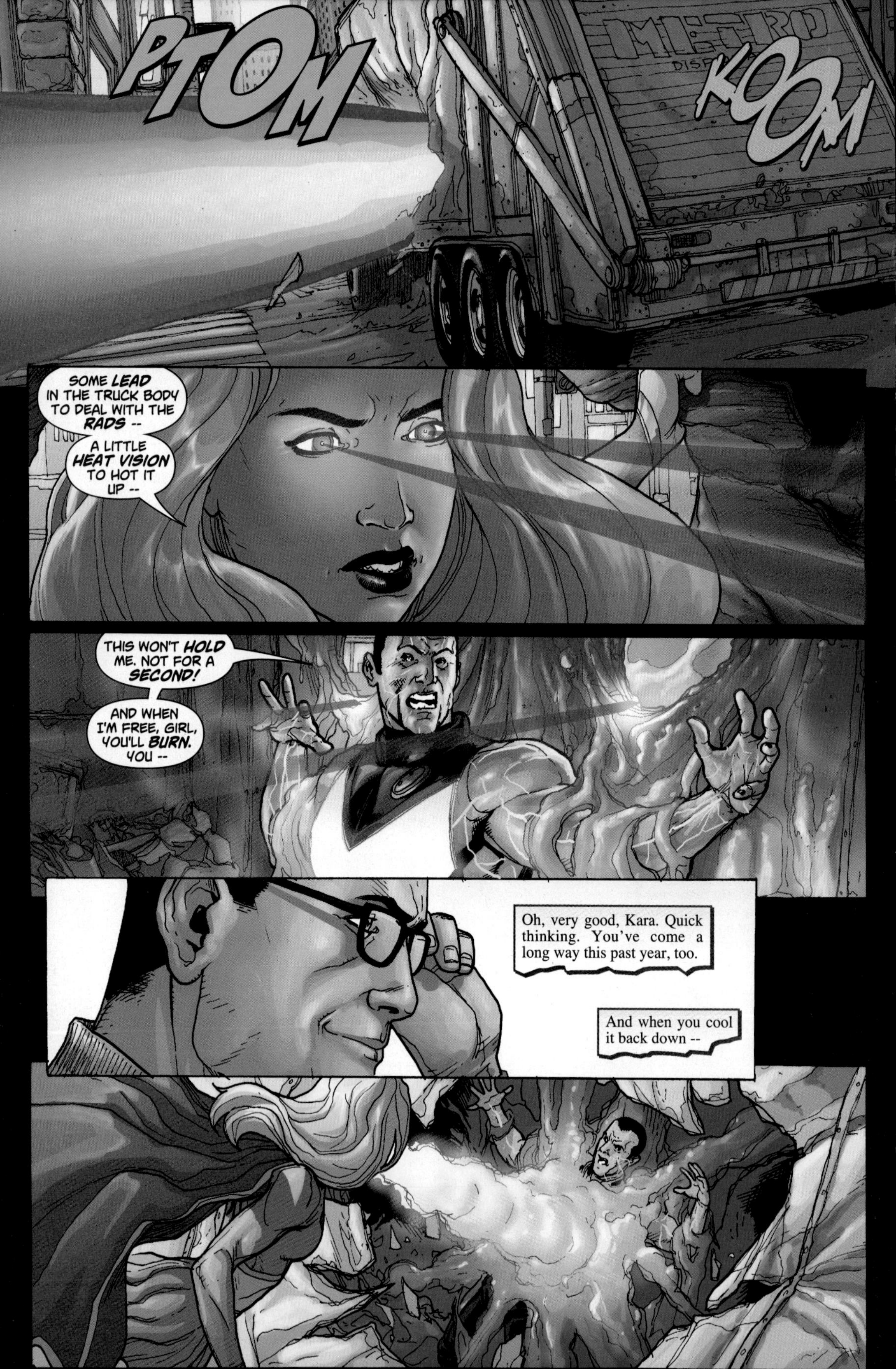
PTOM
KOOM
SOME LEAD IN THE TRUCK BODY TO DEAL WITH THE RADS --
A LITTLE HEAT VISION TO HOT IT UP --
THIS WON'T HOLD ME. NOT FOR A SECOND!
AND WHEN I'M FREE, GIRL, YOU'LL BURN. YOU --
Oh, very good, Kara. Quick thinking. You've come a long way this past year, too.
And when you cool it back down --

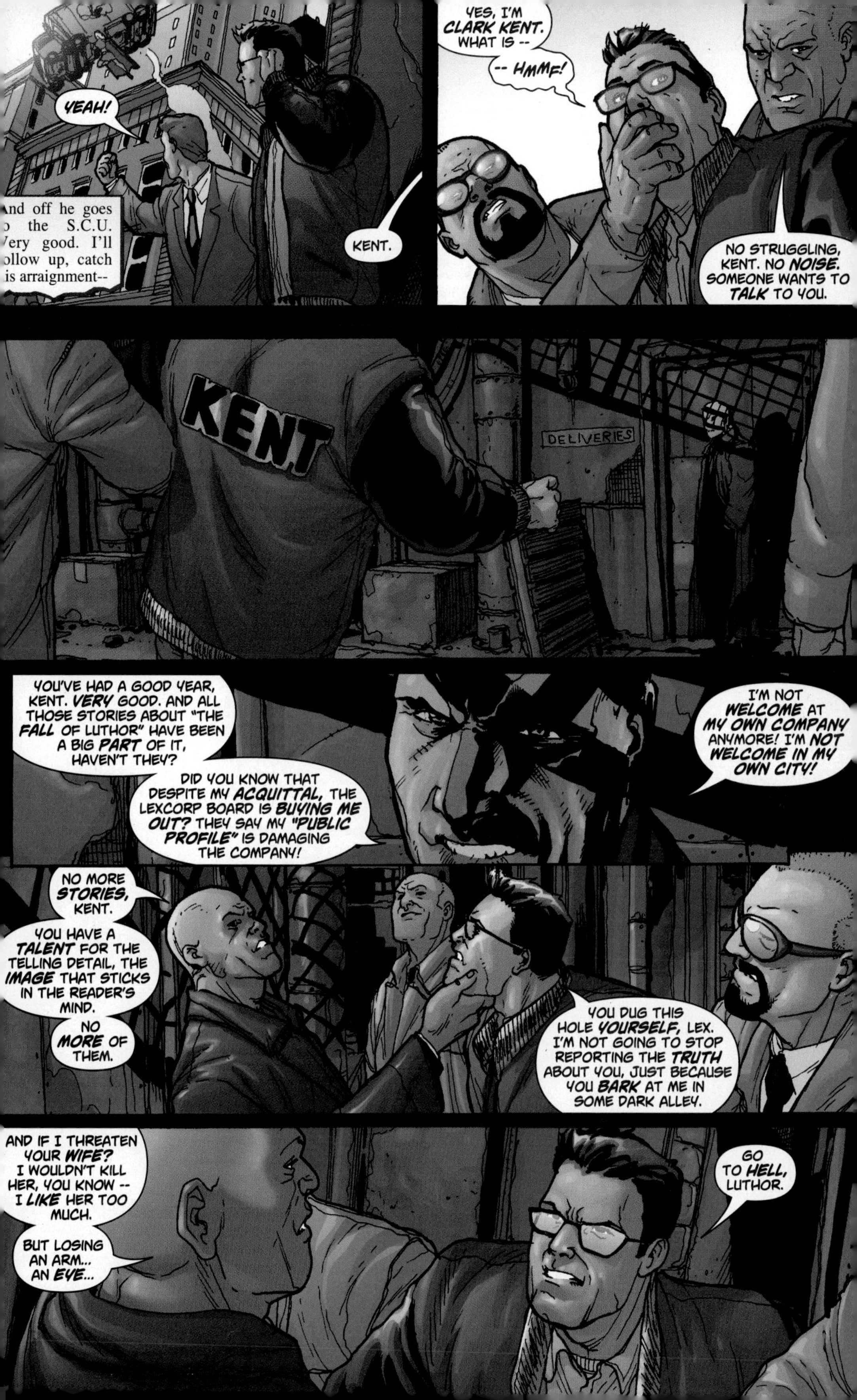
YEAH!
And off he goes
o the S.C.U.
Very good. I'll
ollow up, catch
is arraignment--
KENT.
YES, I'M CLARK KENT. WHAT IS --
-- HMMF!
NO STRUGGLING, KENT. NO NOISE. SOMEONE WANTS TO TALK TO YOU.
KENT
DELIVERIES
YOU'VE HAD A GOOD YEAR, KENT. VERY GOOD. AND ALL THOSE STORIES ABOUT "THE FALL OF LUTHOR" HAVE BEEN A BIG PART OF IT, HAVEN'T THEY?
DID YOU KNOW THAT DESPITE MY ACQUITTAL, THE LEXCORP BOARD IS BUYING ME OUT? THEY SAY MY "PUBLIC PROFILE" IS DAMAGING THE COMPANY!
I'M NOT WELCOME AT MY OWN COMPANY ANYMORE! I'M NOT WELCOME IN MY OWN CITY!
NO MORE STORIES, KENT.
YOU HAVE A TALENT FOR THE TELLING DETAIL, THE IMAGE THAT STICKS IN THE READER'S MIND.
NO MORE OF THEM.
YOU DUG THIS HOLE YOURSELF, LEX. I'M NOT GOING TO STOP REPORTING THE TRUTH ABOUT YOU, JUST BECAUSE YOU BARK AT ME IN SOME DARK ALLEY.
AND IF I THREATEN YOUR WIFE? I WOULDN'T KILL HER, YOU KNOW -- I LIKE HER TOO MUCH.
BUT LOSING AN ARM... AN EYE...
GO TO HELL, LUTHOR.

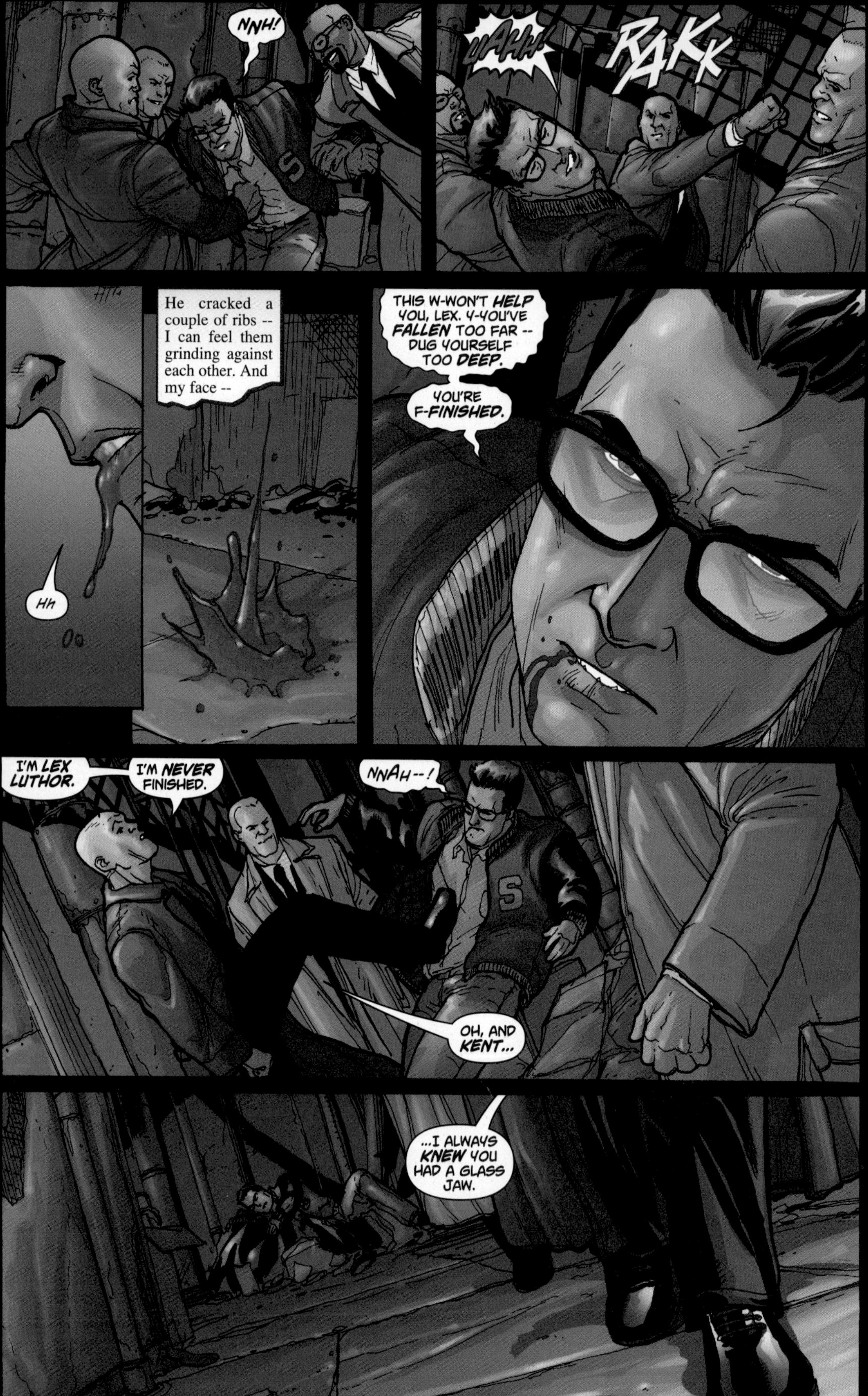
NNH!
UAHH!
RAKK
He cracked a couple of ribs -- I can feel them grinding against each other. And my face --
Hh
THIS W-WON'T HELP YOU, LEX. Y-YOU'VE FALLEN TOO FAR -- DUG YOURSELF TOO DEEP.
YOU'RE F-FINISHED.
I'M LEX LUTHOR.
I'M NEVER FINISHED.
NNAH--!
OH, AND KENT...
...I ALWAYS KNEW YOU HAD A GLASS JAW.

Art by: Pete Woods

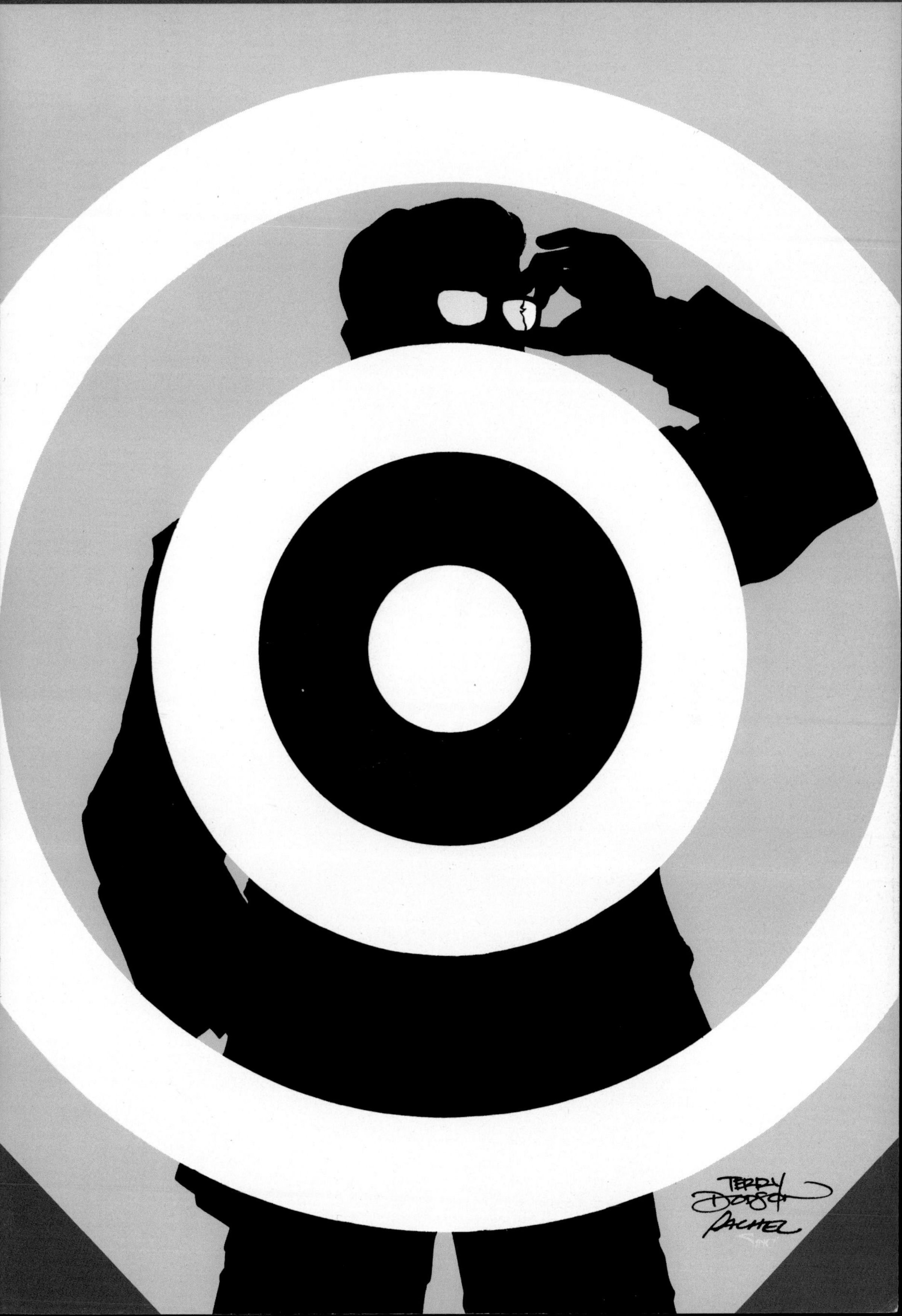
TERRY DODSON
RACHEL

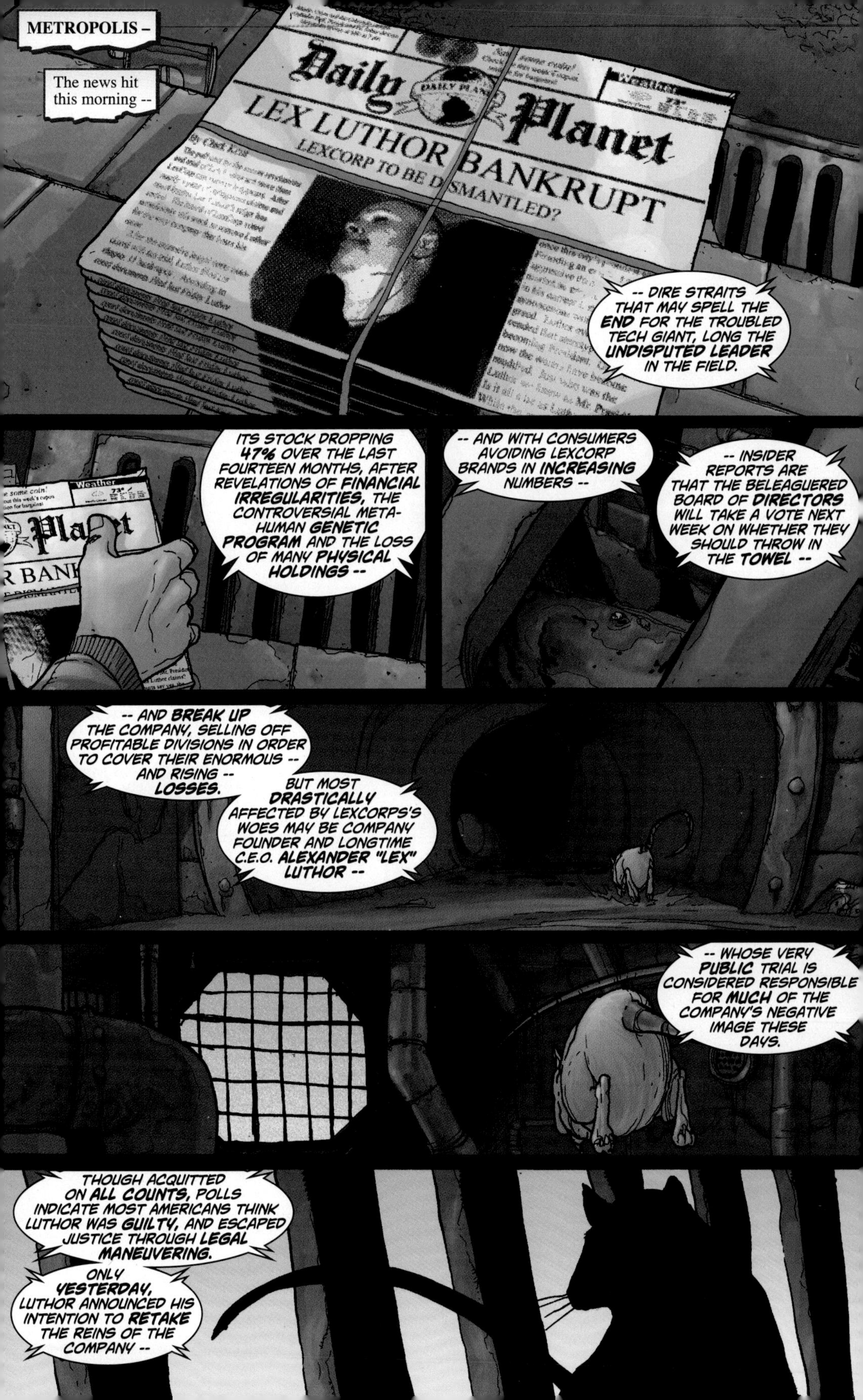
METROPOLIS –
The news hit this morning --
Daily Planet
LEX LUTHOR BANKRUPT
LEXCORP TO BE DISMANTLED?
-- DIRE STRAITS THAT MAY SPELL THE END FOR THE TROUBLED TECH GIANT, LONG THE UNDISPUTED LEADER IN THE FIELD.
ITS STOCK DROPPING 47% OVER THE LAST FOURTEEN MONTHS, AFTER REVELATIONS OF FINANCIAL IRREGULARITIES, THE CONTROVERSIAL META-HUMAN GENETIC PROGRAM AND THE LOSS OF MANY PHYSICAL HOLDINGS --
-- AND WITH CONSUMERS AVOIDING LEXCORP BRANDS IN INCREASING NUMBERS --
-- INSIDER REPORTS ARE THAT THE BELEAGUERED BOARD OF DIRECTORS WILL TAKE A VOTE NEXT WEEK ON WHETHER THEY SHOULD THROW IN THE TOWEL --
-- AND BREAK UP THE COMPANY, SELLING OFF PROFITABLE DIVISIONS IN ORDER TO COVER THEIR ENORMOUS -- AND RISING -- LOSSES.
BUT MOST DRASTICALLY AFFECTED BY LEXCORPS'S WOES MAY BE COMPANY FOUNDER AND LONGTIME C.E.O. ALEXANDER "LEX" LUTHOR --
-- WHOSE VERY PUBLIC TRIAL IS CONSIDERED RESPONSIBLE FOR MUCH OF THE COMPANY'S NEGATIVE IMAGE THESE DAYS.
THOUGH ACQUITTED ON ALL COUNTS, POLLS INDICATE MOST AMERICANS THINK LUTHOR WAS GUILTY, AND ESCAPED JUSTICE THROUGH LEGAL MANEUVERING.
ONLY YESTERDAY, LUTHOR ANNOUNCED HIS INTENTION TO RETAKE THE REINS OF THE COMPANY --

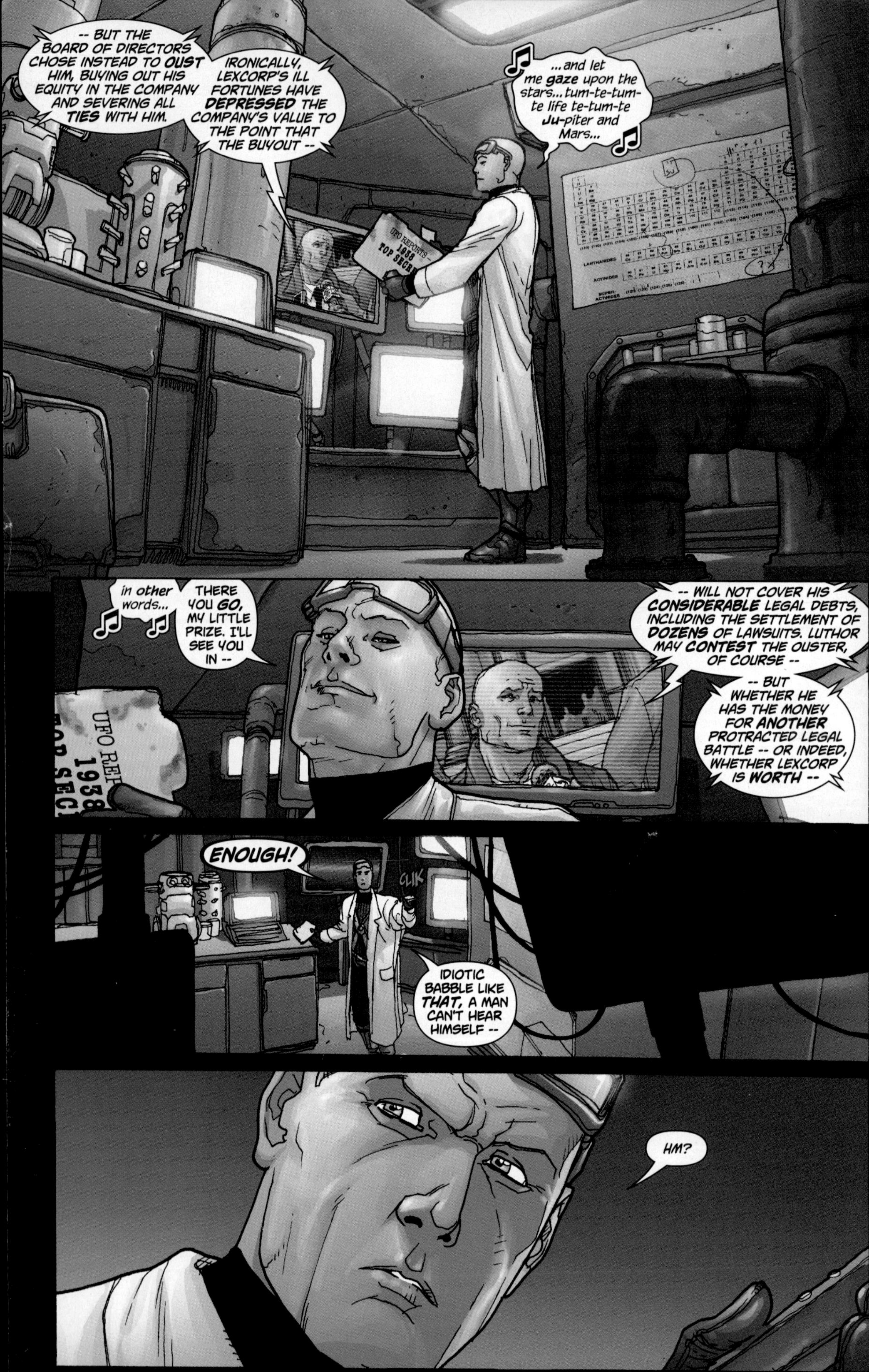
-- BUT THE BOARD OF DIRECTORS CHOSE INSTEAD TO OUST HIM, BUYING OUT HIS EQUITY IN THE COMPANY AND SEVERING ALL TIES WITH HIM.
IRONICALLY, LEXCORP'S ILL FORTUNES HAVE DEPRESSED THE COMPANY'S VALUE TO THE POINT THAT THE BUYOUT --
...and let me gaze upon the stars...tum-te-tum-te life te-tum-te Ju-piter and Mars...
UFO REPORTS 1938 TOP SECRET
LANTHANIDES
ACTINIDES
SUPER-ACTINIDES
in other words...
THERE YOU GO, MY LITTLE PRIZE. I'LL SEE YOU IN --
-- WILL NOT COVER HIS CONSIDERABLE LEGAL DEBTS, INCLUDING THE SETTLEMENT OF DOZENS OF LAWSUITS. LUTHOR MAY CONTEST THE OUSTER, OF COURSE --
-- BUT WHETHER HE HAS THE MONEY FOR ANOTHER PROTRACTED LEGAL BATTLE -- OR INDEED, WHETHER LEXCORP IS WORTH --
ENOUGH!
CLIK
IDIOTIC BABBLE LIKE THAT, A MAN CAN'T HEAR HIMSELF --
HM?

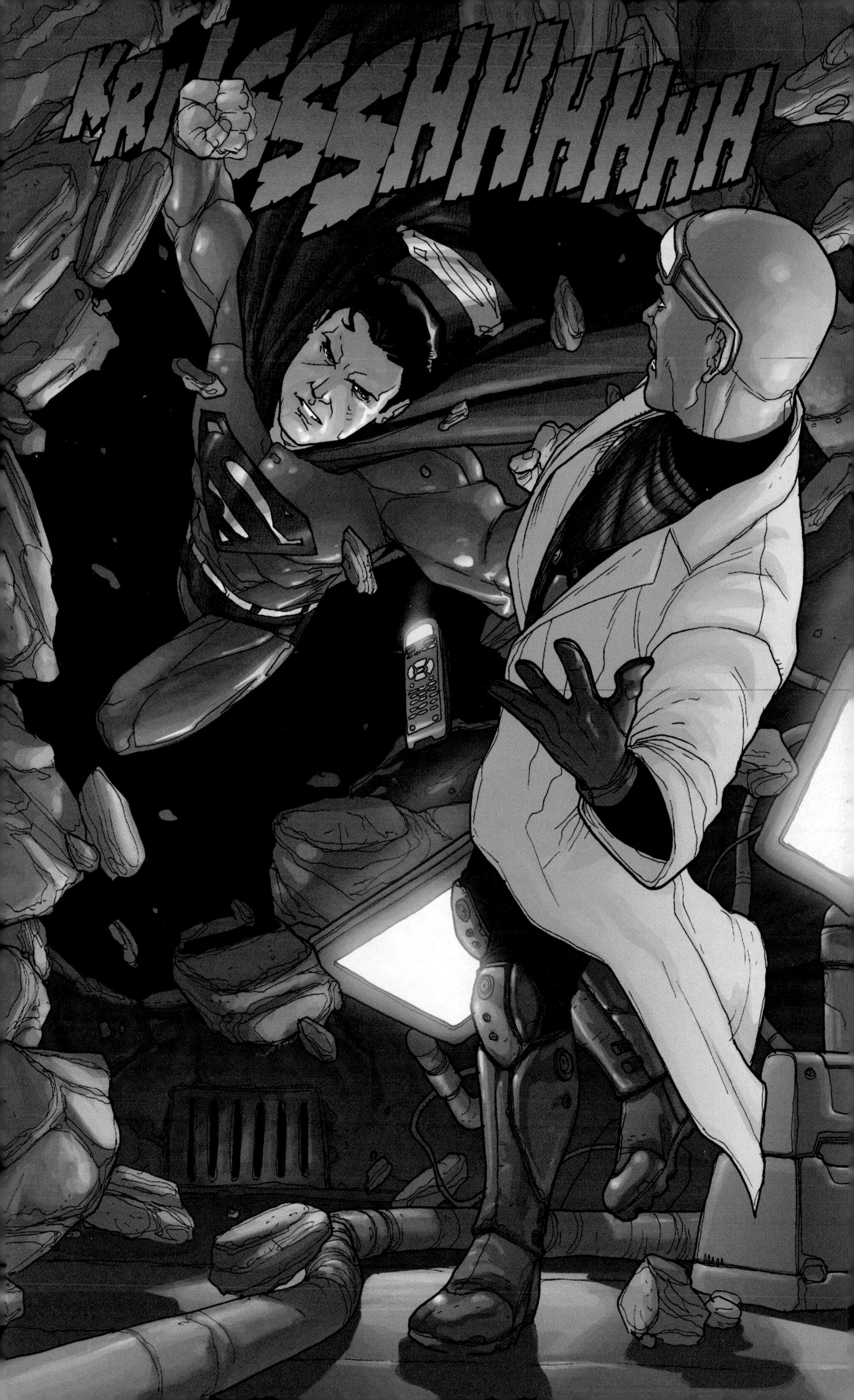

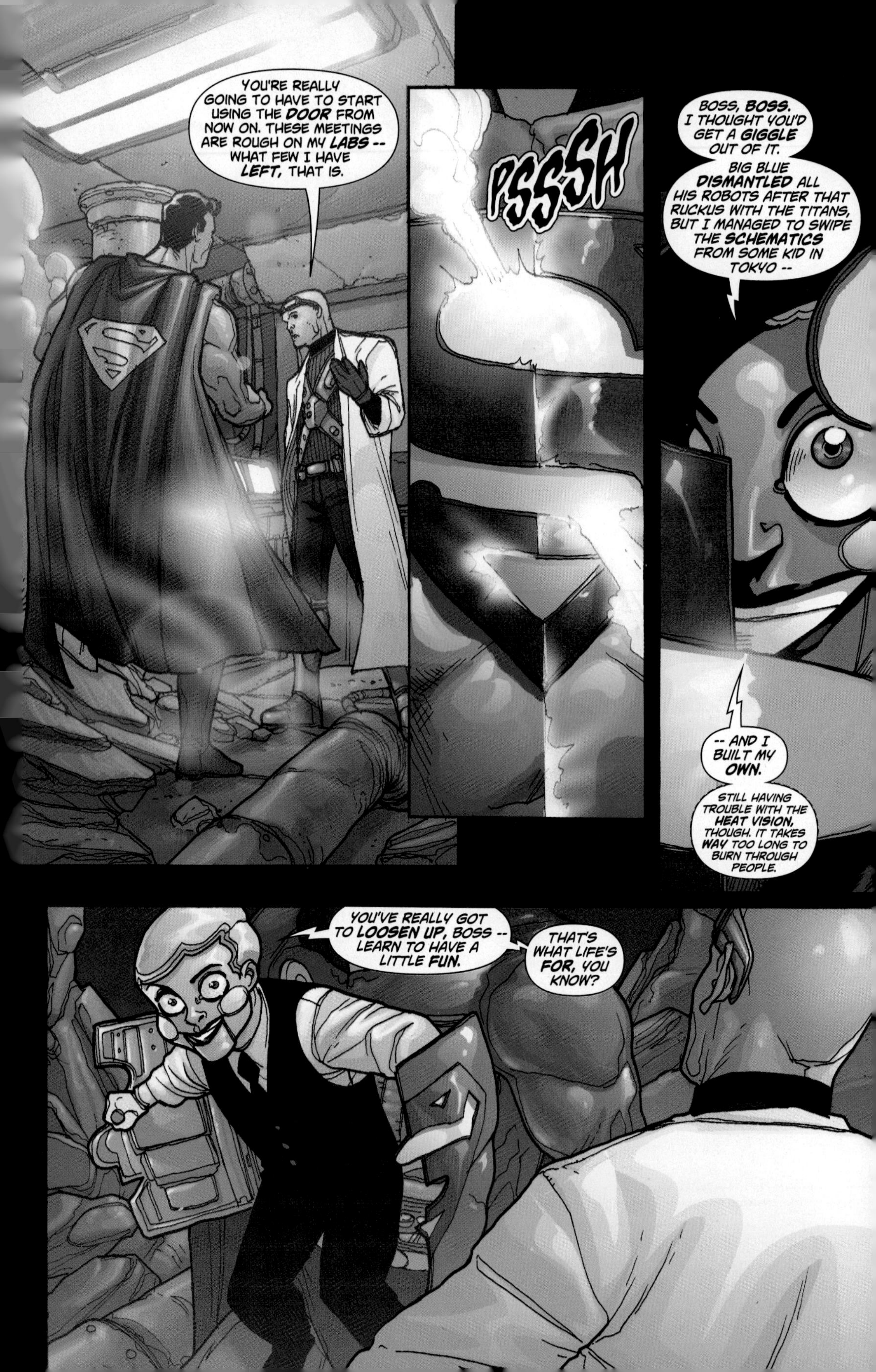
YOU'RE REALLY GOING TO HAVE TO START USING THE DOOR FROM NOW ON. THESE MEETINGS ARE ROUGH ON MY LABS -- WHAT FEW I HAVE LEFT, THAT IS.
PSSSH
BOSS, BOSS. I THOUGHT YOU'D GET A GIGGLE OUT OF IT.
BIG BLUE DISMANTLED ALL HIS ROBOTS AFTER THAT RUCKUS WITH THE TITANS, BUT I MANAGED TO SWIPE THE SCHEMATICS FROM SOME KID IN TOKYO --
-- AND I BUILT MY OWN.
STILL HAVING TROUBLE WITH THE HEAT VISION, THOUGH. IT TAKES WAY TOO LONG TO BURN THROUGH PEOPLE.
YOU'VE REALLY GOT TO LOOSEN UP, BOSS -- LEARN TO HAVE A LITTLE FUN.
THAT'S WHAT LIFE'S FOR, YOU KNOW?

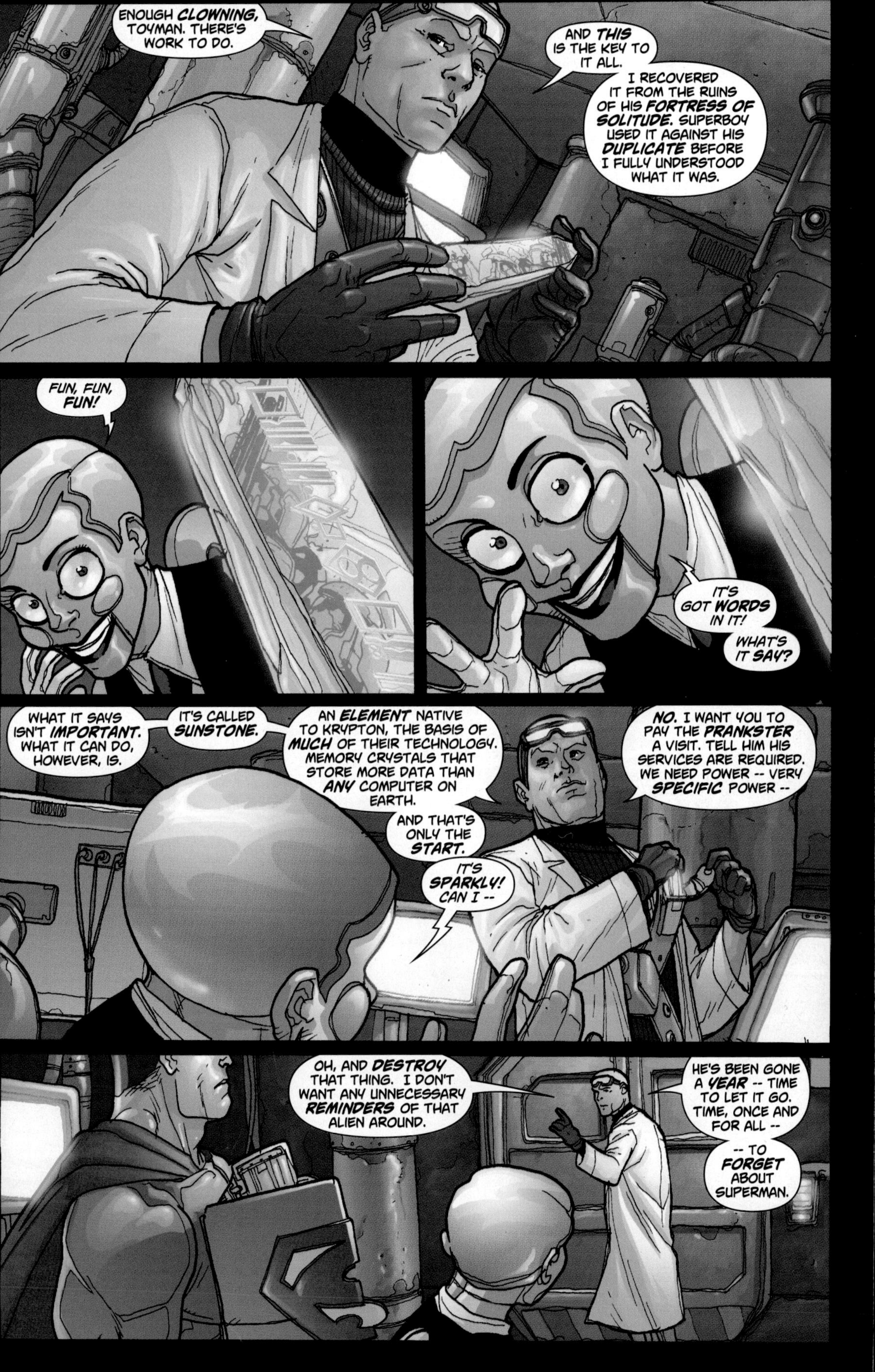

ENOUGH CLOWNING, TOYMAN. THERE'S WORK TO DO.
AND THIS IS THE KEY TO IT ALL.
I RECOVERED IT FROM THE RUINS OF HIS FORTRESS OF SOLITUDE. SUPERBOY USED IT AGAINST HIS DUPLICATE BEFORE I FULLY UNDERSTOOD WHAT IT WAS.
FUN, FUN, FUN!
IT'S GOT WORDS IN IT!
WHAT'S IT SAY?
WHAT IT SAYS ISN'T IMPORTANT. WHAT IT CAN DO, HOWEVER, IS.
IT'S CALLED SUNSTONE.
AN ELEMENT NATIVE TO KRYPTON, THE BASIS OF MUCH OF THEIR TECHNOLOGY. MEMORY CRYSTALS THAT STORE MORE DATA THAN ANY COMPUTER ON EARTH.
AND THAT'S ONLY THE START.
IT'S SPARKLY! CAN I --
NO. I WANT YOU TO PAY THE PRANKSTER A VISIT. TELL HIM HIS SERVICES ARE REQUIRED. WE NEED POWER -- VERY SPECIFIC POWER --
OH, AND DESTROY THAT THING. I DON'T WANT ANY UNNECESSARY REMINDERS OF THAT ALIEN AROUND.
HE'S BEEN GONE A YEAR -- TIME TO LET IT GO. TIME, ONCE AND FOR ALL --
-- TO FORGET ABOUT SUPERMAN.

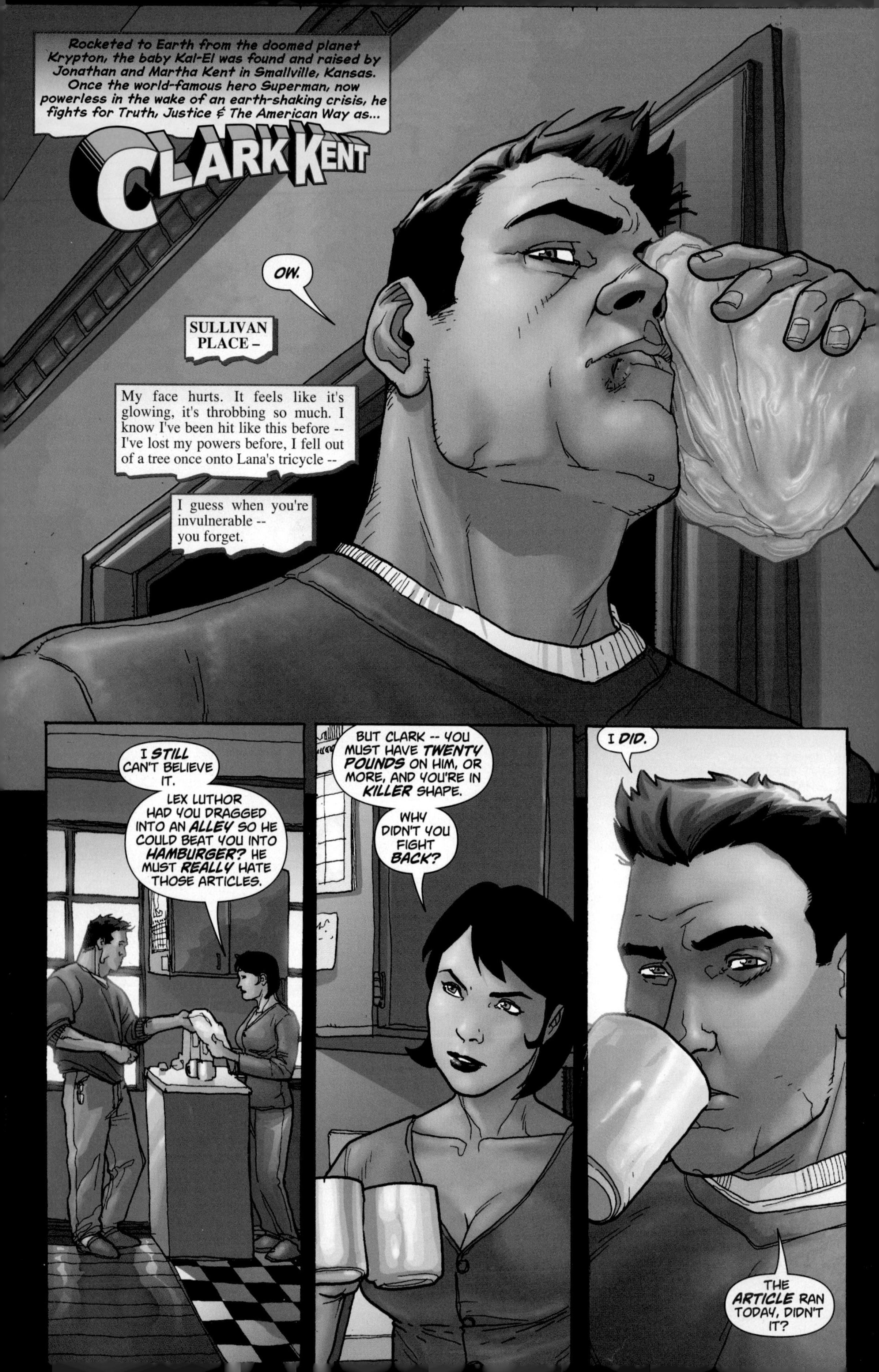
Rocketed to Earth from the doomed planet Krypton, the baby Kal-El was found and raised by Jonathan and Martha Kent in Smallville, Kansas. Once the world-famous hero Superman, now powerless in the wake of an earth-shaking crisis, he fights for Truth, Justice & The American Way as...
CLARK KENT
OW.
SULLIVAN PLACE –
My face hurts. It feels like it's glowing, it's throbbing so much. I know I've been hit like this before -- I've lost my powers before, I fell out of a tree once onto Lana's tricycle --
I guess when you're invulnerable -- you forget.
I STILL CAN'T BELIEVE IT.
LEX LUTHOR HAD YOU DRAGGED INTO AN ALLEY SO HE COULD BEAT YOU INTO HAMBURGER? HE MUST REALLY HATE THOSE ARTICLES.
BUT CLARK -- YOU MUST HAVE TWENTY POUNDS ON HIM, OR MORE, AND YOU'RE IN KILLER SHAPE.
WHY DIDN'T YOU FIGHT BACK?
I DID.
THE ARTICLE RAN TODAY, DIDN'T IT?

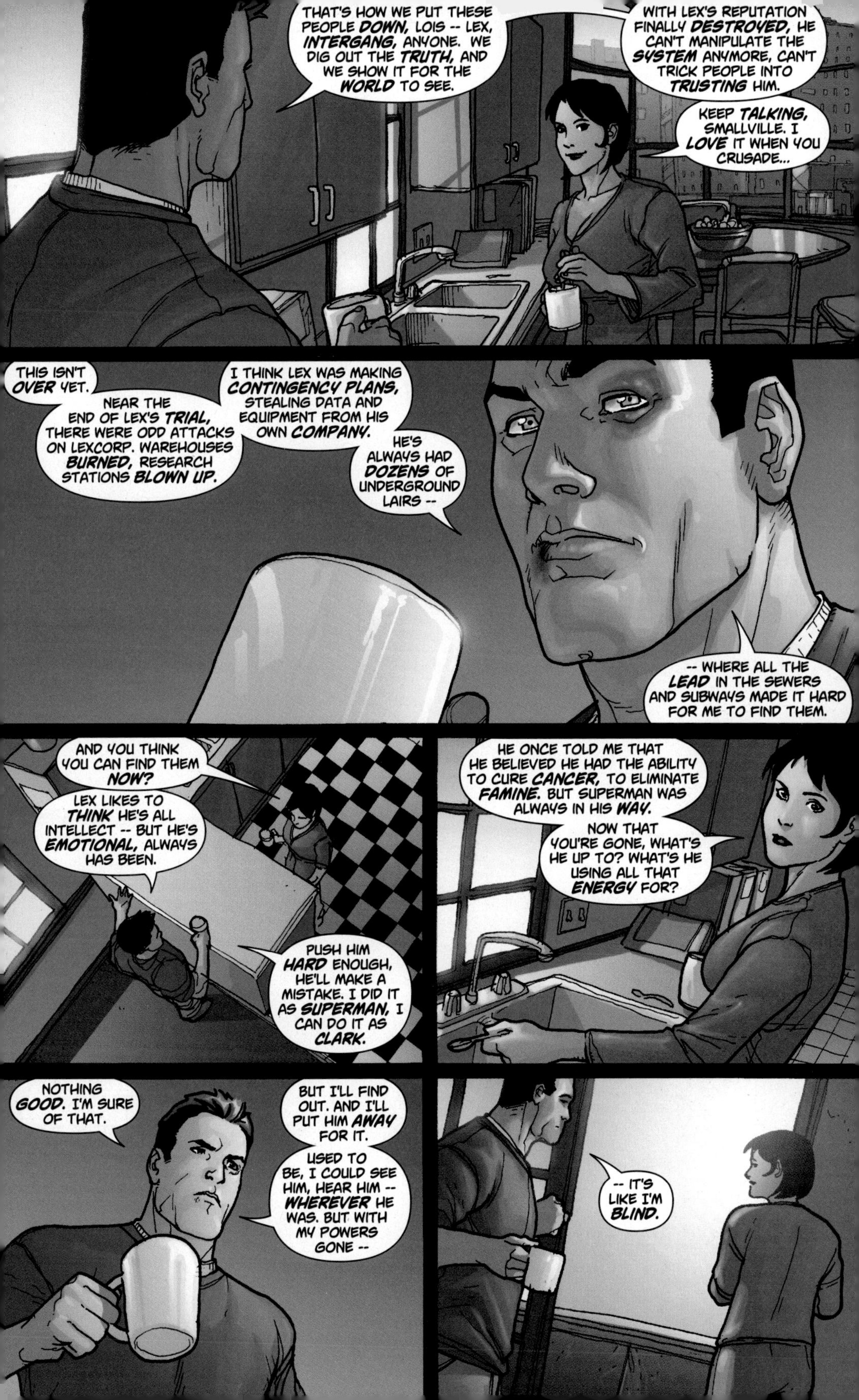
THAT'S HOW WE PUT THESE PEOPLE DOWN, LOIS -- LEX, INTERGANG, ANYONE. WE DIG OUT THE TRUTH, AND WE SHOW IT FOR THE WORLD TO SEE.
WITH LEX'S REPUTATION FINALLY DESTROYED, HE CAN'T MANIPULATE THE SYSTEM ANYMORE, CAN'T TRICK PEOPLE INTO TRUSTING HIM.
KEEP TALKING, SMALLVILLE. I LOVE IT WHEN YOU CRUSADE...
THIS ISN'T OVER YET.
NEAR THE END OF LEX'S TRIAL, THERE WERE ODD ATTACKS ON LEXCORP. WAREHOUSES BURNED, RESEARCH STATIONS BLOWN UP.
I THINK LEX WAS MAKING CONTINGENCY PLANS, STEALING DATA AND EQUIPMENT FROM HIS OWN COMPANY.
HE'S ALWAYS HAD DOZENS OF UNDERGROUND LAIRS --
-- WHERE ALL THE LEAD IN THE SEWERS AND SUBWAYS MADE IT HARD FOR ME TO FIND THEM.
AND YOU THINK YOU CAN FIND THEM NOW?
LEX LIKES TO THINK HE'S ALL INTELLECT -- BUT HE'S EMOTIONAL, ALWAYS HAS BEEN.
PUSH HIM HARD ENOUGH, HE'LL MAKE A MISTAKE. I DID IT AS SUPERMAN, I CAN DO IT AS CLARK.
HE ONCE TOLD ME THAT HE BELIEVED HE HAD THE ABILITY TO CURE CANCER, TO ELIMINATE FAMINE. BUT SUPERMAN WAS ALWAYS IN HIS WAY.
NOW THAT YOU'RE GONE, WHAT'S HE UP TO? WHAT'S HE USING ALL THAT ENERGY FOR?
NOTHING GOOD. I'M SURE OF THAT.
BUT I'LL FIND OUT. AND I'LL PUT HIM AWAY FOR IT.
USED TO BE, I COULD SEE HIM, HEAR HIM -- WHEREVER HE WAS. BUT WITH MY POWERS GONE --
-- IT'S LIKE I'M BLIND.

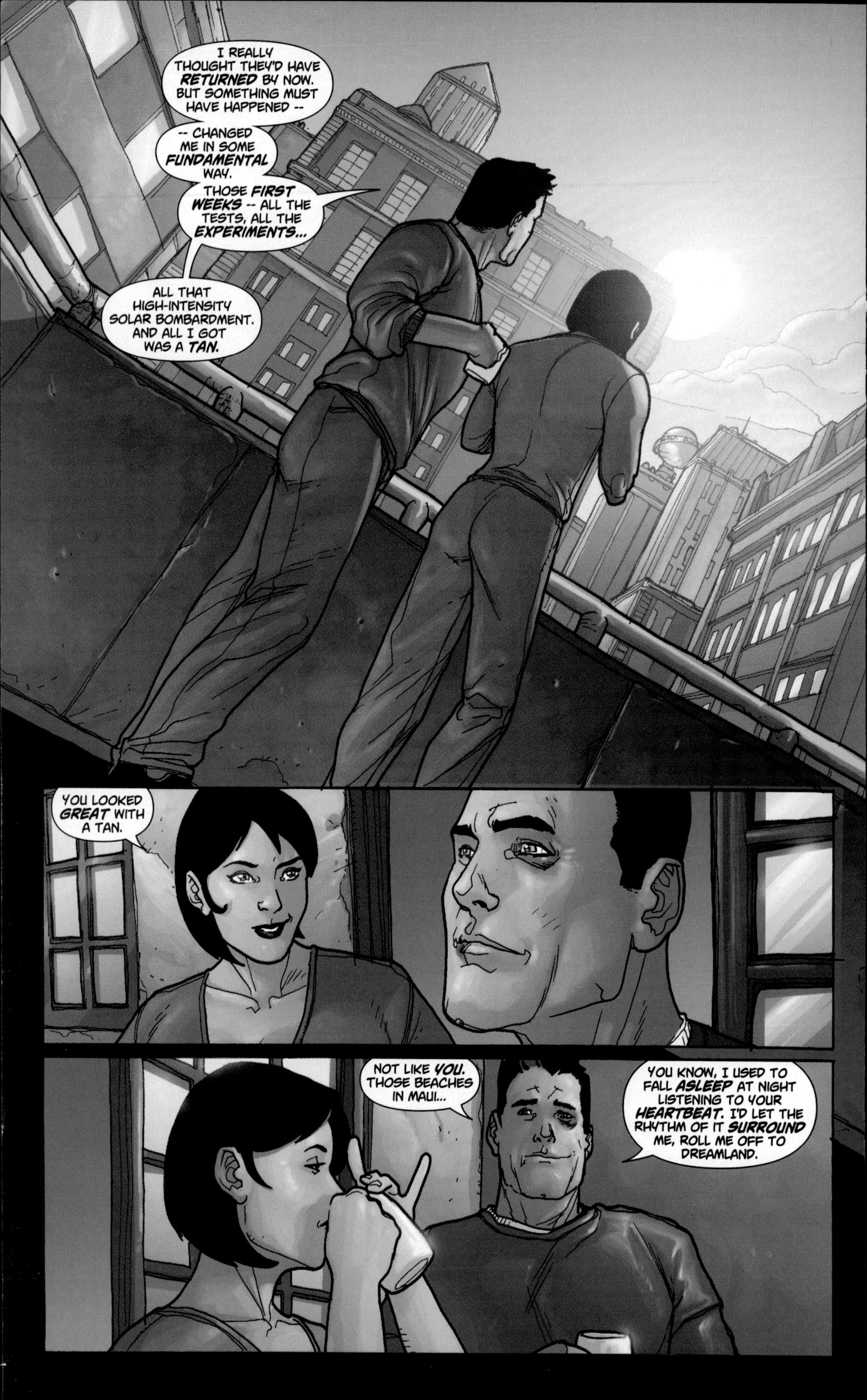
I REALLY THOUGHT THEY'D HAVE RETURNED BY NOW. BUT SOMETHING MUST HAVE HAPPENED --
-- CHANGED ME IN SOME FUNDAMENTAL WAY.
THOSE FIRST WEEKS -- ALL THE TESTS, ALL THE EXPERIMENTS...
ALL THAT HIGH-INTENSITY SOLAR BOMBARDMENT. AND ALL I GOT WAS A TAN.
YOU LOOKED GREAT WITH A TAN.
NOT LIKE YOU. THOSE BEACHES IN MAUI...
YOU KNOW, I USED TO FALL ASLEEP AT NIGHT LISTENING TO YOUR HEARTBEAT. I'D LET THE RHYTHM OF IT SURROUND ME, ROLL ME OFF TO DREAMLAND.

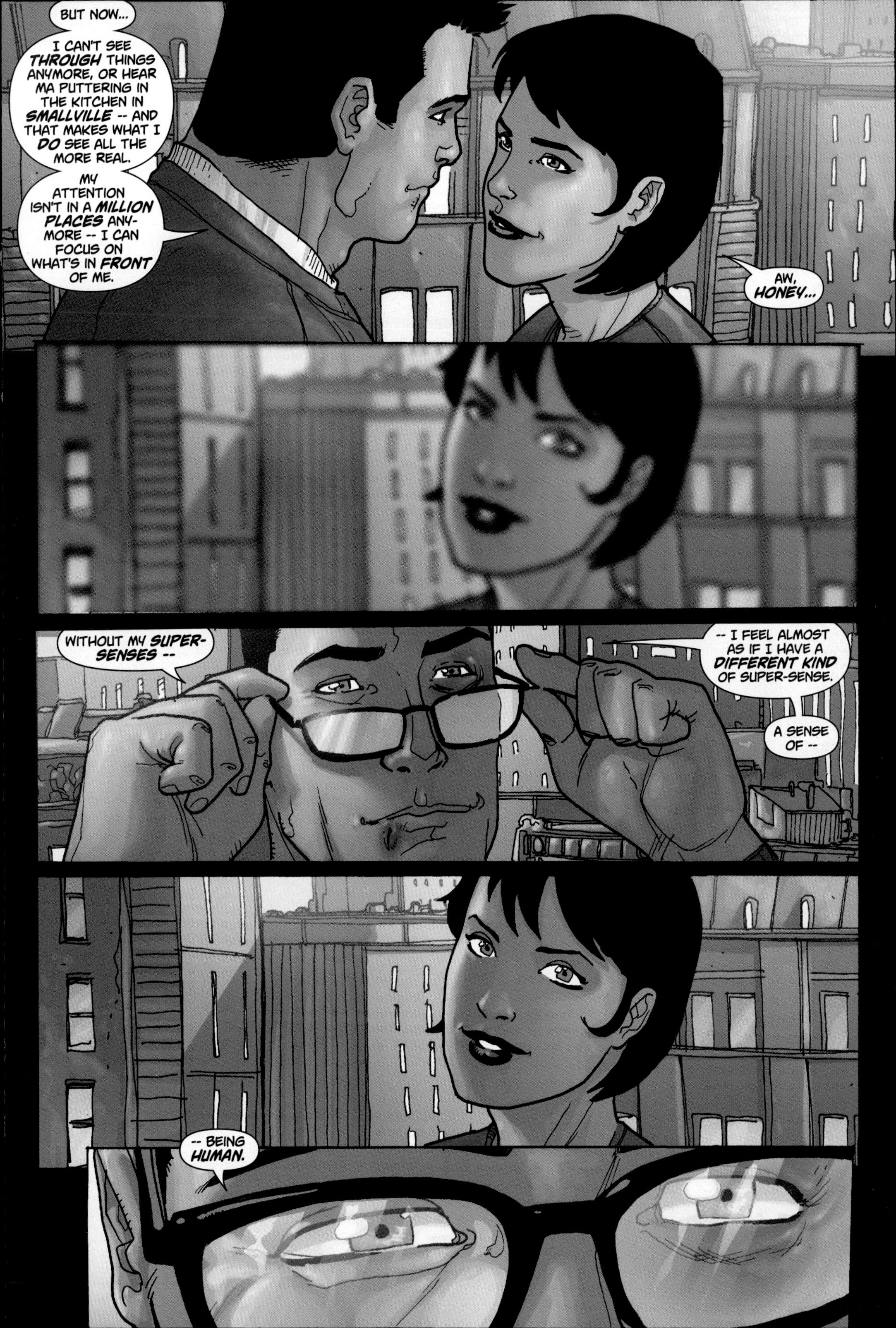

BUT NOW...
I CAN'T SEE THROUGH THINGS ANYMORE, OR HEAR MA PUTTERING IN THE KITCHEN IN SMALLVILLE -- AND THAT MAKES WHAT I DO SEE ALL THE MORE REAL.
MY ATTENTION ISN'T IN A MILLION PLACES ANY-MORE -- I CAN FOCUS ON WHAT'S IN FRONT OF ME.
AW, HONEY...
WITHOUT MY SUPER-SENSES --
-- I FEEL ALMOST AS IF I HAVE A DIFFERENT KIND OF SUPER-SENSE.
A SENSE OF --
-- BEING HUMAN.

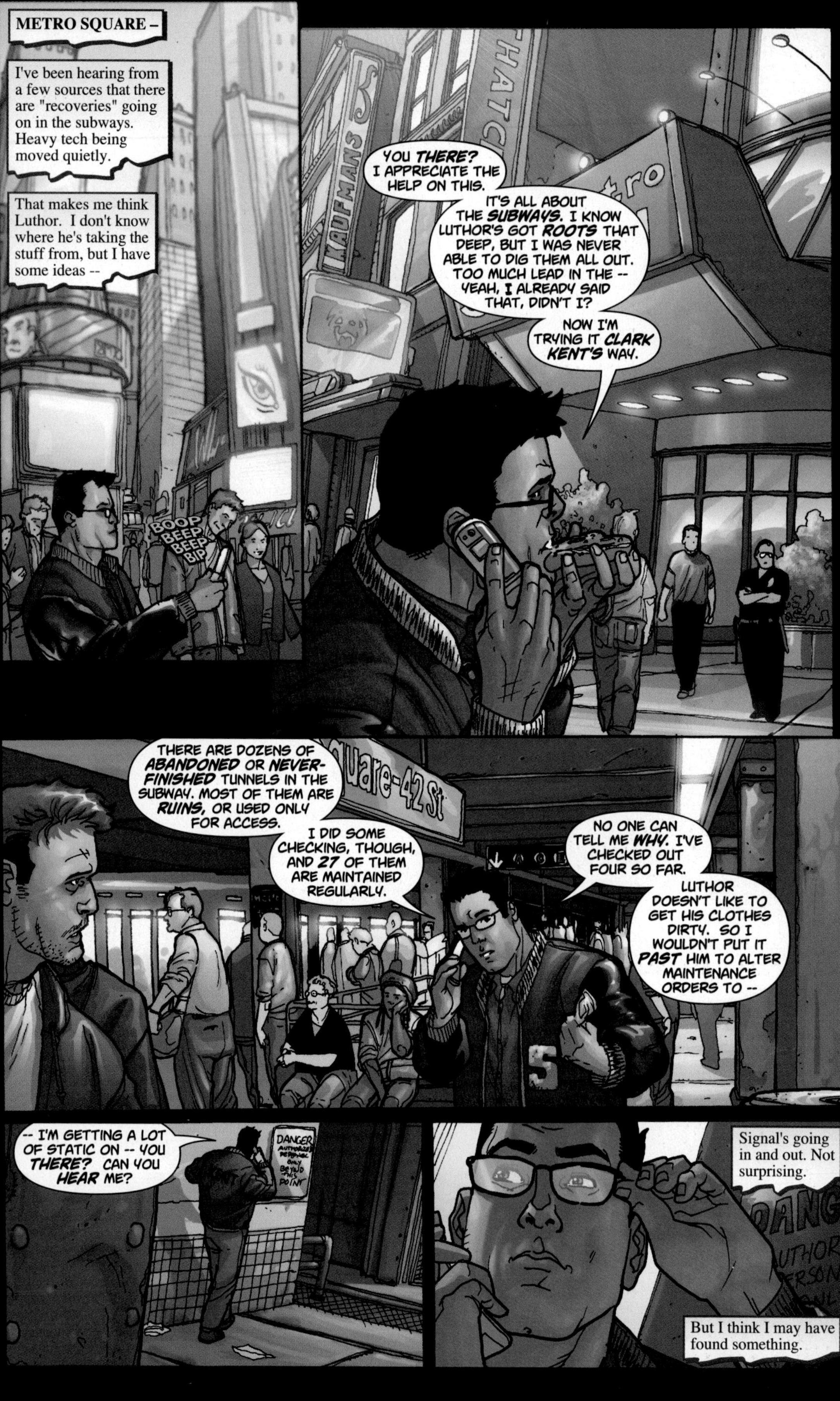
METRO SQUARE –
I've been hearing from a few sources that there are "recoveries" going on in the subways. Heavy tech being moved quietly.
That makes me think Luthor. I don't know where he's taking the stuff from, but I have some ideas --
BOOP BEEP BEEP BIP
YOU THERE? I APPRECIATE THE HELP ON THIS.
IT'S ALL ABOUT THE SUBWAYS. I KNOW LUTHOR'S GOT ROOTS THAT DEEP, BUT I WAS NEVER ABLE TO DIG THEM ALL OUT. TOO MUCH LEAD IN THE -- YEAH, I ALREADY SAID THAT, DIDN'T I?
NOW I'M TRYING IT CLARK KENT'S WAY.
THERE ARE DOZENS OF ABANDONED OR NEVER-FINISHED TUNNELS IN THE SUBWAY. MOST OF THEM ARE RUINS, OR USED ONLY FOR ACCESS.
I DID SOME CHECKING, THOUGH, AND 27 OF THEM ARE MAINTAINED REGULARLY.
NO ONE CAN TELL ME WHY. I'VE CHECKED OUT FOUR SO FAR.
LUTHOR DOESN'T LIKE TO GET HIS CLOTHES DIRTY. SO I WOULDN'T PUT IT PAST HIM TO ALTER MAINTENANCE ORDERS TO --
-- I'M GETTING A LOT OF STATIC ON -- YOU THERE? CAN YOU HEAR ME?
DANGER
Signal's going in and out. Not surprising.
But I think I may have found something.

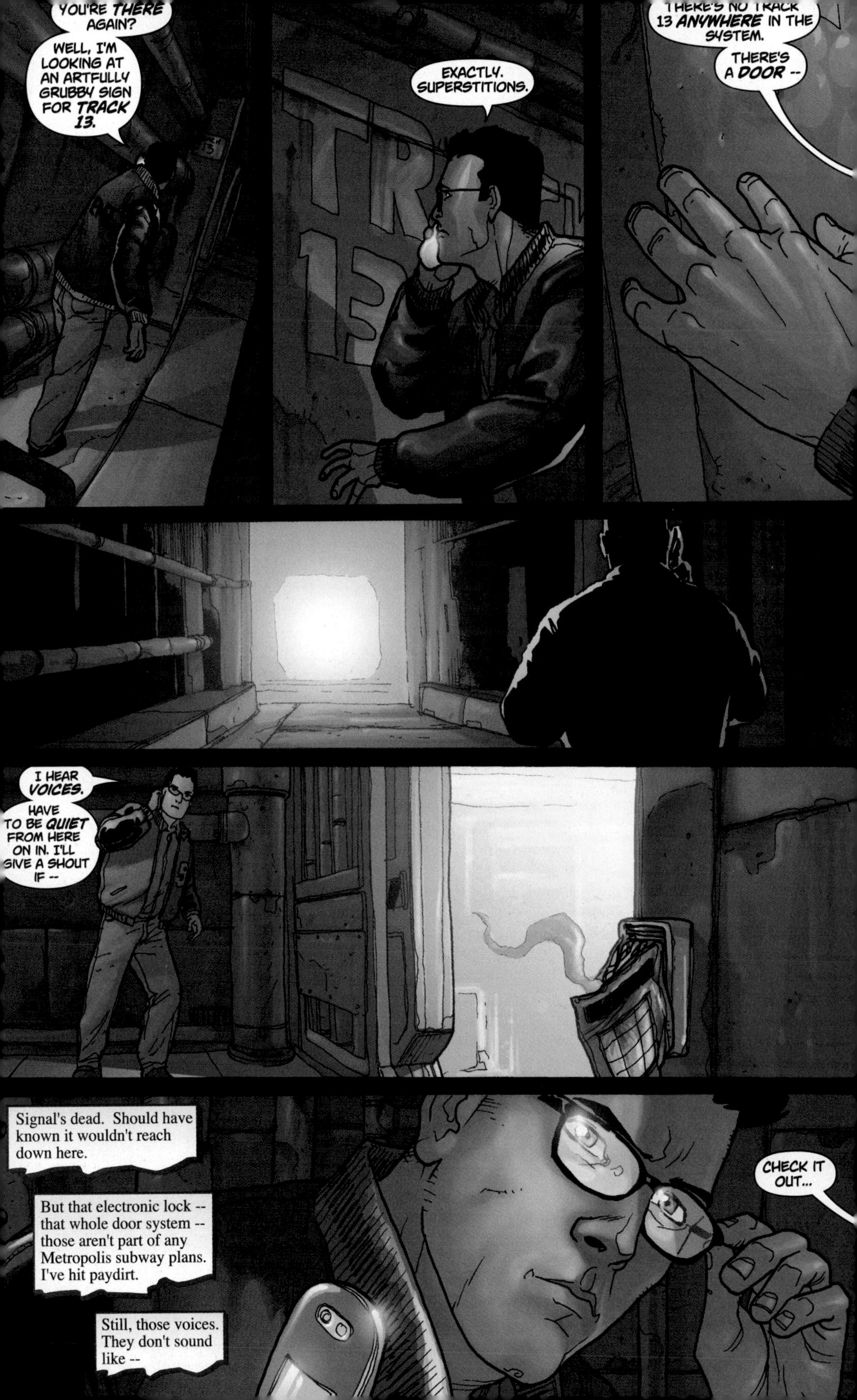
YOU'RE THERE AGAIN?
WELL, I'M LOOKING AT AN ARTFULLY GRUBBY SIGN FOR TRACK 13.
EXACTLY. SUPERSTITIONS.
THERE'S NO TRACK 13 ANYWHERE IN THE SYSTEM.
THERE'S A DOOR --
I HEAR VOICES.
HAVE TO BE QUIET FROM HERE ON IN. I'LL GIVE A SHOUT IF --
Signal's dead. Should have known it wouldn't reach down here.
But that electronic lock -- that whole door system -- those aren't part of any Metropolis subway plans. I've hit paydirt.
Still, those voices. They don't sound like --
CHECK IT OUT...

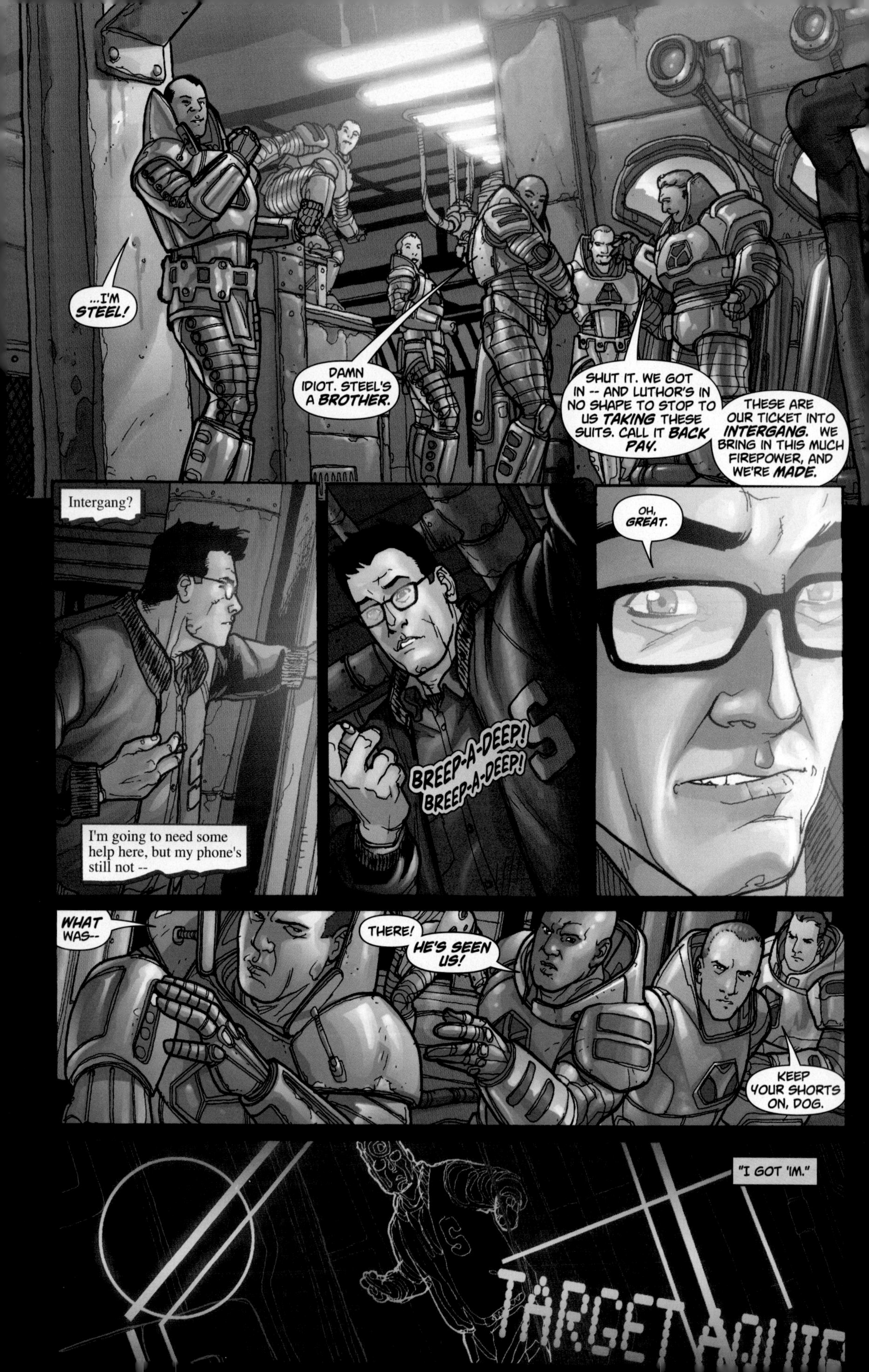
...I'M STEEL!
DAMN IDIOT. STEEL'S A BROTHER.
SHUT IT. WE GOT IN -- AND LUTHOR'S IN NO SHAPE TO STOP TO US TAKING THESE SUITS. CALL IT BACK PAY.
THESE ARE OUR TICKET INTO INTERGANG. WE BRING IN THIS MUCH FIREPOWER, AND WE'RE MADE.
Intergang?
I'm going to need some help here, but my phone's still not --
BREEP-A-DEEP! BREEP-A-DEEP!
OH, GREAT.
WHAT WAS--
THERE!
HE'S SEEN US!
KEEP YOUR SHORTS ON, DOG.
"I GOT 'IM."
TARGET

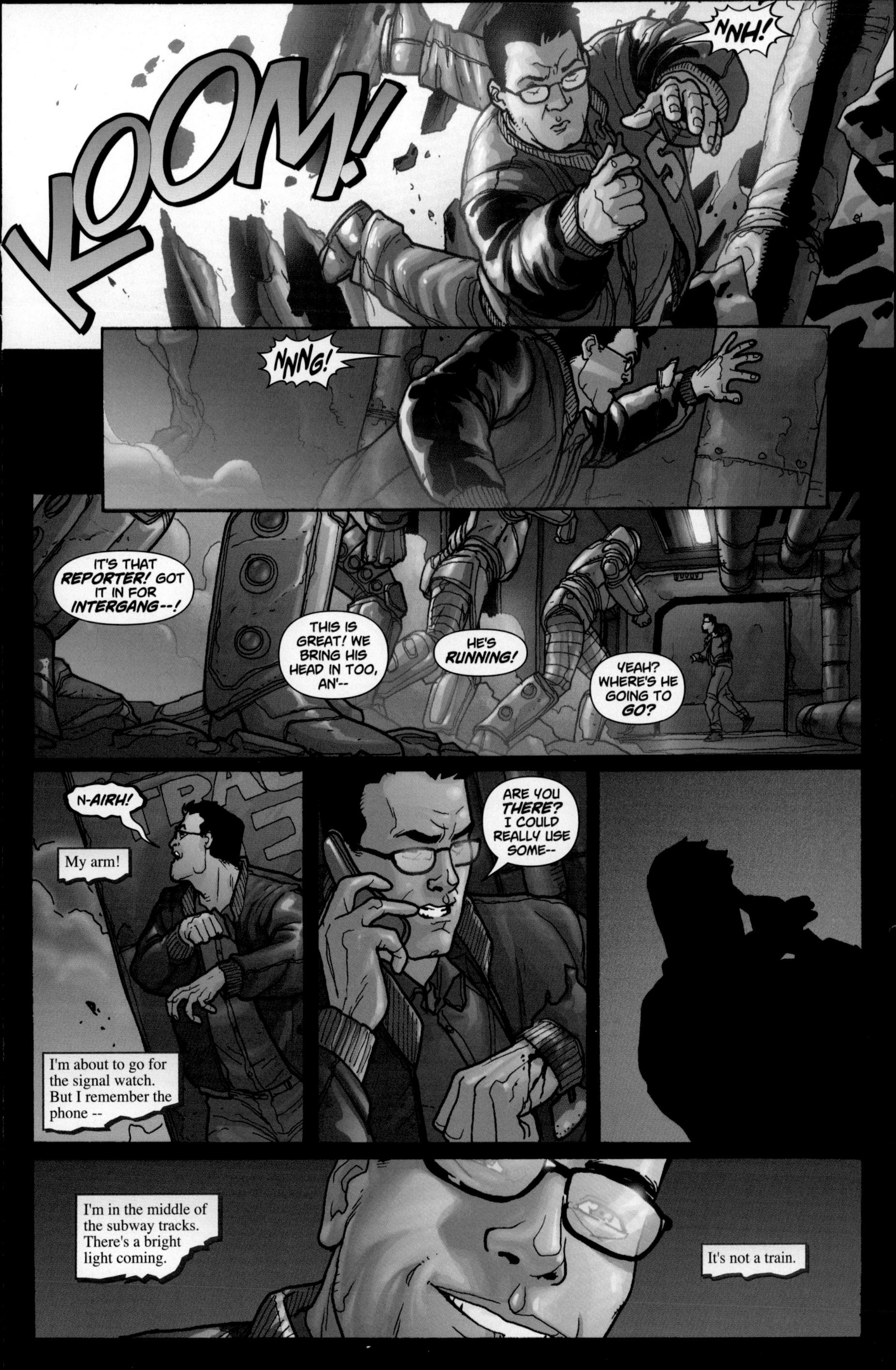
KOOM!
NNH!
NNNG!
IT'S THAT REPORTER! GOT IT IN FOR INTERGANG--!
THIS IS GREAT! WE BRING HIS HEAD IN TOO, AN'--
HE'S RUNNING!
YEAH? WHERE'S HE GOING TO GO?
N-AIRH!
My arm!
I'm about to go for the signal watch. But I remember the phone --
ARE YOU THERE? I COULD REALLY USE SOME--
I'm in the middle of the subway tracks. There's a bright light coming.
It's not a train.

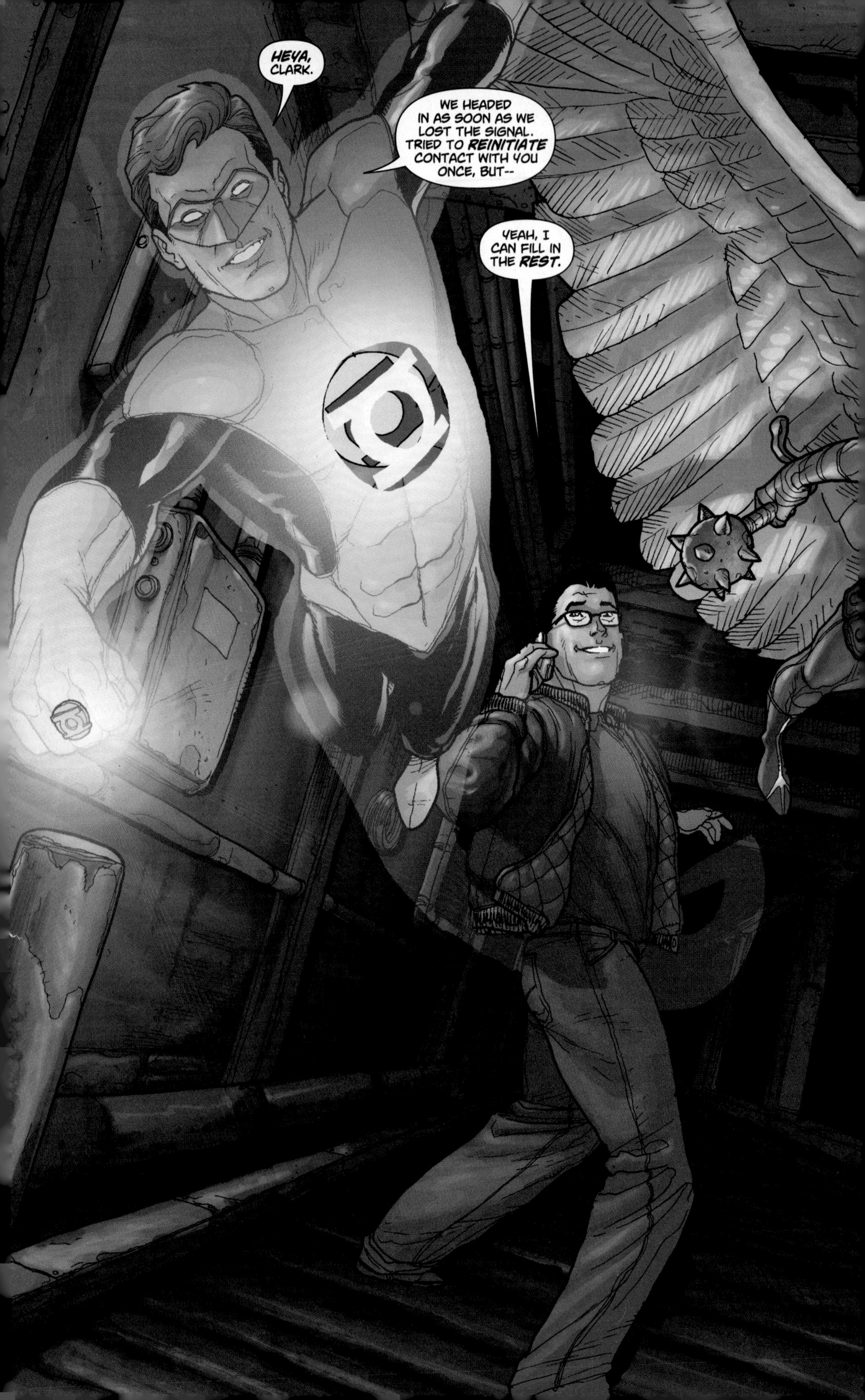
HEYA, CLARK.
WE HEADED IN AS SOON AS WE LOST THE SIGNAL. TRIED TO REINITIATE CONTACT WITH YOU ONCE, BUT--
YEAH, I CAN FILL IN THE REST.

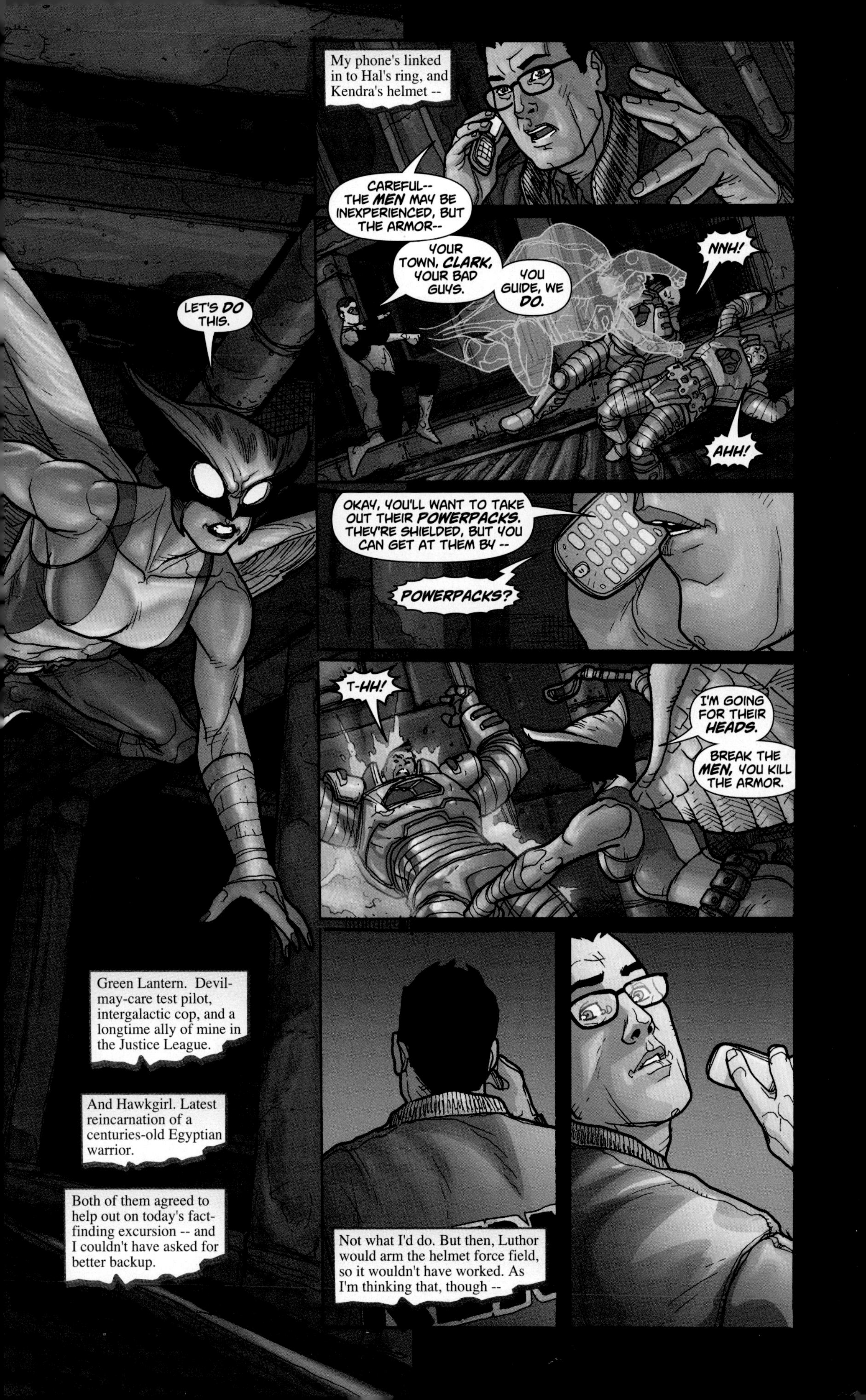
My phone's linked in to Hal's ring, and Kendra's helmet --
CAREFUL-- THE MEN MAY BE INEXPERIENCED, BUT THE ARMOR--
YOUR TOWN, CLARK, YOUR BAD GUYS.
YOU GUIDE, WE DO.
NNH!
AHH!
LET'S DO THIS.
OKAY, YOU'LL WANT TO TAKE OUT THEIR POWERPACKS. THEY'RE SHIELDED, BUT YOU CAN GET AT THEM BY --
POWERPACKS?
T-HH!
I'M GOING FOR THEIR HEADS.
BREAK THE MEN, YOU KILL THE ARMOR.
Green Lantern. Devil-may-care test pilot, intergalactic cop, and a longtime ally of mine in the Justice League.
And Hawkgirl. Latest reincarnation of a centuries-old Egyptian warrior.
Both of them agreed to help out on today's fact-finding excursion -- and I couldn't have asked for better backup.
Not what I'd do. But then, Luthor would arm the helmet force field, so it wouldn't have worked. As I'm thinking that, though --

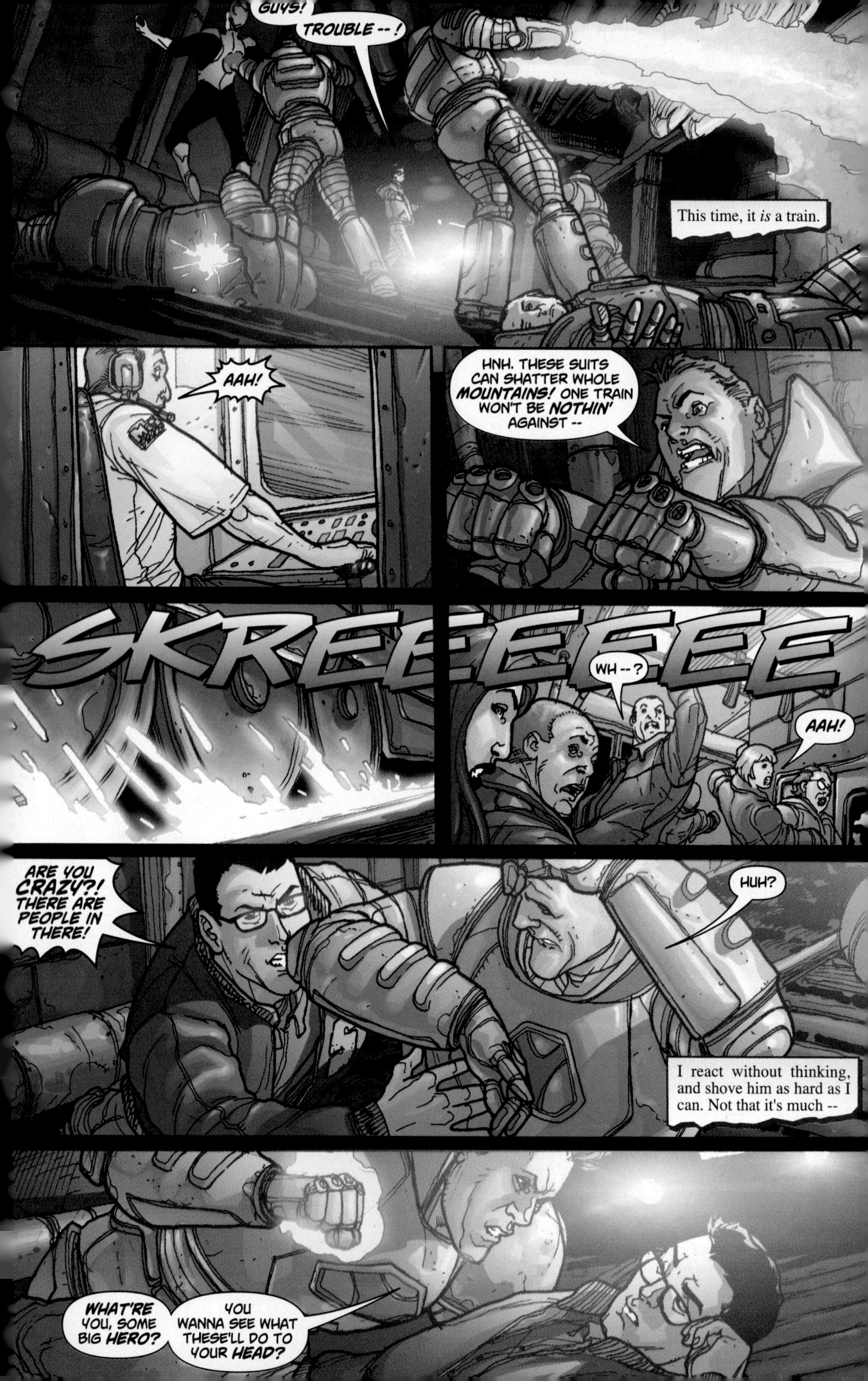
GUYS!
TROUBLE --!
This time, it *is* a train.
AAH!
HNH. THESE SUITS CAN SHATTER WHOLE MOUNTAINS! ONE TRAIN WON'T BE NOTHIN' AGAINST --
SKREEEEEEE
WH --?
AAH!
ARE YOU CRAZY?! THERE ARE PEOPLE IN THERE!
HUH?
I react without thinking, and shove him as hard as I can. Not that it's much --
WHAT'RE YOU, SOME BIG HERO?
YOU WANNA SEE WHAT THESE'LL DO TO YOUR HEAD?

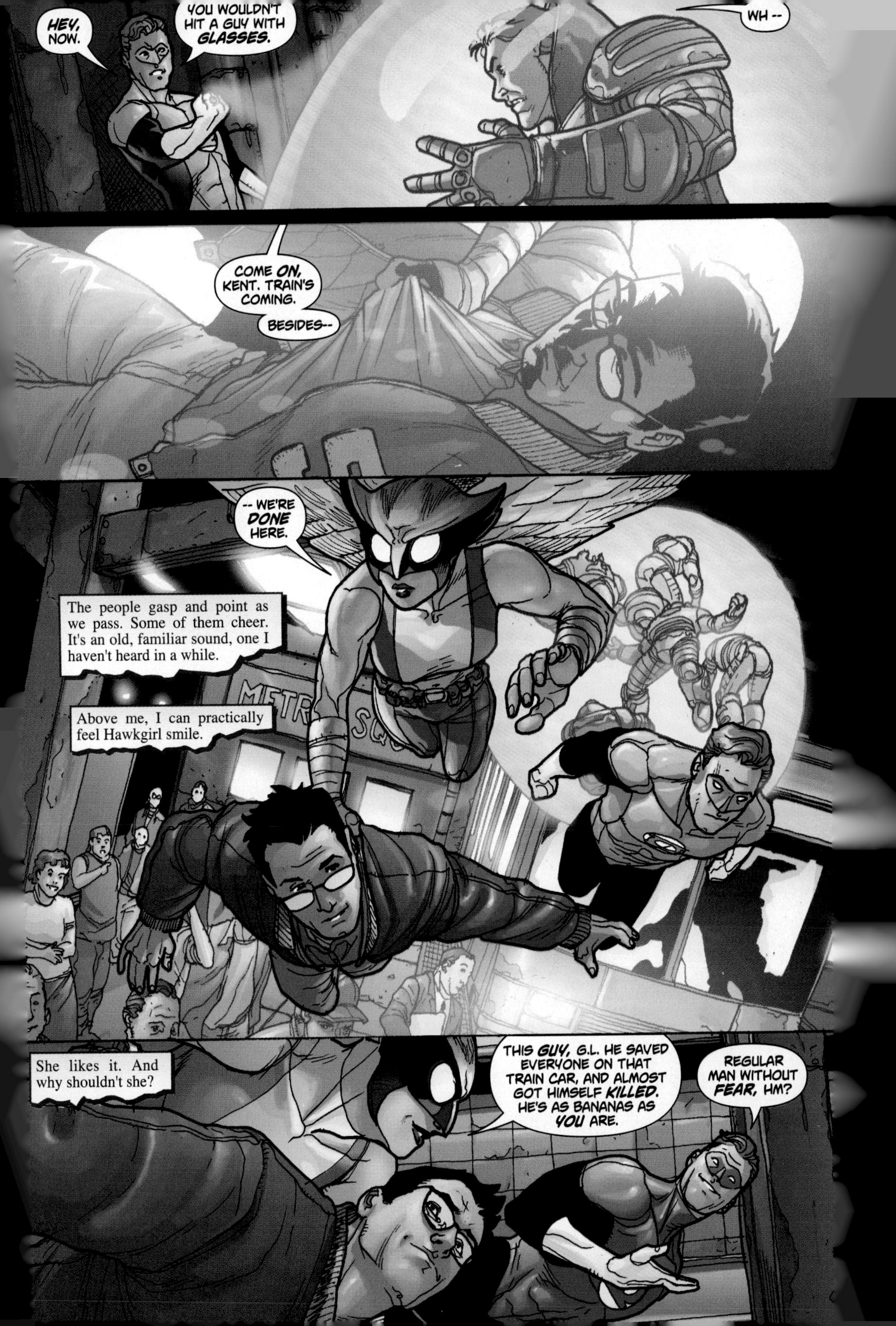

HEY, NOW.
YOU WOULDN'T HIT A GUY WITH GLASSES.
WH --
COME ON, KENT. TRAIN'S COMING.
BESIDES--
-- WE'RE DONE HERE.
The people gasp and point as we pass. Some of them cheer. It's an old, familiar sound, one I haven't heard in a while.
Above me, I can practically feel Hawkgirl smile.
She likes it. And why shouldn't she?
THIS GUY, G.L. HE SAVED EVERYONE ON THAT TRAIN CAR, AND ALMOST GOT HIMSELF KILLED. HE'S AS BANANAS AS YOU ARE.
REGULAR MAN WITHOUT FEAR, HM?

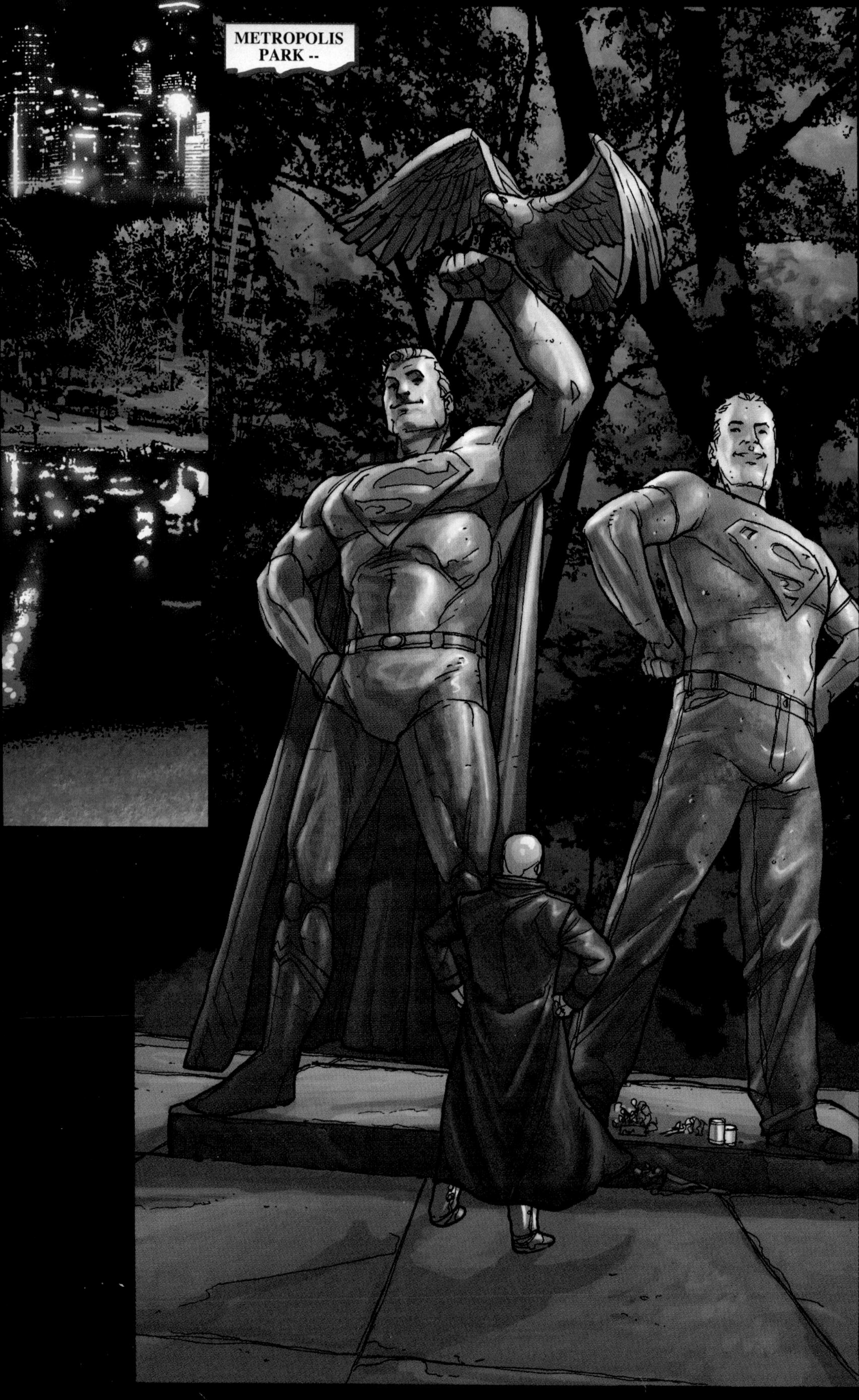
METROPOLIS PARK --

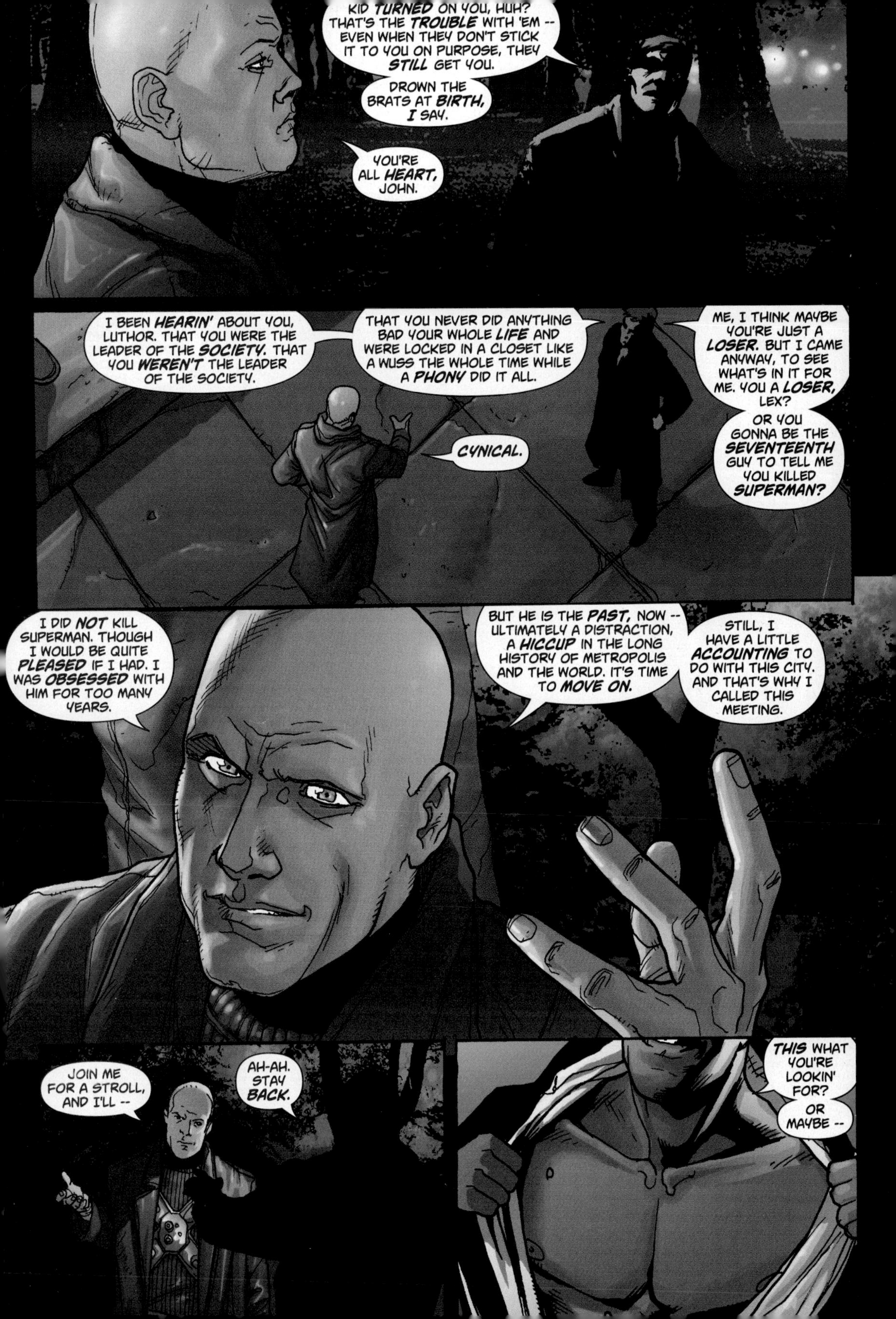
KID TURNED ON YOU, HUH? THAT'S THE TROUBLE WITH 'EM -- EVEN WHEN THEY DON'T STICK IT TO YOU ON PURPOSE, THEY STILL GET YOU.
DROWN THE BRATS AT BIRTH, I SAY.
YOU'RE ALL HEART, JOHN.
I BEEN HEARIN' ABOUT YOU, LUTHOR. THAT YOU WERE THE LEADER OF THE SOCIETY. THAT YOU WEREN'T THE LEADER OF THE SOCIETY.
THAT YOU NEVER DID ANYTHING BAD YOUR WHOLE LIFE AND WERE LOCKED IN A CLOSET LIKE A WUSS THE WHOLE TIME WHILE A PHONY DID IT ALL.
ME, I THINK MAYBE YOU'RE JUST A LOSER. BUT I CAME ANYWAY, TO SEE WHAT'S IN IT FOR ME. YOU A LOSER, LEX?
OR YOU GONNA BE THE SEVENTEENTH GUY TO TELL ME YOU KILLED SUPERMAN?
CYNICAL.
I DID NOT KILL SUPERMAN. THOUGH I WOULD BE QUITE PLEASED IF I HAD. I WAS OBSESSED WITH HIM FOR TOO MANY YEARS.
BUT HE IS THE PAST, NOW -- ULTIMATELY A DISTRACTION, A HICCUP IN THE LONG HISTORY OF METROPOLIS AND THE WORLD. IT'S TIME TO MOVE ON.
STILL, I HAVE A LITTLE ACCOUNTING TO DO WITH THIS CITY. AND THAT'S WHY I CALLED THIS MEETING.
JOIN ME FOR A STROLL, AND I'LL --
AH-AH. STAY BACK.
THIS WHAT YOU'RE LOOKIN' FOR?
OR MAYBE --

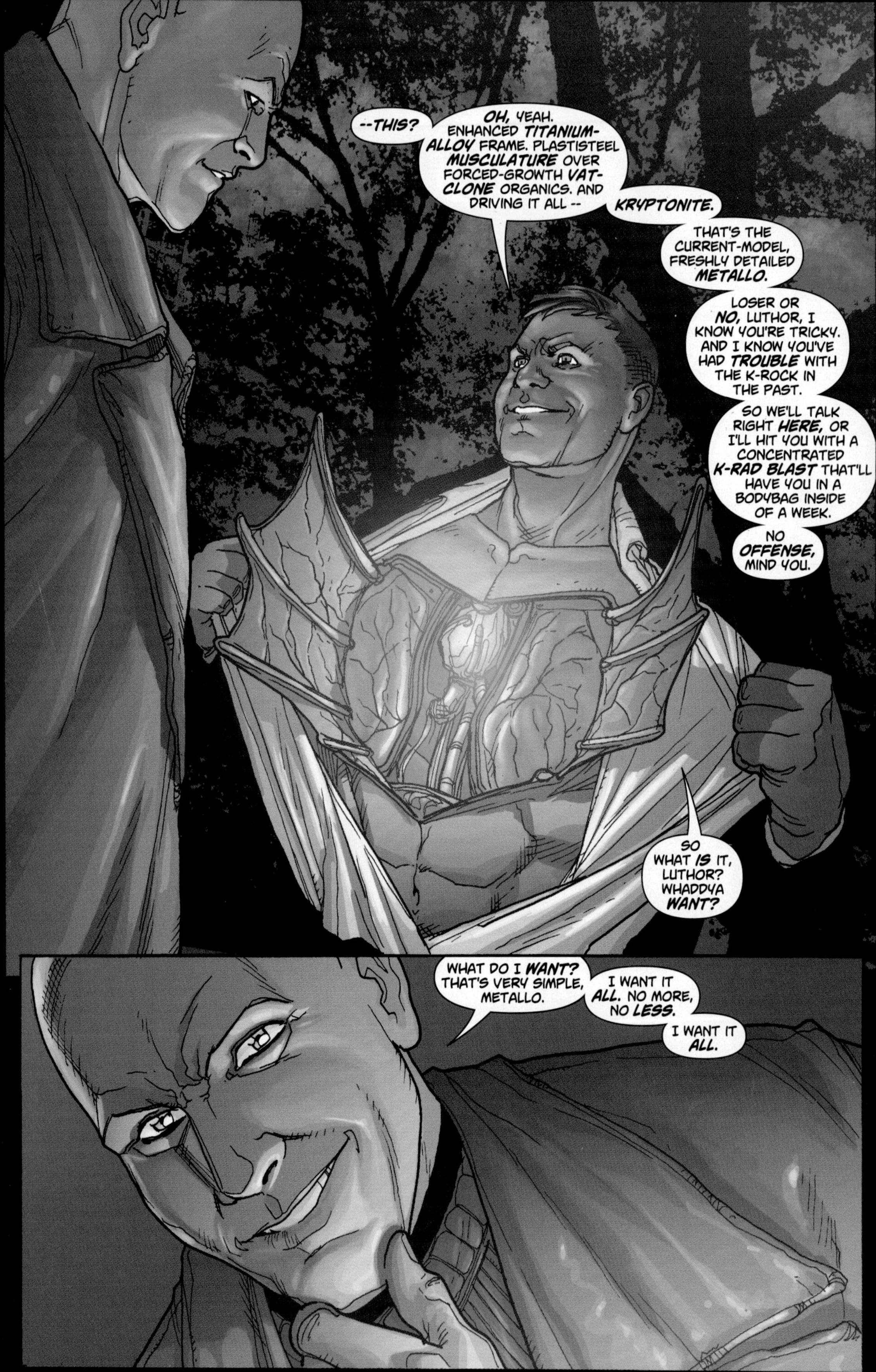
--THIS?
OH, YEAH. ENHANCED TITANIUM-ALLOY FRAME. PLASTISTEEL MUSCULATURE OVER FORCED-GROWTH VAT-CLONE ORGANICS. AND DRIVING IT ALL --
KRYPTONITE.
THAT'S THE CURRENT-MODEL, FRESHLY DETAILED METALLO.
LOSER OR NO, LUTHOR, I KNOW YOU'RE TRICKY. AND I KNOW YOU'VE HAD TROUBLE WITH THE K-ROCK IN THE PAST.
SO WE'LL TALK RIGHT HERE, OR I'LL HIT YOU WITH A CONCENTRATED K-RAD BLAST THAT'LL HAVE YOU IN A BODYBAG INSIDE OF A WEEK.
NO OFFENSE, MIND YOU.
SO WHAT IS IT, LUTHOR? WHADDYA WANT?
WHAT DO I WANT? THAT'S VERY SIMPLE, METALLO.
I WANT IT ALL. NO MORE, NO LESS.
I WANT IT ALL.

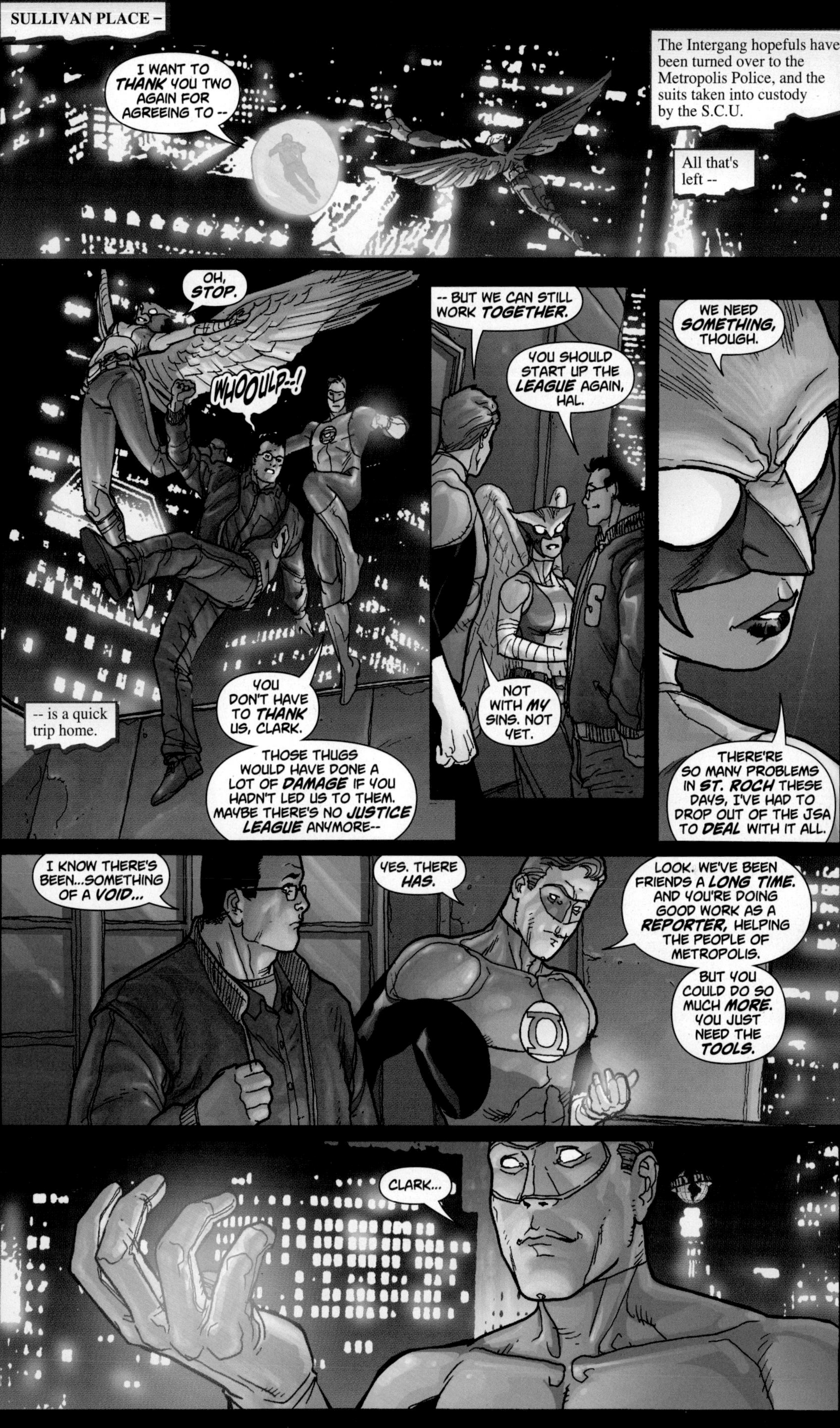
SULLIVAN PLACE –
I WANT TO THANK YOU TWO AGAIN FOR AGREEING TO --
The Intergang hopefuls have been turned over to the Metropolis Police, and the suits taken into custody by the S.C.U.
All that's left --
OH, STOP.
WHOOULP--!
-- is a quick trip home.
YOU DON'T HAVE TO THANK US, CLARK.
THOSE THUGS WOULD HAVE DONE A LOT OF DAMAGE IF YOU HADN'T LED US TO THEM. MAYBE THERE'S NO JUSTICE LEAGUE ANYMORE--
-- BUT WE CAN STILL WORK TOGETHER.
YOU SHOULD START UP THE LEAGUE AGAIN, HAL.
NOT WITH MY SINS. NOT YET.
WE NEED SOMETHING, THOUGH.
THERE'RE SO MANY PROBLEMS IN ST. ROCH THESE DAYS, I'VE HAD TO DROP OUT OF THE JSA TO DEAL WITH IT ALL.
I KNOW THERE'S BEEN...SOMETHING OF A VOID...
YES. THERE HAS.
LOOK. WE'VE BEEN FRIENDS A LONG TIME. AND YOU'RE DOING GOOD WORK AS A REPORTER, HELPING THE PEOPLE OF METROPOLIS.
BUT YOU COULD DO SO MUCH MORE. YOU JUST NEED THE TOOLS.
CLARK...

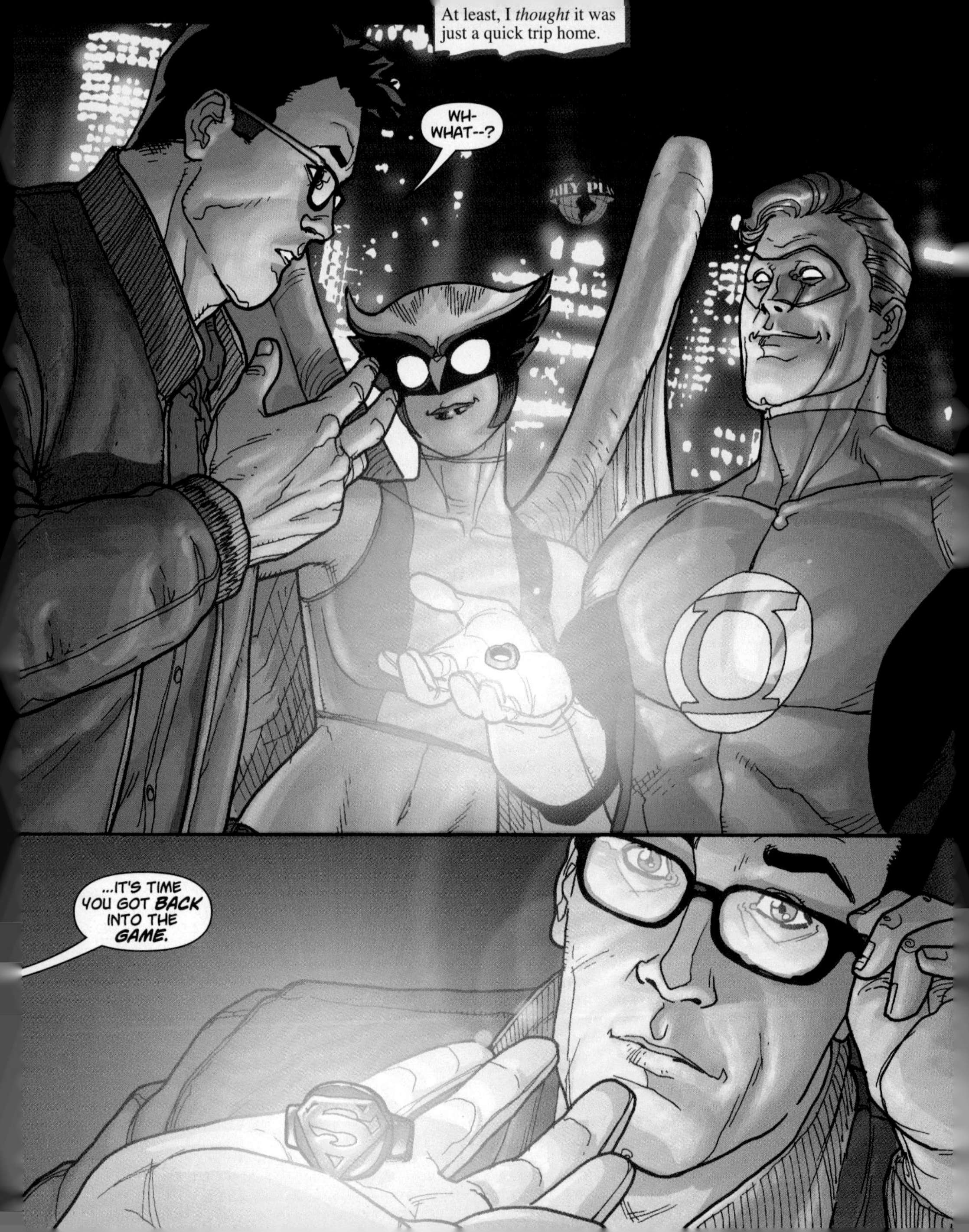
At least, I *thought* it was just a quick trip home.
WH- WHAT--?
...IT'S TIME YOU GOT **BACK** INTO THE **GAME.**

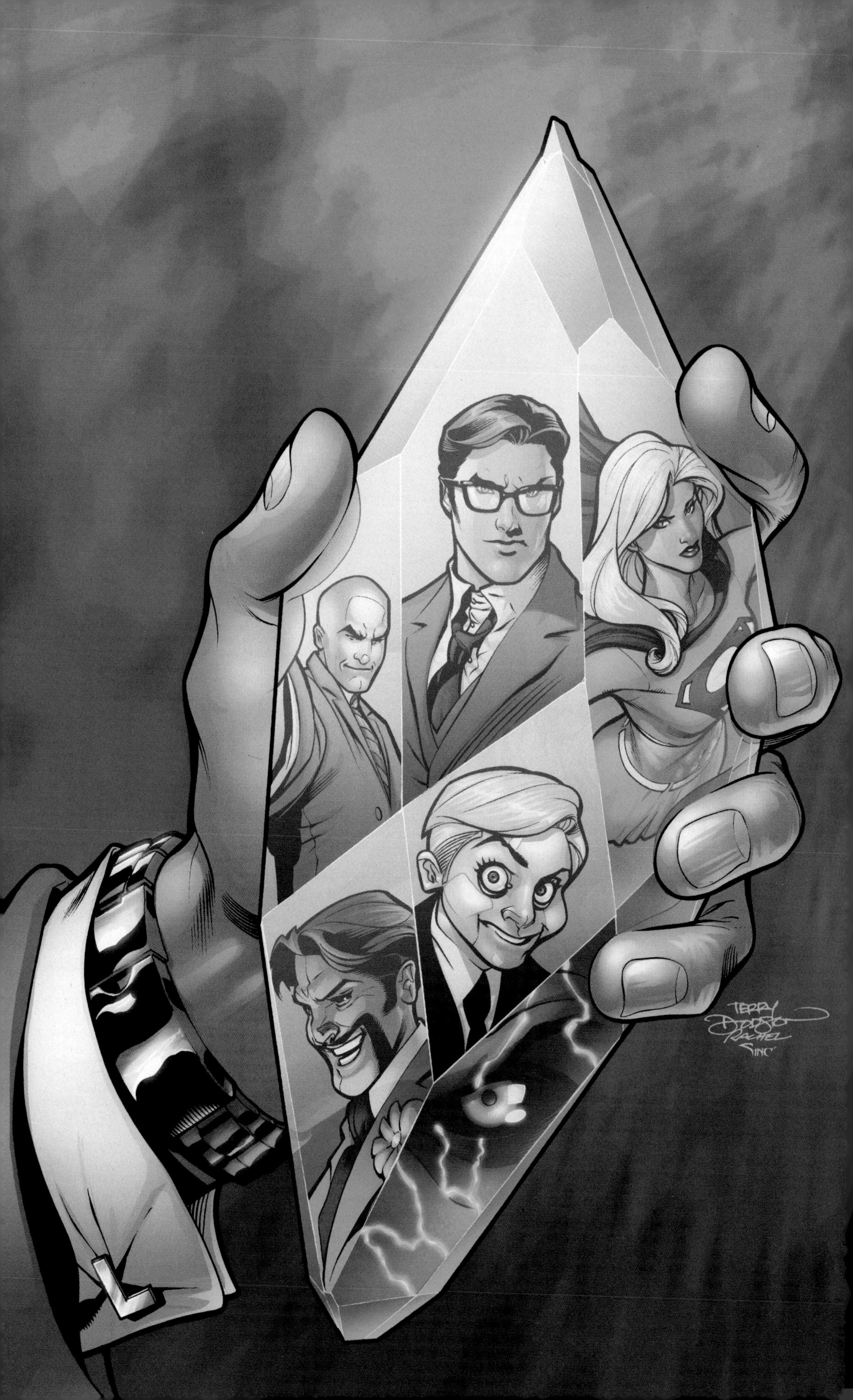

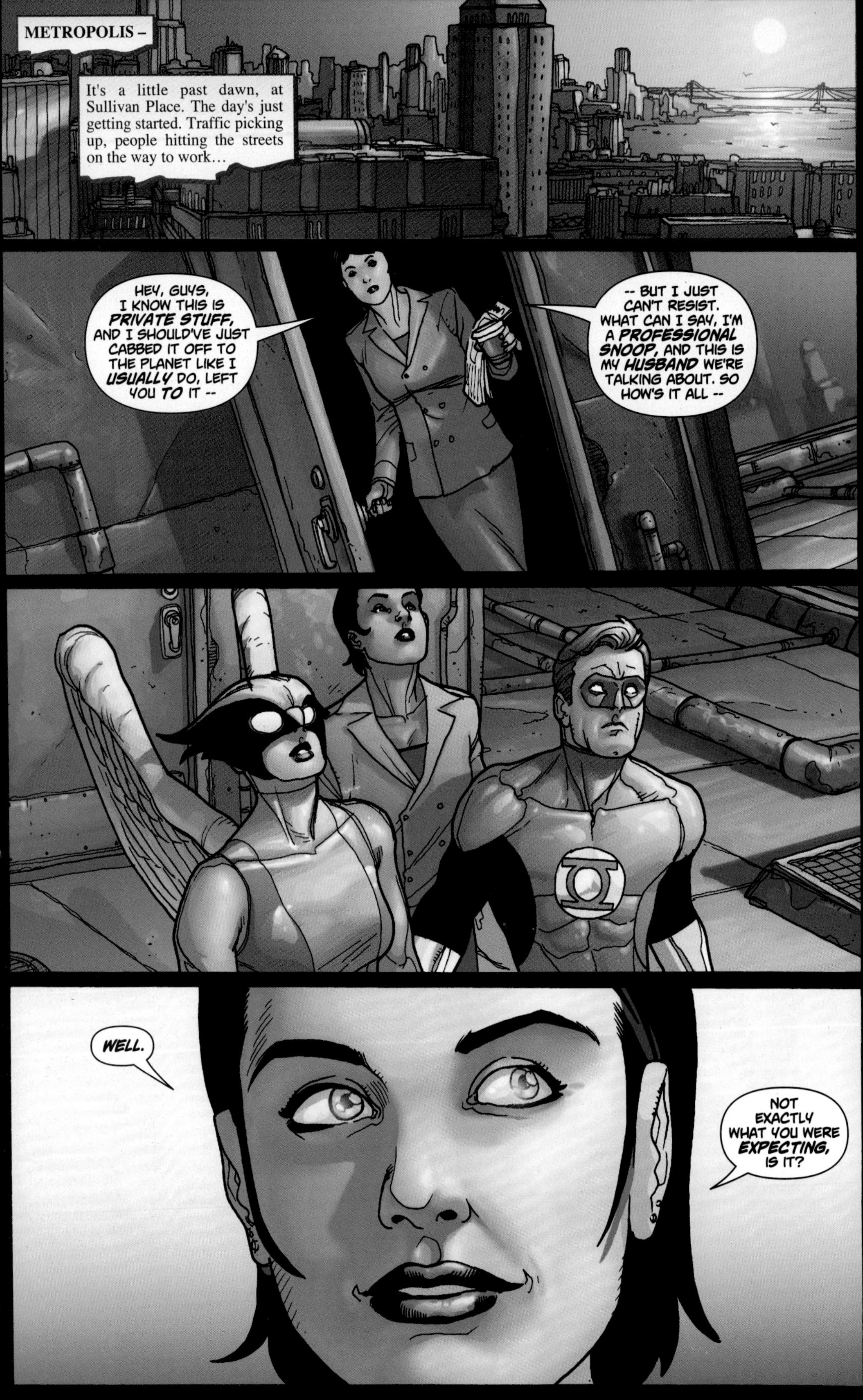
METROPOLIS –
It's a little past dawn, at Sullivan Place. The day's just getting started. Traffic picking up, people hitting the streets on the way to work…
HEY, GUYS, I KNOW THIS IS PRIVATE STUFF, AND I SHOULD'VE JUST CABBED IT OFF TO THE PLANET LIKE I USUALLY DO, LEFT YOU TO IT --
-- BUT I JUST CAN'T RESIST. WHAT CAN I SAY, I'M A PROFESSIONAL SNOOP, AND THIS IS MY HUSBAND WE'RE TALKING ABOUT. SO HOW'S IT ALL --
WELL.
NOT EXACTLY WHAT YOU WERE EXPECTING, IS IT?

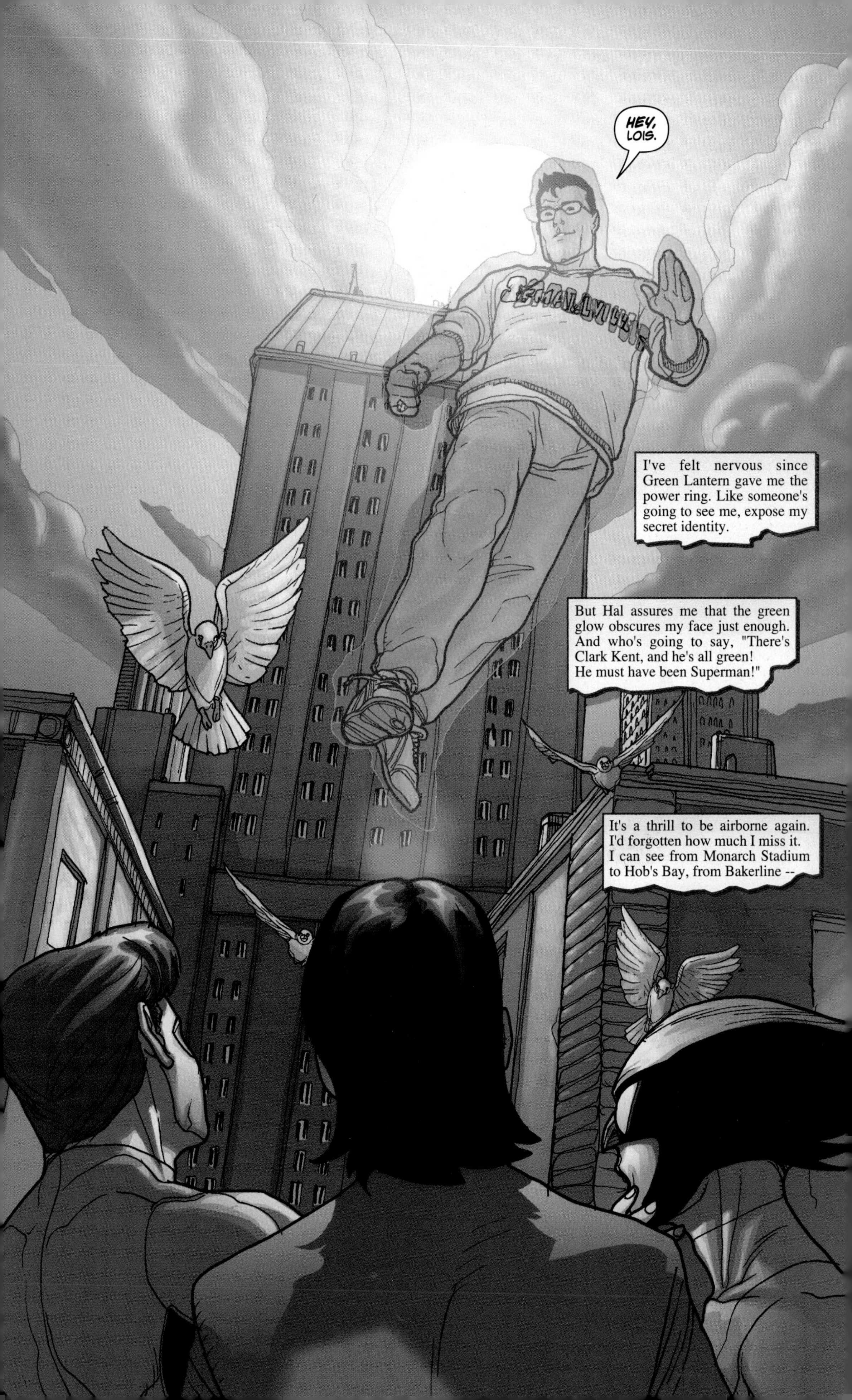
HEY, LOIS.
I've felt nervous since Green Lantern gave me the power ring. Like someone's going to see me, expose my secret identity.
But Hal assures me that the green glow obscures my face just enough. And who's going to say, "There's Clark Kent, and he's all green! He must have been Superman!"
It's a thrill to be airborne again. I'd forgotten how much I miss it. I can see from Monarch Stadium to Hob's Bay, from Bakerline --

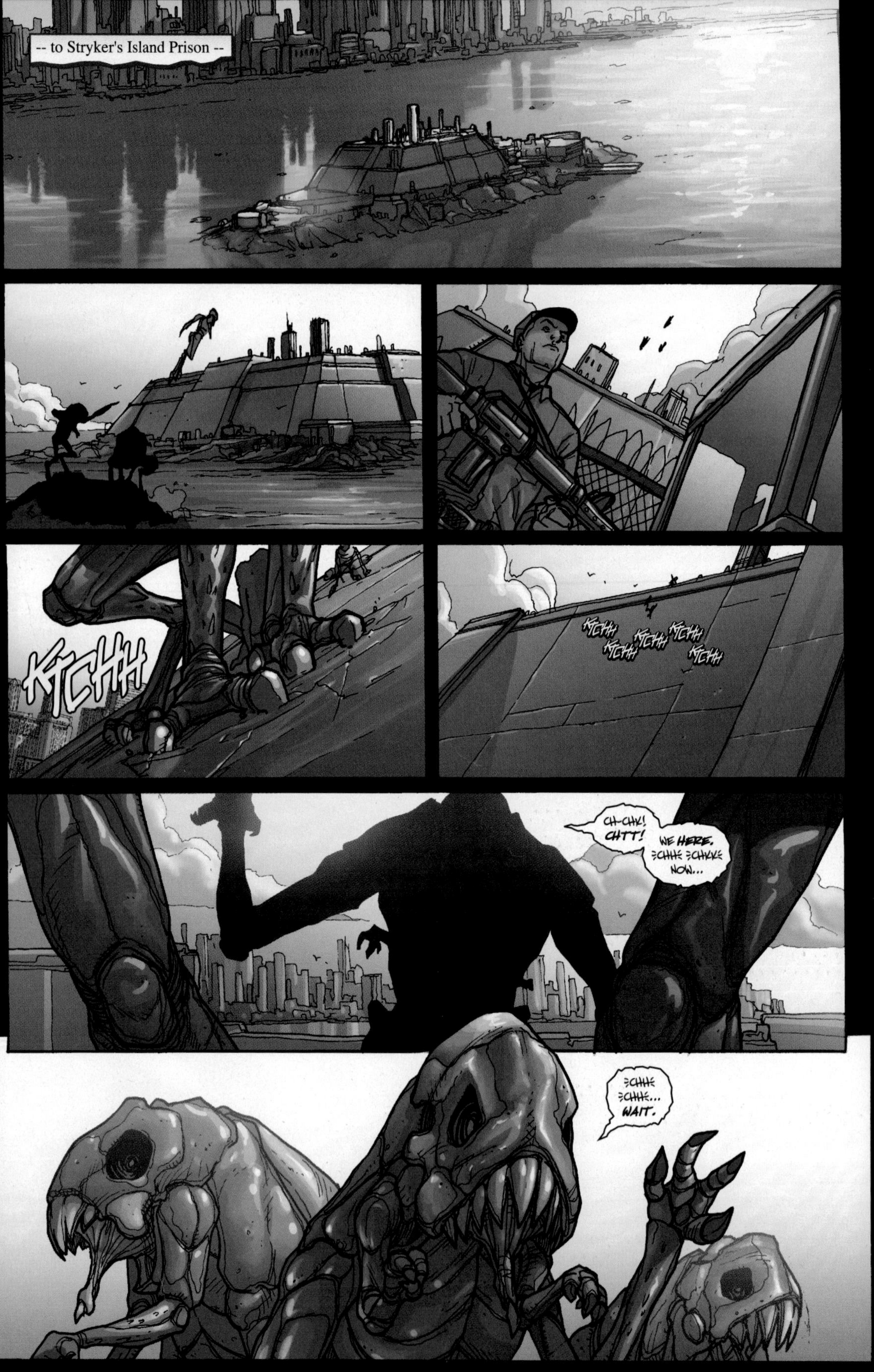
-- to Stryker's Island Prison --
KTCHH
KTCHH KTCHH KTCHH KTCHH KTCHH
CH-CHK! CHTT!
WE HERE. ≡CHH≡ ≡CHKK≡ NOW...
≡CHH≡ ≡CHH≡... WAIT.

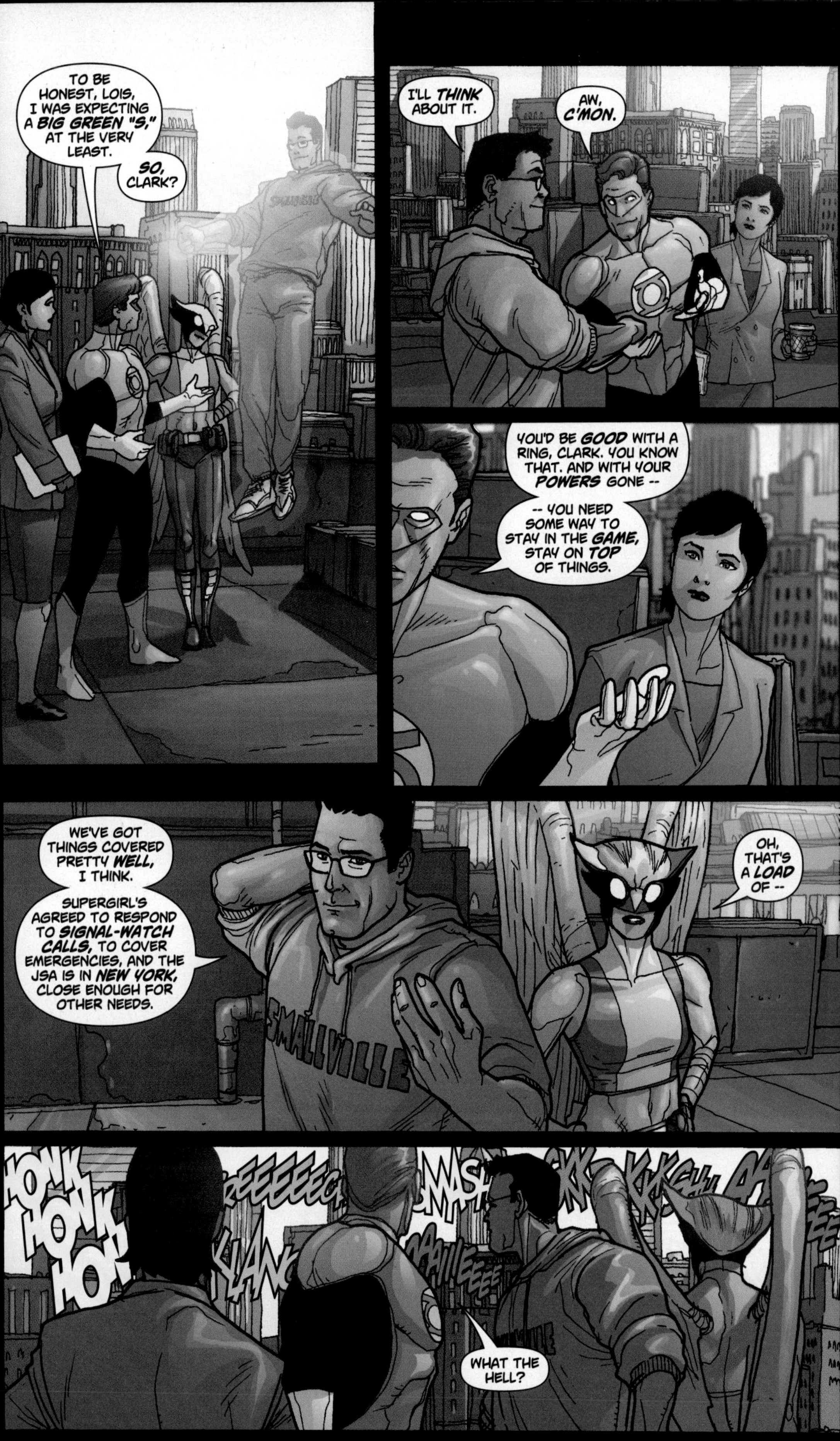
TO BE HONEST, LOIS, I WAS EXPECTING A BIG GREEN "S," AT THE VERY LEAST.
SO, CLARK?
I'LL THINK ABOUT IT.
AW, C'MON.
YOU'D BE GOOD WITH A RING, CLARK. YOU KNOW THAT. AND WITH YOUR POWERS GONE --
-- YOU NEED SOME WAY TO STAY IN THE GAME, STAY ON TOP OF THINGS.
WE'VE GOT THINGS COVERED PRETTY WELL, I THINK.
SUPERGIRL'S AGREED TO RESPOND TO SIGNAL-WATCH CALLS, TO COVER EMERGENCIES, AND THE JSA IS IN NEW YORK, CLOSE ENOUGH FOR OTHER NEEDS.
OH, THAT'S A LOAD OF --
HONK
HONK
WHAT THE HELL?

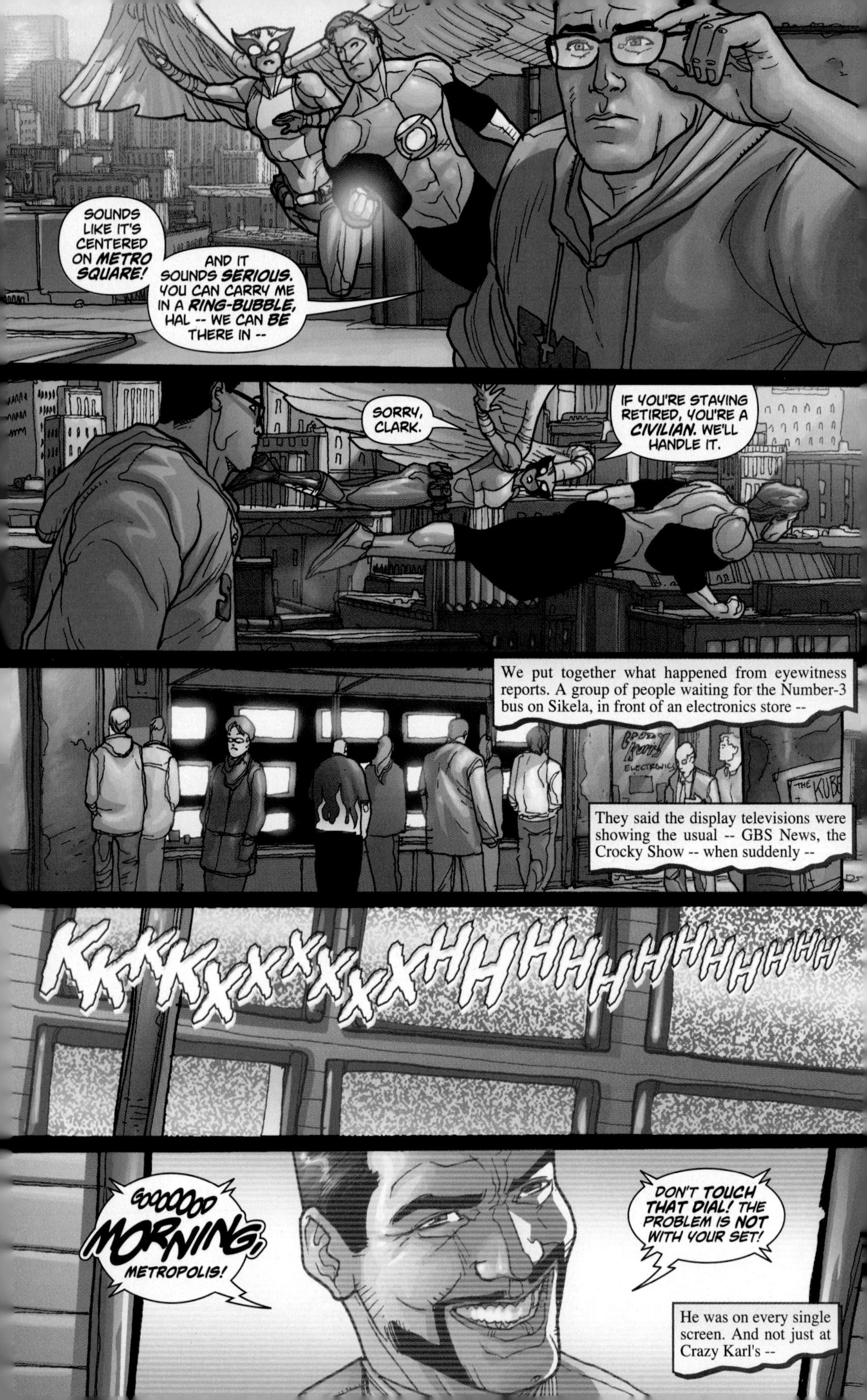
SOUNDS LIKE IT'S CENTERED ON METRO SQUARE!
AND IT SOUNDS SERIOUS. YOU CAN CARRY ME IN A RING-BUBBLE, HAL -- WE CAN BE THERE IN --
SORRY, CLARK.
IF YOU'RE STAYING RETIRED, YOU'RE A CIVILIAN. WE'LL HANDLE IT.
We put together what happened from eyewitness reports. A group of people waiting for the Number-3 bus on Sikela, in front of an electronics store --
They said the display televisions were showing the usual -- GBS News, the Crocky Show -- when suddenly --
KKKKXXXXXXXHHHHHHHHHHHHHHH
GOOOOOOD MORNING, METROPOLIS!
DON'T TOUCH THAT DIAL! THE PROBLEM IS NOT WITH YOUR SET!
He was on every single screen. And not just at Crazy Karl's --

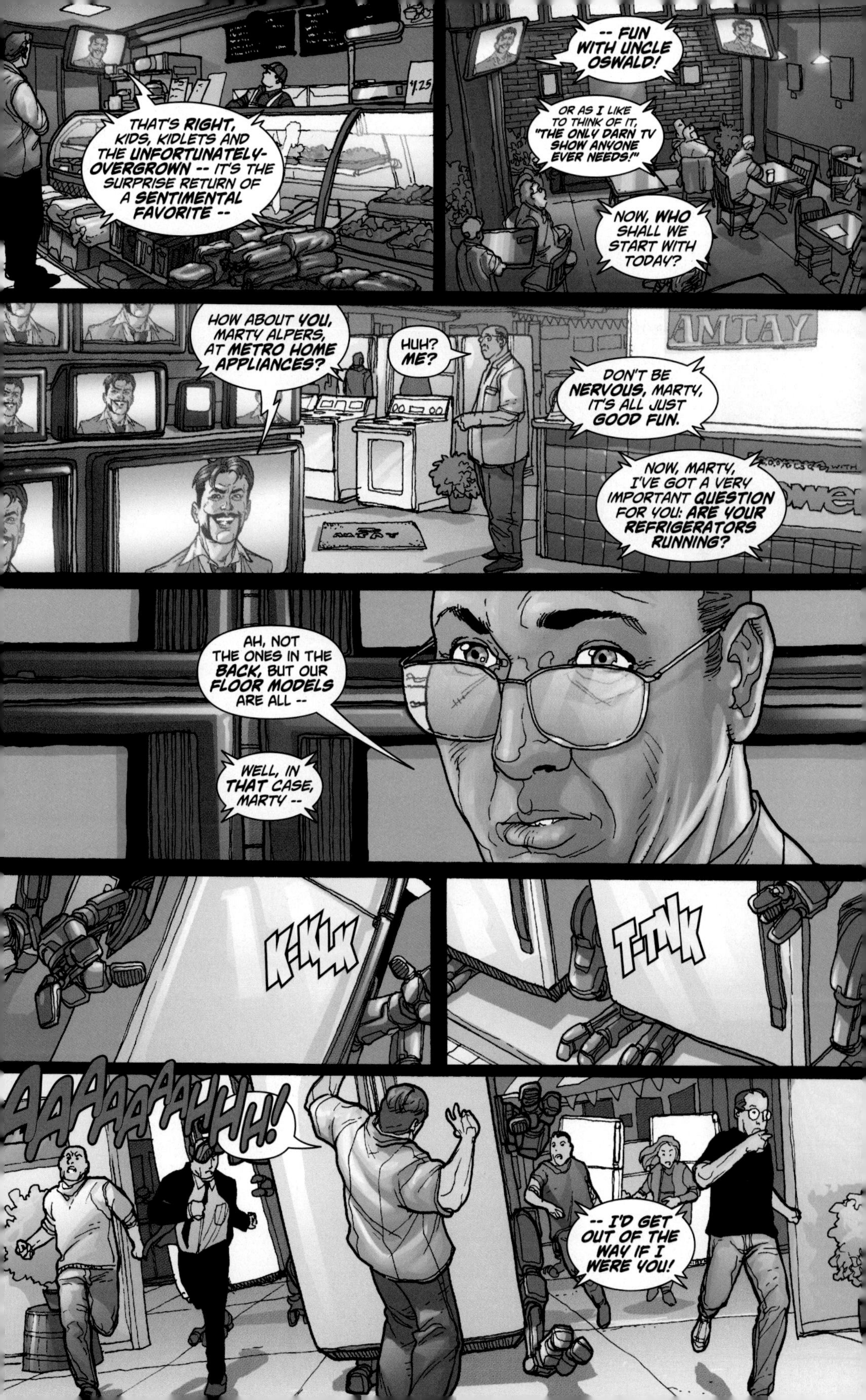

THAT'S RIGHT, KIDS, KIDLETS AND THE UNFORTUNATELY-OVERGROWN -- IT'S THE SURPRISE RETURN OF A SENTIMENTAL FAVORITE --
-- FUN WITH UNCLE OSWALD!
OR AS I LIKE TO THINK OF IT, "THE ONLY DARN TV SHOW ANYONE EVER NEEDS!"
NOW, WHO SHALL WE START WITH TODAY?
HOW ABOUT YOU, MARTY ALPERS, AT METRO HOME APPLIANCES?
HUH? ME?
AMTAY
DON'T BE NERVOUS, MARTY, IT'S ALL JUST GOOD FUN.
NOW, MARTY, I'VE GOT A VERY IMPORTANT QUESTION FOR YOU: ARE YOUR REFRIGERATORS RUNNING?
AH, NOT THE ONES IN THE BACK, BUT OUR FLOOR MODELS ARE ALL --
WELL, IN THAT CASE, MARTY --
K-KLIK
T-TNK
AAAAAAHHHH!
-- I'D GET OUT OF THE WAY IF I WERE YOU!

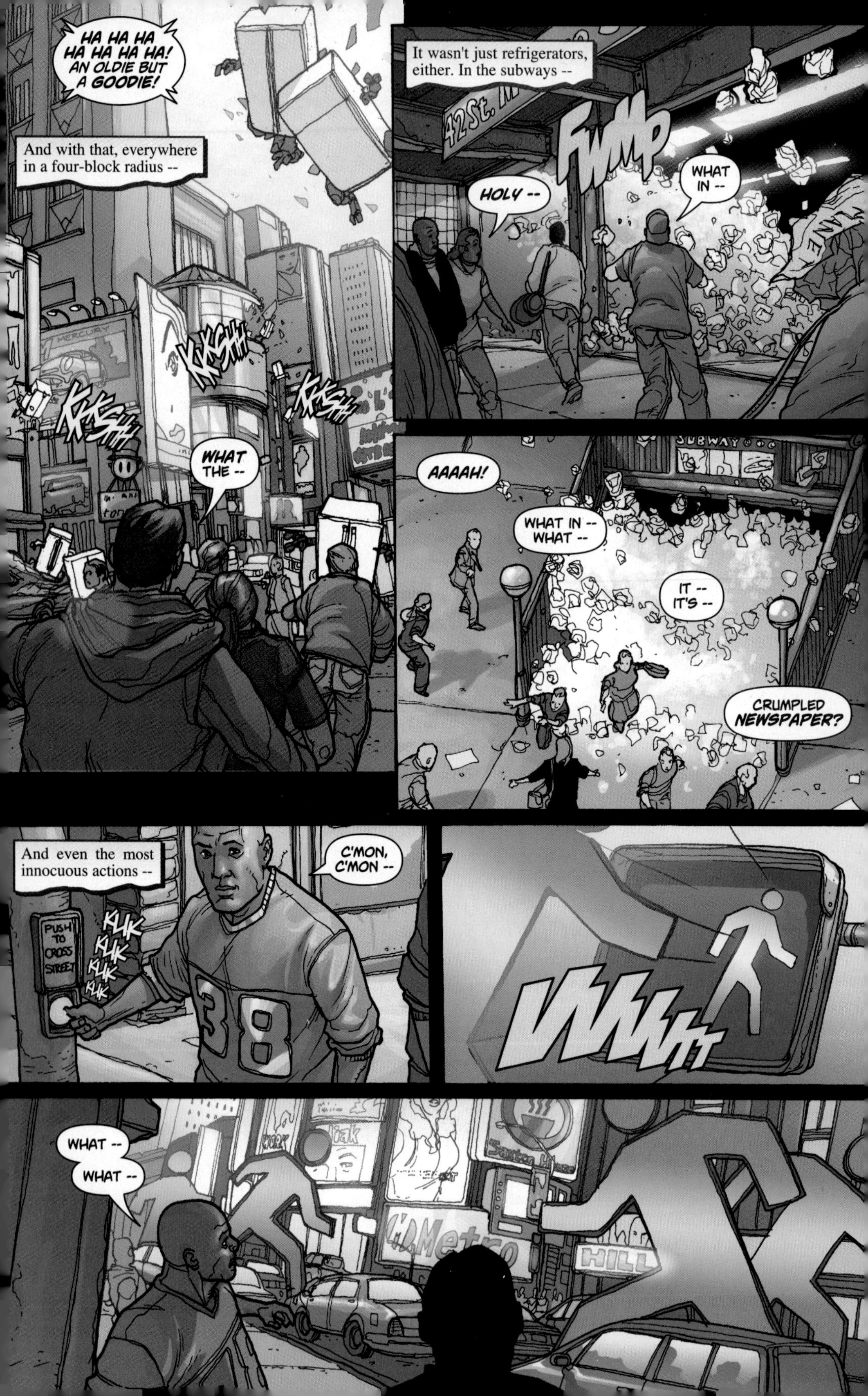

HA HA HA
HA HA HA HA! AN OLDIE BUT A GOODIE!
And with that, everywhere in a four-block radius --
KRKSHH
KRKSHH
KRKSHH
WHAT THE --
It wasn't just refrigerators, either. In the subways --
42 St.
FWMP
HOLY --
WHAT IN --
AAAAH!
SUBWAY
WHAT IN -- WHAT --
IT -- IT'S --
CRUMPLED NEWSPAPER?
And even the most innocuous actions --
C'MON, C'MON --
PUSH TO CROSS STREET
KLIK KLIK KLIK KLIK
VMMTT
WHAT --
WHAT --
Metro
HILL

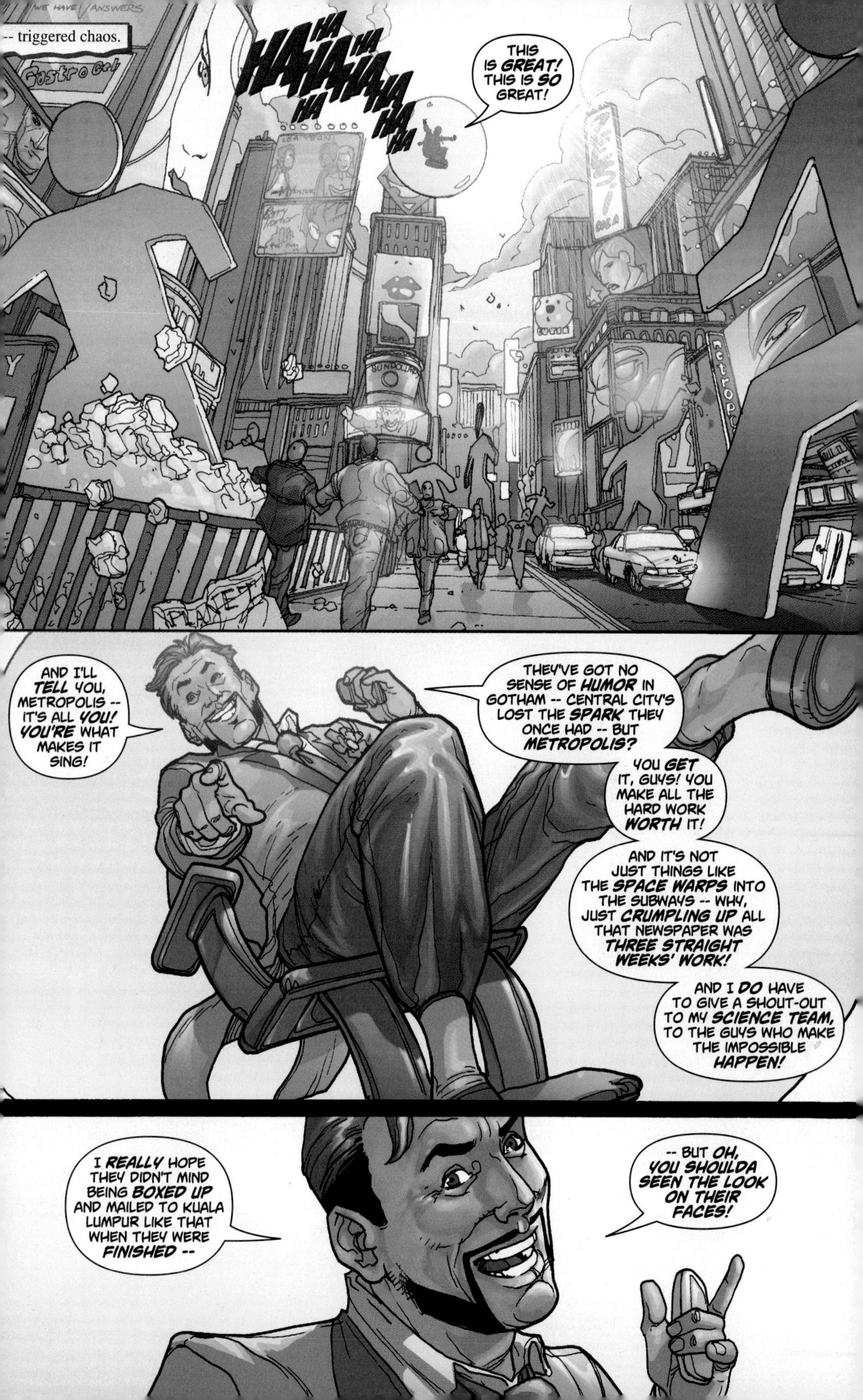
-- triggered chaos.
HAHAHAHAHAHAHAHAHAHA
THIS IS GREAT! THIS IS SO GREAT!
AND I'LL TELL YOU, METROPOLIS -- IT'S ALL YOU! YOU'RE WHAT MAKES IT SING!
THEY'VE GOT NO SENSE OF HUMOR IN GOTHAM -- CENTRAL CITY'S LOST THE SPARK THEY ONCE HAD -- BUT METROPOLIS?
YOU GET IT, GUYS! YOU MAKE ALL THE HARD WORK WORTH IT!
AND IT'S NOT JUST THINGS LIKE THE SPACE WARPS INTO THE SUBWAYS -- WHY, JUST CRUMPLING UP ALL THAT NEWSPAPER WAS THREE STRAIGHT WEEKS' WORK!
AND I DO HAVE TO GIVE A SHOUT-OUT TO MY SCIENCE TEAM, TO THE GUYS WHO MAKE THE IMPOSSIBLE HAPPEN!
I REALLY HOPE THEY DIDN'T MIND BEING BOXED UP AND MAILED TO KUALA LUMPUR LIKE THAT WHEN THEY WERE FINISHED --
-- BUT OH, YOU SHOULDA SEEN THE LOOK ON THEIR FACES!

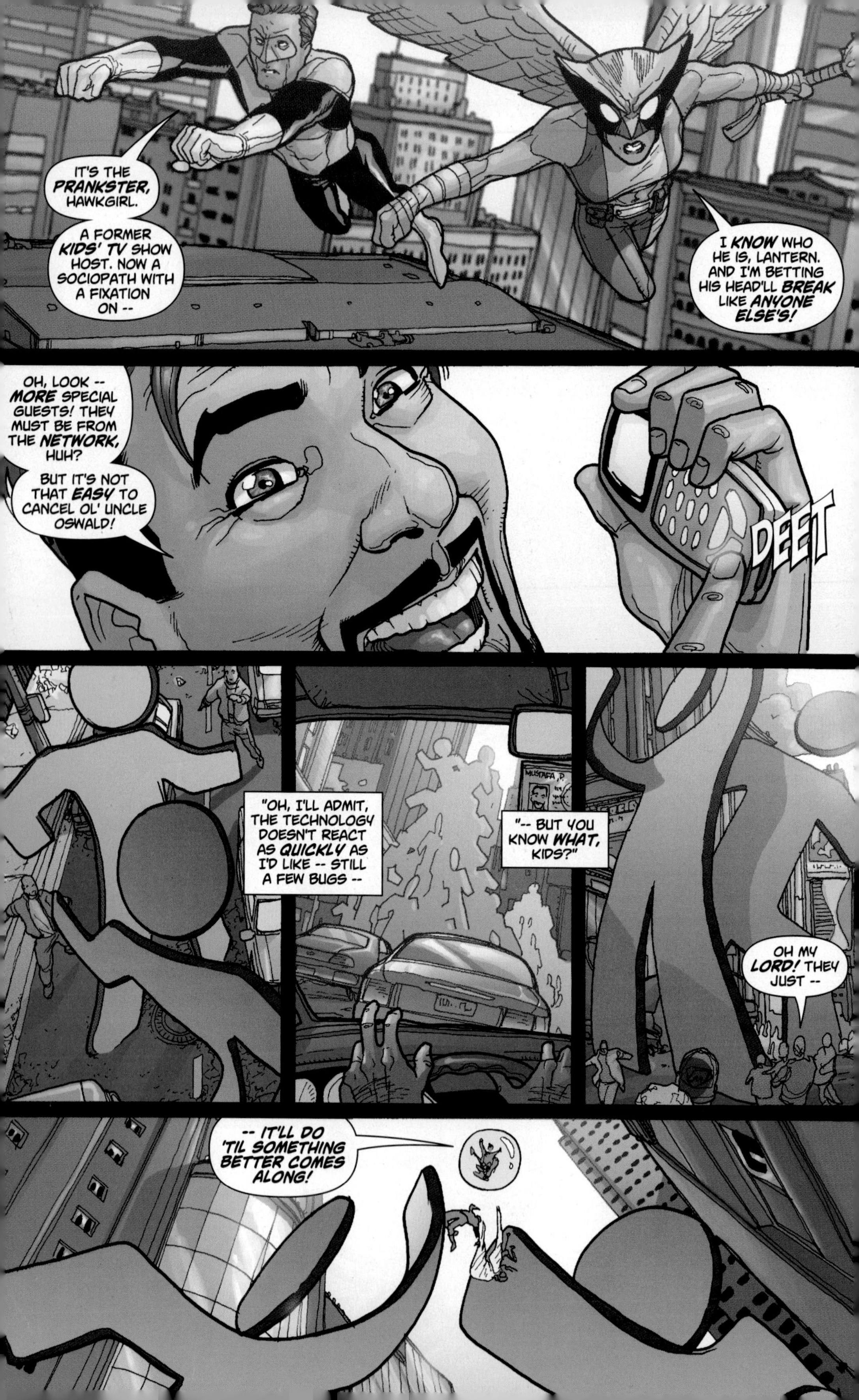
IT'S THE PRANKSTER, HAWKGIRL.
A FORMER KIDS' TV SHOW HOST. NOW A SOCIOPATH WITH A FIXATION ON --
I KNOW WHO HE IS, LANTERN. AND I'M BETTING HIS HEAD'LL BREAK LIKE ANYONE ELSE'S!
OH, LOOK -- MORE SPECIAL GUESTS! THEY MUST BE FROM THE NETWORK, HUH?
BUT IT'S NOT THAT EASY TO CANCEL OL' UNCLE OSWALD!
DEEET
"OH, I'LL ADMIT, THE TECHNOLOGY DOESN'T REACT AS QUICKLY AS I'D LIKE -- STILL A FEW BUGS --
"-- BUT YOU KNOW WHAT, KIDS?"
OH MY LORD! THEY JUST --
-- IT'LL DO 'TIL SOMETHING BETTER COMES ALONG!

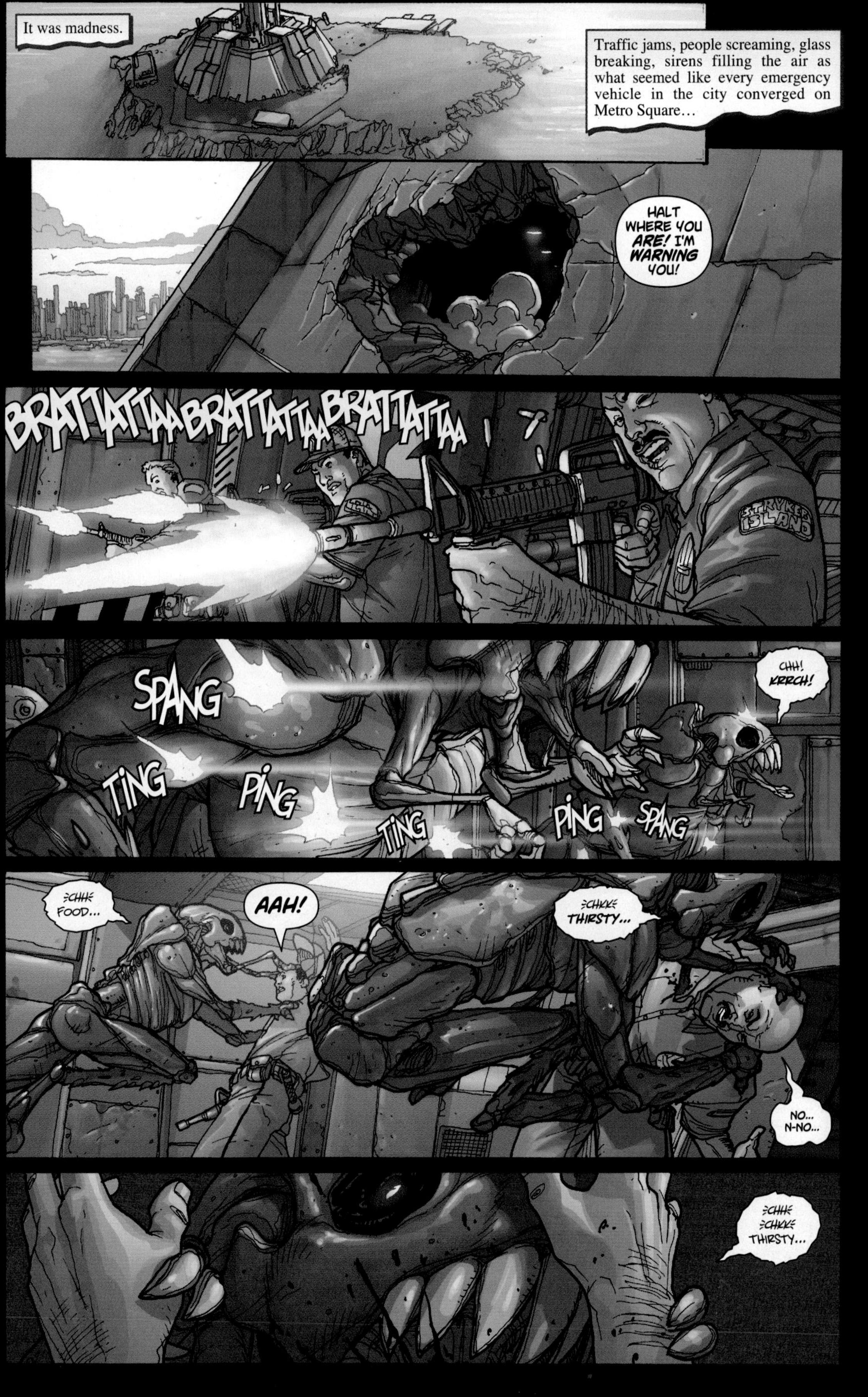
It was madness.
Traffic jams, people screaming, glass breaking, sirens filling the air as what seemed like every emergency vehicle in the city converged on Metro Square…
HALT WHERE YOU ARE! I'M WARNING YOU!
BRATTATTAA BRATTATTAA BRATTATTAA
STRYKER ISLAND
SPANG
CHH! KRRCH!
TING
PING
TING
PING
SPANG
CHH FOOD...
AAH!
CHKK THIRSTY...
NO... N-NO...
CHH CHKK THIRSTY...

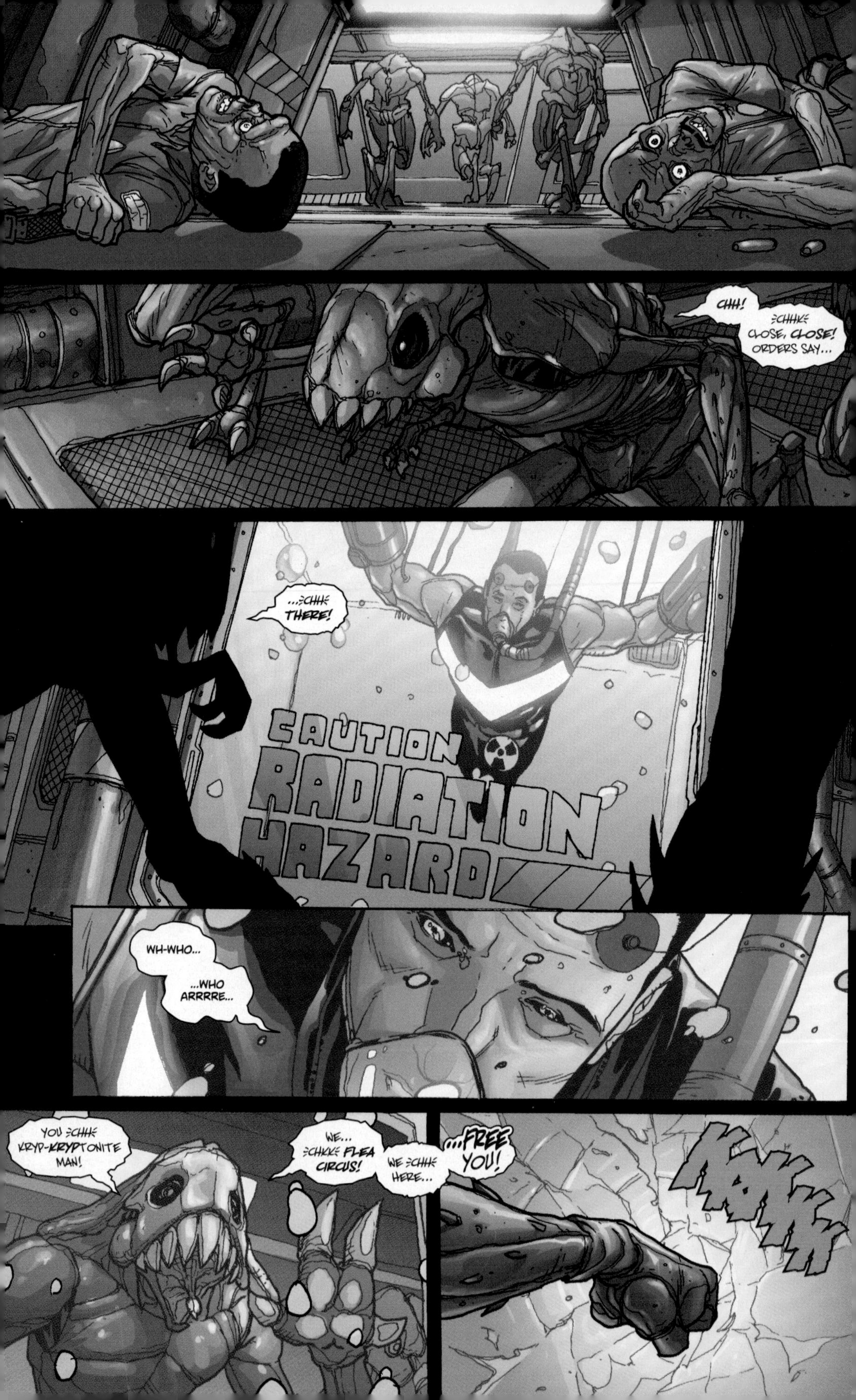
CHH!
≡CHHK≡ CLOSE, CLOSE! ORDERS SAY...
...≡CHH≡ THERE!
CAUTION RADIATION HAZARD
WH-WHO...
...WHO ARRRRE...
YOU ≡CHH≡ KRYP-KRYPTONITE MAN!
WE... ≡CHKK≡ FLEA CIRCUS!
WE ≡CHH≡ HERE...
...FREE YOU!

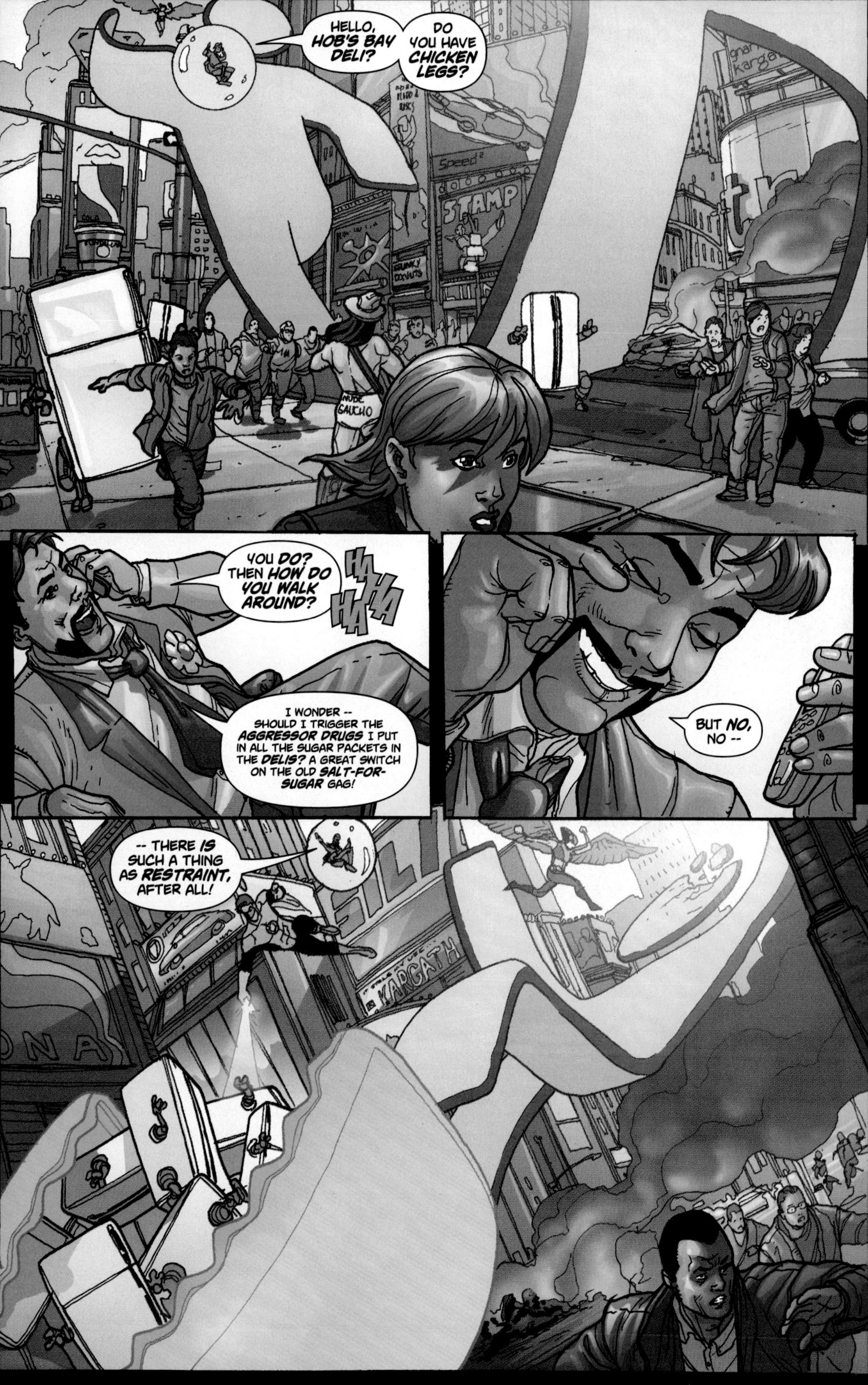
HELLO, HOB'S BAY DELI?
DO YOU HAVE CHICKEN LEGS?
STAMP
NUDE GAUCHO
YOU DO? THEN HOW DO YOU WALK AROUND?
HA HA HA HA
I WONDER -- SHOULD I TRIGGER THE AGGRESSOR DRUGS I PUT IN ALL THE SUGAR PACKETS IN THE DELIS? A GREAT SWITCH ON THE OLD SALT-FOR-SUGAR GAG!
BUT NO, NO --
-- THERE IS SUCH A THING AS RESTRAINT, AFTER ALL!
KARGATH

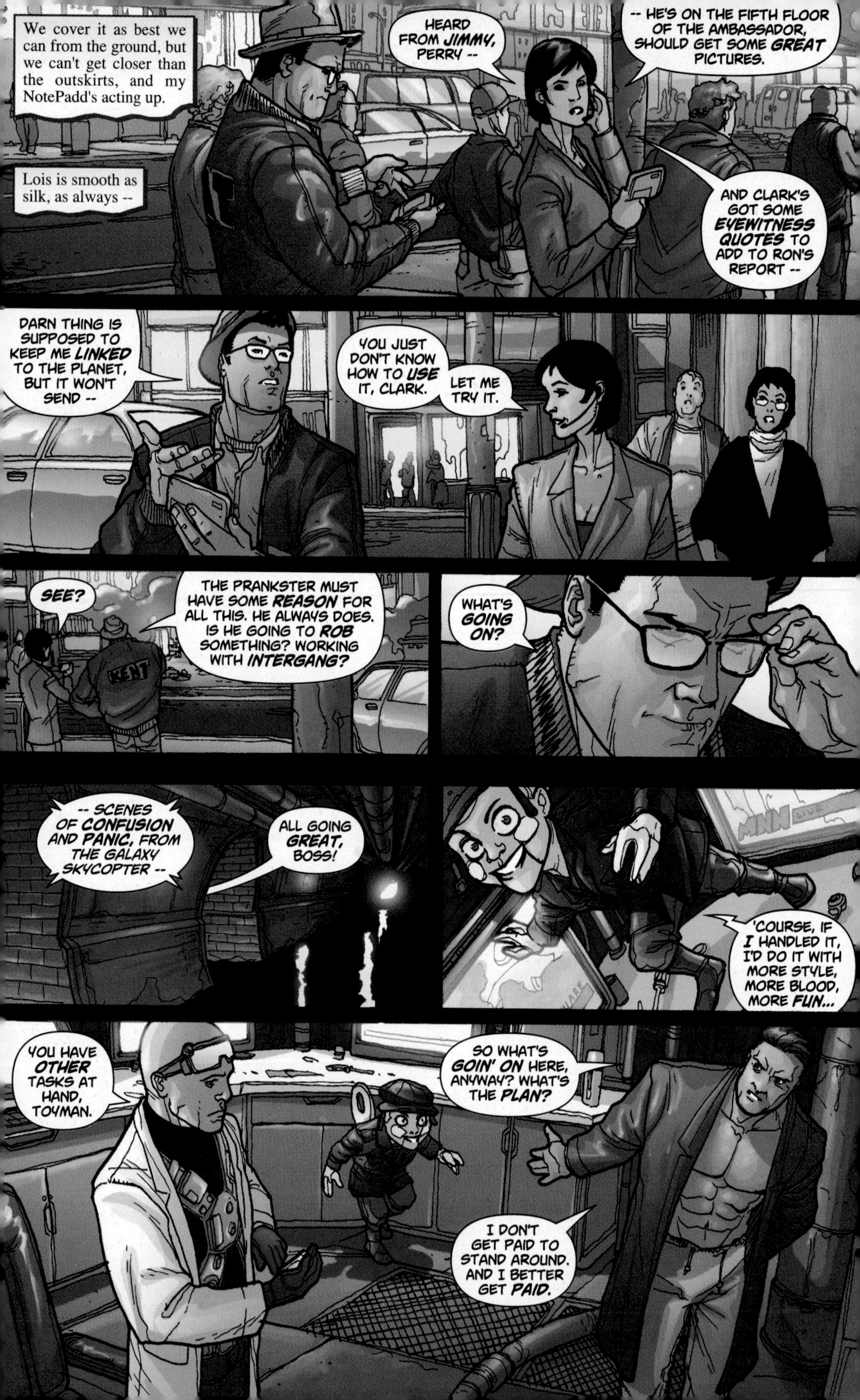
We cover it as best we can from the ground, but we can't get closer than the outskirts, and my NotePadd's acting up.
HEARD FROM JIMMY, PERRY --
-- HE'S ON THE FIFTH FLOOR OF THE AMBASSADOR, SHOULD GET SOME GREAT PICTURES.
Lois is smooth as silk, as always --
AND CLARK'S GOT SOME EYEWITNESS QUOTES TO ADD TO RON'S REPORT --
DARN THING IS SUPPOSED TO KEEP ME LINKED TO THE PLANET, BUT IT WON'T SEND --
YOU JUST DON'T KNOW HOW TO USE IT, CLARK.
LET ME TRY IT.
SEE?
THE PRANKSTER MUST HAVE SOME REASON FOR ALL THIS. HE ALWAYS DOES. IS HE GOING TO ROB SOMETHING? WORKING WITH INTERGANG?
KENT
WHAT'S GOING ON?
-- SCENES OF CONFUSION AND PANIC, FROM THE GALAXY SKYCOPTER --
ALL GOING GREAT, BOSS!
MNN LIVE
'COURSE, IF I HANDLED IT, I'D DO IT WITH MORE STYLE, MORE BLOOD, MORE FUN...
YOU HAVE OTHER TASKS AT HAND, TOYMAN.
SO WHAT'S GOIN' ON HERE, ANYWAY? WHAT'S THE PLAN?
I DON'T GET PAID TO STAND AROUND. AND I BETTER GET PAID.

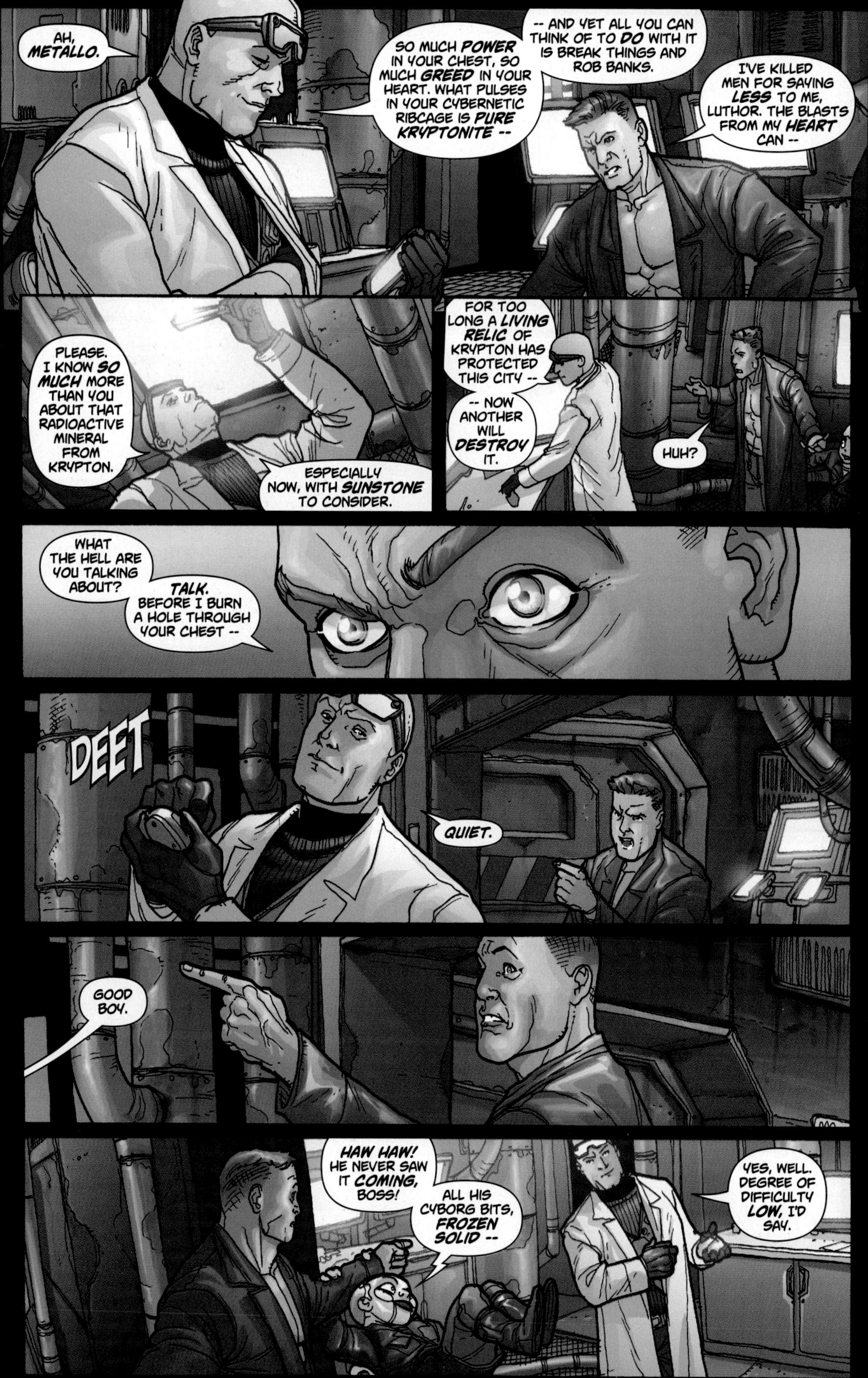
AH, METALLO.
SO MUCH POWER IN YOUR CHEST, SO MUCH GREED IN YOUR HEART. WHAT PULSES IN YOUR CYBERNETIC RIBCAGE IS PURE KRYPTONITE --
-- AND YET ALL YOU CAN THINK OF TO DO WITH IT IS BREAK THINGS AND ROB BANKS.
I'VE KILLED MEN FOR SAYING LESS TO ME, LUTHOR. THE BLASTS FROM MY HEART CAN --
PLEASE. I KNOW SO MUCH MORE THAN YOU ABOUT THAT RADIOACTIVE MINERAL FROM KRYPTON.
ESPECIALLY NOW, WITH SUNSTONE TO CONSIDER.
FOR TOO LONG A LIVING RELIC OF KRYPTON HAS PROTECTED THIS CITY --
-- NOW ANOTHER WILL DESTROY IT.
HUH?
WHAT THE HELL ARE YOU TALKING ABOUT?
TALK. BEFORE I BURN A HOLE THROUGH YOUR CHEST --
DEET
QUIET.
GOOD BOY.
HAW HAW! HE NEVER SAW IT COMING, BOSS!
ALL HIS CYBORG BITS, FROZEN SOLID --
YES, WELL. DEGREE OF DIFFICULTY LOW, I'D SAY.

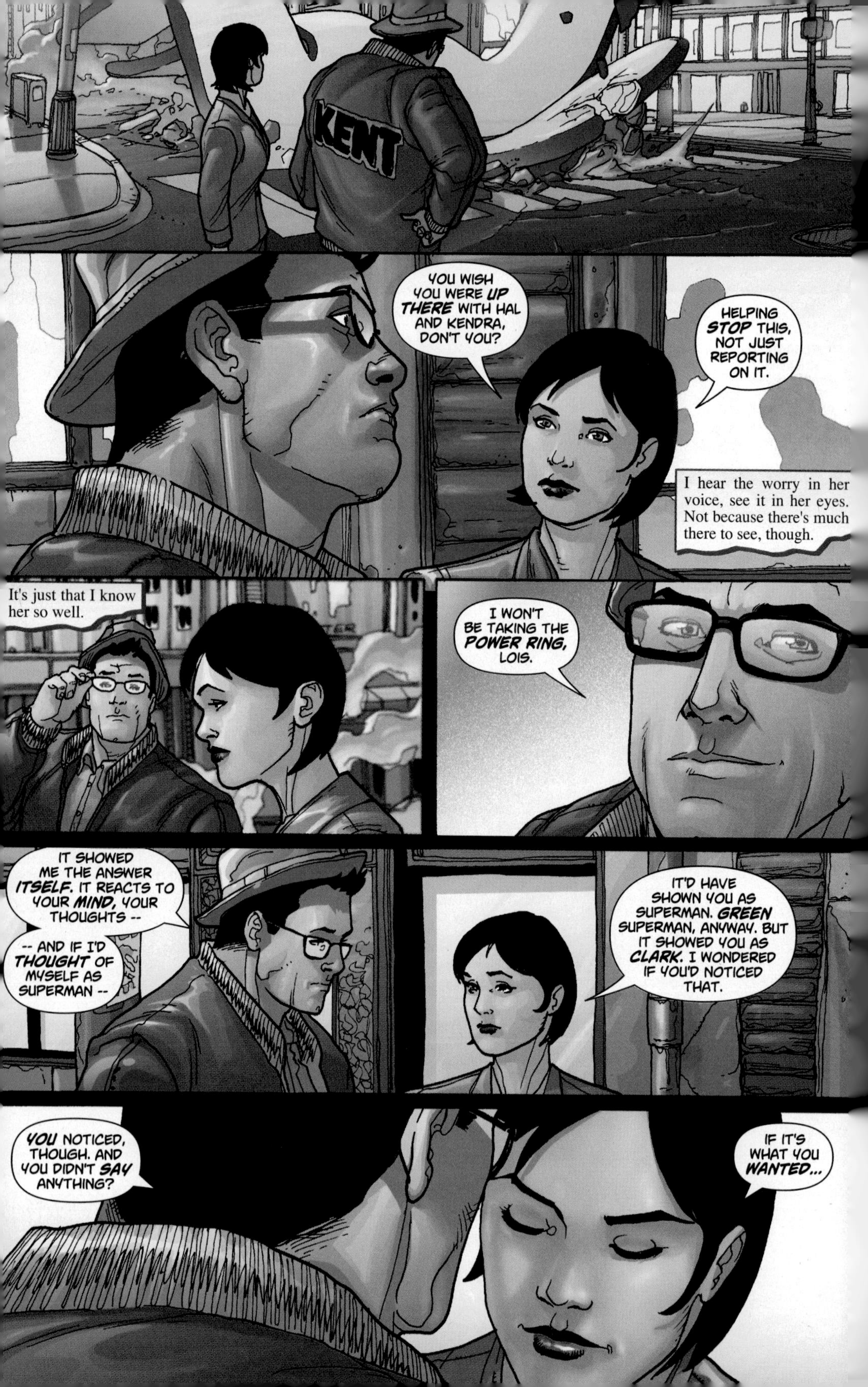
KENT
YOU WISH YOU WERE UP THERE WITH HAL AND KENDRA, DON'T YOU?
HELPING STOP THIS, NOT JUST REPORTING ON IT.
I hear the worry in her voice, see it in her eyes. Not because there's much there to see, though.
It's just that I know her so well.
I WON'T BE TAKING THE POWER RING, LOIS.
IT SHOWED ME THE ANSWER ITSELF. IT REACTS TO YOUR MIND, YOUR THOUGHTS --
-- AND IF I'D THOUGHT OF MYSELF AS SUPERMAN --
IT'D HAVE SHOWN YOU AS SUPERMAN. GREEN SUPERMAN, ANYWAY. BUT IT SHOWED YOU AS CLARK. I WONDERED IF YOU'D NOTICED THAT.
YOU NOTICED, THOUGH. AND YOU DIDN'T SAY ANYTHING?
IF IT'S WHAT YOU WANTED...

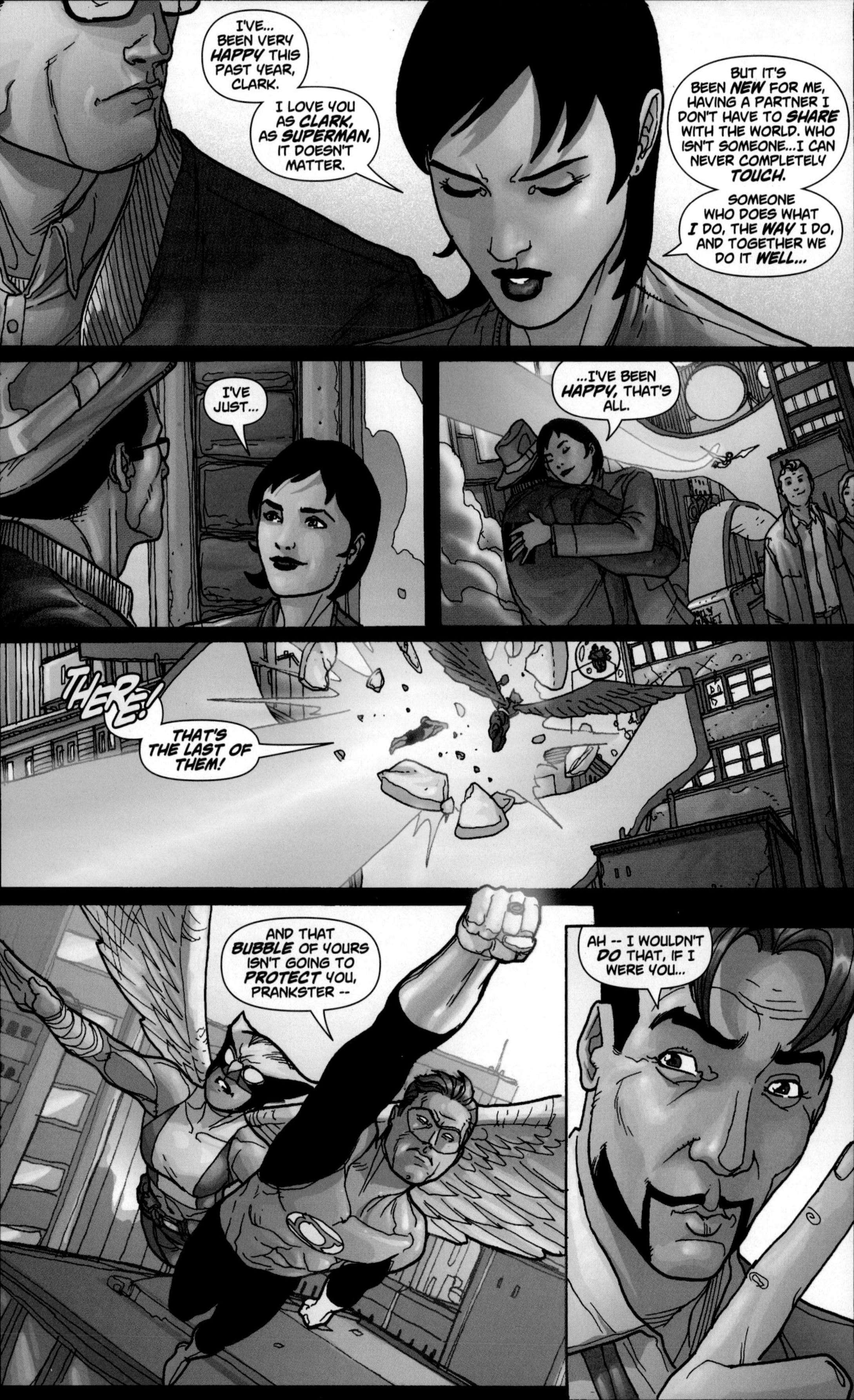
I'VE... BEEN VERY HAPPY THIS PAST YEAR, CLARK.
I LOVE YOU AS CLARK, AS SUPERMAN, IT DOESN'T MATTER.
BUT IT'S BEEN NEW FOR ME, HAVING A PARTNER I DON'T HAVE TO SHARE WITH THE WORLD. WHO ISN'T SOMEONE...I CAN NEVER COMPLETELY TOUCH.
SOMEONE WHO DOES WHAT I DO, THE WAY I DO, AND TOGETHER WE DO IT WELL...
I'VE JUST...
...I'VE BEEN HAPPY, THAT'S ALL.
THERE!
THAT'S THE LAST OF THEM!
AND THAT BUBBLE OF YOURS ISN'T GOING TO PROTECT YOU, PRANKSTER --
AH -- I WOULDN'T DO THAT, IF I WERE YOU...

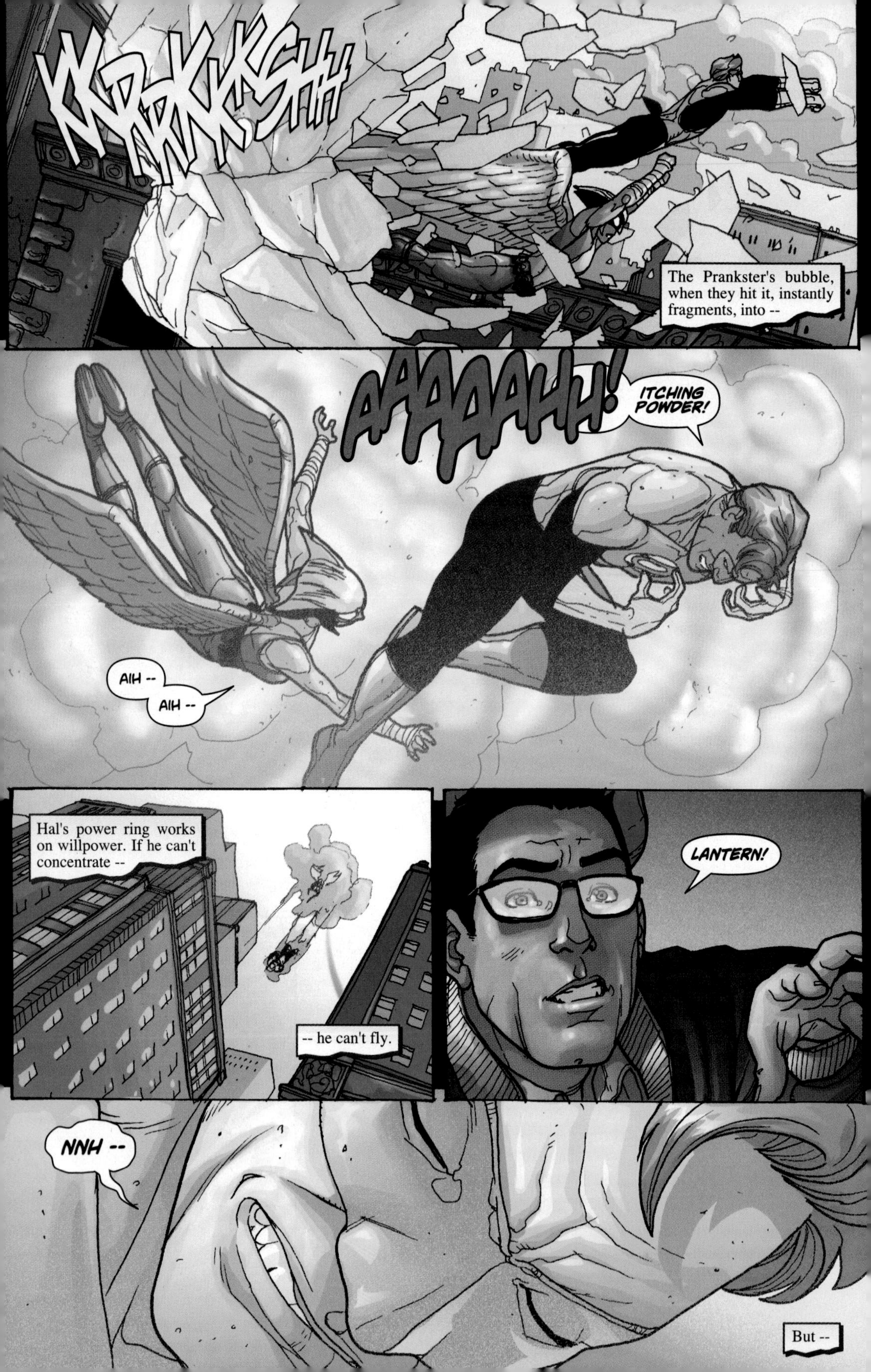
KKRRKKKSHH
The Prankster's bubble, when they hit it, instantly fragments, into --
AAAAAHH!
ITCHING POWDER!
AIH --
AIH --
Hal's power ring works on willpower. If he can't concentrate --
-- he can't fly.
LANTERN!
NNH --
But --

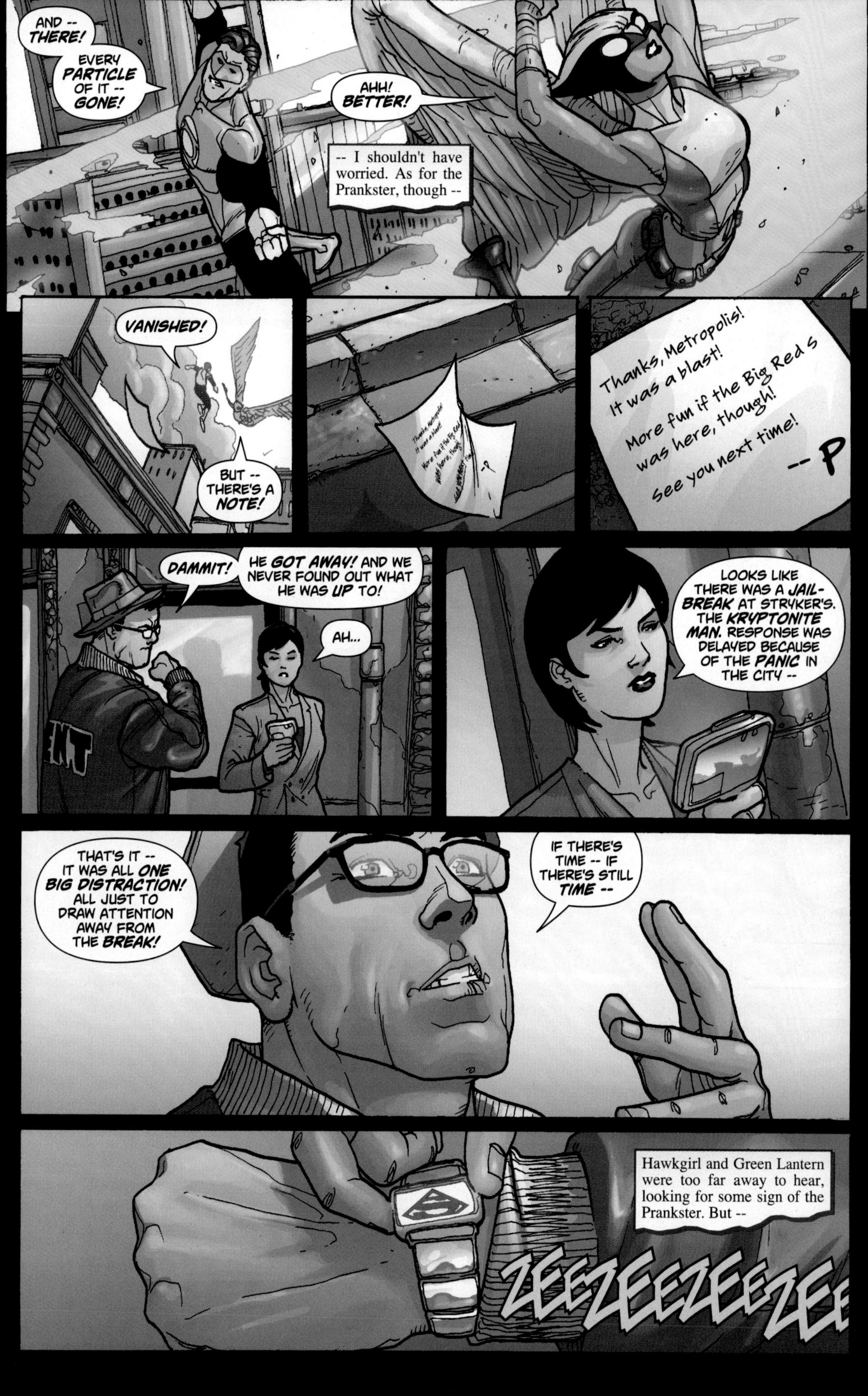
AND -- THERE! EVERY PARTICLE OF IT -- GONE!
AHH! BETTER!
-- I shouldn't have worried. As for the Prankster, though --
VANISHED!
BUT -- THERE'S A NOTE!
Thanks, Metropolis! It was a blast!
More fun if the Big Red S was here, though!
See you next time!
-- P
DAMMIT!
HE GOT AWAY! AND WE NEVER FOUND OUT WHAT HE WAS UP TO!
AH...
LOOKS LIKE THERE WAS A JAIL-BREAK AT STRYKER'S. THE KRYPTONITE MAN. RESPONSE WAS DELAYED BECAUSE OF THE PANIC IN THE CITY --
THAT'S IT -- IT WAS ALL ONE BIG DISTRACTION! ALL JUST TO DRAW ATTENTION AWAY FROM THE BREAK!
IF THERE'S TIME -- IF THERE'S STILL TIME --
Hawkgirl and Green Lantern were too far away to hear, looking for some sign of the Prankster. But --
ZEEZEEZEEZEEZEE

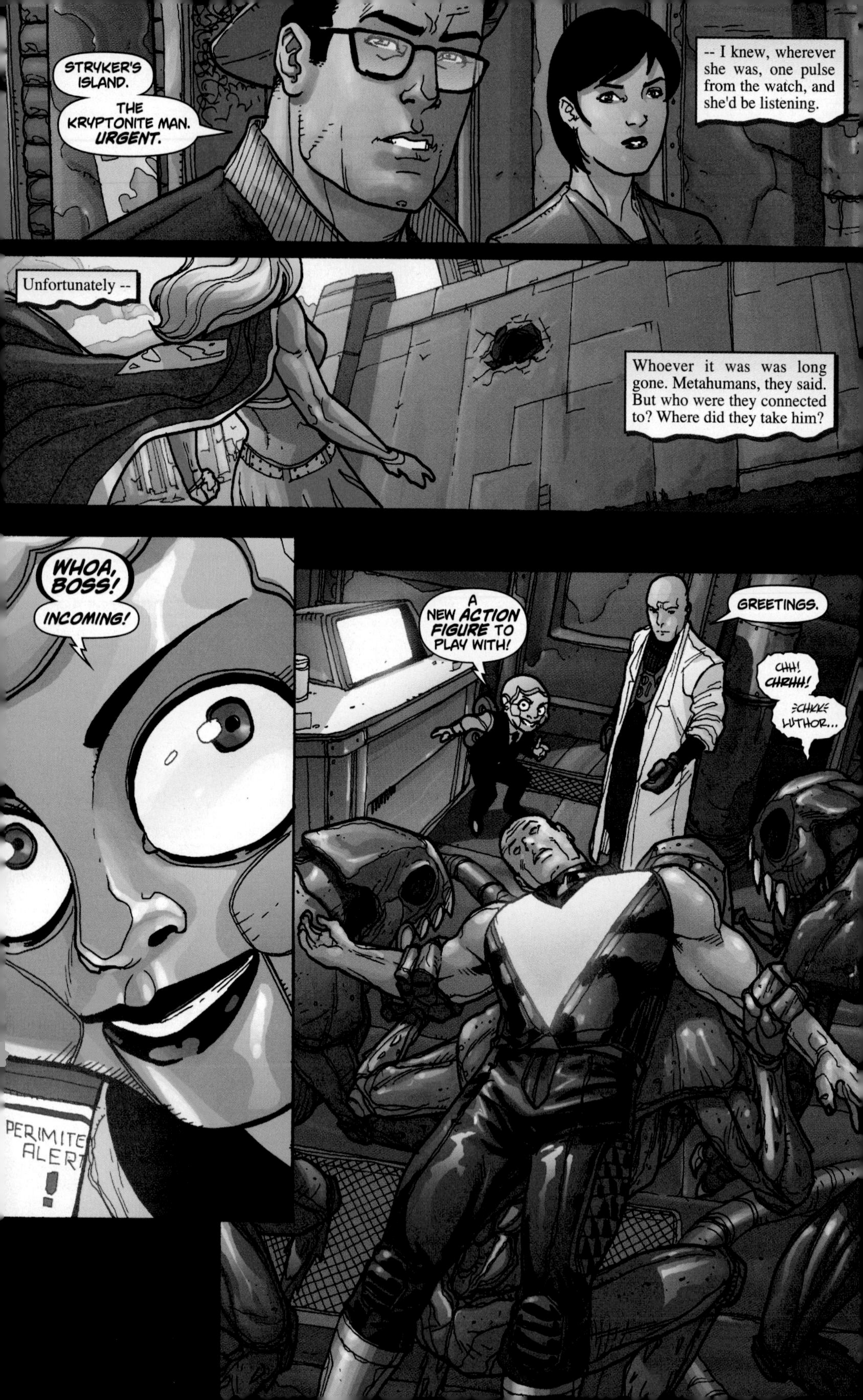

STRYKER'S ISLAND.
THE KRYPTONITE MAN. URGENT.
-- I knew, wherever she was, one pulse from the watch, and she'd be listening.
Unfortunately --
Whoever it was was long gone. Metahumans, they said. But who were they connected to? Where did they take him?
WHOA, BOSS!
INCOMING!
PERIMITE ALERT
!
A NEW ACTION FIGURE TO PLAY WITH!
GREETINGS.
CHH! CHRHH!
CHKK LUTHOR...

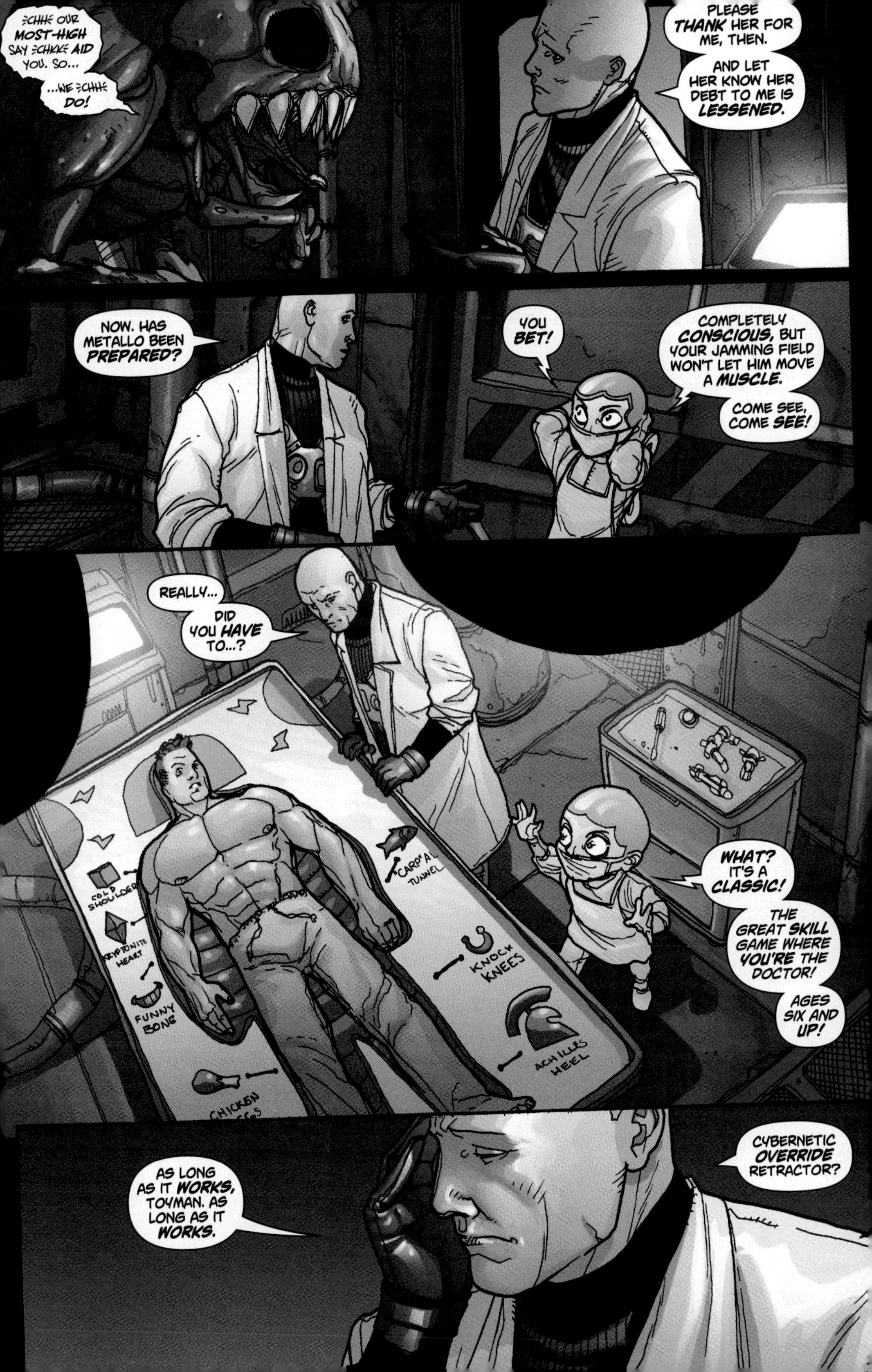

ƷCHHE OUR MOST-HIGH SAY ƷCHKKE AID YOU. SO...
...WE ƷCHHE DO!
PLEASE THANK HER FOR ME, THEN.
AND LET HER KNOW HER DEBT TO ME IS LESSENED.
NOW. HAS METALLO BEEN PREPARED?
YOU BET!
COMPLETELY CONSCIOUS, BUT YOUR JAMMING FIELD WON'T LET HIM MOVE A MUSCLE.
COME SEE, COME SEE!
REALLY...
DID YOU HAVE TO...?
COLD SHOULDER
KRYPTONITE HEART
FUNNY BONE
CHICKEN
"CARP"AL TUNNEL
KNOCK KNEES
ACHILLES HEEL
WHAT? IT'S A CLASSIC!
THE GREAT SKILL GAME WHERE YOU'RE THE DOCTOR!
AGES SIX AND UP!
CYBERNETIC OVERRIDE RETRACTOR?
AS LONG AS IT WORKS, TOYMAN. AS LONG AS IT WORKS.

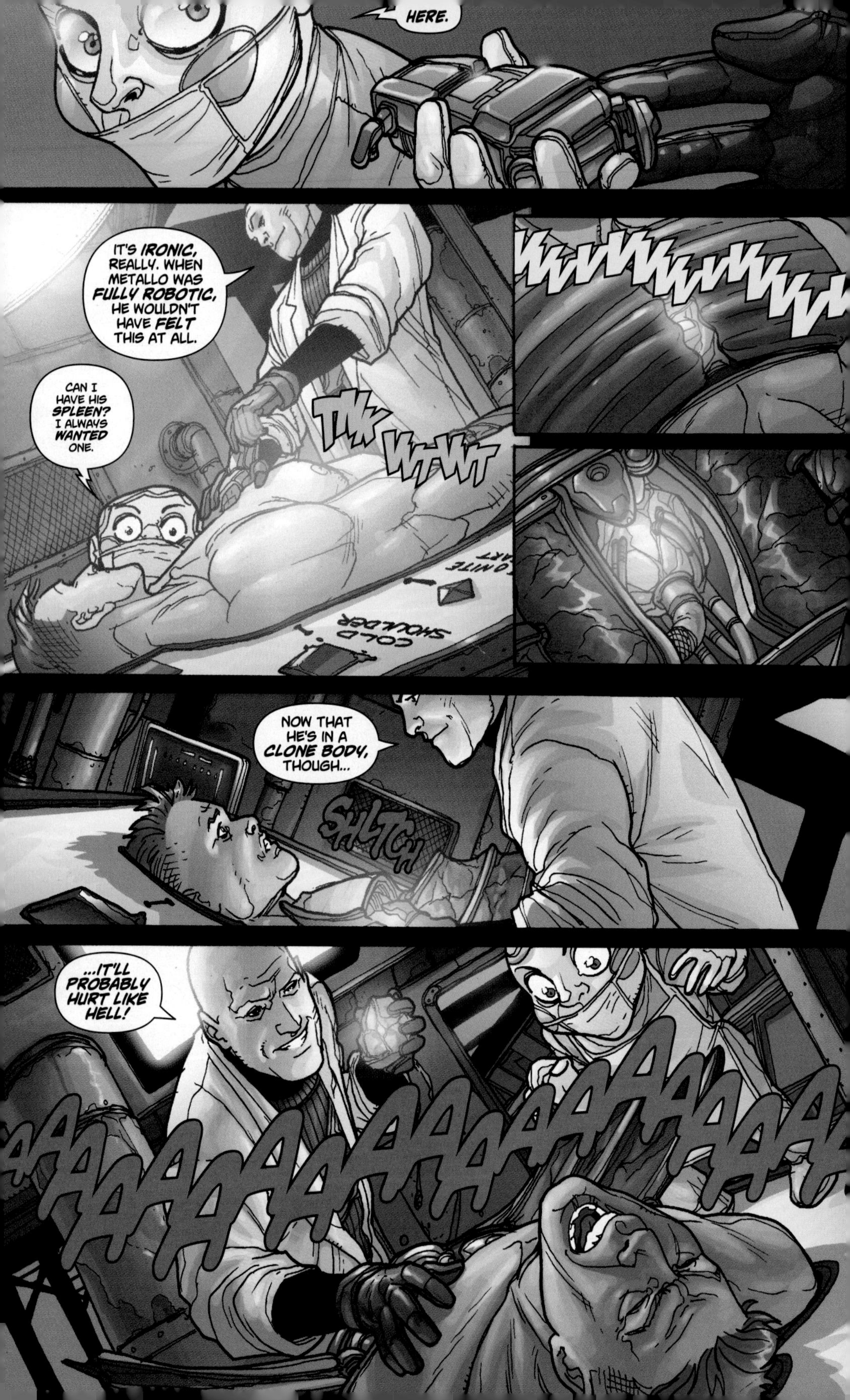
HERE.
IT'S IRONIC, REALLY. WHEN METALLO WAS FULLY ROBOTIC, HE WOULDN'T HAVE FELT THIS AT ALL.
CAN I HAVE HIS SPLEEN? I ALWAYS WANTED ONE.
TNK
WTWT
COLD SHOULDER
KWWWWWWWWWW
NOW THAT HE'S IN A CLONE BODY, THOUGH...
SHLTCH
...IT'LL PROBABLY HURT LIKE HELL!
AAAAAAAAAAAAAAAAAAAAAAA

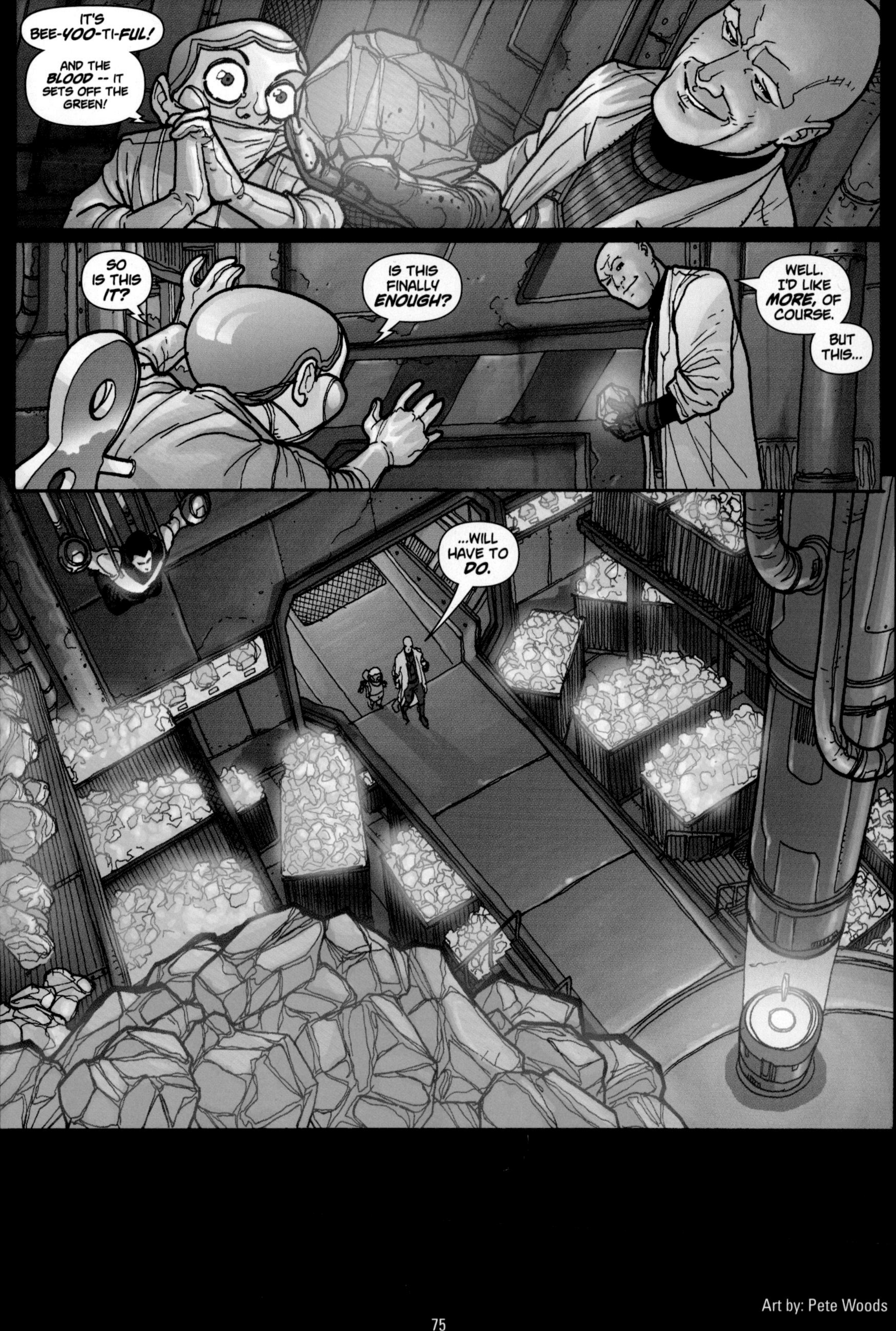
IT'S BEE-YOO-TI-FUL!
AND THE BLOOD -- IT SETS OFF THE GREEN!
SO IS THIS IT?
IS THIS FINALLY ENOUGH?
WELL. I'D LIKE MORE, OF COURSE.
BUT THIS...
...WILL HAVE TO DO.

Art by: Pete Woods

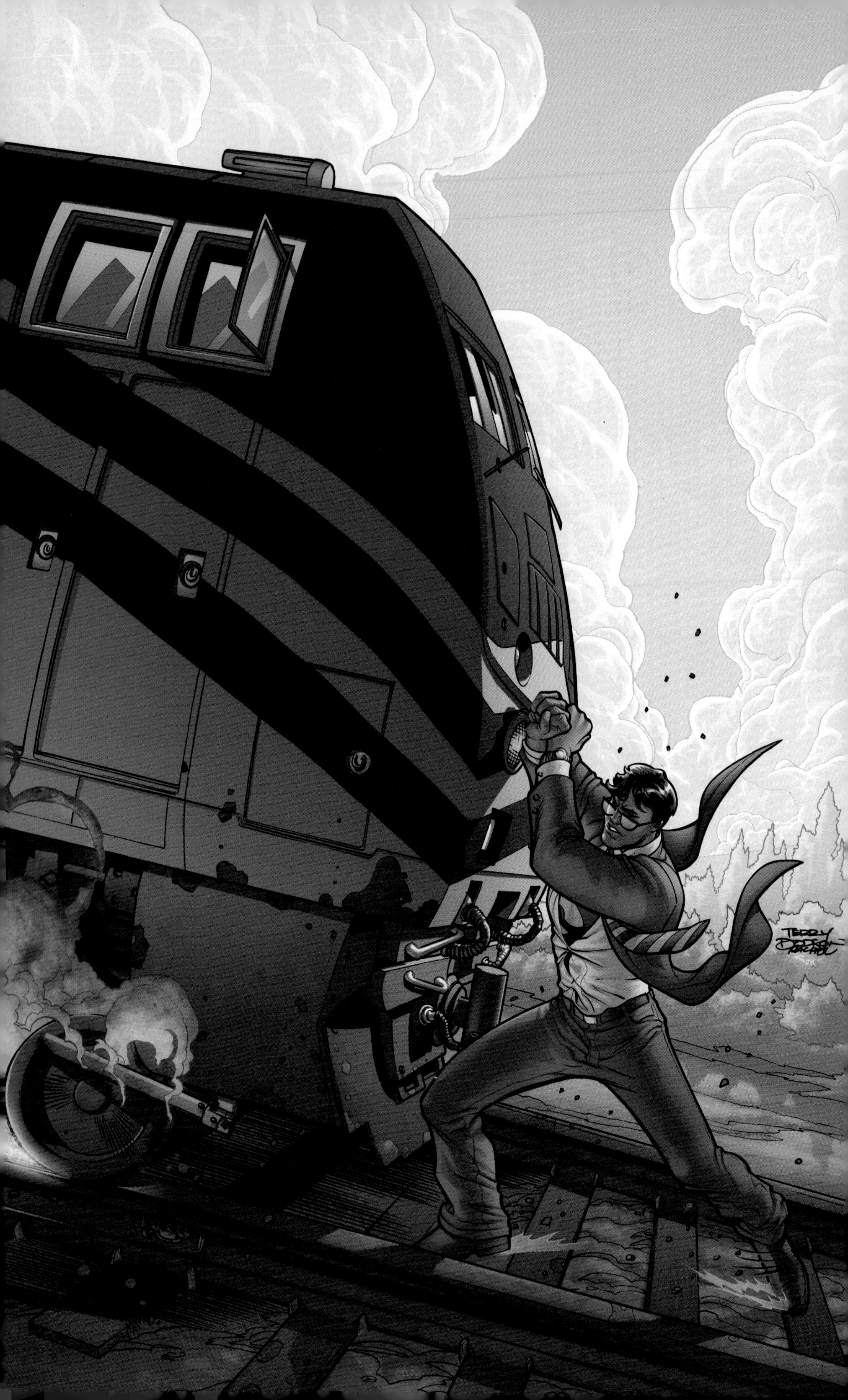

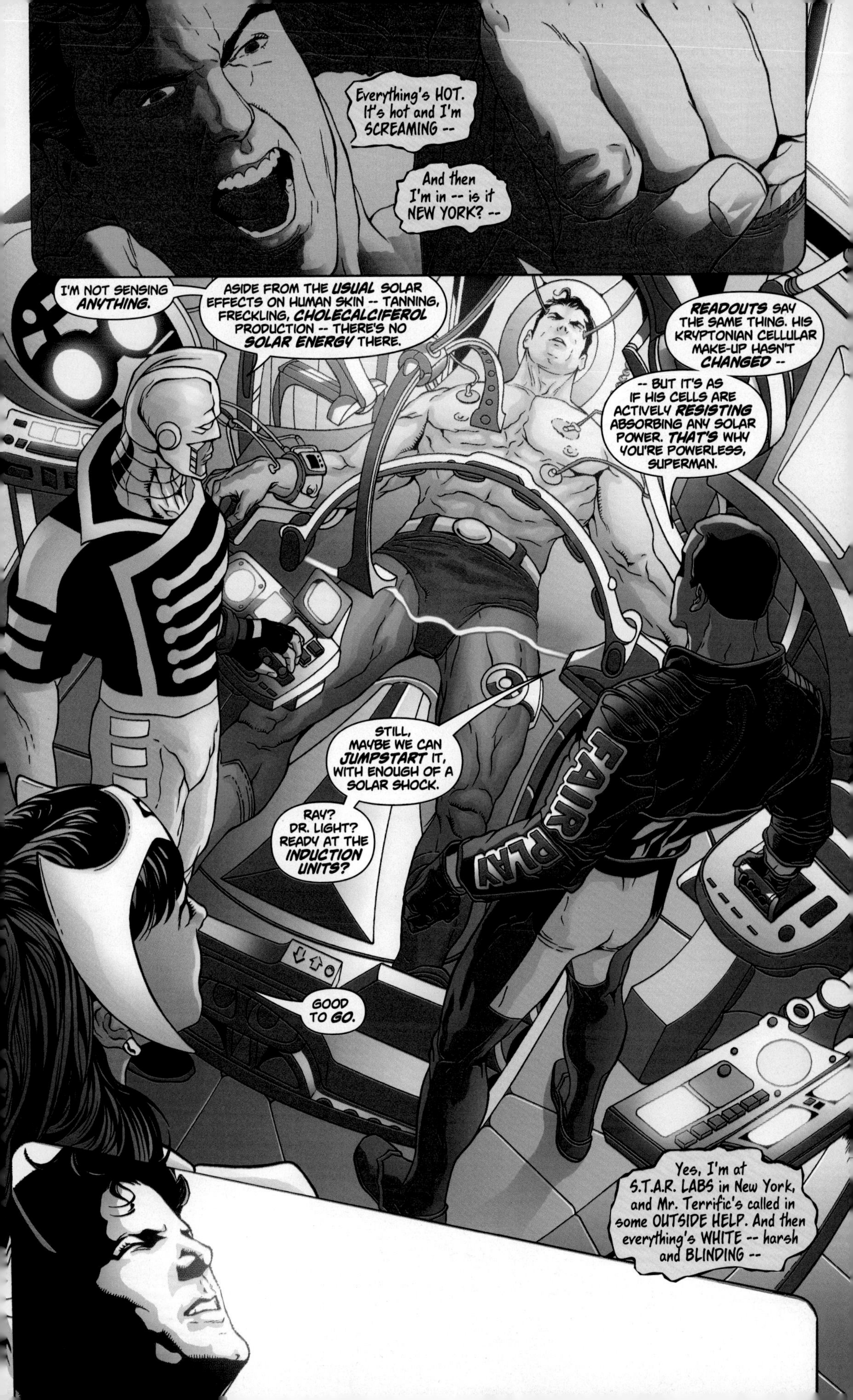
Everything's HOT. It's hot and I'm SCREAMING --
And then I'm in -- is it NEW YORK? --
I'M NOT SENSING ANYTHING.
ASIDE FROM THE USUAL SOLAR EFFECTS ON HUMAN SKIN -- TANNING, FRECKLING, CHOLECALCIFEROL PRODUCTION -- THERE'S NO SOLAR ENERGY THERE.
READOUTS SAY THE SAME THING. HIS KRYPTONIAN CELLULAR MAKE-UP HASN'T CHANGED --
-- BUT IT'S AS IF HIS CELLS ARE ACTIVELY RESISTING ABSORBING ANY SOLAR POWER. THAT'S WHY YOU'RE POWERLESS, SUPERMAN.
FAIR PLAY
STILL, MAYBE WE CAN JUMPSTART IT, WITH ENOUGH OF A SOLAR SHOCK.
RAY? DR. LIGHT? READY AT THE INDUCTION UNITS?
GOOD TO GO.
Yes, I'm at S.T.A.R. LABS in New York, and Mr. Terrific's called in some OUTSIDE HELP. And then everything's WHITE -- harsh and BLINDING --

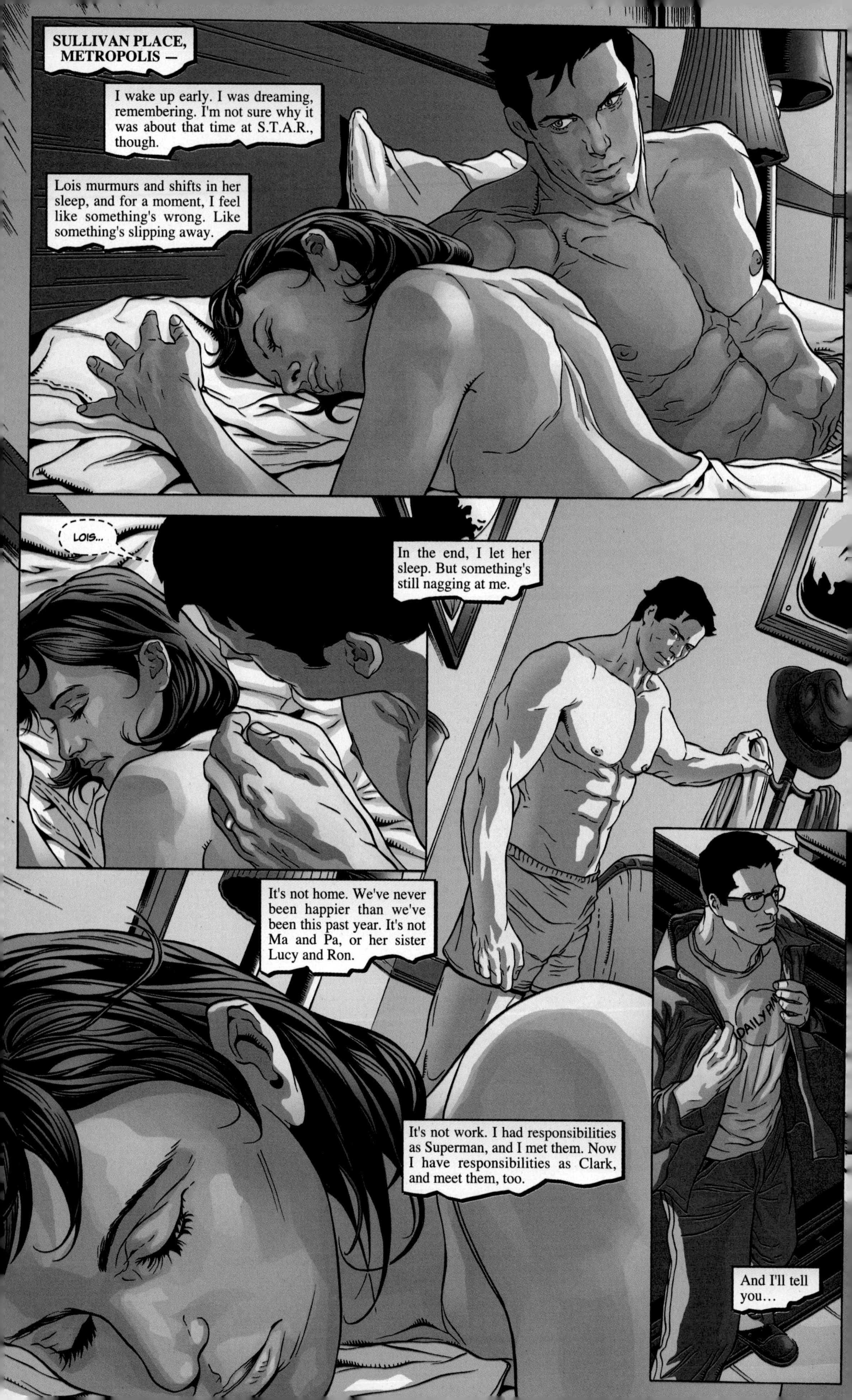
SULLIVAN PLACE, METROPOLIS —
I wake up early. I was dreaming, remembering. I'm not sure why it was about that time at S.T.A.R., though.
Lois murmurs and shifts in her sleep, and for a moment, I feel like something's wrong. Like something's slipping away.
LOIS...
In the end, I let her sleep. But something's still nagging at me.
It's not home. We've never been happier than we've been this past year. It's not Ma and Pa, or her sister Lucy and Ron.
It's not work. I had responsibilities as Superman, and I met them. Now I have responsibilities as Clark, and meet them, too.
And I'll tell you…

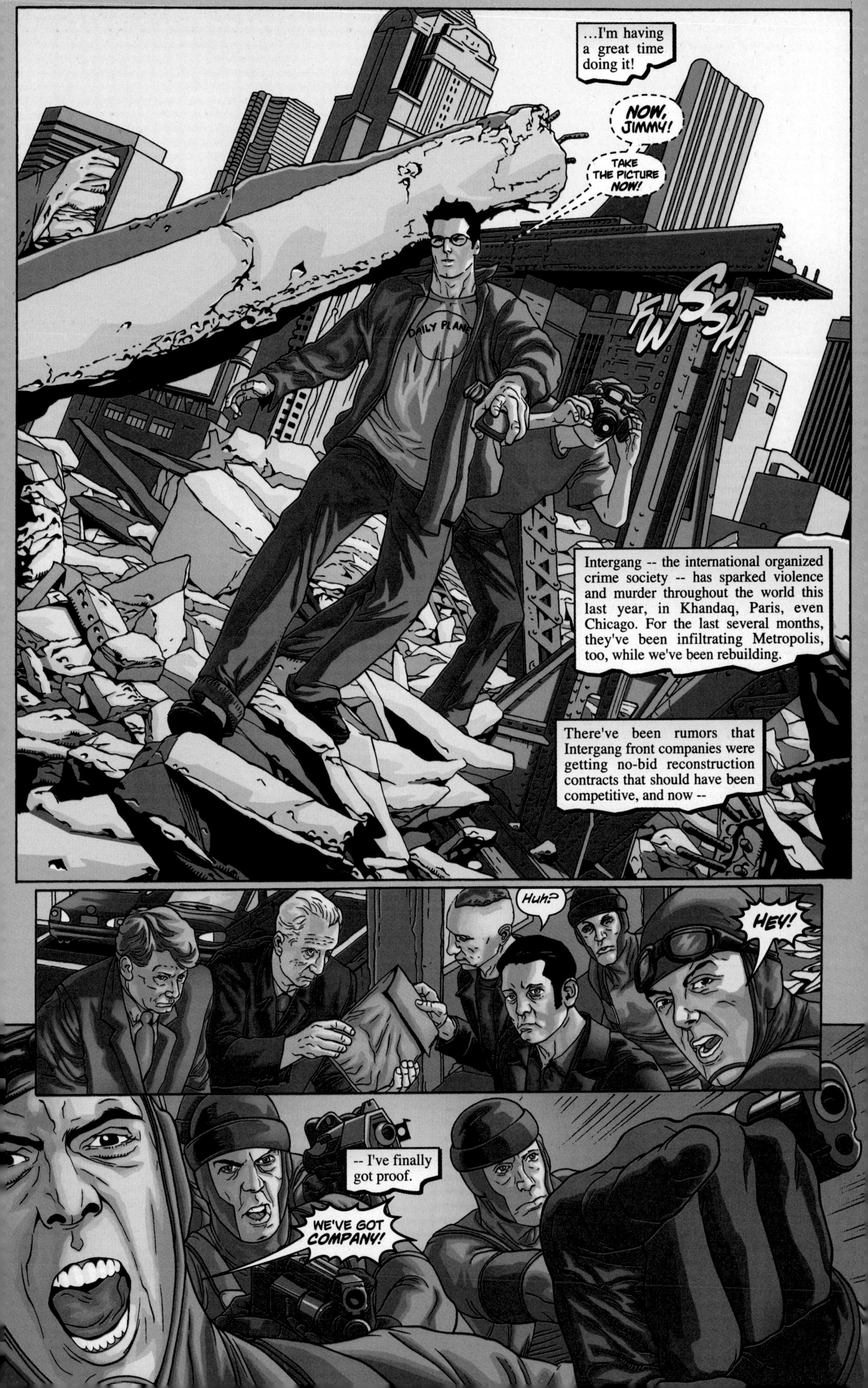

...I'm having a great time doing it!
NOW, JIMMY!
TAKE THE PICTURE NOW!
FWSSSH
Intergang -- the international organized crime society -- has sparked violence and murder throughout the world this last year, in Khandaq, Paris, even Chicago. For the last several months, they've been infiltrating Metropolis, too, while we've been rebuilding.
There've been rumors that Intergang front companies were getting no-bid reconstruction contracts that should have been competitive, and now --
Huh?
HEY!
-- I've finally got proof.
WE'VE GOT COMPANY!

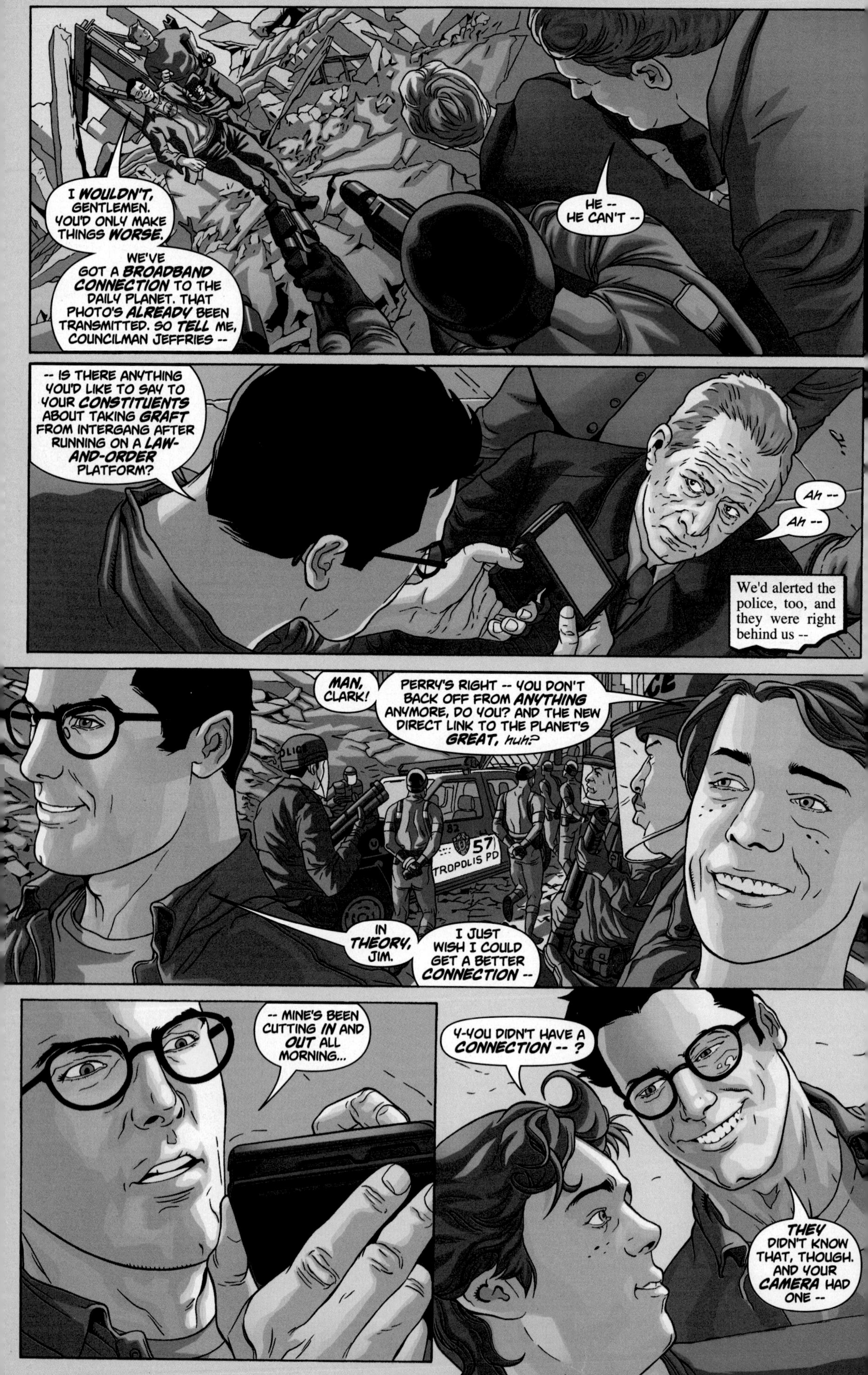
I WOULDN'T, GENTLEMEN. YOU'D ONLY MAKE THINGS WORSE.
WE'VE GOT A BROADBAND CONNECTION TO THE DAILY PLANET. THAT PHOTO'S ALREADY BEEN TRANSMITTED. SO TELL ME, COUNCILMAN JEFFRIES --
HE -- HE CAN'T --
-- IS THERE ANYTHING YOU'D LIKE TO SAY TO YOUR CONSTITUENTS ABOUT TAKING GRAFT FROM INTERGANG AFTER RUNNING ON A LAW-AND-ORDER PLATFORM?
Ah --
Ah --
We'd alerted the police, too, and they were right behind us --
MAN, CLARK!
PERRY'S RIGHT -- YOU DON'T BACK OFF FROM ANYTHING ANYMORE, DO YOU? AND THE NEW DIRECT LINK TO THE PLANET'S GREAT, huh?
57
TROPOLIS PD
IN THEORY, JIM.
I JUST WISH I COULD GET A BETTER CONNECTION --
-- MINE'S BEEN CUTTING IN AND OUT ALL MORNING...
Y-YOU DIDN'T HAVE A CONNECTION -- ?
THEY DIDN'T KNOW THAT, THOUGH. AND YOUR CAMERA HAD ONE --

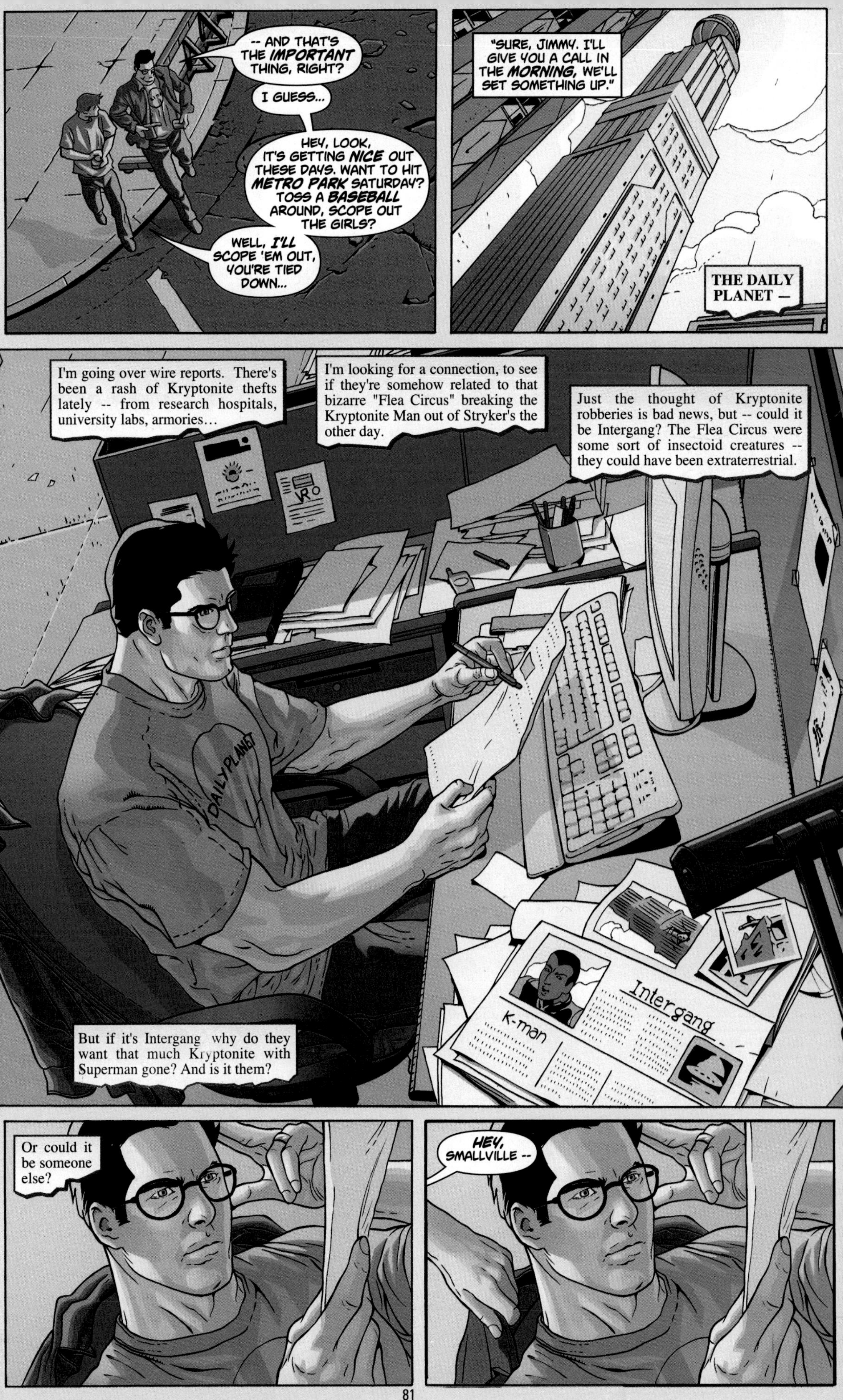
-- AND THAT'S THE IMPORTANT THING, RIGHT?
I GUESS...
HEY, LOOK, IT'S GETTING NICE OUT THESE DAYS. WANT TO HIT METRO PARK SATURDAY? TOSS A BASEBALL AROUND, SCOPE OUT THE GIRLS?
WELL, I'LL SCOPE 'EM OUT, YOU'RE TIED DOWN...
"SURE, JIMMY. I'LL GIVE YOU A CALL IN THE MORNING, WE'LL SET SOMETHING UP."
THE DAILY PLANET —
I'm going over wire reports. There's been a rash of Kryptonite thefts lately -- from research hospitals, university labs, armories…
I'm looking for a connection, to see if they're somehow related to that bizarre "Flea Circus" breaking the Kryptonite Man out of Stryker's the other day.
Just the thought of Kryptonite robberies is bad news, but -- could it be Intergang? The Flea Circus were some sort of insectoid creatures -- they could have been extraterrestrial.
DAILY PLANET
Intergang
K-man
But if it's Intergang why do they want that much Kryptonite with Superman gone? And is it them?
Or could it be someone else?
HEY, SMALLVILLE --

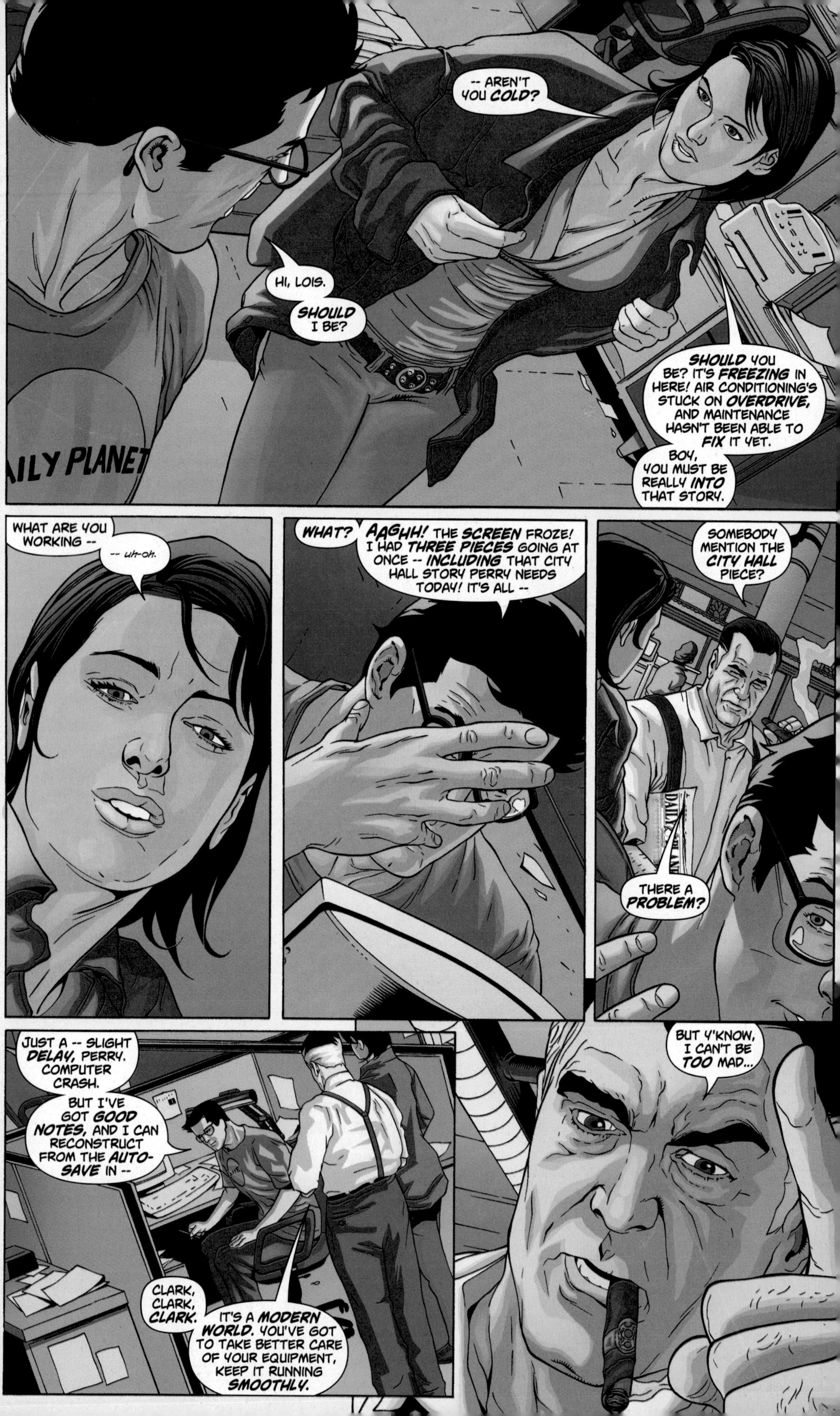
-- AREN'T YOU COLD?
HI, LOIS. SHOULD I BE?
SHOULD YOU BE? IT'S FREEZING IN HERE! AIR CONDITIONING'S STUCK ON OVERDRIVE, AND MAINTENANCE HASN'T BEEN ABLE TO FIX IT YET.
BOY, YOU MUST BE REALLY INTO THAT STORY.
DAILY PLANET
WHAT ARE YOU WORKING --
-- uh-oh.
WHAT?
AAGHH! THE SCREEN FROZE! I HAD THREE PIECES GOING AT ONCE -- INCLUDING THAT CITY HALL STORY PERRY NEEDS TODAY! IT'S ALL --
SOMEBODY MENTION THE CITY HALL PIECE?
THERE A PROBLEM?
JUST A -- SLIGHT DELAY, PERRY. COMPUTER CRASH.
BUT I'VE GOT GOOD NOTES, AND I CAN RECONSTRUCT FROM THE AUTO-SAVE IN --
CLARK, CLARK, CLARK.
IT'S A MODERN WORLD. YOU'VE GOT TO TAKE BETTER CARE OF YOUR EQUIPMENT, KEEP IT RUNNING SMOOTHLY.
BUT Y'KNOW, I CAN'T BE TOO MAD...

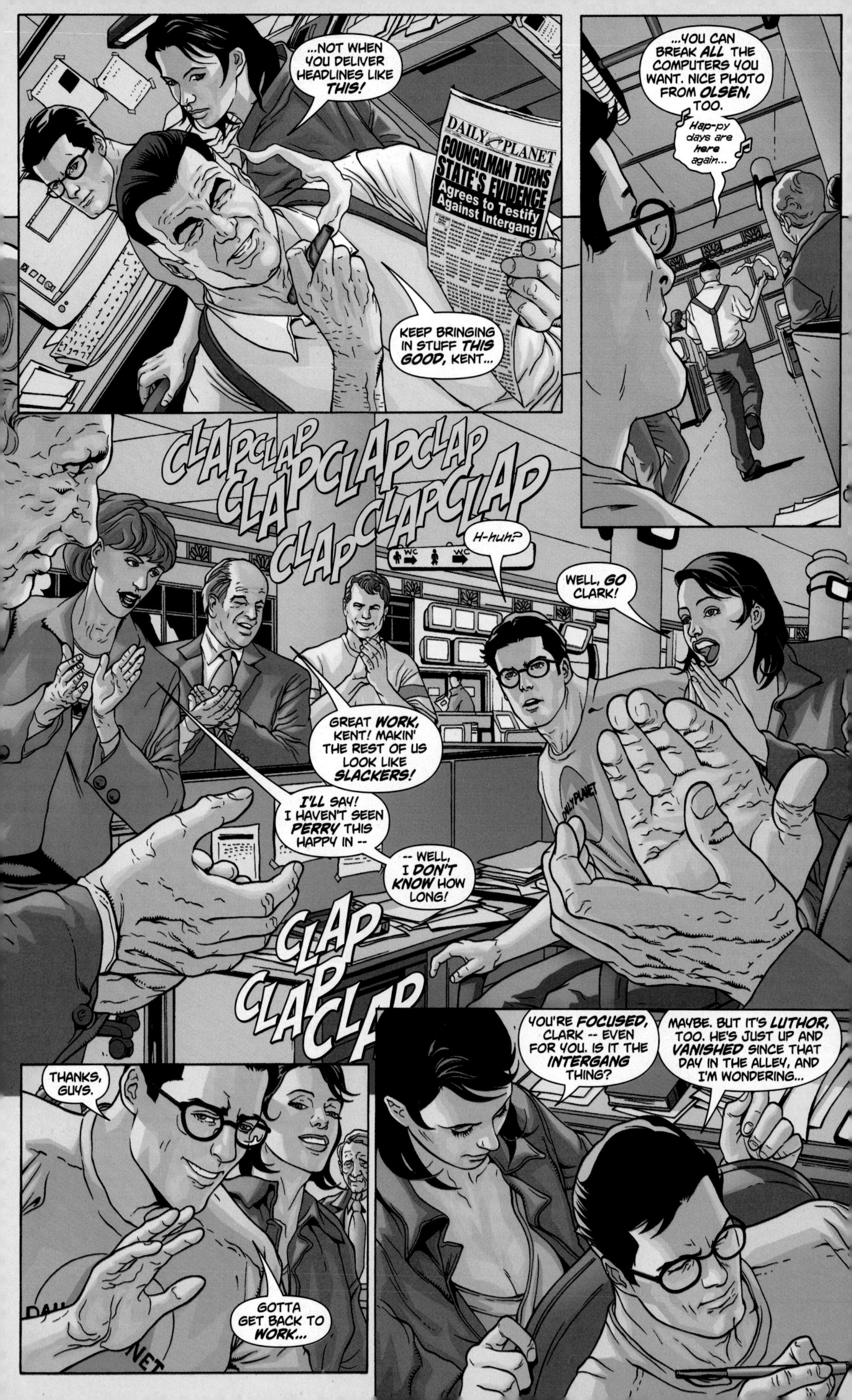
...NOT WHEN YOU DELIVER HEADLINES LIKE THIS!
DAILY PLANET
COUNCILMAN TURNS STATE'S EVIDENCE
Agrees to Testify Against Intergang
KEEP BRINGING IN STUFF THIS GOOD, KENT...
...YOU CAN BREAK ALL THE COMPUTERS YOU WANT. NICE PHOTO FROM OLSEN, TOO.
Hap-py days are here again...
CLAPCLAP CLAPCLAPCLAP CLAPCLAPCLAP
H-huh?
WC
WC
WELL, GO CLARK!
GREAT WORK, KENT! MAKIN' THE REST OF US LOOK LIKE SLACKERS!
I'LL SAY! I HAVEN'T SEEN PERRY THIS HAPPY IN --
-- WELL, I DON'T KNOW HOW LONG!
DAILY PLANET
CLAP CLAP CLAP
THANKS, GUYS.
GOTTA GET BACK TO WORK...
YOU'RE FOCUSED, CLARK -- EVEN FOR YOU. IS IT THE INTERGANG THING?
MAYBE. BUT IT'S LUTHOR, TOO. HE'S JUST UP AND VANISHED SINCE THAT DAY IN THE ALLEY, AND I'M WONDERING...

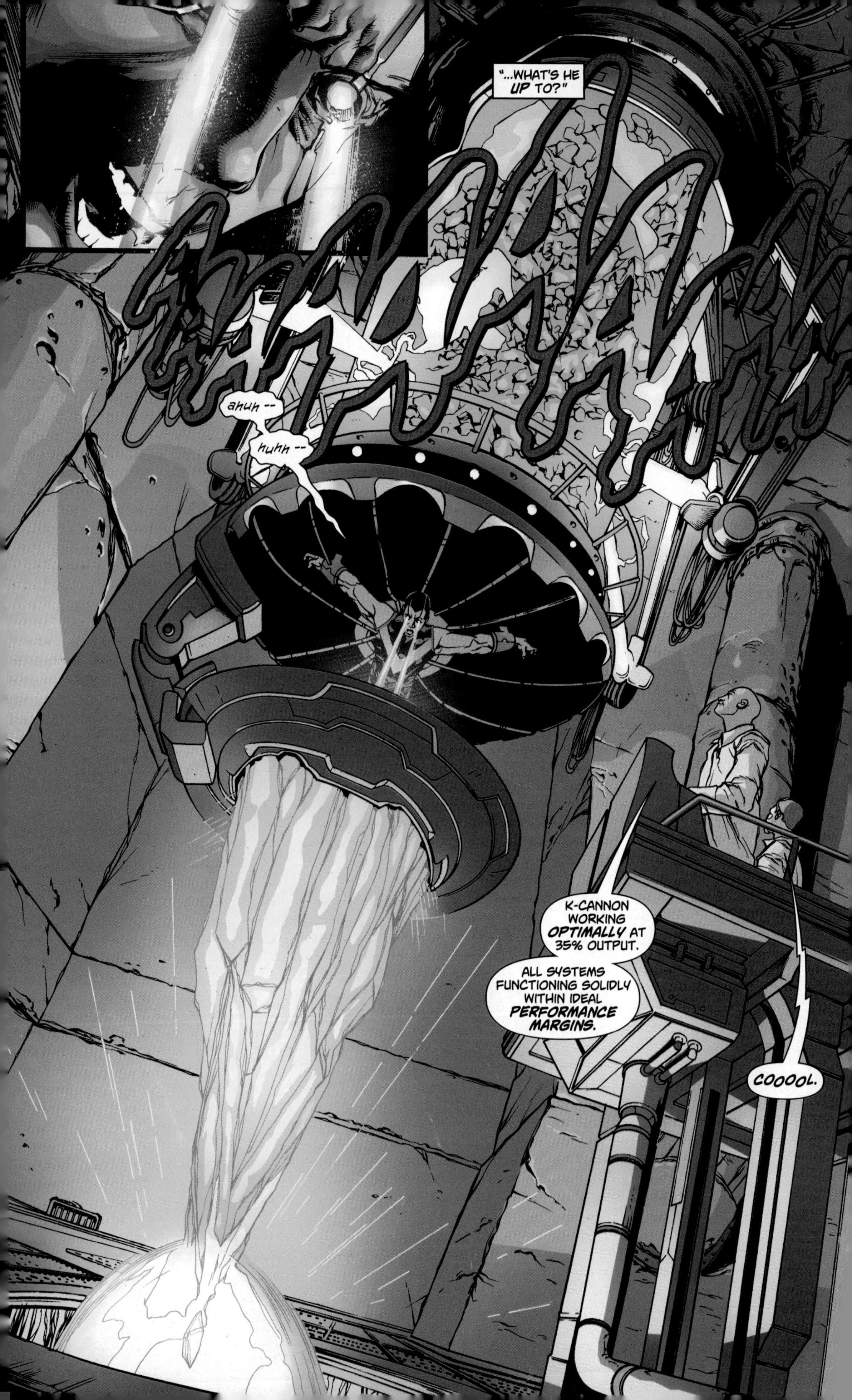
"...WHAT'S HE UP TO?"
ahuh --
huhh --
K-CANNON WORKING OPTIMALLY AT 35% OUTPUT.
ALL SYSTEMS FUNCTIONING SOLIDLY WITHIN IDEAL PERFORMANCE MARGINS.
COOOOL.

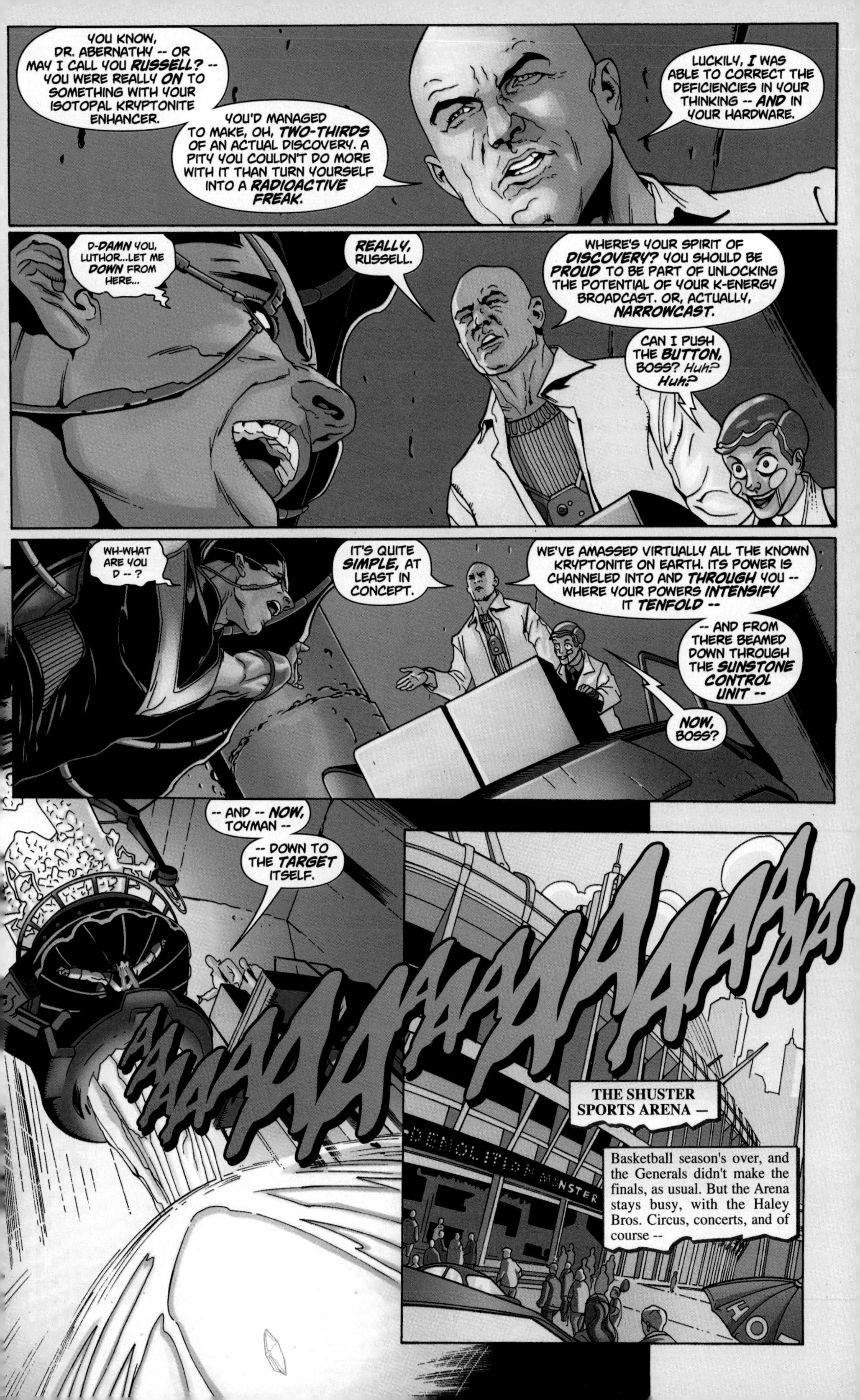
YOU KNOW, DR. ABERNATHY -- OR MAY I CALL YOU RUSSELL? -- YOU WERE REALLY ON TO SOMETHING WITH YOUR ISOTOPAL KRYPTONITE ENHANCER.
YOU'D MANAGED TO MAKE, OH, TWO-THIRDS OF AN ACTUAL DISCOVERY. A PITY YOU COULDN'T DO MORE WITH IT THAN TURN YOURSELF INTO A RADIOACTIVE FREAK.
LUCKILY, I WAS ABLE TO CORRECT THE DEFICIENCIES IN YOUR THINKING -- AND IN YOUR HARDWARE.
D-DAMN YOU, LUTHOR...LET ME DOWN FROM HERE...
REALLY, RUSSELL.
WHERE'S YOUR SPIRIT OF DISCOVERY? YOU SHOULD BE PROUD TO BE PART OF UNLOCKING THE POTENTIAL OF YOUR K-ENERGY BROADCAST. OR, ACTUALLY, NARROWCAST.
CAN I PUSH THE BUTTON, BOSS? Huh? Huh?
WH-WHAT ARE YOU D -- ?
IT'S QUITE SIMPLE, AT LEAST IN CONCEPT.
WE'VE AMASSED VIRTUALLY ALL THE KNOWN KRYPTONITE ON EARTH. ITS POWER IS CHANNELED INTO AND THROUGH YOU -- WHERE YOUR POWERS INTENSIFY IT TENFOLD --
-- AND FROM THERE BEAMED DOWN THROUGH THE SUNSTONE CONTROL UNIT --
NOW, BOSS?
-- AND -- NOW, TOYMAN --
-- DOWN TO THE TARGET ITSELF.
AAAAAAAAAAAAAAAAAAAAAAA
THE SHUSTER SPORTS ARENA —
Basketball season's over, and the Generals didn't make the finals, as usual. But the Arena stays busy, with the Haley Bros. Circus, concerts, and of course --

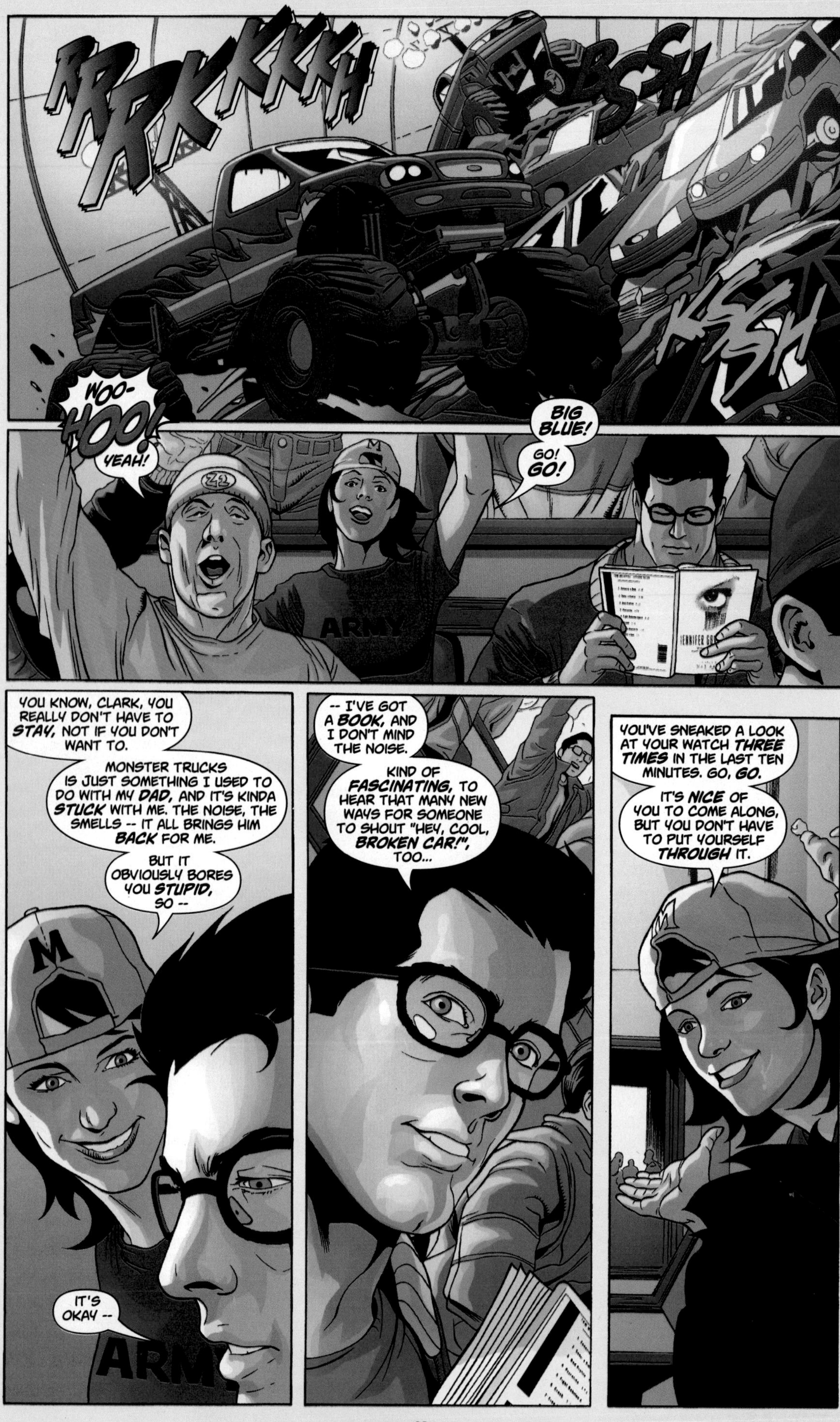
RRRKKKKH
BSCH
KSH
WOO-HOO!
YEAH!
BIG BLUE!
GO! GO!
YOU KNOW, CLARK, YOU REALLY DON'T HAVE TO STAY, NOT IF YOU DON'T WANT TO.
MONSTER TRUCKS IS JUST SOMETHING I USED TO DO WITH MY DAD, AND IT'S KINDA STUCK WITH ME. THE NOISE, THE SMELLS -- IT ALL BRINGS HIM BACK FOR ME.
BUT IT OBVIOUSLY BORES YOU STUPID, SO --
IT'S OKAY --
-- I'VE GOT A BOOK, AND I DON'T MIND THE NOISE.
KIND OF FASCINATING, TO HEAR THAT MANY NEW WAYS FOR SOMEONE TO SHOUT "HEY, COOL, BROKEN CAR!", TOO...
YOU'VE SNEAKED A LOOK AT YOUR WATCH THREE TIMES IN THE LAST TEN MINUTES. GO, GO.
IT'S NICE OF YOU TO COME ALONG, BUT YOU DON'T HAVE TO PUT YOURSELF THROUGH IT.

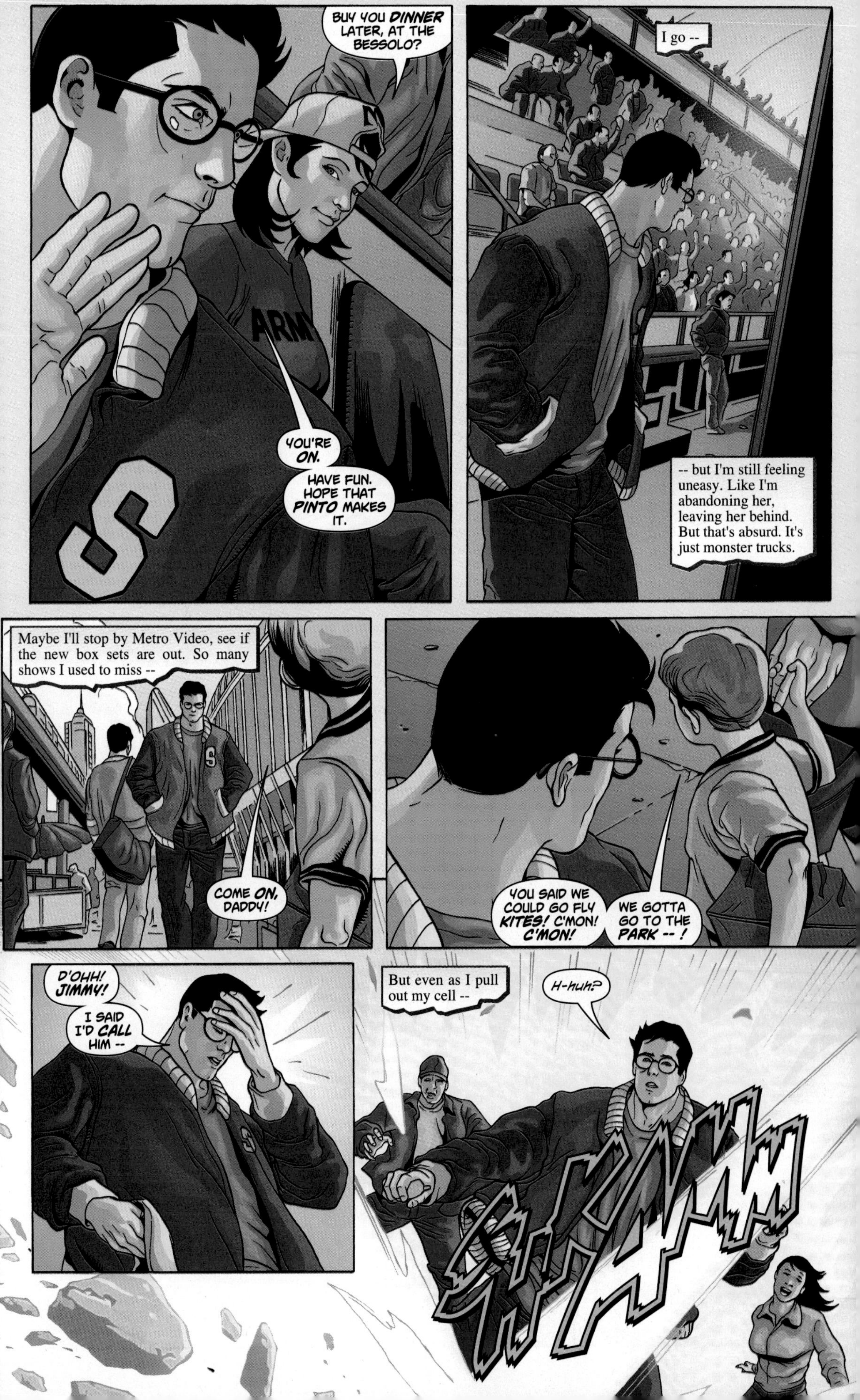
BUY YOU DINNER LATER, AT THE BESSOLO?
YOU'RE ON.
HAVE FUN. HOPE THAT PINTO MAKES IT.
I go --
-- but I'm still feeling uneasy. Like I'm abandoning her, leaving her behind. But that's absurd. It's just monster trucks.
Maybe I'll stop by Metro Video, see if the new box sets are out. So many shows I used to miss --
COME ON, DADDY!
YOU SAID WE COULD GO FLY KITES! C'MON! C'MON!
WE GOTTA GO TO THE PARK -- !
D'OHH! JIMMY!
I SAID I'D CALL HIM --
But even as I pull out my cell --
H-huh?

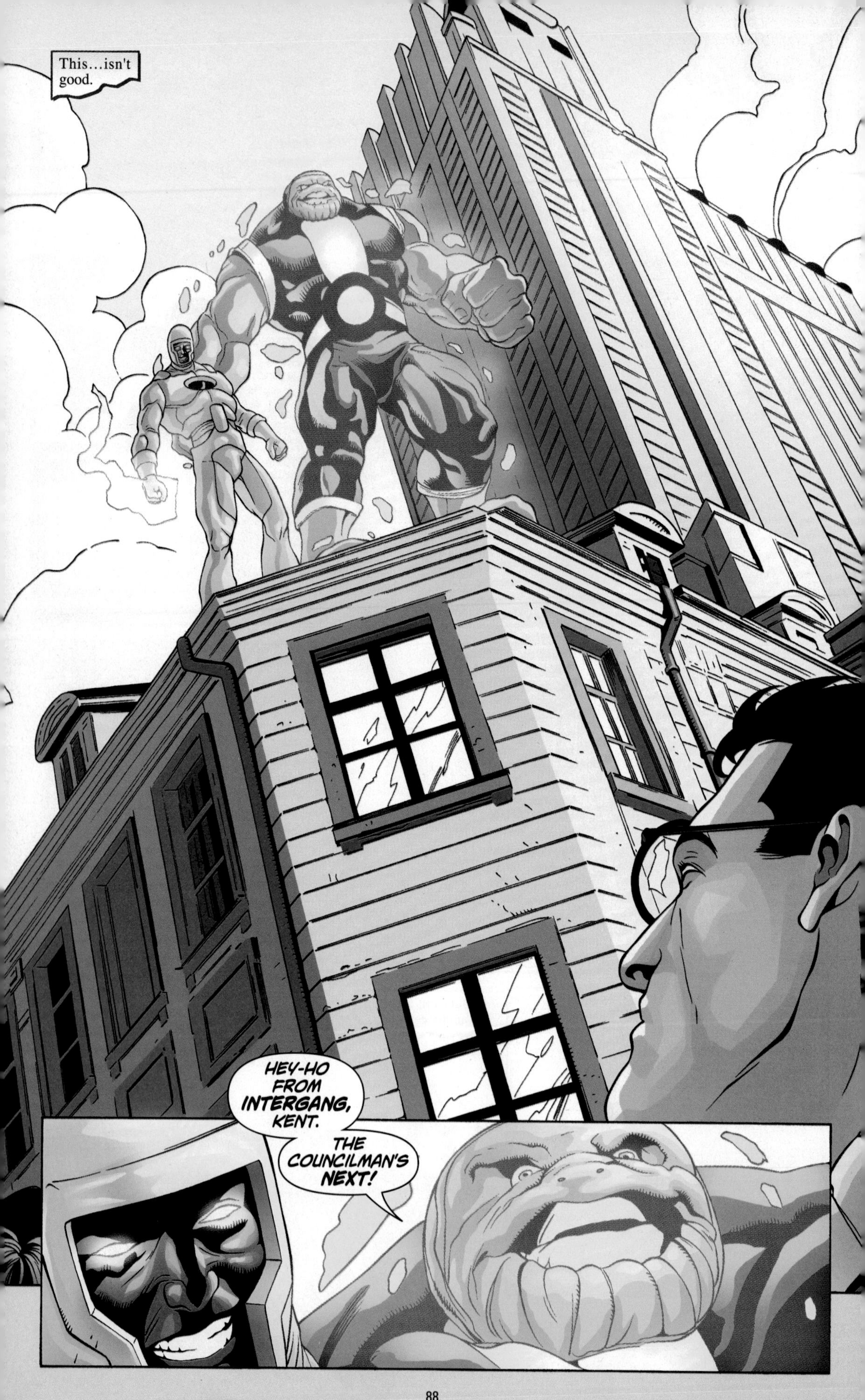

This…isn't good.
HEY-HO FROM INTERGANG, KENT.
THE COUNCILMAN'S NEXT!

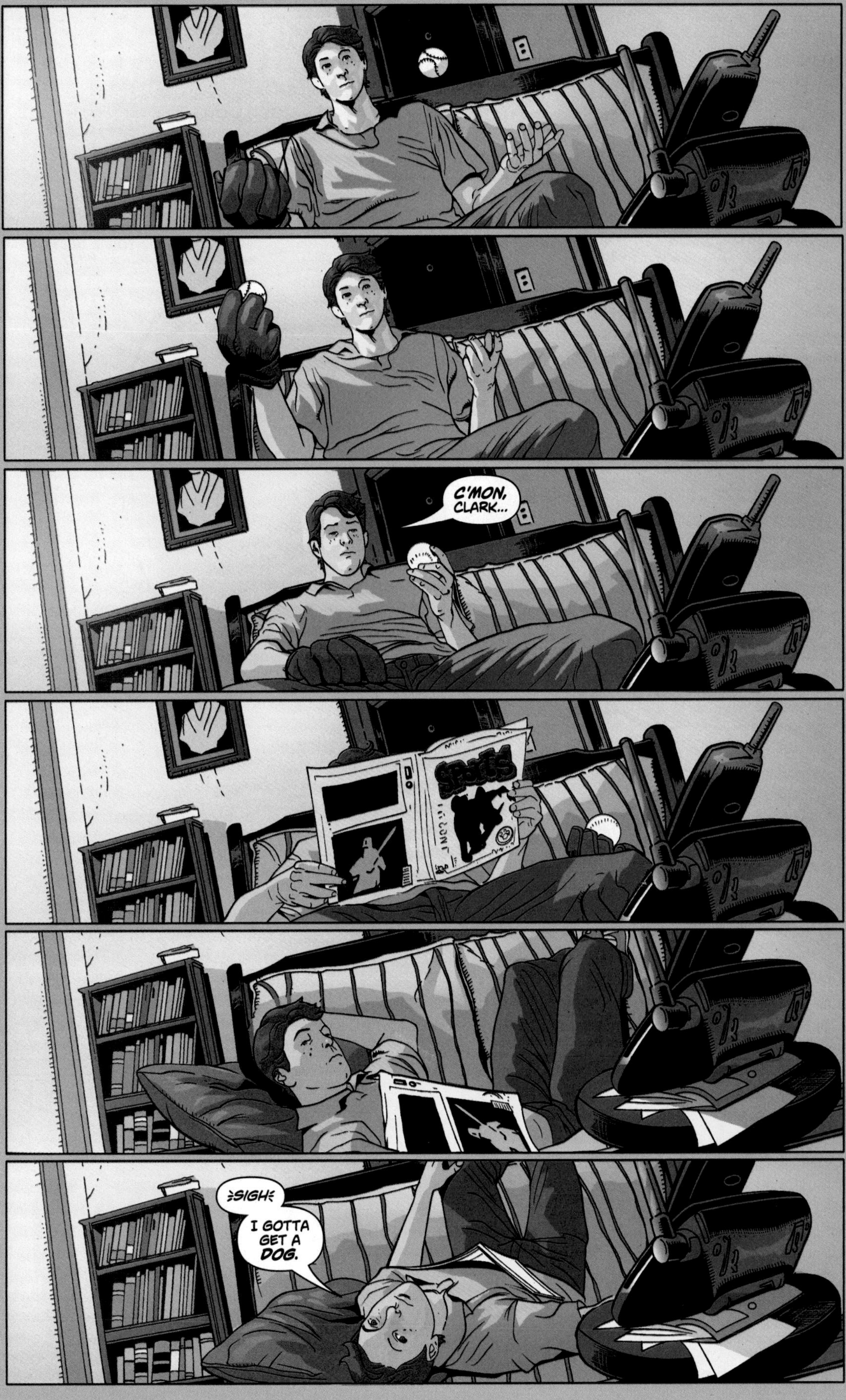
C'MON, CLARK...
SIGH
I GOTTA GET A DOG.

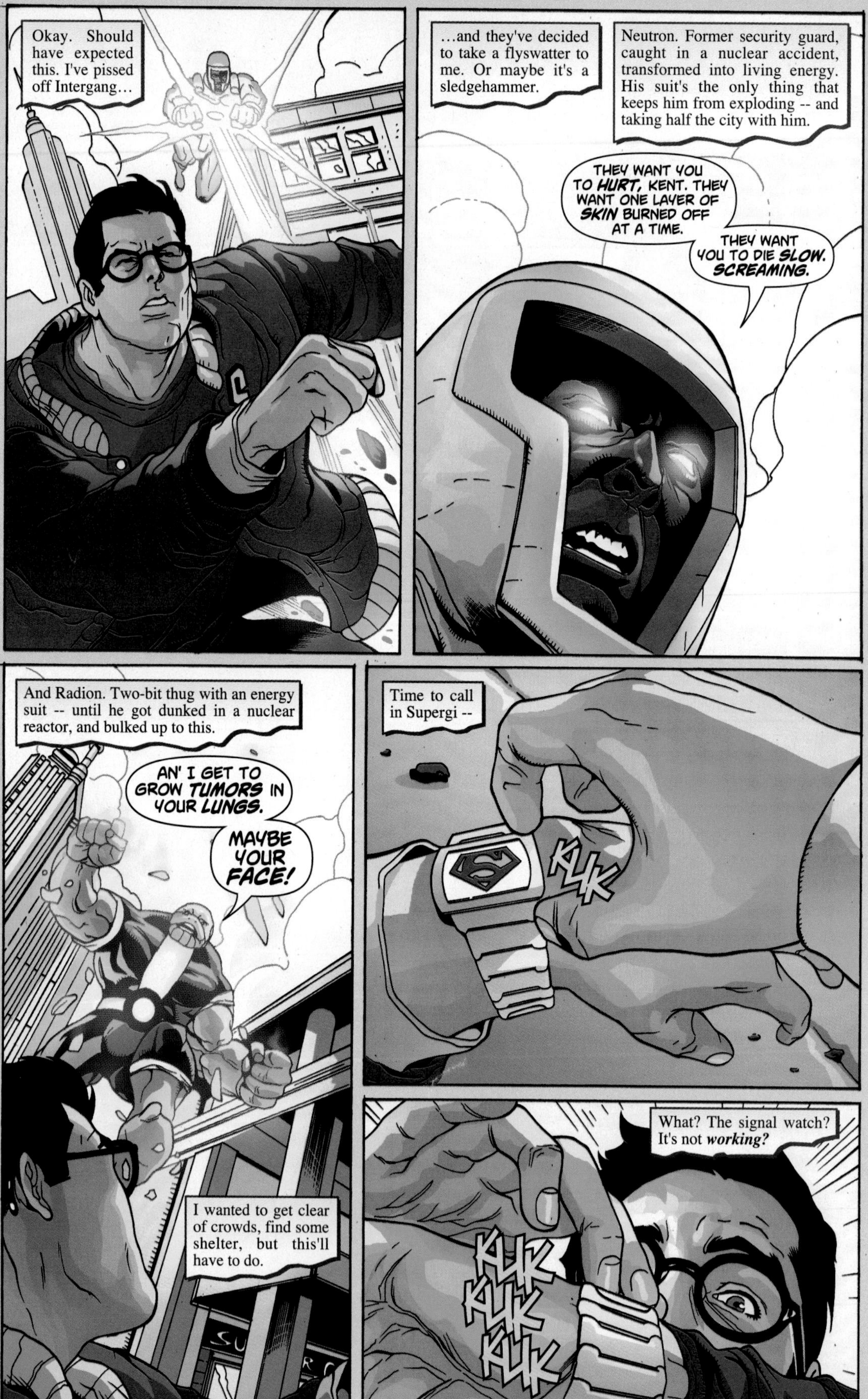
Okay. Should have expected this. I've pissed off Intergang…
…and they've decided to take a flyswatter to me. Or maybe it's a sledgehammer.
Neutron. Former security guard, caught in a nuclear accident, transformed into living energy. His suit's the only thing that keeps him from exploding -- and taking half the city with him.
THEY WANT YOU TO HURT, KENT. THEY WANT ONE LAYER OF SKIN BURNED OFF AT A TIME.
THEY WANT YOU TO DIE SLOW. SCREAMING.
And Radion. Two-bit thug with an energy suit -- until he got dunked in a nuclear reactor, and bulked up to this.
AN' I GET TO GROW TUMORS IN YOUR LUNGS.
MAYBE YOUR FACE!
I wanted to get clear of crowds, find some shelter, but this'll have to do.
Time to call in Supergi --
KLIK
What? The signal watch? It's not working?
KLIK KLIK KLIK

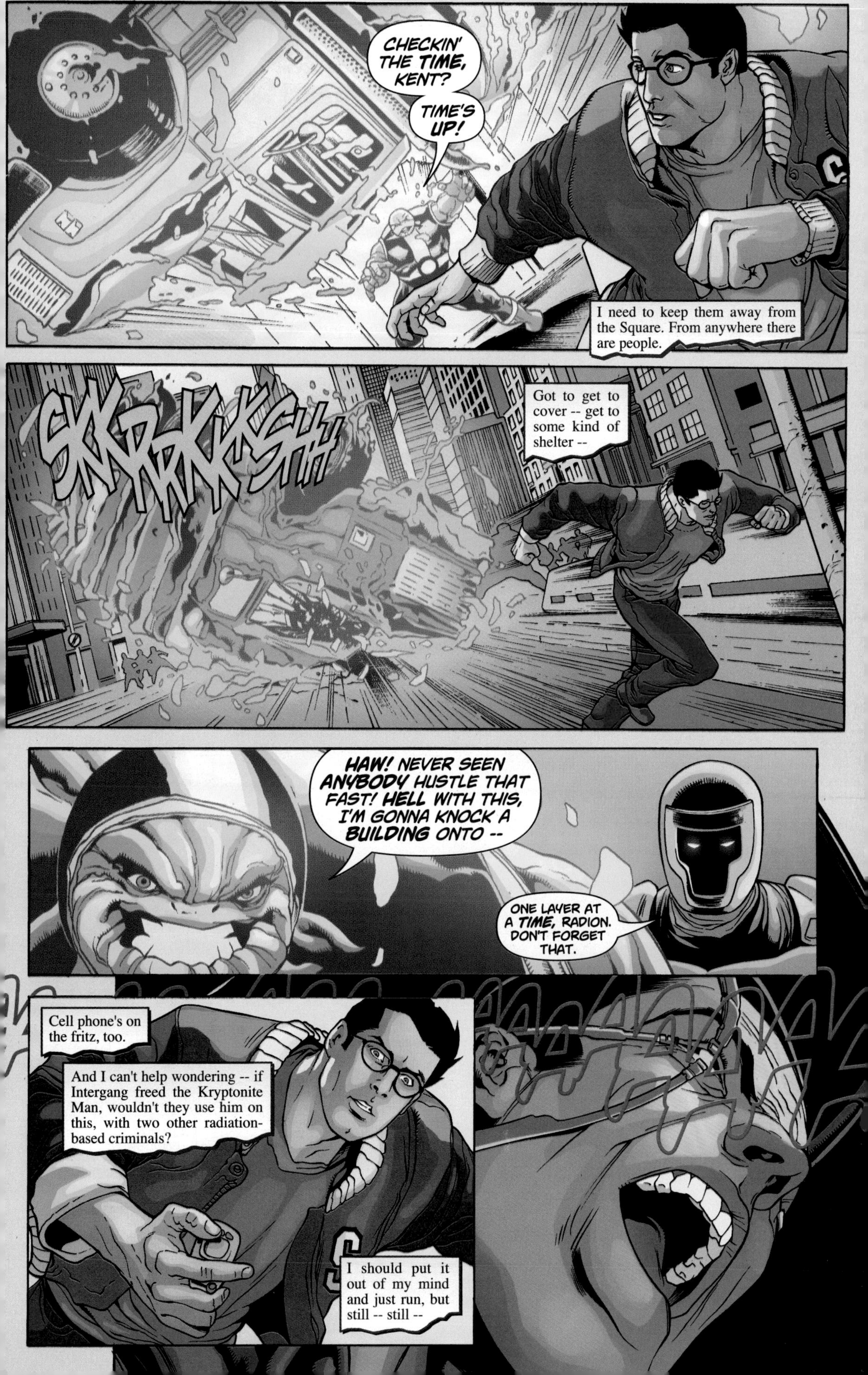
CHECKIN' THE TIME, KENT?
TIME'S UP!
I need to keep them away from the Square. From anywhere there are people.
SKKRRKKKSHH
Got to get to cover -- get to some kind of shelter --
HAW! NEVER SEEN ANYBODY HUSTLE THAT FAST! HELL WITH THIS, I'M GONNA KNOCK A BUILDING ONTO --
ONE LAYER AT A TIME, RADION. DON'T FORGET THAT.
Cell phone's on the fritz, too.
And I can't help wondering -- if Intergang freed the Kryptonite Man, wouldn't they use him on this, with two other radiation-based criminals?
I should put it out of my mind and just run, but still -- still --

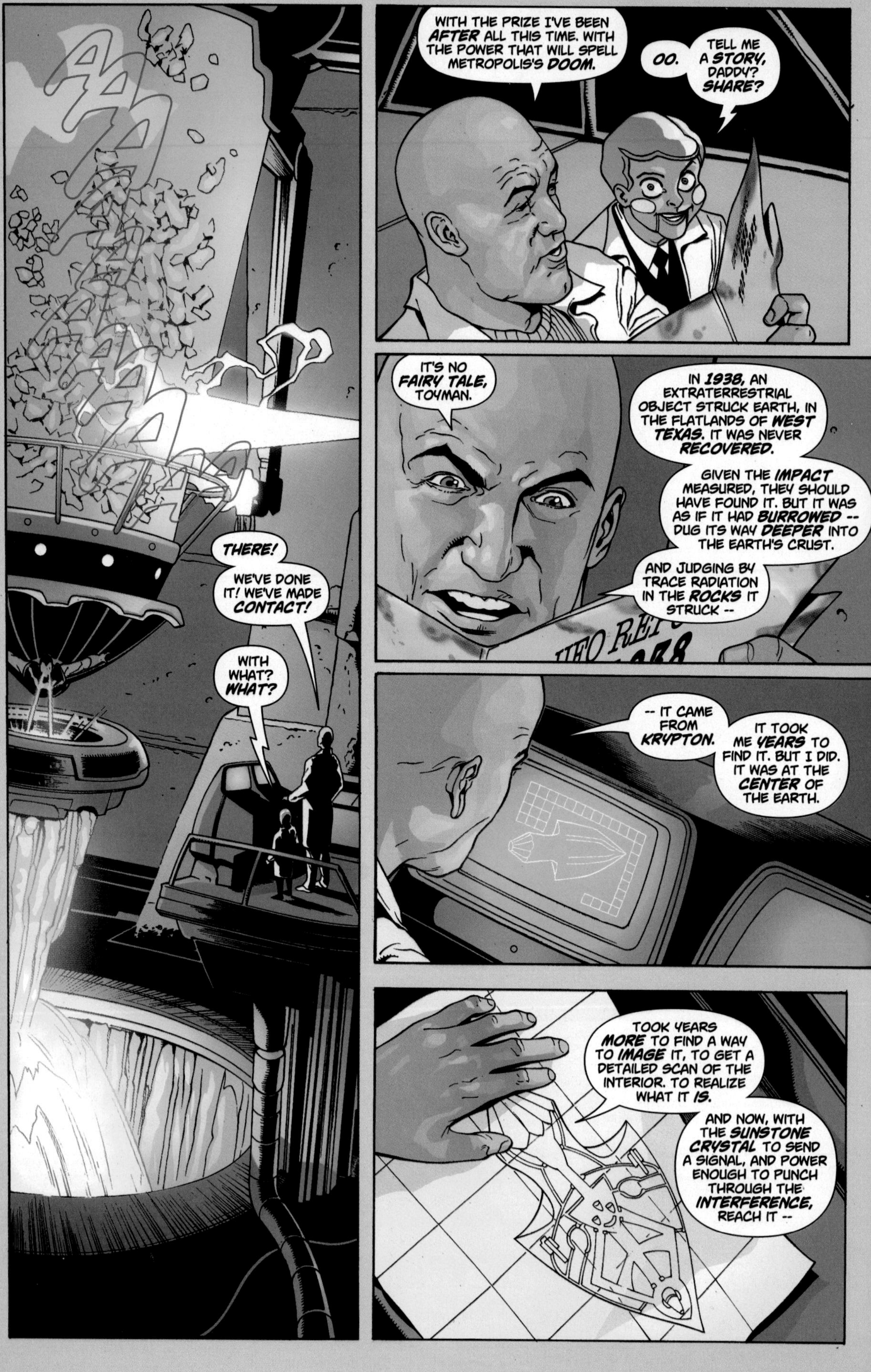

THERE!
WE'VE DONE IT! WE'VE MADE CONTACT!
WITH WHAT? WHAT?
WITH THE PRIZE I'VE BEEN AFTER ALL THIS TIME. WITH THE POWER THAT WILL SPELL METROPOLIS'S DOOM.
OO.
TELL ME A STORY, DADDY? SHARE?
IT'S NO FAIRY TALE, TOYMAN.
IN 1938, AN EXTRATERRESTRIAL OBJECT STRUCK EARTH, IN THE FLATLANDS OF WEST TEXAS. IT WAS NEVER RECOVERED.
GIVEN THE IMPACT MEASURED, THEY SHOULD HAVE FOUND IT. BUT IT WAS AS IF IT HAD BURROWED -- DUG ITS WAY DEEPER INTO THE EARTH'S CRUST.
AND JUDGING BY TRACE RADIATION IN THE ROCKS IT STRUCK --
-- IT CAME FROM KRYPTON.
IT TOOK ME YEARS TO FIND IT. BUT I DID. IT WAS AT THE CENTER OF THE EARTH.
TOOK YEARS MORE TO FIND A WAY TO IMAGE IT, TO GET A DETAILED SCAN OF THE INTERIOR. TO REALIZE WHAT IT IS.
AND NOW, WITH THE SUNSTONE CRYSTAL TO SEND A SIGNAL, AND POWER ENOUGH TO PUNCH THROUGH THE INTERFERENCE, REACH IT --

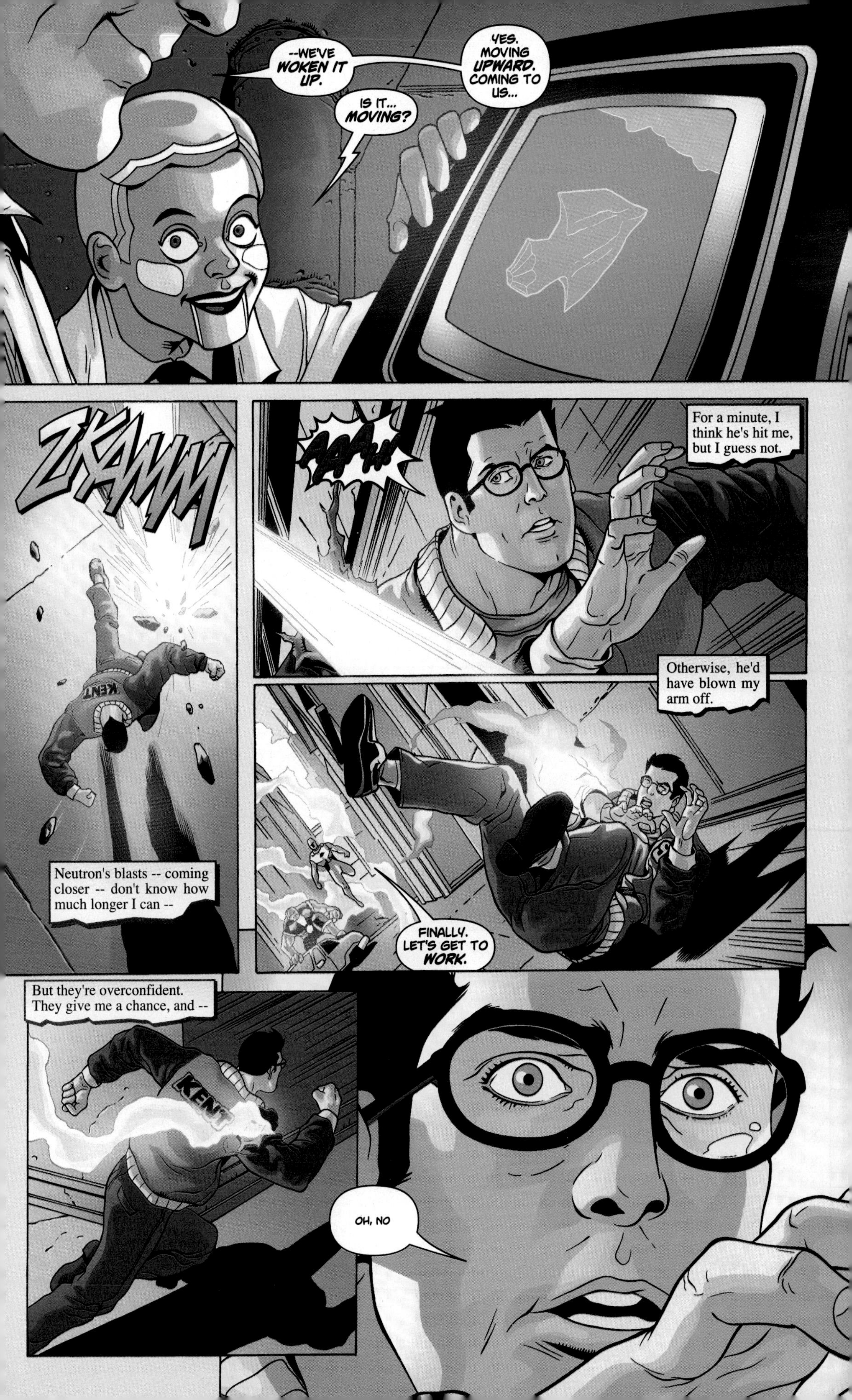
--WE'VE WOKEN IT UP.
IS IT... MOVING?
YES. MOVING UPWARD. COMING TO US...
ZKAMMM
Neutron's blasts -- coming closer -- don't know how much longer I can --
AAAH
For a minute, I think he's hit me, but I guess not.
Otherwise, he'd have blown my arm off.
FINALLY. LET'S GET TO WORK.
But they're overconfident. They give me a chance, and --
OH, NO

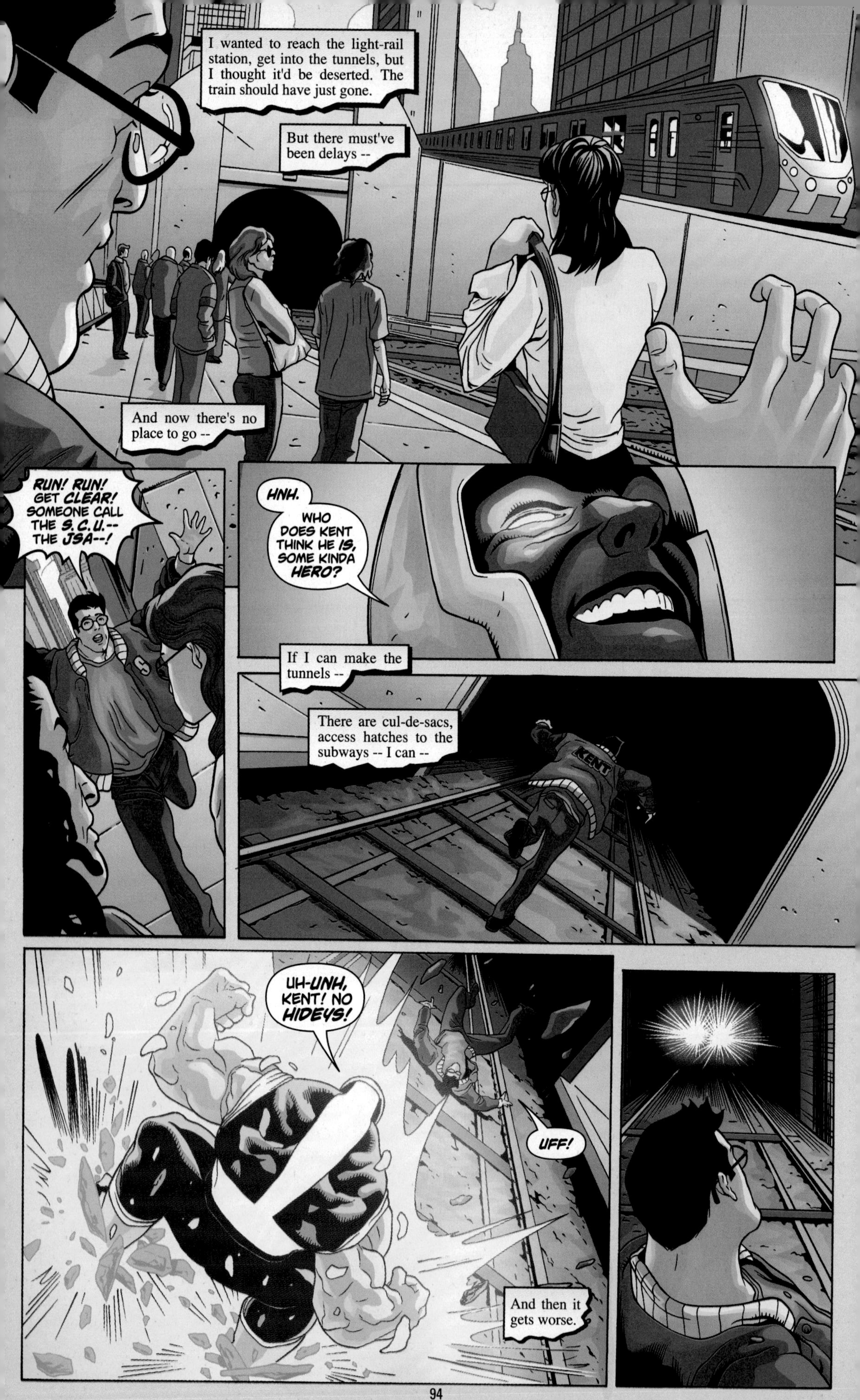

I wanted to reach the light-rail station, get into the tunnels, but I thought it'd be deserted. The train should have just gone.
But there must've been delays --
And now there's no place to go --
RUN! RUN! GET CLEAR! SOMEONE CALL THE S.C.U.-- THE JSA--!
HNH.
WHO DOES KENT THINK HE IS, SOME KINDA HERO?
If I can make the tunnels --
There are cul-de-sacs, access hatches to the subways -- I can --
KENT
UH-UNH, KENT! NO HIDEYS!
UFF!
And then it gets worse.

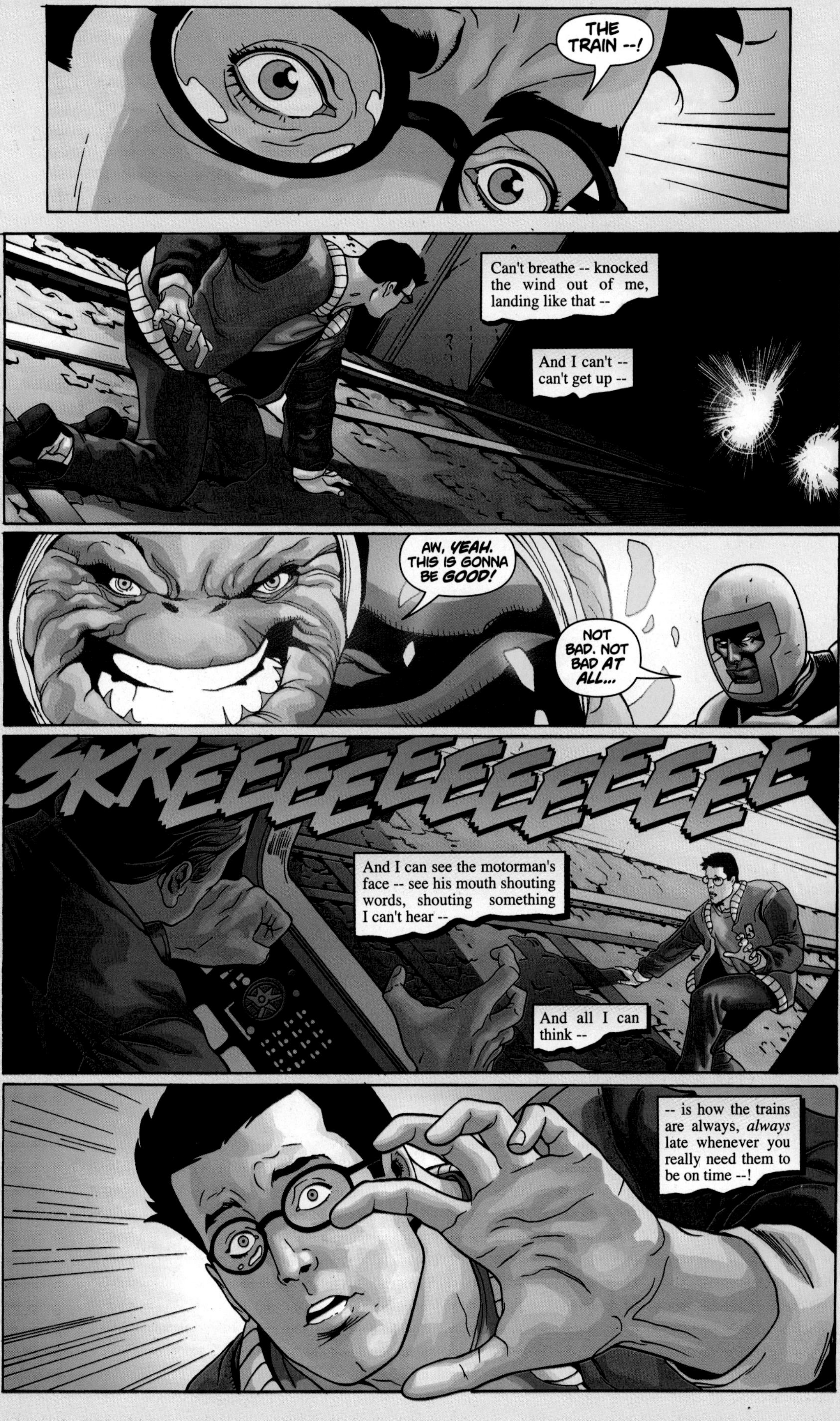
THE TRAIN --!
Can't breathe -- knocked the wind out of me, landing like that --
And I can't -- can't get up --
AW, YEAH. THIS IS GONNA BE GOOD!
NOT BAD. NOT BAD AT ALL...
SKREEEEEEEEEEEEEEE
And I can see the motorman's face -- see his mouth shouting words, shouting something I can't hear --
And all I can think --
-- is how the trains are always, *always* late whenever you really need them to be on time --!

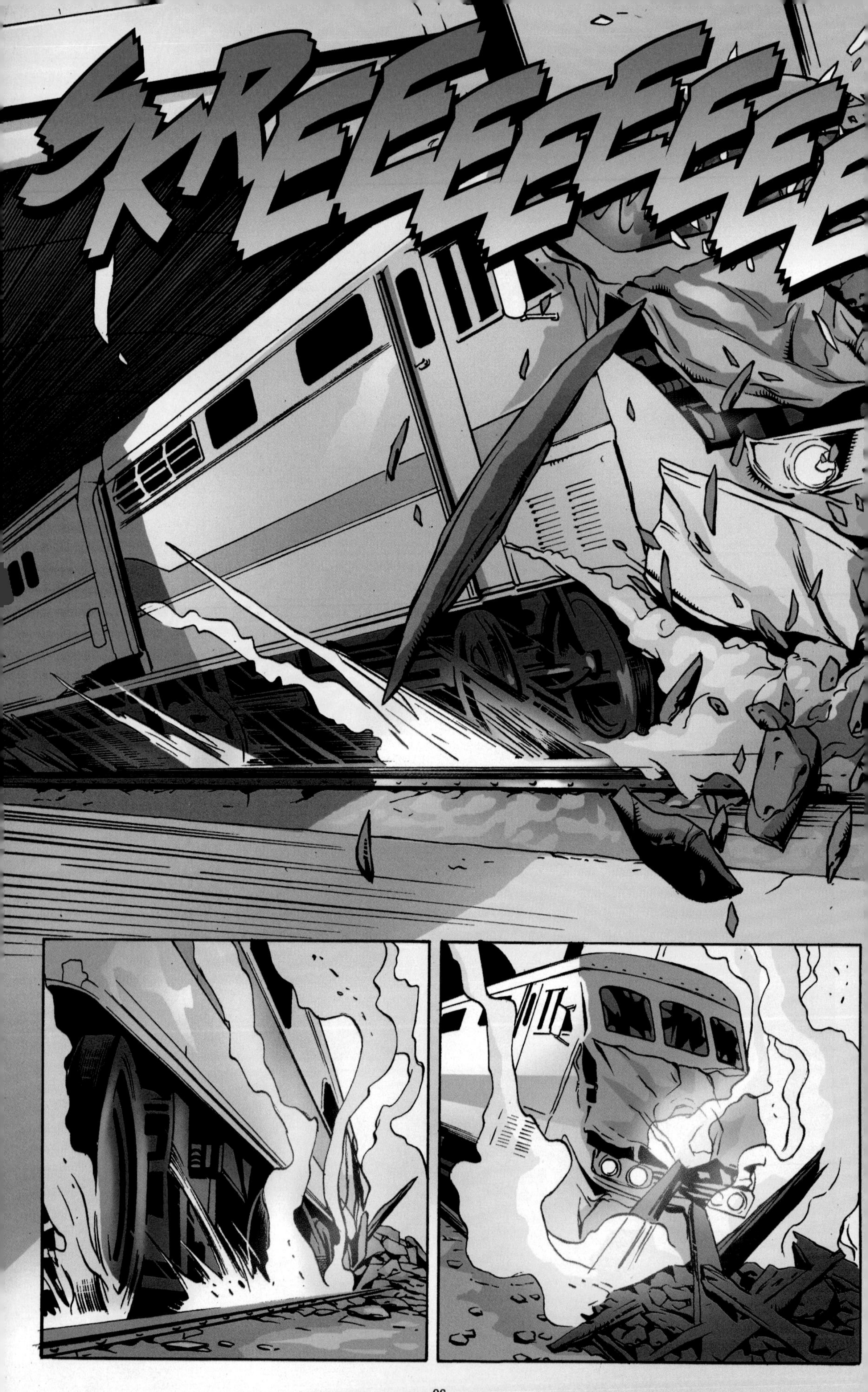
SKREEEEEEE

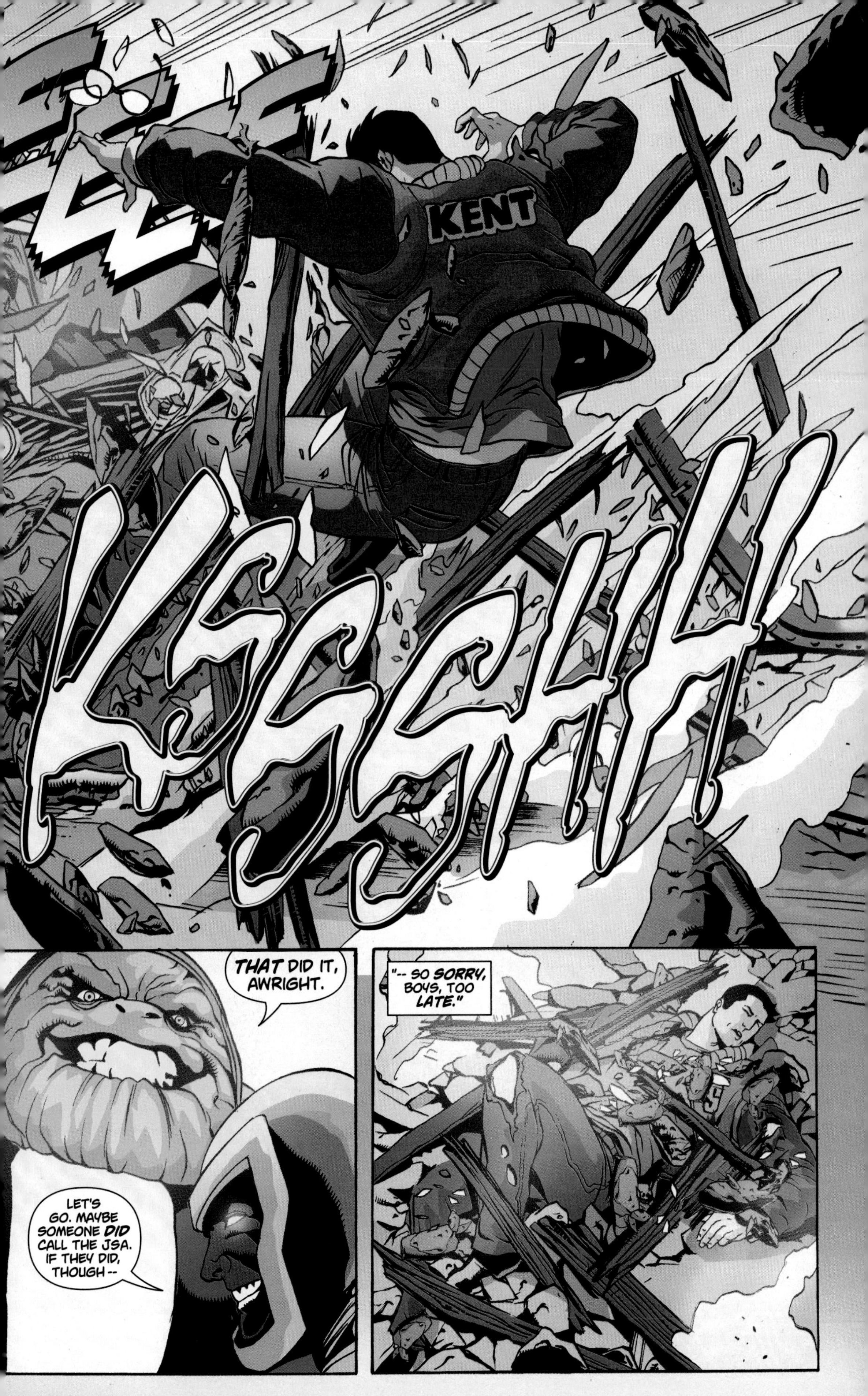

KENT
THAT DID IT, AWRIGHT.
LET'S GO. MAYBE SOMEONE DID CALL THE JSA. IF THEY DID, THOUGH --
"-- SO SORRY, BOYS, TOO LATE."

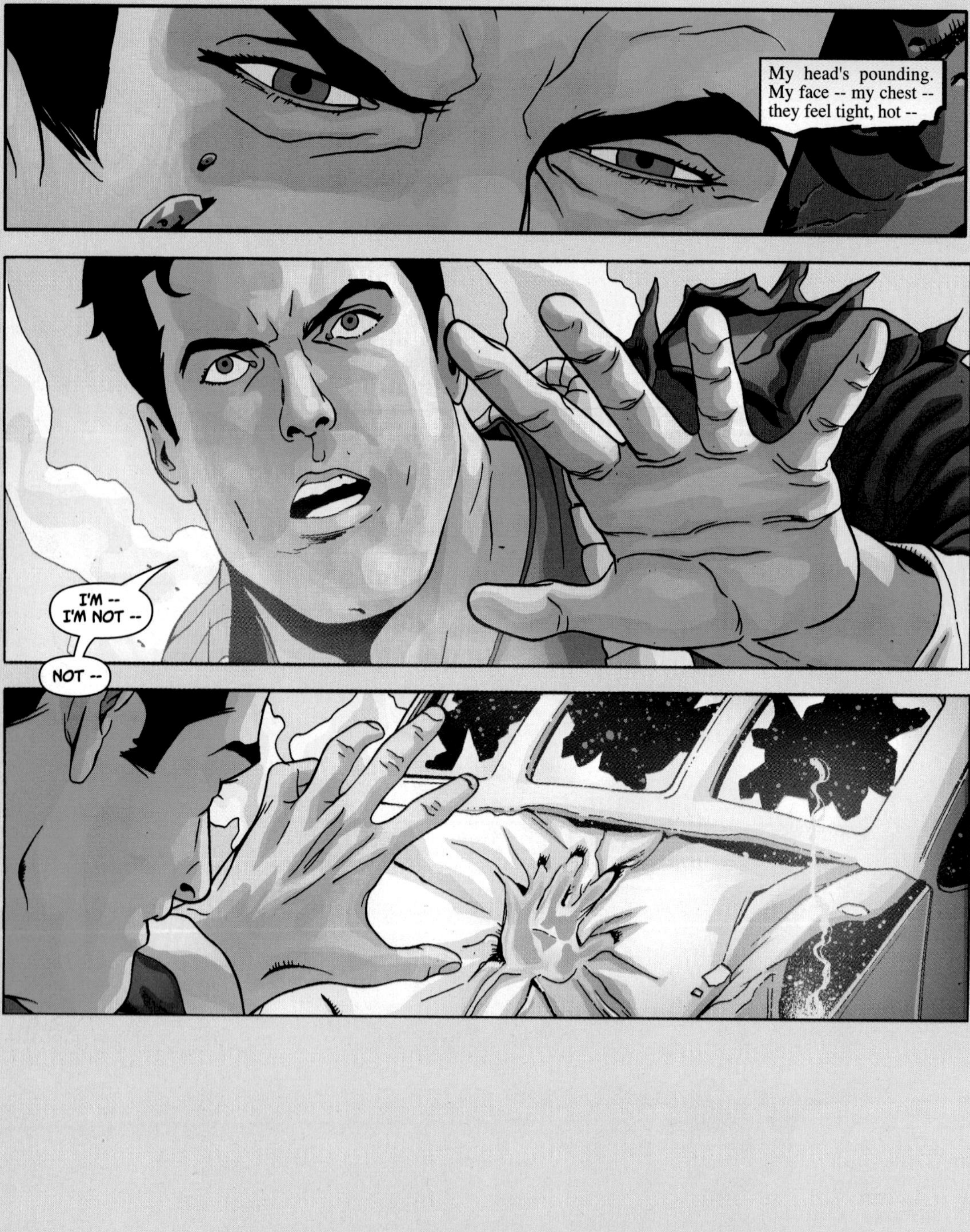
My head's pounding. My face -- my chest -- they feel tight, hot --
I'M -- I'M NOT --
NOT --

Art by: Renato Guedes

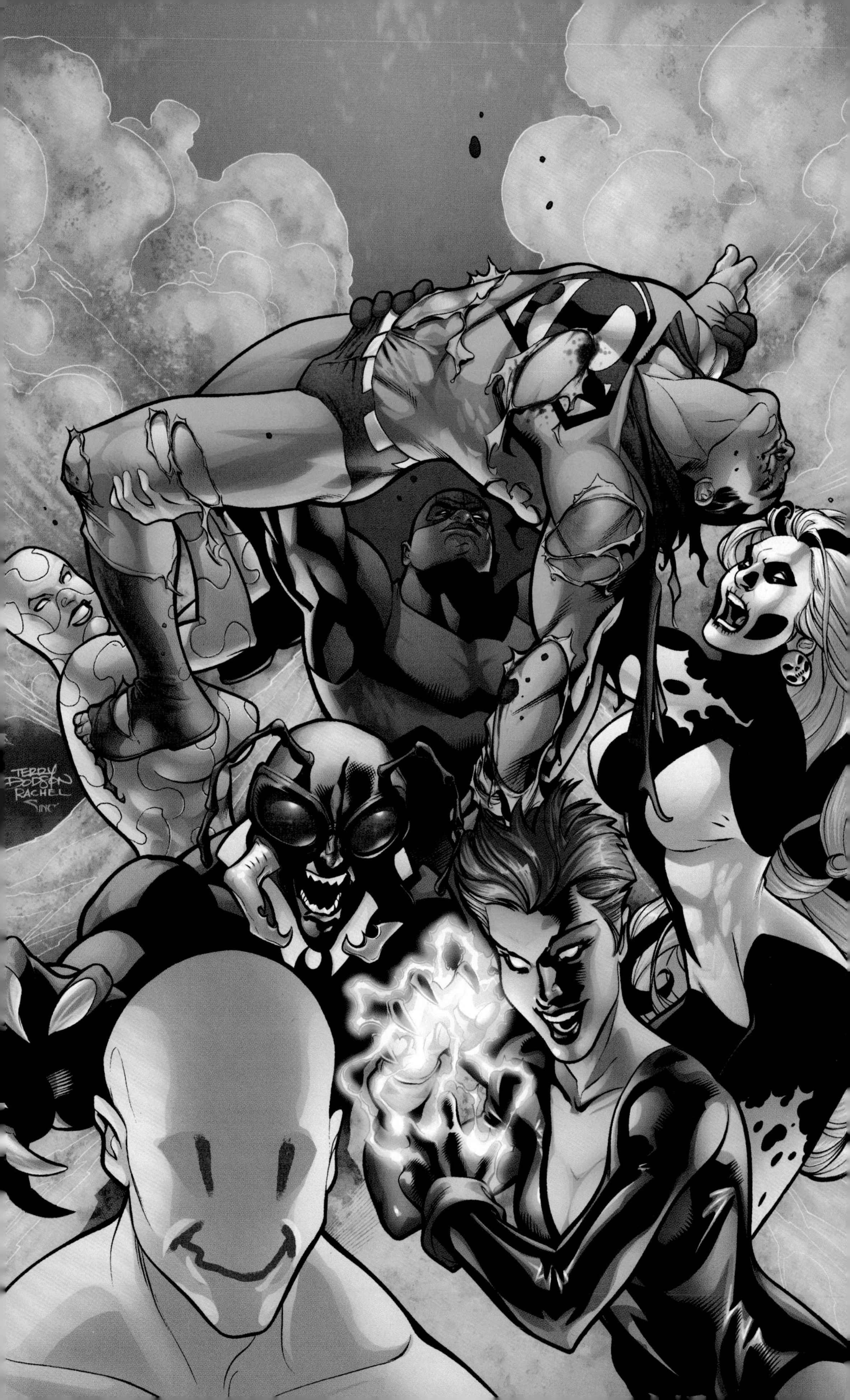
TERRY
DODSON
RACHEL

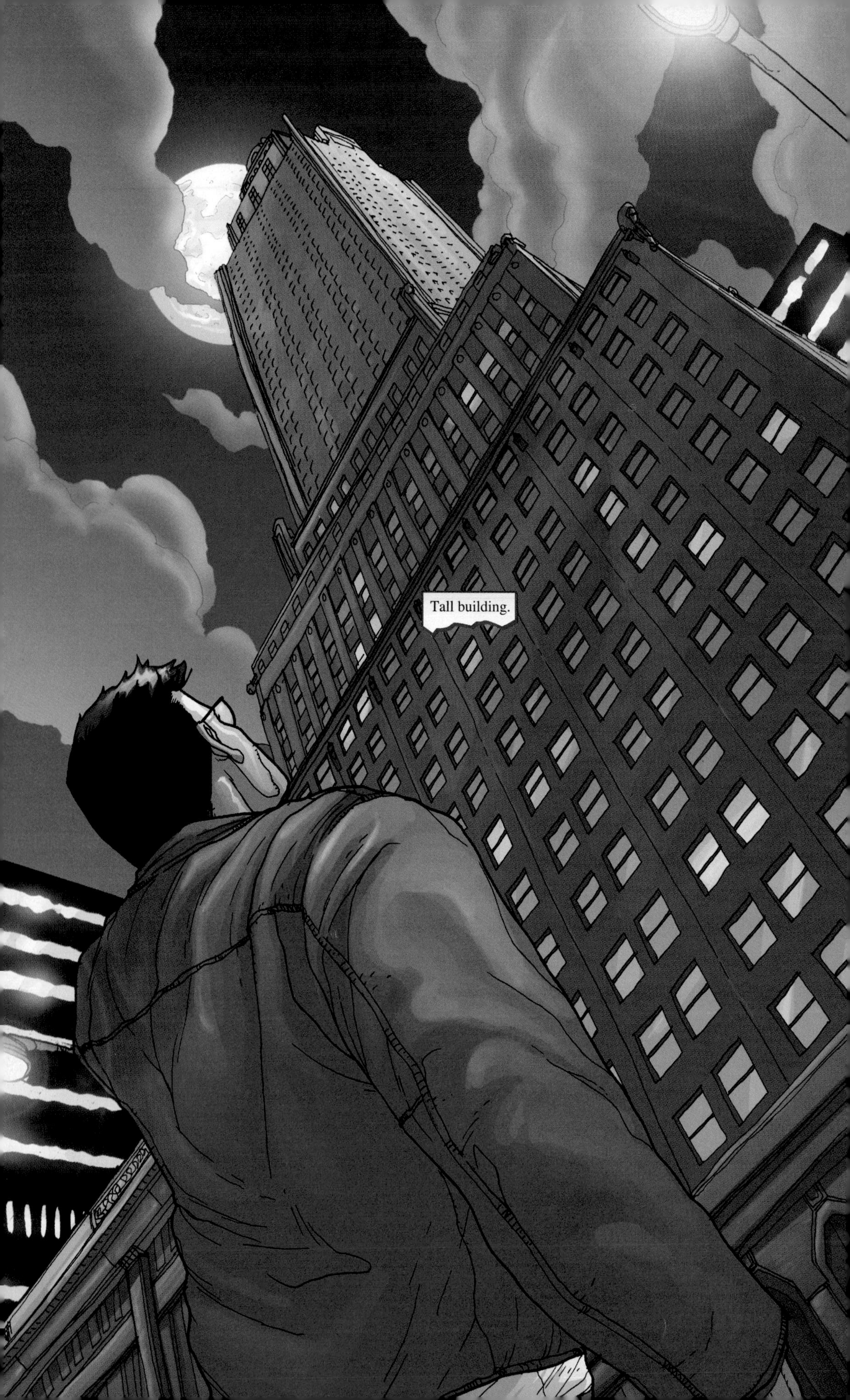
Tall building.

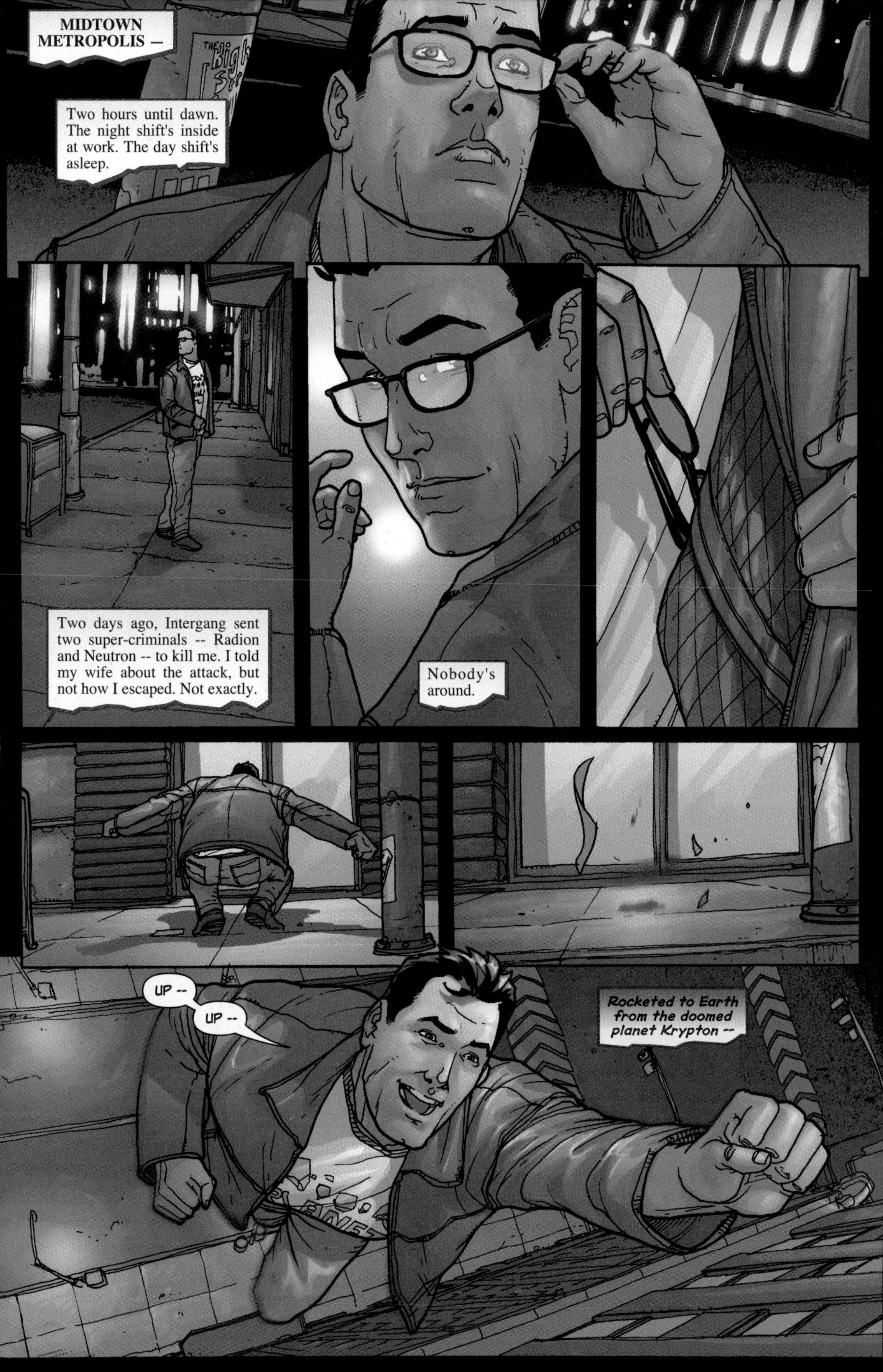
MIDTOWN METROPOLIS —
Two hours until dawn. The night shift's inside at work. The day shift's asleep.
Two days ago, Intergang sent two super-criminals -- Radion and Neutron -- to kill me. I told my wife about the attack, but not how I escaped. Not exactly.
Nobody's around.
UP --
UP --
Rocketed to Earth from the doomed planet Krypton --

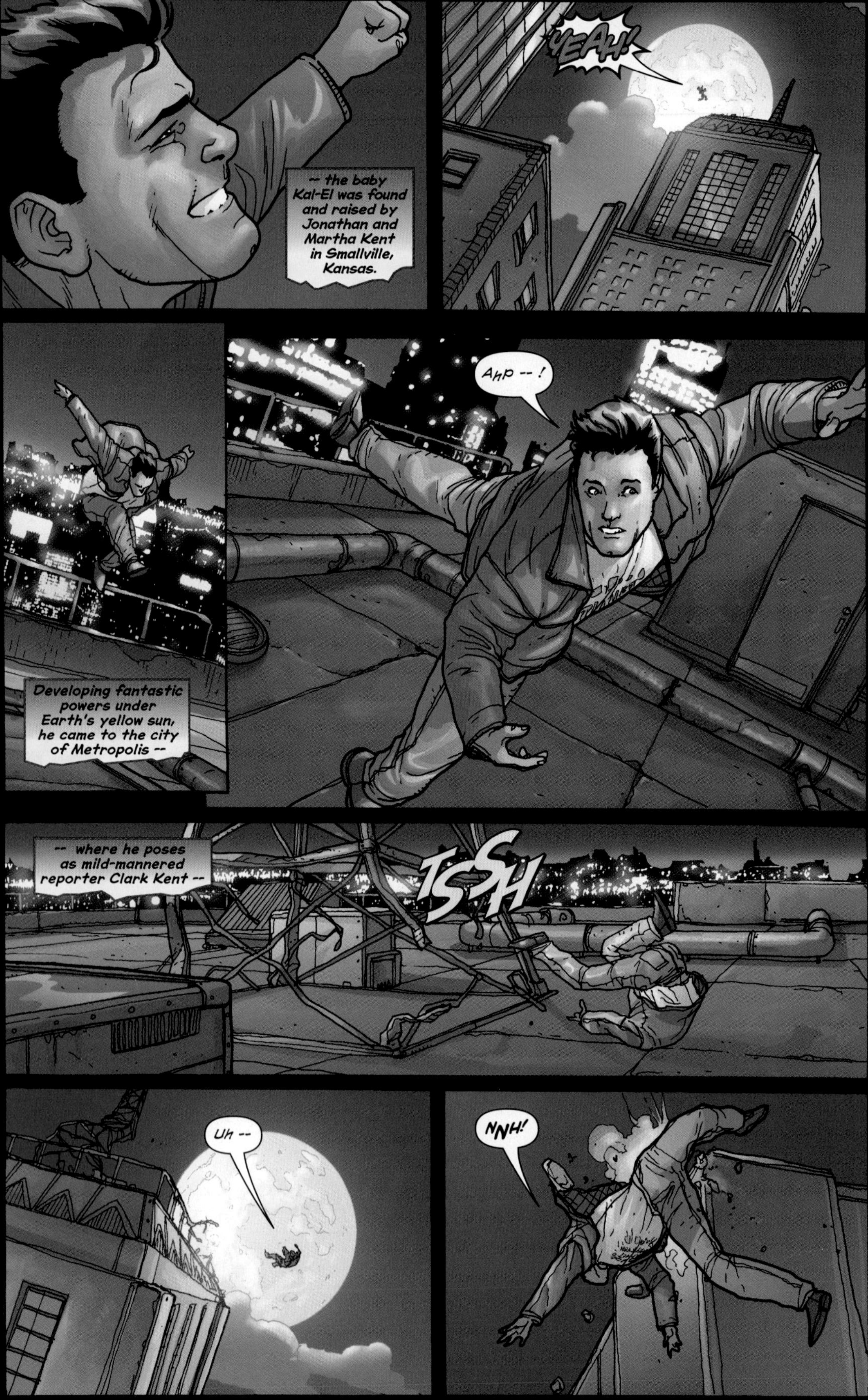
YEAH!
-- the baby Kal-El was found and raised by Jonathan and Martha Kent in Smallville, Kansas.
Developing fantastic powers under Earth's yellow sun, he came to the city of Metropolis --
Ahp --!
-- where he poses as mild-mannered reporter Clark Kent --
TSSH
Uh --
NNH!

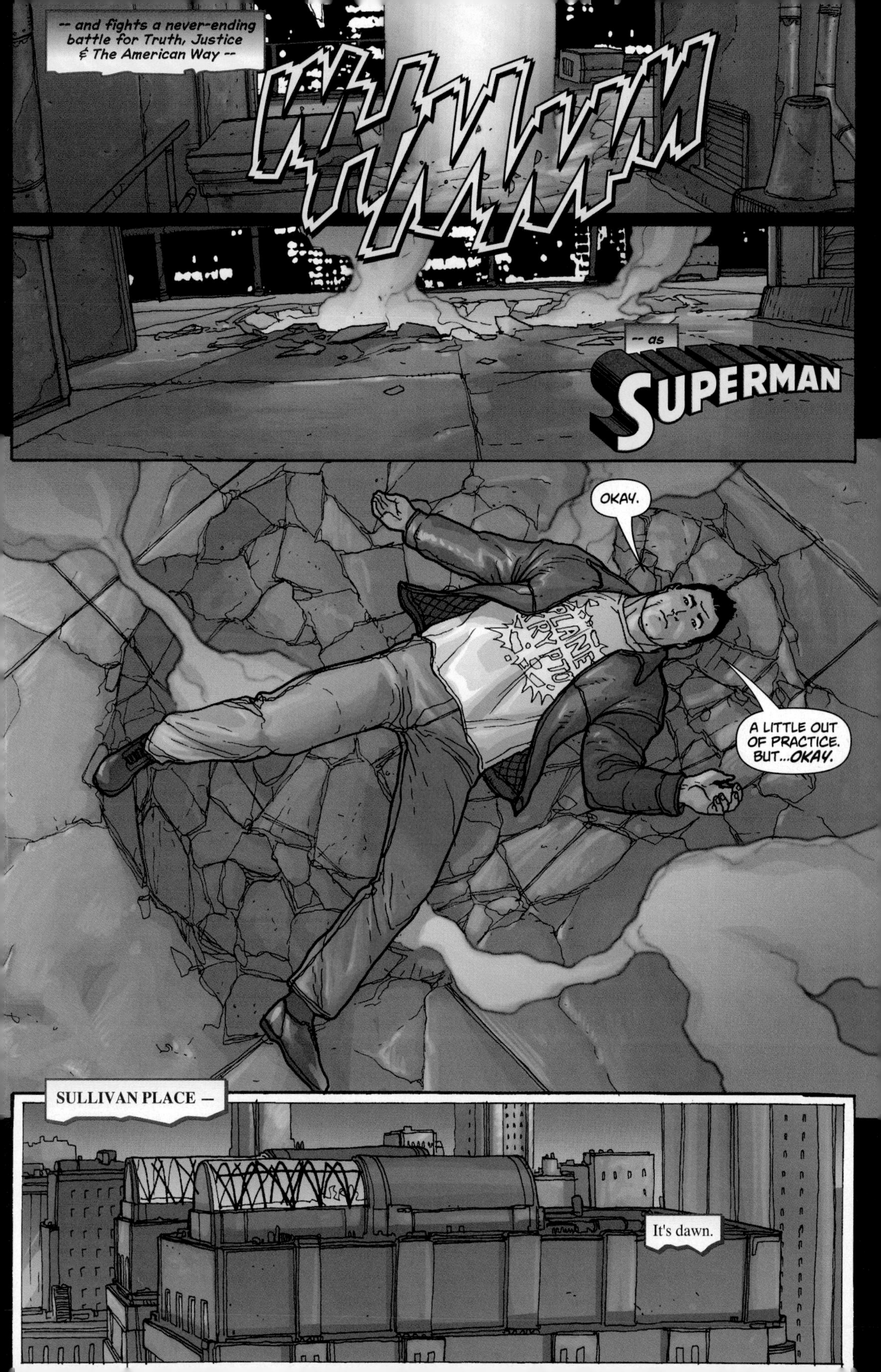
-- and fights a never-ending battle for Truth, Justice & The American Way --
-- as
SUPERMAN
OKAY.
A LITTLE OUT OF PRACTICE. BUT...OKAY.
SULLIVAN PLACE —
It's dawn.

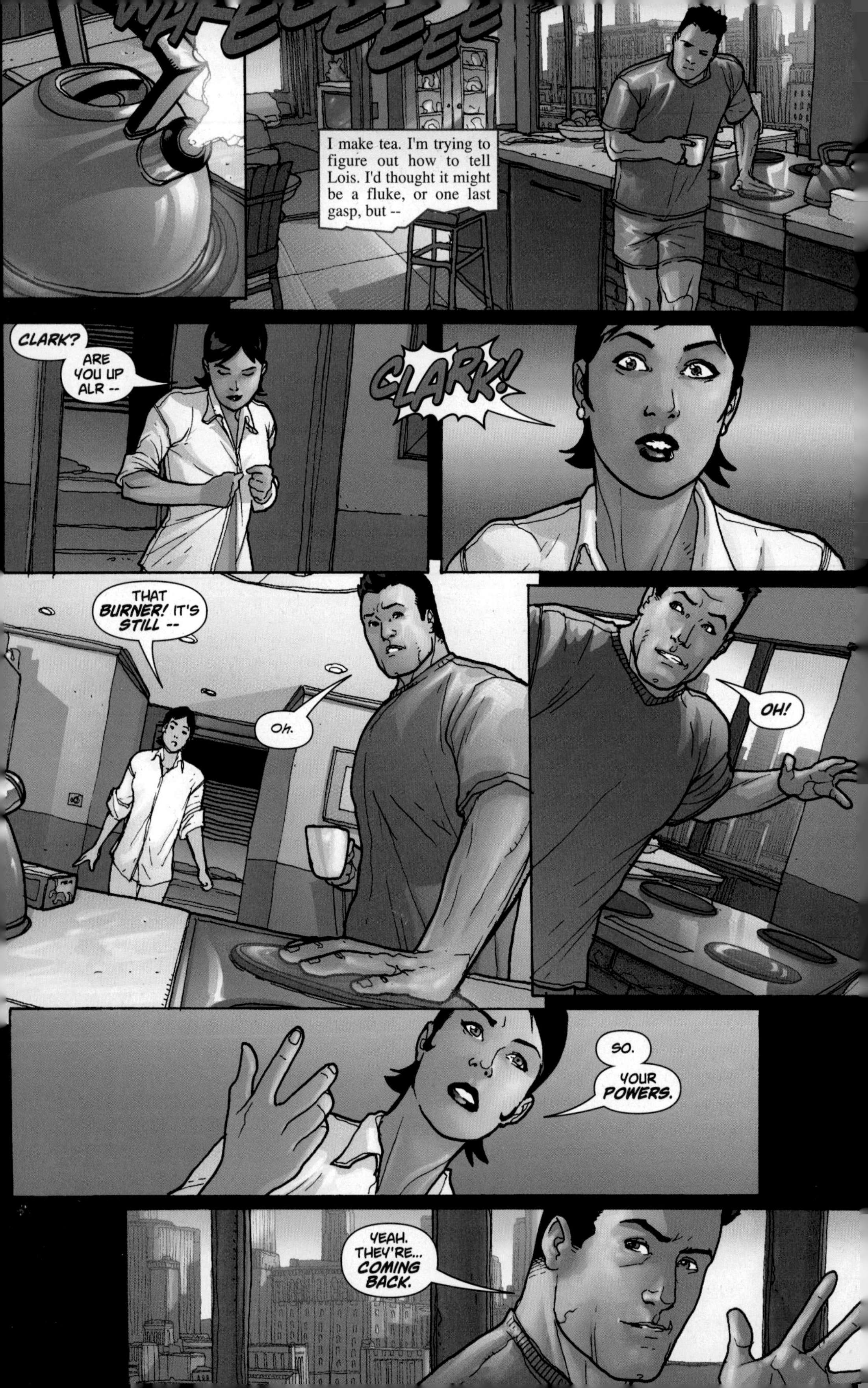
I make tea. I'm trying to figure out how to tell Lois. I'd thought it might be a fluke, or one last gasp, but --
CLARK?
ARE YOU UP ALR --
CLARK!
THAT BURNER! IT'S STILL --
Oh.
OH!
SO.
YOUR POWERS.
YEAH. THEY'RE... COMING BACK.

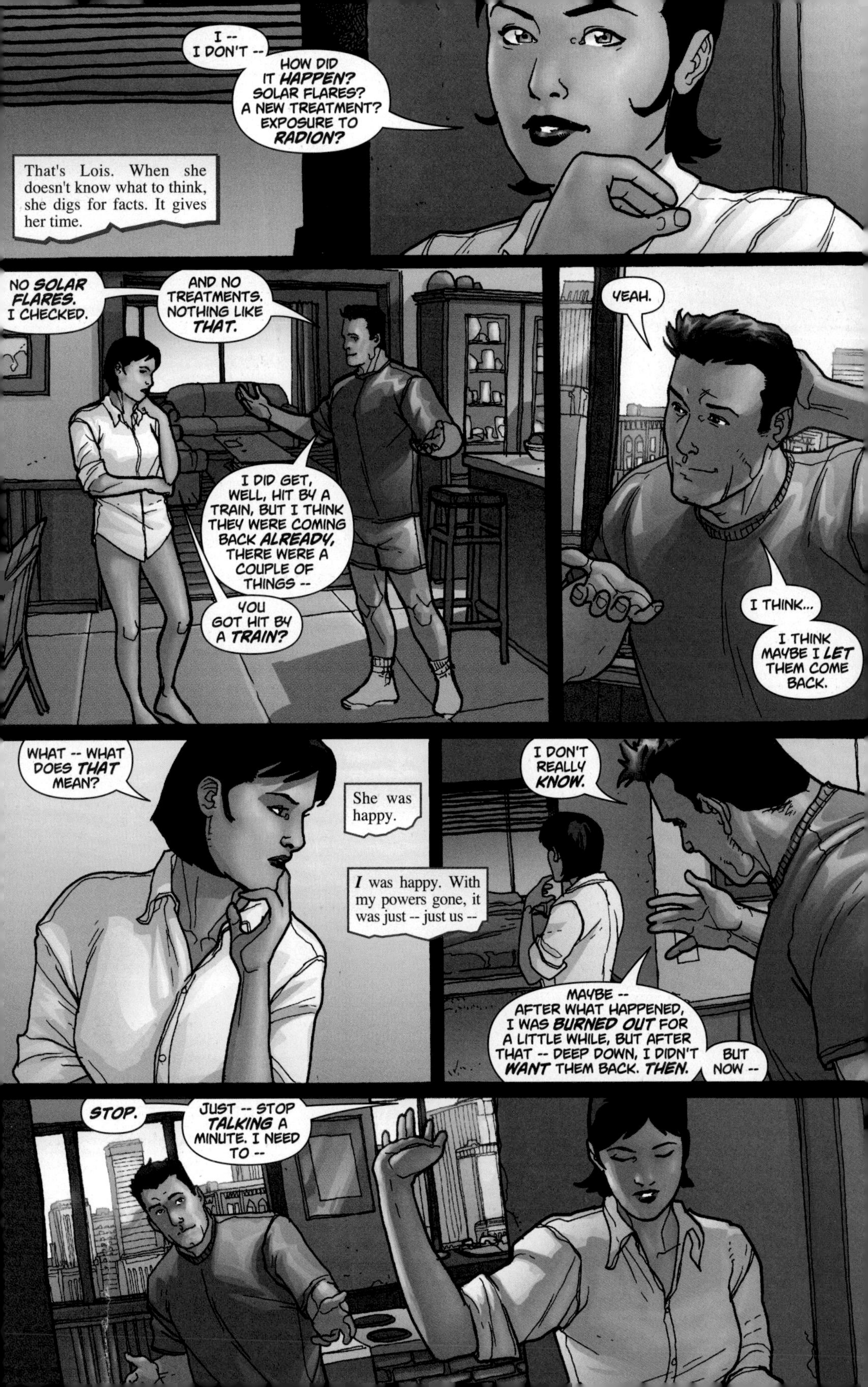
I -- I DON'T --
HOW DID IT HAPPEN? SOLAR FLARES? A NEW TREATMENT? EXPOSURE TO RADION?
That's Lois. When she doesn't know what to think, she digs for facts. It gives her time.
NO SOLAR FLARES. I CHECKED.
AND NO TREATMENTS. NOTHING LIKE THAT.
I DID GET, WELL, HIT BY A TRAIN, BUT I THINK THEY WERE COMING BACK ALREADY, THERE WERE A COUPLE OF THINGS --
YOU GOT HIT BY A TRAIN?
YEAH.
I THINK...
I THINK MAYBE I LET THEM COME BACK.
WHAT -- WHAT DOES THAT MEAN?
She was happy.
I was happy. With my powers gone, it was just -- just us --
I DON'T REALLY KNOW.
MAYBE -- AFTER WHAT HAPPENED, I WAS BURNED OUT FOR A LITTLE WHILE, BUT AFTER THAT -- DEEP DOWN, I DIDN'T WANT THEM BACK. THEN.
BUT NOW --
STOP.
JUST -- STOP TALKING A MINUTE. I NEED TO --

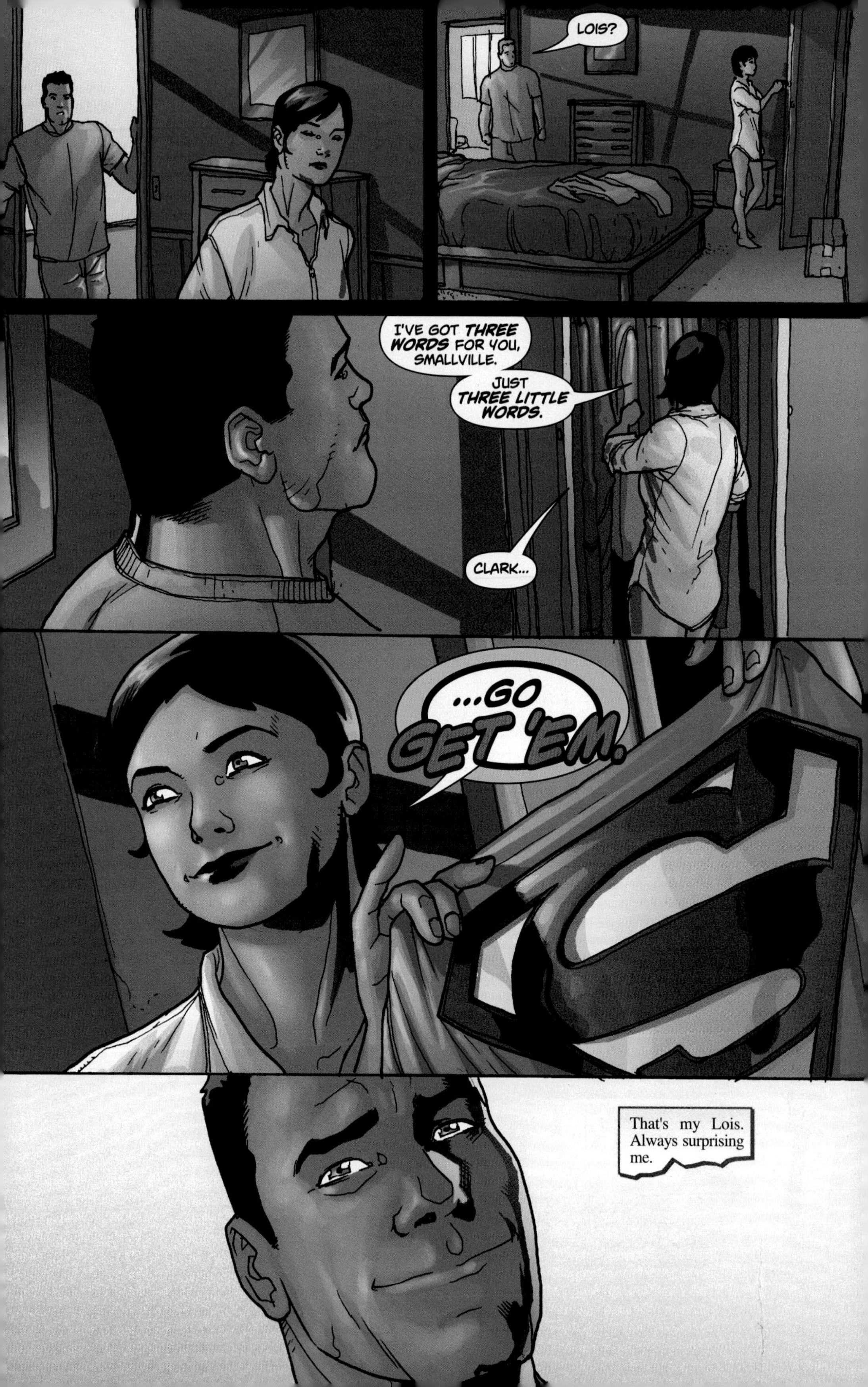
LOIS?
I'VE GOT THREE WORDS FOR YOU, SMALLVILLE.
JUST THREE LITTLE WORDS.
CLARK...
...GO GET 'EM.
That's my Lois. Always surprising me.

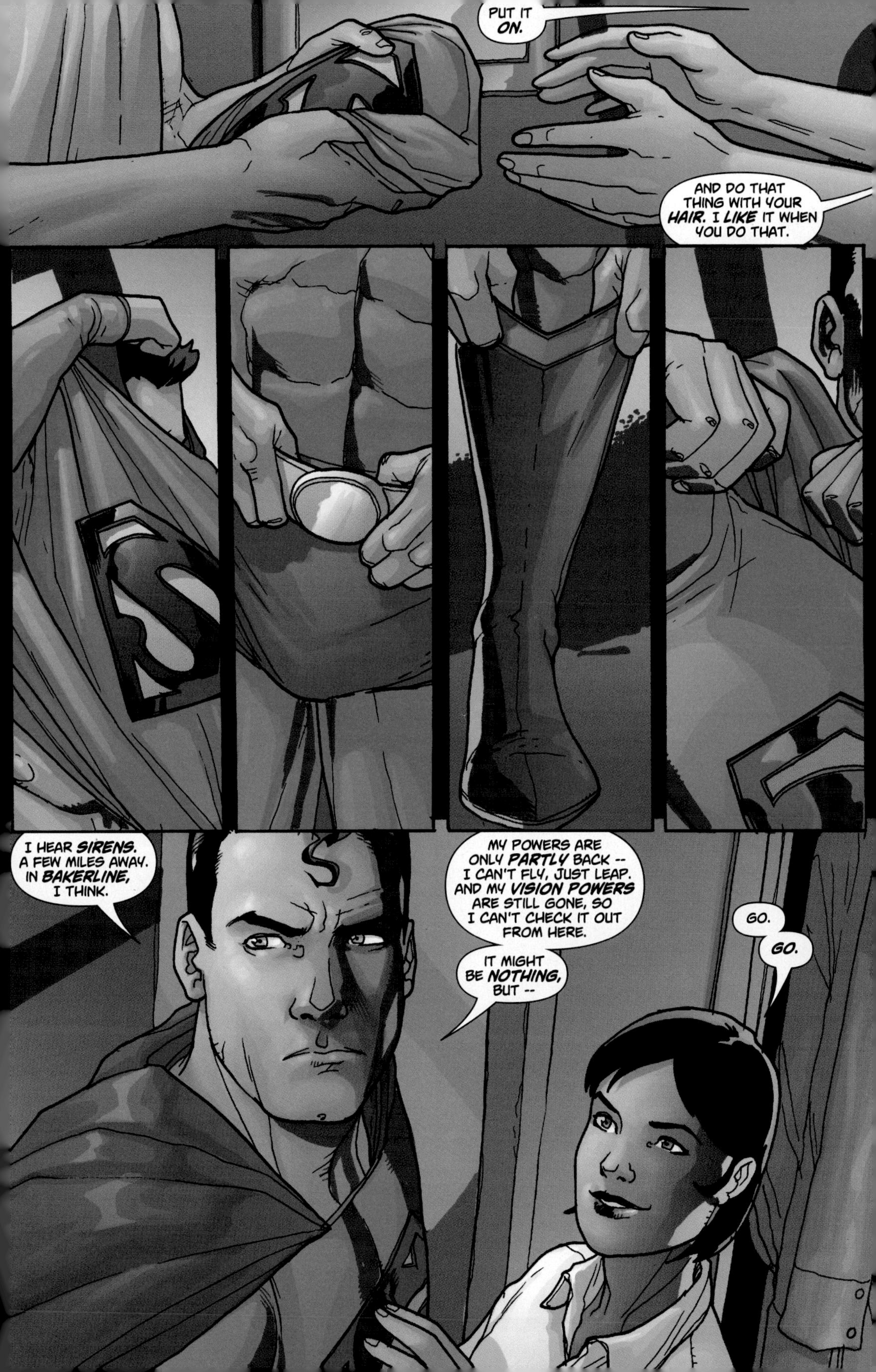
PUT IT ON.
AND DO THAT THING WITH YOUR HAIR. I LIKE IT WHEN YOU DO THAT.
I HEAR SIRENS. A FEW MILES AWAY. IN BAKERLINE, I THINK.
MY POWERS ARE ONLY PARTLY BACK -- I CAN'T FLY, JUST LEAP. AND MY VISION POWERS ARE STILL GONE, SO I CAN'T CHECK IT OUT FROM HERE.
IT MIGHT BE NOTHING, BUT --
GO.
GO.

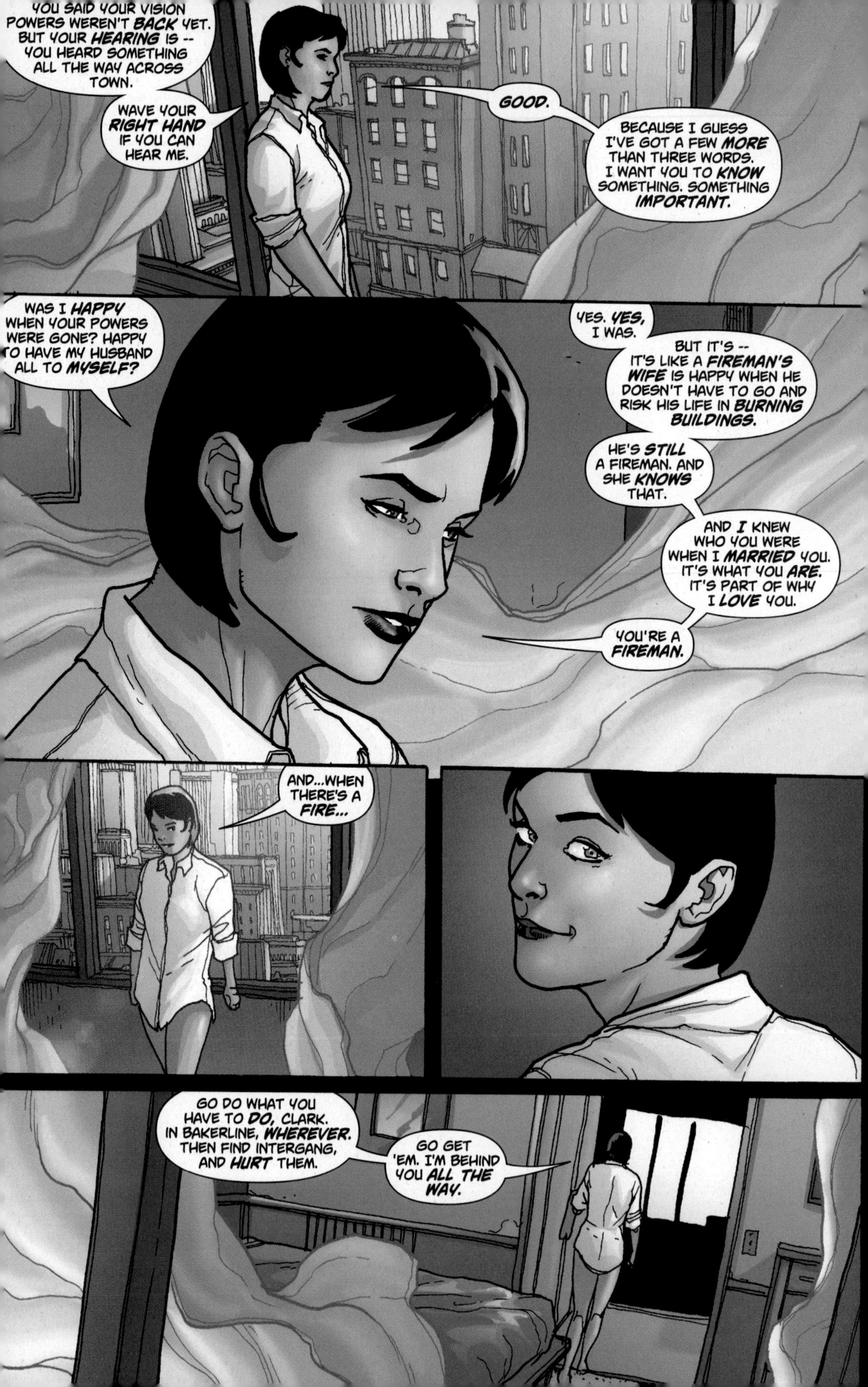
YOU SAID YOUR VISION POWERS WEREN'T BACK YET. BUT YOUR HEARING IS -- YOU HEARD SOMETHING ALL THE WAY ACROSS TOWN.
WAVE YOUR RIGHT HAND IF YOU CAN HEAR ME.
GOOD.
BECAUSE I GUESS I'VE GOT A FEW MORE THAN THREE WORDS. I WANT YOU TO KNOW SOMETHING. SOMETHING IMPORTANT.
WAS I HAPPY WHEN YOUR POWERS WERE GONE? HAPPY TO HAVE MY HUSBAND ALL TO MYSELF?
YES. YES, I WAS.
BUT IT'S -- IT'S LIKE A FIREMAN'S WIFE IS HAPPY WHEN HE DOESN'T HAVE TO GO AND RISK HIS LIFE IN BURNING BUILDINGS.
HE'S STILL A FIREMAN. AND SHE KNOWS THAT.
AND I KNEW WHO YOU WERE WHEN I MARRIED YOU. IT'S WHAT YOU ARE. IT'S PART OF WHY I LOVE YOU.
YOU'RE A FIREMAN.
AND...WHEN THERE'S A FIRE...
GO DO WHAT YOU HAVE TO DO, CLARK. IN BAKERLINE, WHEREVER. THEN FIND INTERGANG, AND HURT THEM.
GO GET 'EM. I'M BEHIND YOU ALL THE WAY.

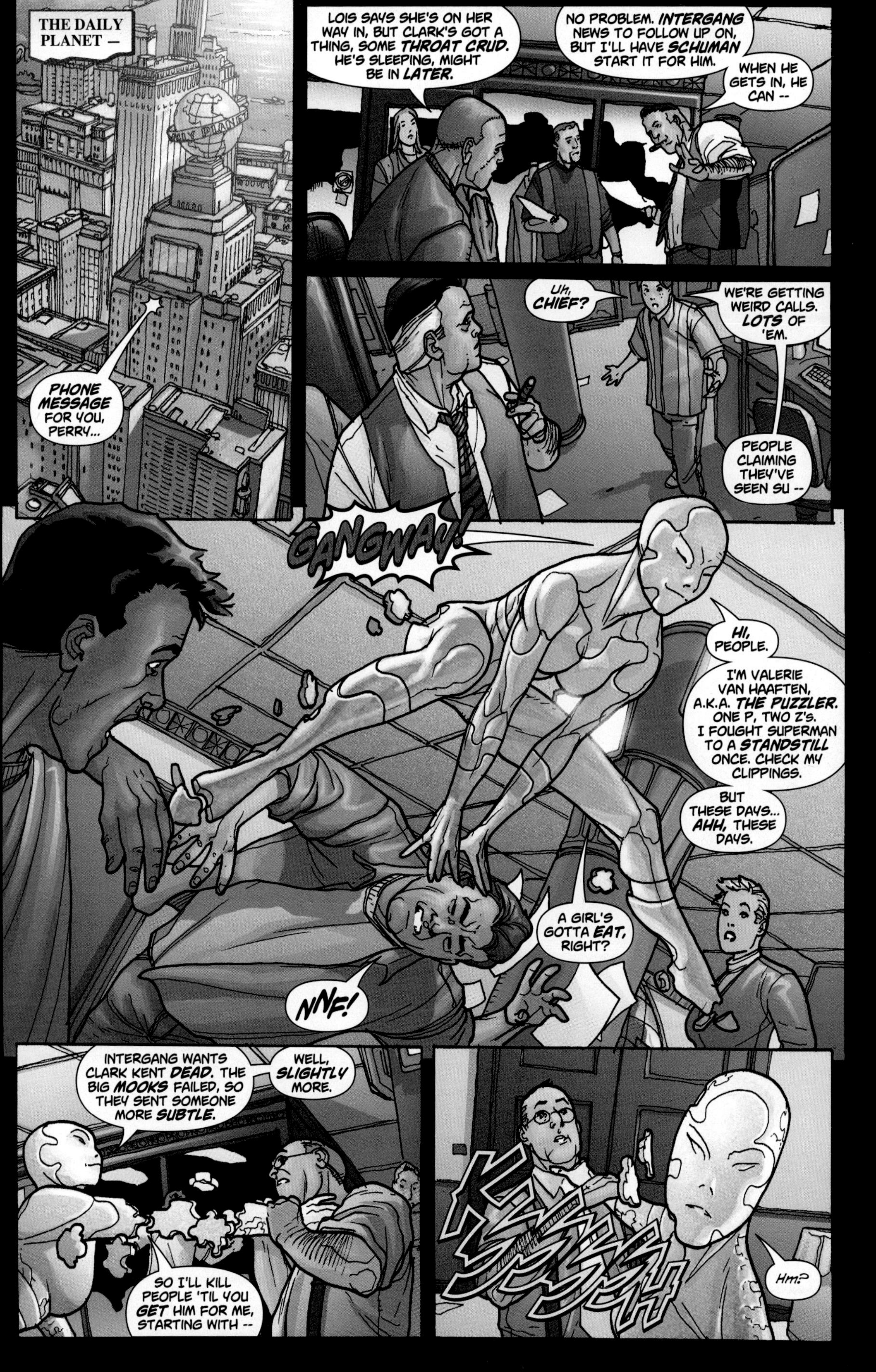
THE DAILY PLANET —
PHONE MESSAGE FOR YOU, PERRY...
LOIS SAYS SHE'S ON HER WAY IN, BUT CLARK'S GOT A THING, SOME THROAT CRUD. HE'S SLEEPING, MIGHT BE IN LATER.
NO PROBLEM. INTERGANG NEWS TO FOLLOW UP ON, BUT I'LL HAVE SCHUMAN START IT FOR HIM.
WHEN HE GETS IN, HE CAN --
UH, CHIEF?
WE'RE GETTING WEIRD CALLS. LOTS OF 'EM.
PEOPLE CLAIMING THEY'VE SEEN SU --
GANGWAY!
HI, PEOPLE.
I'M VALERIE VAN HAAFTEN, A.K.A. THE PUZZLER. ONE P, TWO Z'S. I FOUGHT SUPERMAN TO A STANDSTILL ONCE. CHECK MY CLIPPINGS.
BUT THESE DAYS... AHH, THESE DAYS.
A GIRL'S GOTTA EAT, RIGHT?
NNF!
INTERGANG WANTS CLARK KENT DEAD. THE BIG MOOKS FAILED, SO THEY SENT SOMEONE MORE SUBTLE.
WELL, SLIGHTLY MORE.
SO I'LL KILL PEOPLE 'TIL YOU GET HIM FOR ME, STARTING WITH --
Hm?

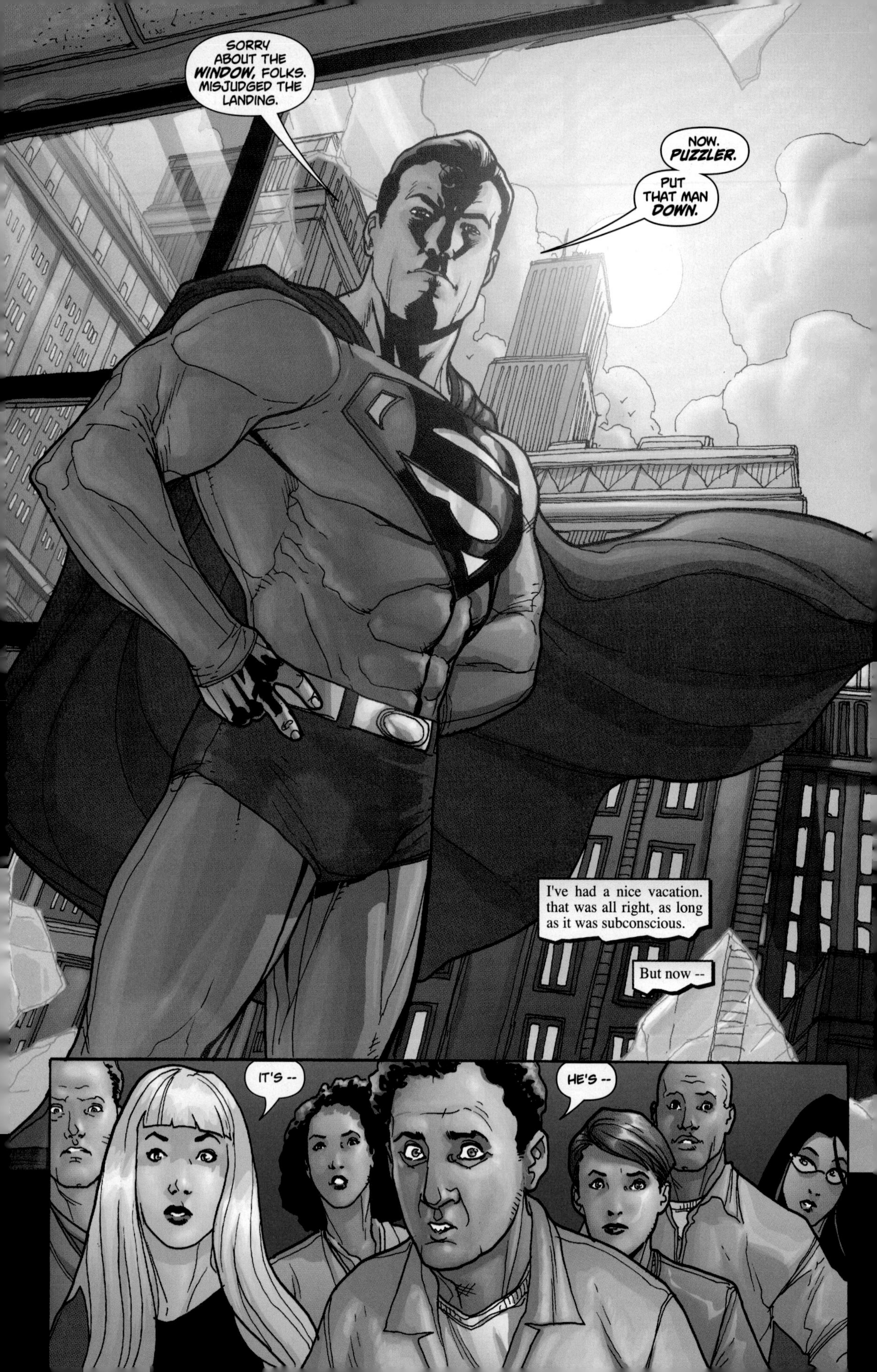
SORRY ABOUT THE WINDOW, FOLKS. MISJUDGED THE LANDING.
NOW. PUZZLER.
PUT THAT MAN DOWN.
I've had a nice vacation. that was all right, as long as it was subconscious.
But now --
IT'S --
HE'S --

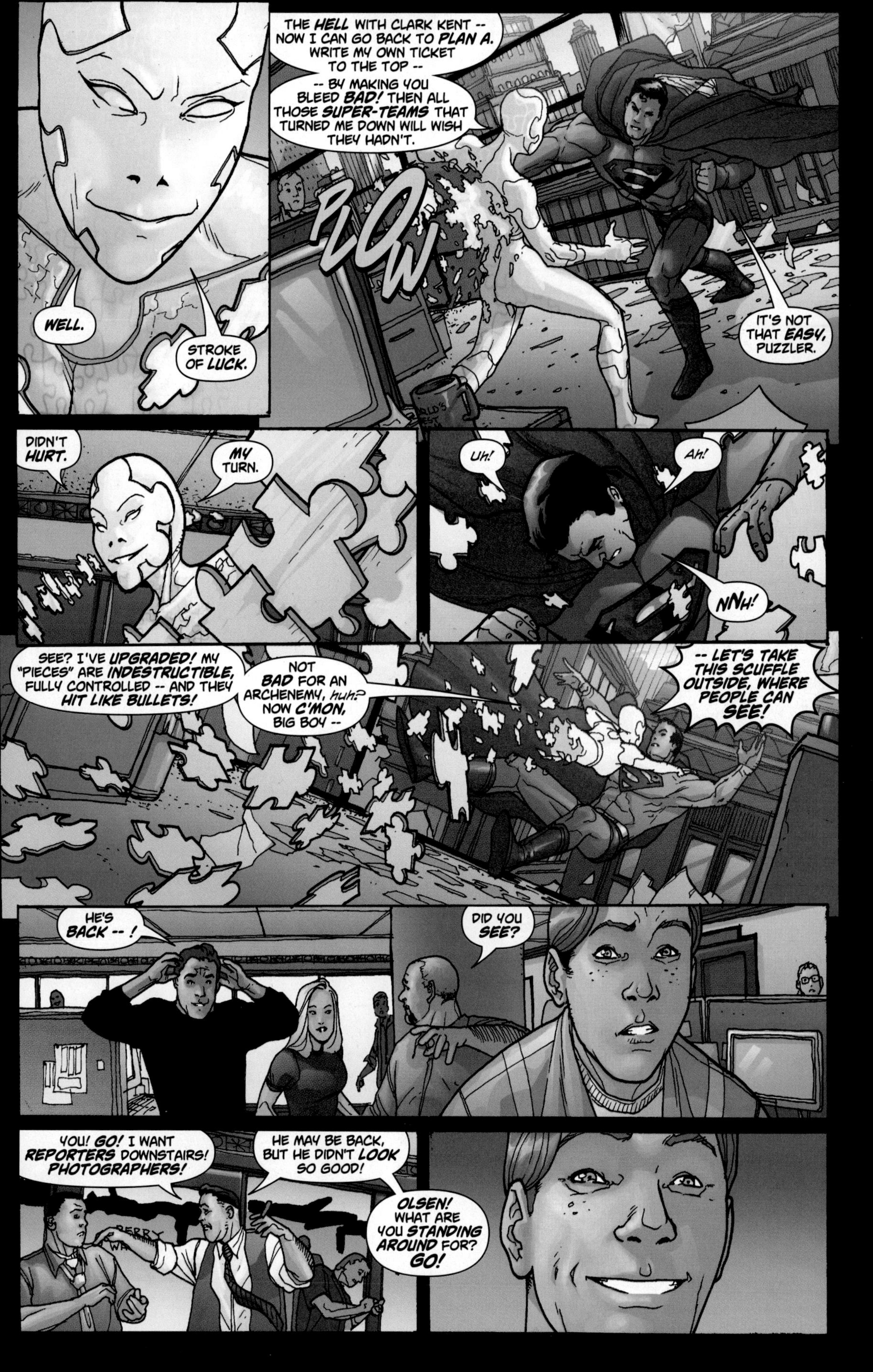
WELL.
STROKE OF LUCK.
THE HELL WITH CLARK KENT -- NOW I CAN GO BACK TO PLAN A. WRITE MY OWN TICKET TO THE TOP --
-- BY MAKING YOU BLEED BAD! THEN ALL THOSE SUPER-TEAMS THAT TURNED ME DOWN WILL WISH THEY HADN'T.
PLOW
IT'S NOT THAT EASY, PUZZLER.
DIDN'T HURT.
MY TURN.
Uh!
Ah!
NNH!
SEE? I'VE UPGRADED! MY "PIECES" ARE INDESTRUCTIBLE, FULLY CONTROLLED -- AND THEY HIT LIKE BULLETS!
NOT BAD FOR AN ARCHENEMY, huh? NOW C'MON, BIG BOY --
-- LET'S TAKE THIS SCUFFLE OUTSIDE, WHERE PEOPLE CAN SEE!
HE'S BACK -- !
DID YOU SEE?
YOU! GO! I WANT REPORTERS DOWNSTAIRS! PHOTOGRAPHERS!
HE MAY BE BACK, BUT HE DIDN'T LOOK SO GOOD!
OLSEN! WHAT ARE YOU STANDING AROUND FOR? GO!

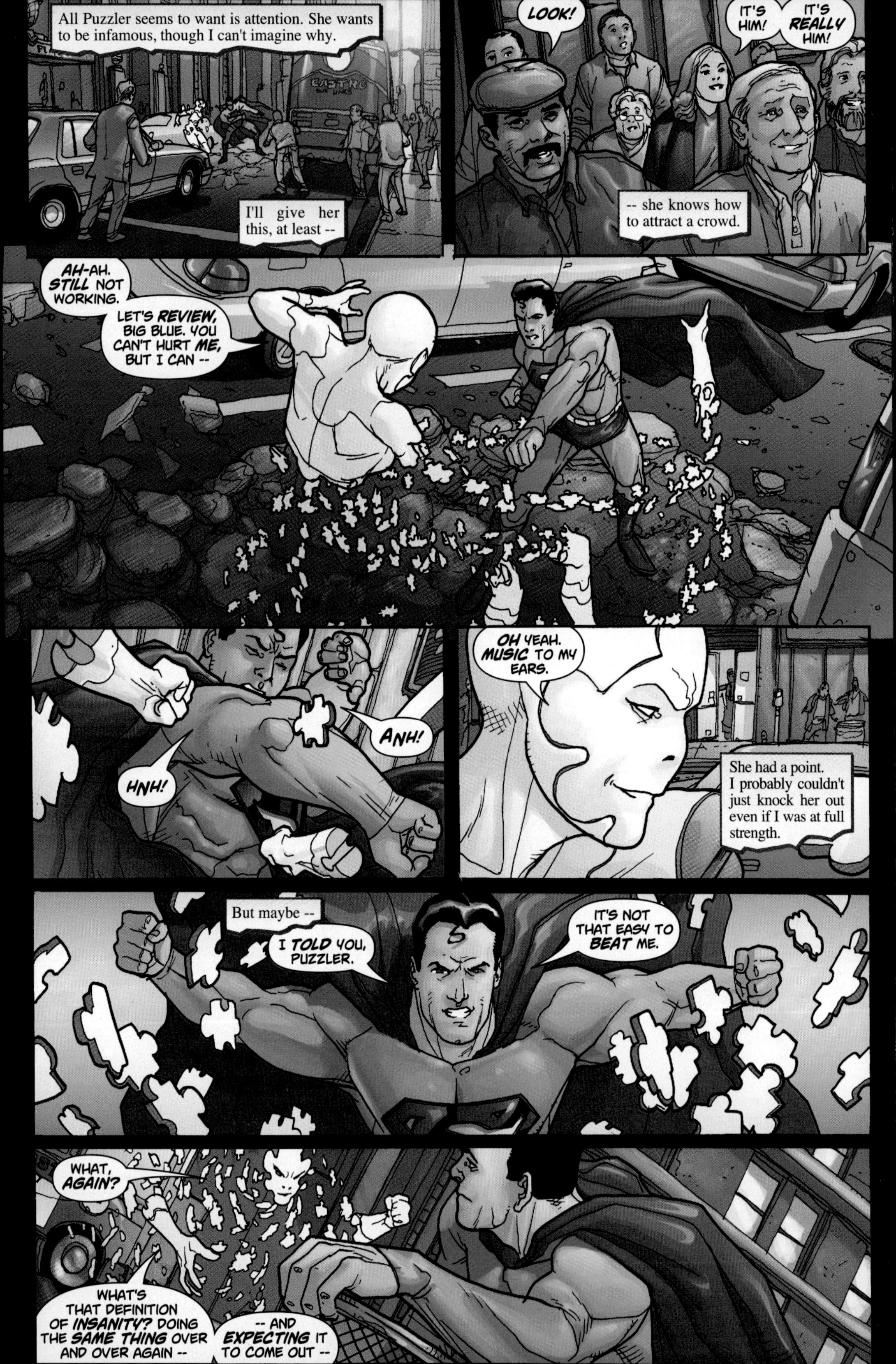

All Puzzler seems to want is attention. She wants to be infamous, though I can't imagine why.
I'll give her this, at least --
LOOK!
IT'S HIM!
IT'S REALLY HIM!
-- she knows how to attract a crowd.
AH-AH. STILL NOT WORKING.
LET'S REVIEW, BIG BLUE. YOU CAN'T HURT ME, BUT I CAN --
ANH!
HNH!
OH YEAH. MUSIC TO MY EARS.
She had a point. I probably couldn't just knock her out even if I was at full strength.
But maybe --
I TOLD YOU, PUZZLER.
IT'S NOT THAT EASY TO BEAT ME.
WHAT, AGAIN?
WHAT'S THAT DEFINITION OF INSANITY? DOING THE SAME THING OVER AND OVER AGAIN --
-- AND EXPECTING IT TO COME OUT --

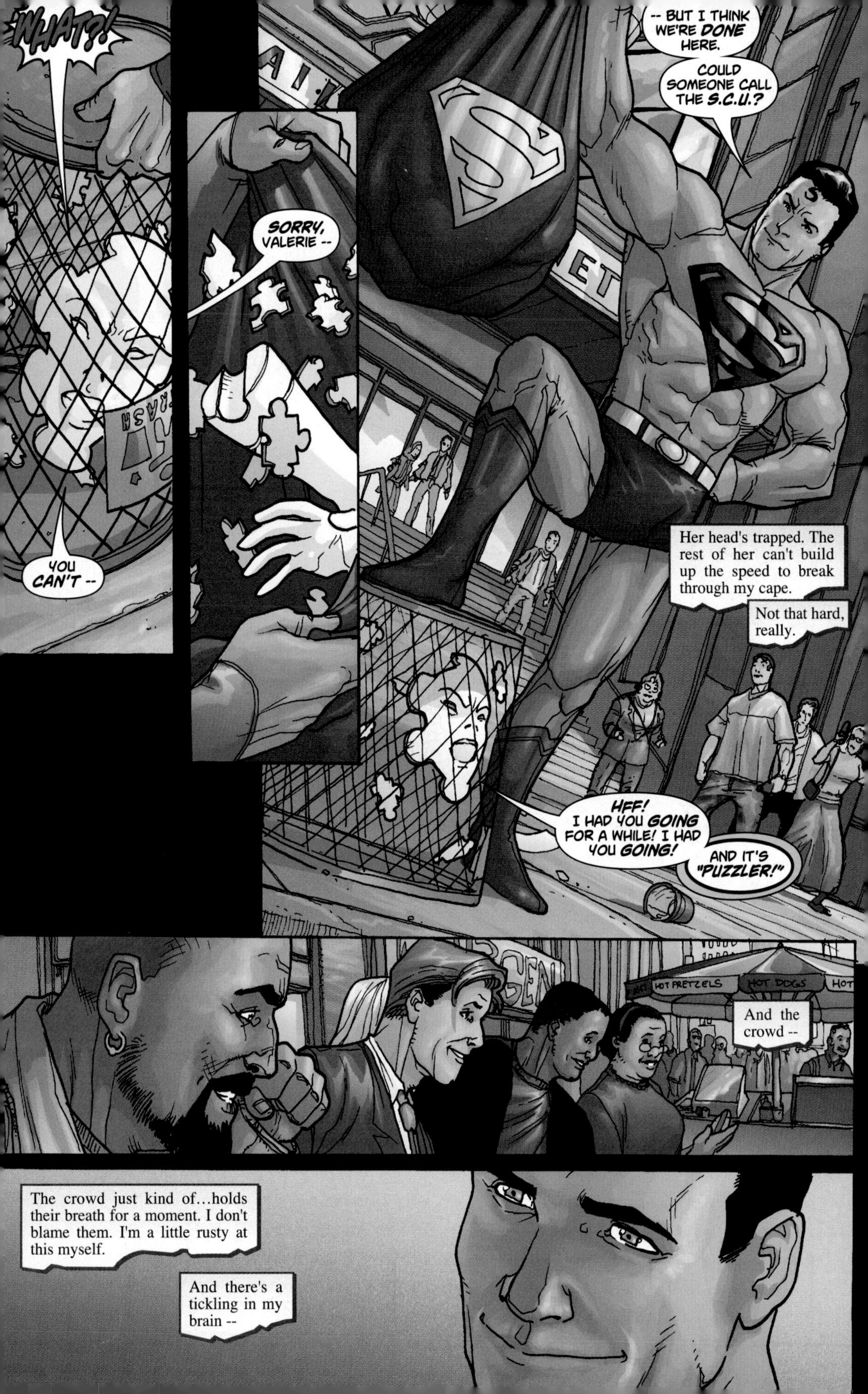
WHAT?!
SORRY, VALERIE --
YOU CAN'T --
-- BUT I THINK WE'RE DONE HERE.
COULD SOMEONE CALL THE S.C.U.?
Her head's trapped. The rest of her can't build up the speed to break through my cape.
Not that hard, really.
HFF! I HAD YOU GOING FOR A WHILE! I HAD YOU GOING!
AND IT'S "PUZZLER!"
HOT PRETZELS
HOT DOGS
And the crowd --
The crowd just kind of…holds their breath for a moment. I don't blame them. I'm a little rusty at this myself.
And there's a tickling in my brain --

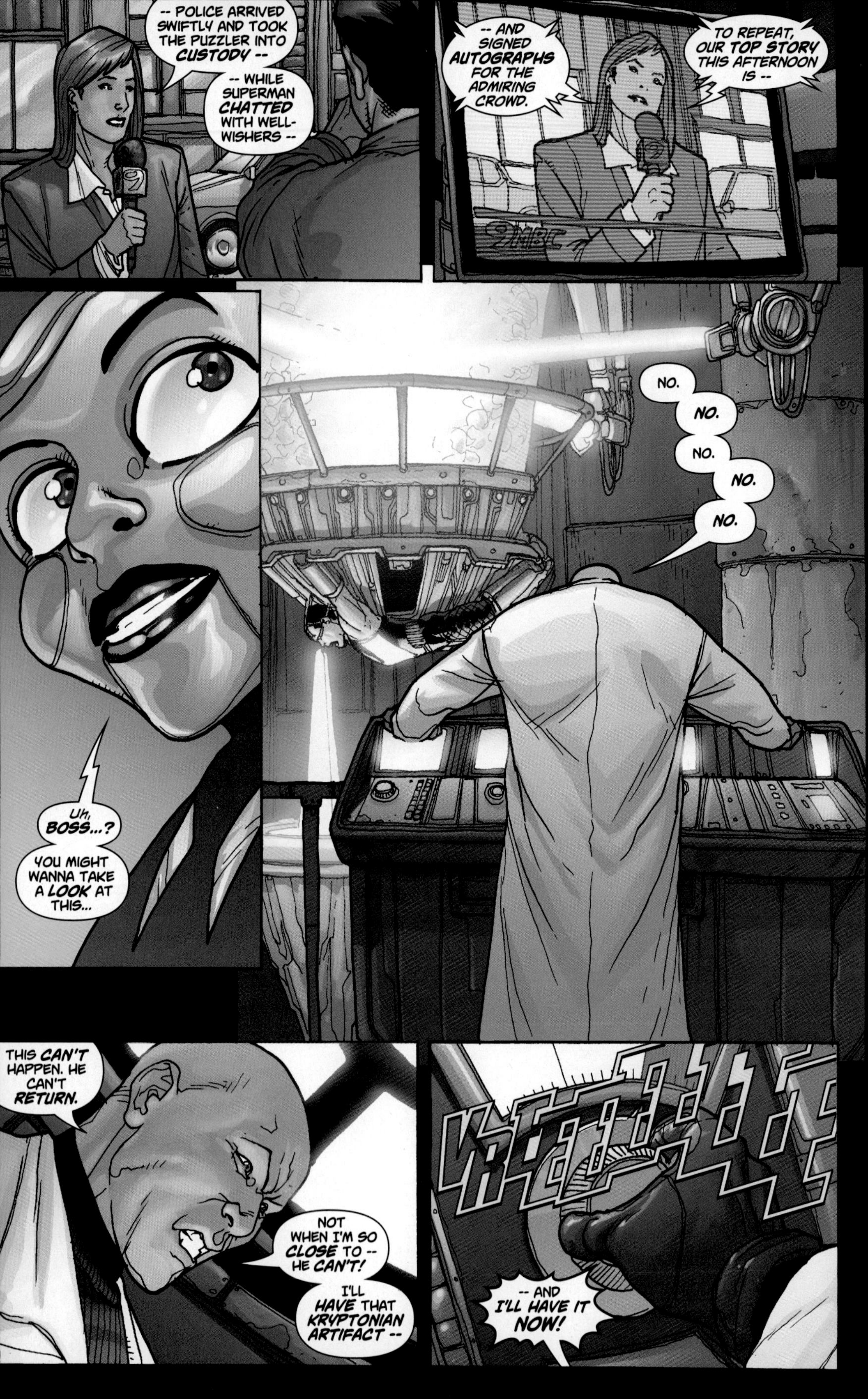
-- POLICE ARRIVED SWIFTLY AND TOOK THE PUZZLER INTO CUSTODY --
-- WHILE SUPERMAN CHATTED WITH WELL-WISHERS --
-- AND SIGNED AUTOGRAPHS FOR THE ADMIRING CROWD.
TO REPEAT, OUR TOP STORY THIS AFTERNOON IS --
NO.
NO.
NO.
NO.
NO.
UH, BOSS...?
YOU MIGHT WANNA TAKE A LOOK AT THIS...
THIS CAN'T HAPPEN. HE CAN'T RETURN.
NOT WHEN I'M SO CLOSE TO -- HE CAN'T!
I'LL HAVE THAT KRYPTONIAN ARTIFACT --
-- AND I'LL HAVE IT NOW!

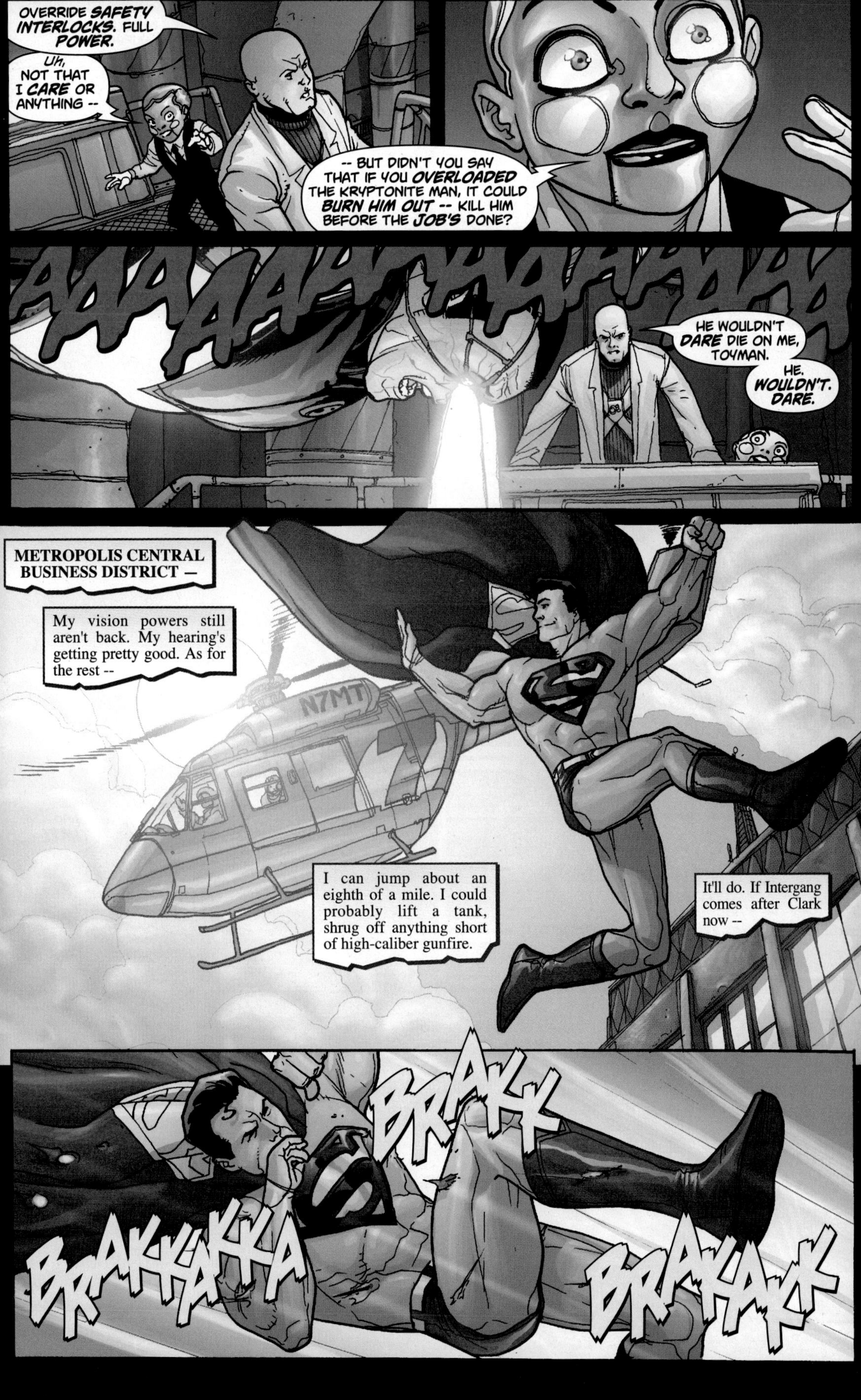
OVERRIDE SAFETY INTERLOCKS. FULL POWER.
Uh, NOT THAT I CARE OR ANYTHING --
-- BUT DIDN'T YOU SAY THAT IF YOU OVERLOADED THE KRYPTONITE MAN, IT COULD BURN HIM OUT -- KILL HIM BEFORE THE JOB'S DONE?
AAAAAAAAAAAAAA
HE WOULDN'T DARE DIE ON ME, TOYMAN.
HE. WOULDN'T. DARE.
METROPOLIS CENTRAL BUSINESS DISTRICT —
My vision powers still aren't back. My hearing's getting pretty good. As for the rest --
N7MT
I can jump about an eighth of a mile. I could probably lift a tank, shrug off anything short of high-caliber gunfire.
It'll do. If Intergang comes after Clark now --
BRAKK
BRAKAKKA
BRAKAKK

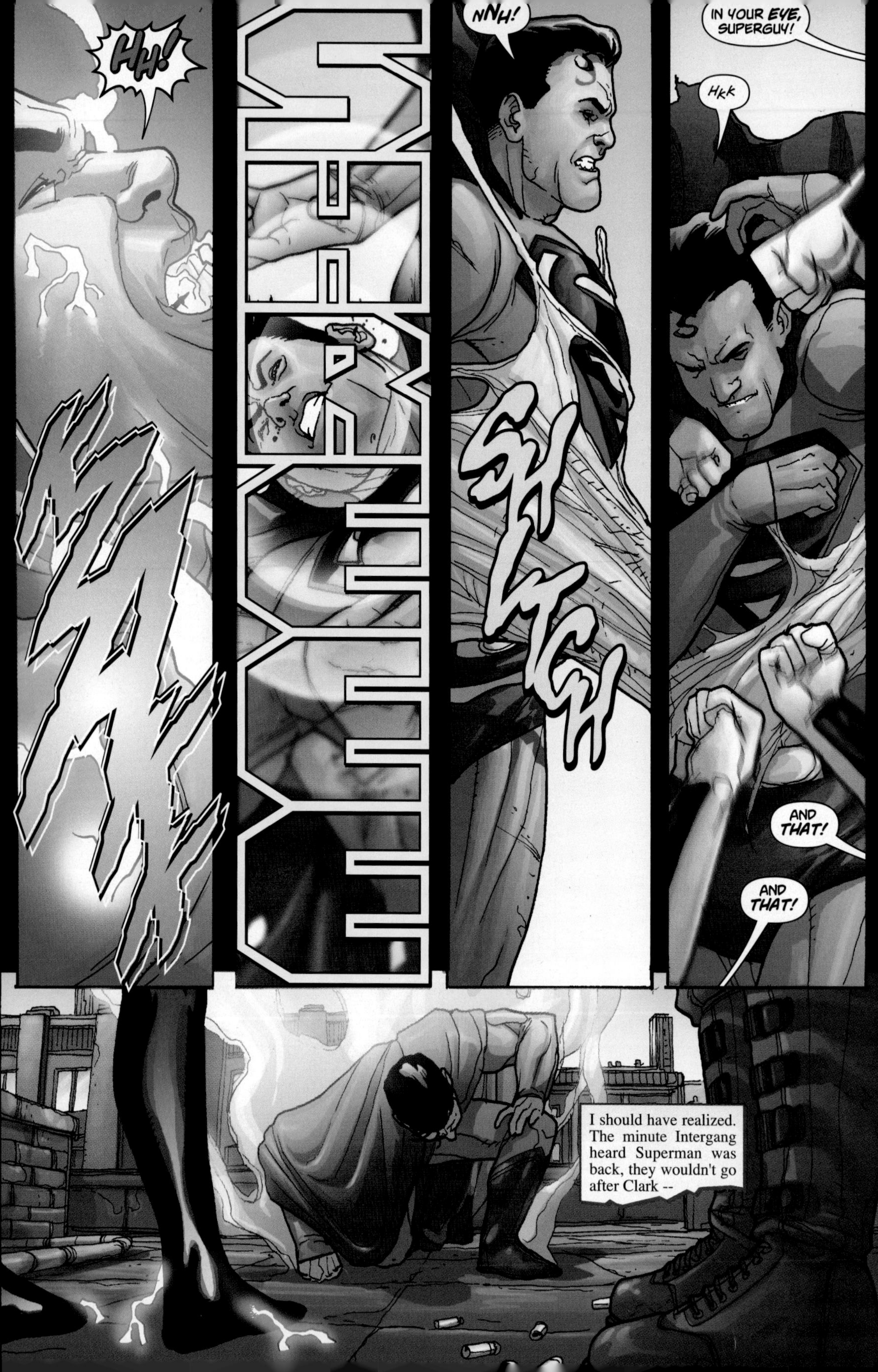
HH!
NNH!
IN YOUR EYE, SUPERGUY!
HKK
AND THAT!
AND THAT!
I should have realized. The minute Intergang heard Superman was back, they wouldn't go after Clark --

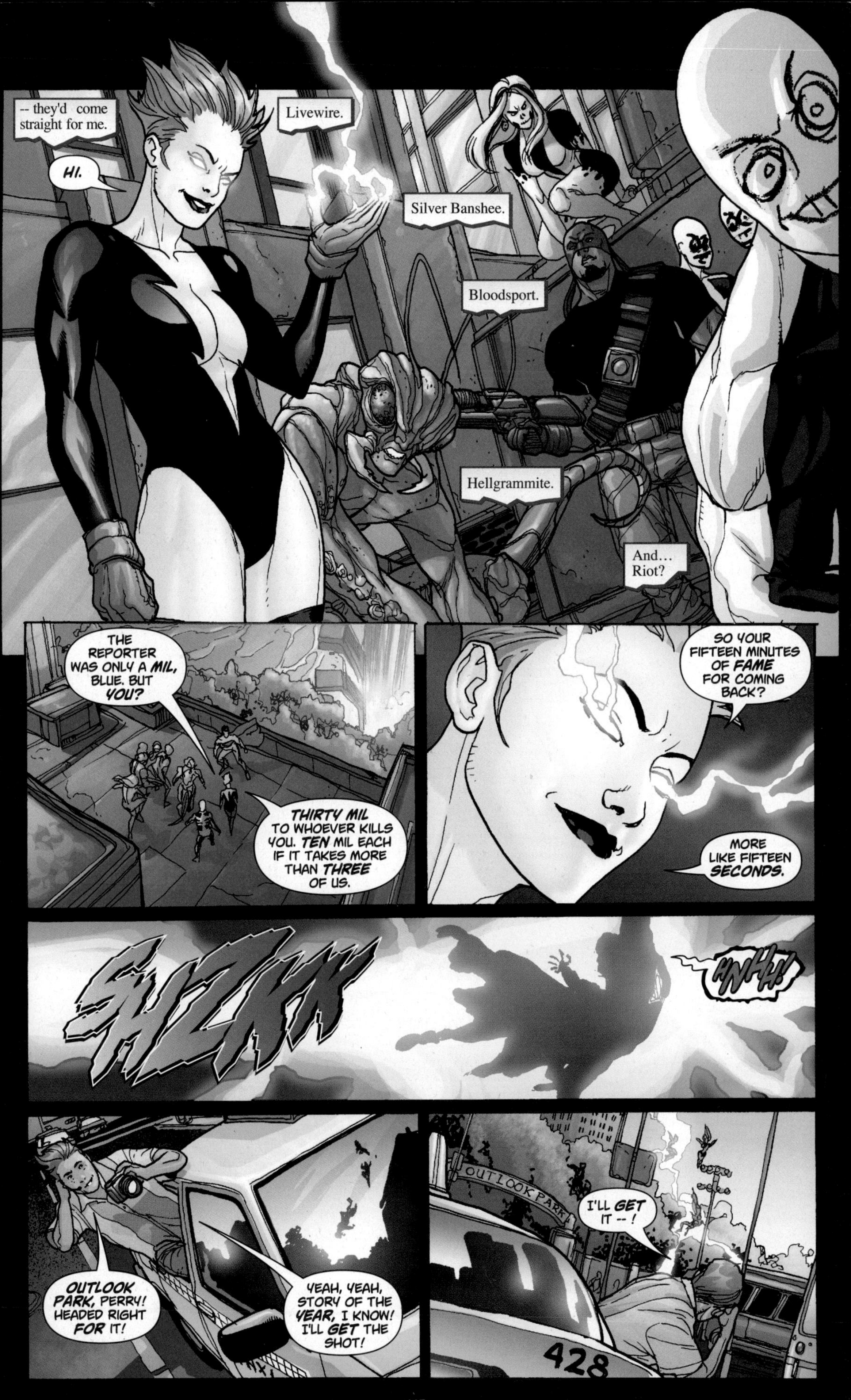
-- they'd come straight for me.
HI.
Livewire.
Silver Banshee.
Bloodsport.
Hellgrammite.
And… Riot?
THE REPORTER WAS ONLY A MIL, BLUE. BUT YOU?
THIRTY MIL TO WHOEVER KILLS YOU. TEN MIL EACH IF IT TAKES MORE THAN THREE OF US.
SO YOUR FIFTEEN MINUTES OF FAME FOR COMING BACK?
MORE LIKE FIFTEEN SECONDS.
SHZKK
UNH!
OUTLOOK PARK, PERRY! HEADED RIGHT FOR IT!
YEAH, YEAH, STORY OF THE YEAR, I KNOW! I'LL GET THE SHOT!
OUTLOOK PARK
I'LL GET IT -- !
428

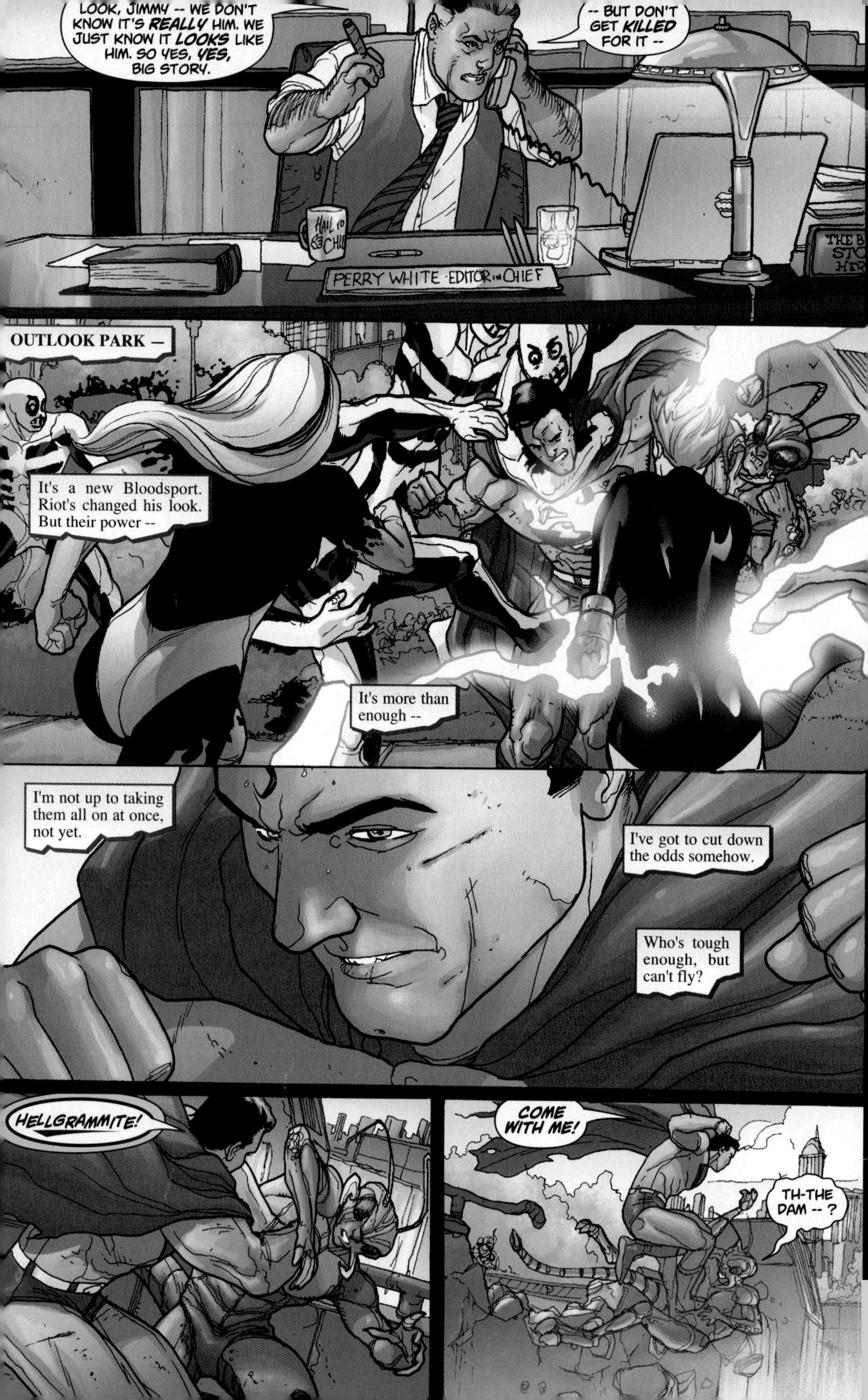
LOOK, JIMMY -- WE DON'T KNOW IT'S REALLY HIM. WE JUST KNOW IT LOOKS LIKE HIM. SO YES, YES, BIG STORY.
-- BUT DON'T GET KILLED FOR IT --
HAIL TO CHIEF
PERRY WHITE · EDITOR IN CHIEF
OUTLOOK PARK --
It's a new Bloodsport. Riot's changed his look. But their power --
It's more than enough --
I'm not up to taking them all on at once, not yet.
I've got to cut down the odds somehow.
Who's tough enough, but can't fly?
HELLGRAMMITE!
COME WITH ME!
TH-THE DAM -- ?

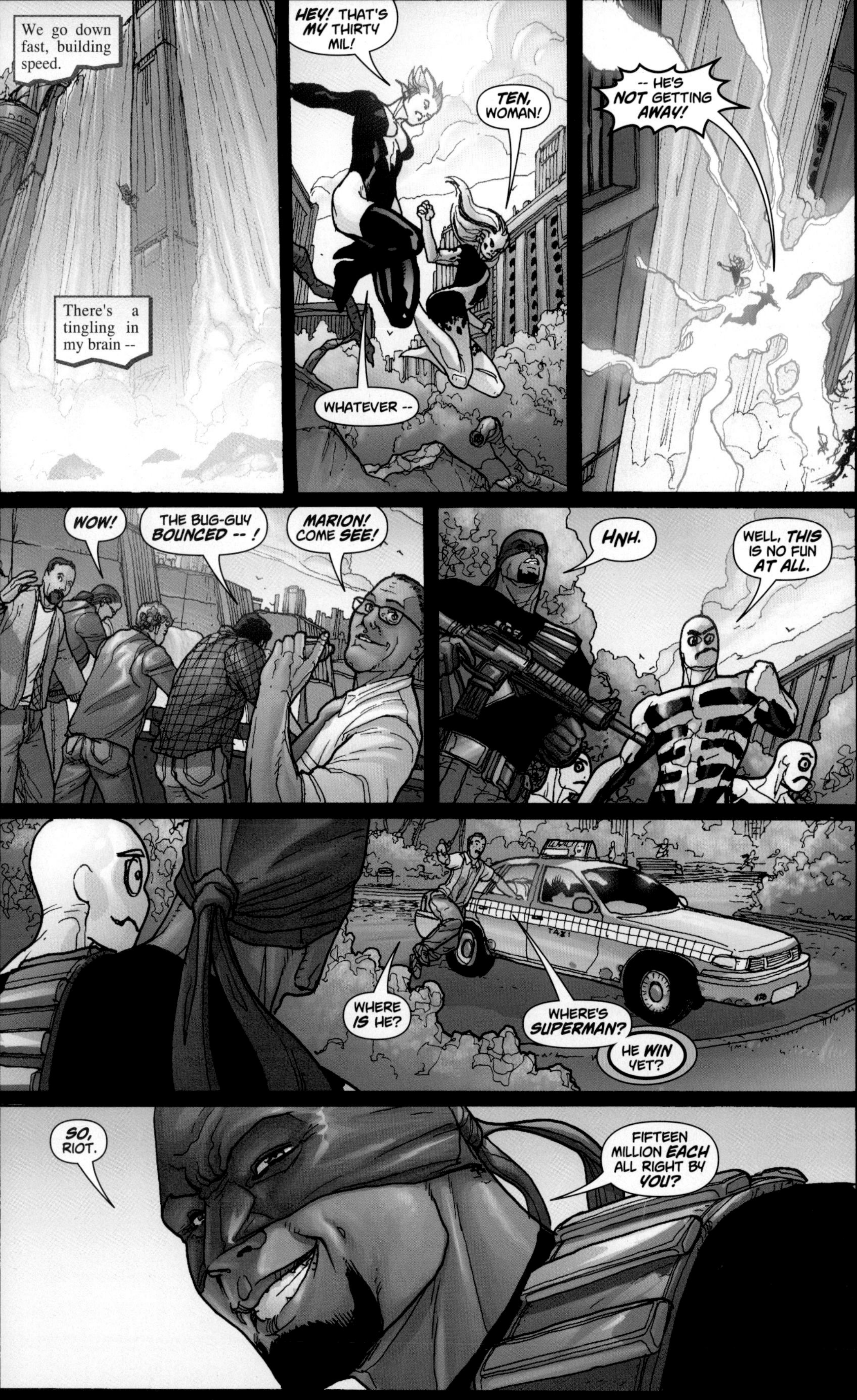
We go down fast, building speed.
There's a tingling in my brain --
HEY! THAT'S MY THIRTY MIL!
TEN, WOMAN!
WHATEVER --
-- HE'S NOT GETTING AWAY!
WOW!
THE BUG-GUY BOUNCED -- !
MARION! COME SEE!
HNH.
WELL, THIS IS NO FUN AT ALL.
WHERE IS HE?
WHERE'S SUPERMAN?
HE WIN YET?
SO, RIOT.
FIFTEEN MILLION EACH ALL RIGHT BY YOU?

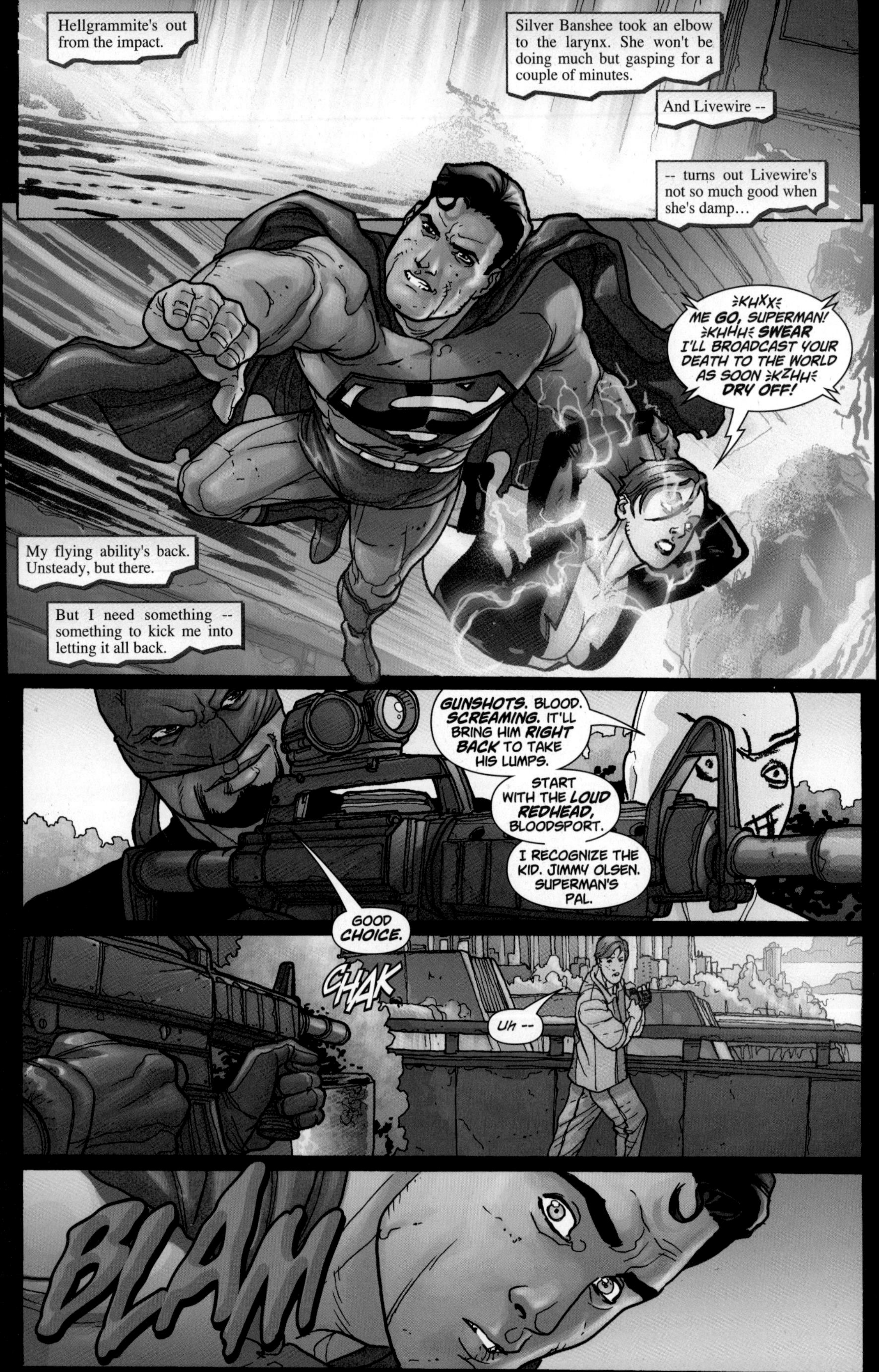
Hellgrammite's out from the impact.
Silver Banshee took an elbow to the larynx. She won't be doing much but gasping for a couple of minutes.
And Livewire --
-- turns out Livewire's not so much good when she's damp…
KHXX ME GO, SUPERMAN! KHHH SWEAR I'LL BROADCAST YOUR DEATH TO THE WORLD AS SOON KZHH DRY OFF!
My flying ability's back. Unsteady, but there.
But I need something -- something to kick me into letting it all back.
GUNSHOTS. BLOOD. SCREAMING. IT'LL BRING HIM RIGHT BACK TO TAKE HIS LUMPS.
START WITH THE LOUD REDHEAD, BLOODSPORT.
I RECOGNIZE THE KID. JIMMY OLSEN. SUPERMAN'S PAL.
GOOD CHOICE.
CHAK
UH --
BLAM

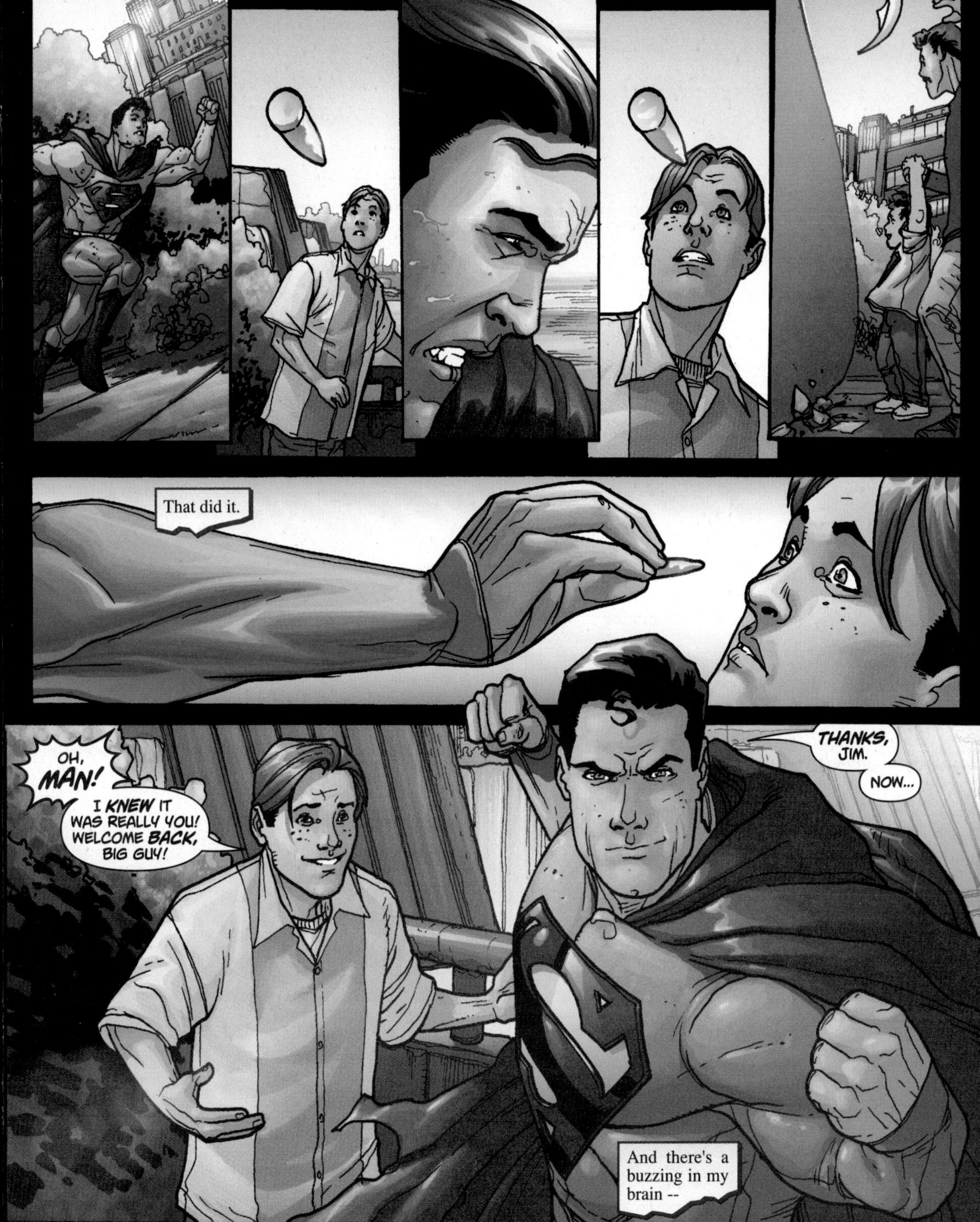
That did it.
OH, MAN!
I KNEW IT WAS REALLY YOU! WELCOME BACK, BIG GUY!
THANKS, JIM.
NOW...
And there's a buzzing in my brain --

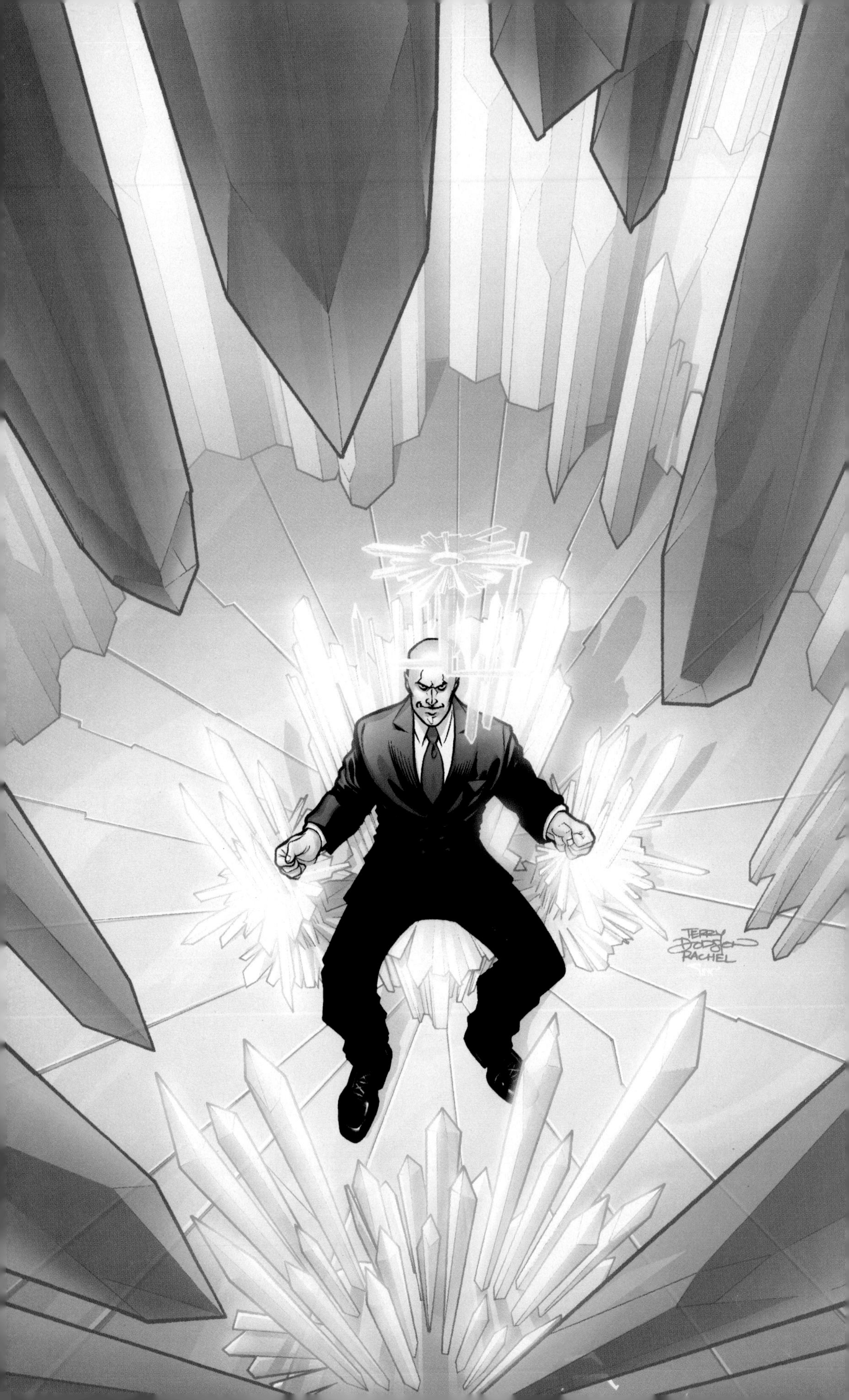
TERRY
DODSON
RACHEL

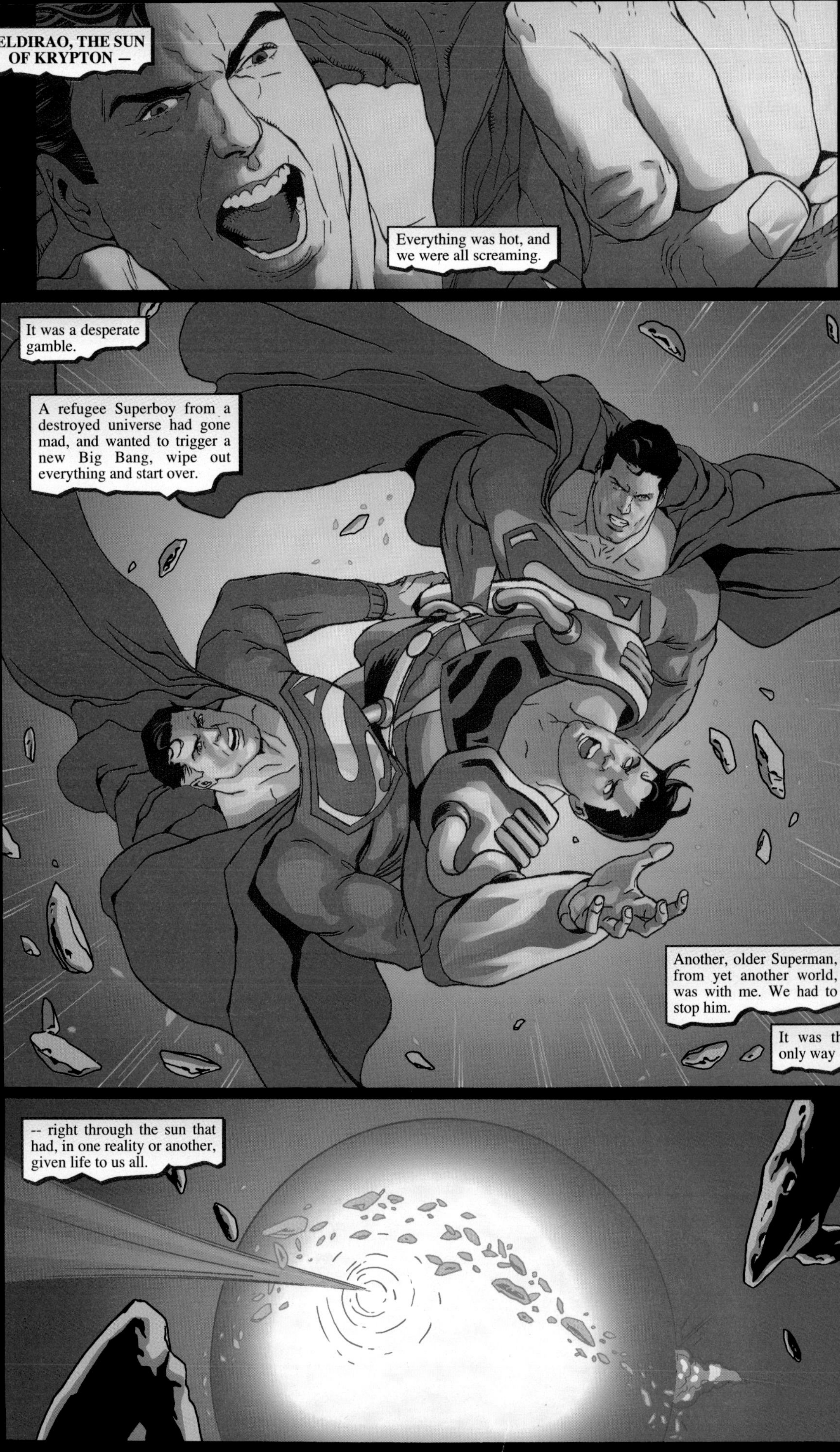

ELDIRAO, THE SUN OF KRYPTON —
Everything was hot, and we were all screaming.
It was a desperate gamble.
A refugee Superboy from a destroyed universe had gone mad, and wanted to trigger a new Big Bang, wipe out everything and start over.
Another, older Superman, from yet another world, was with me. We had to stop him.
It was the only way --
-- right through the sun that had, in one reality or another, given life to us all.

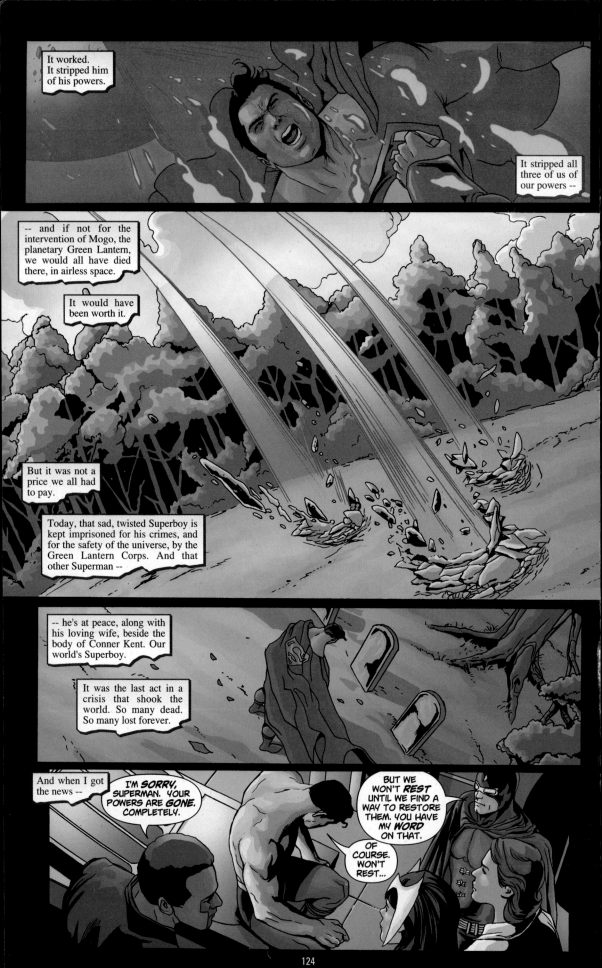

It worked. It stripped him of his powers.

It stripped all three of us of our powers --

-- and if not for the intervention of Mogo, the planetary Green Lantern, we would all have died there, in airless space.

It would have been worth it.

But it was not a price we all had to pay.

Today, that sad, twisted Superboy is kept imprisoned for his crimes, and for the safety of the universe, by the Green Lantern Corps. And that other Superman --

-- he's at peace, along with his loving wife, beside the body of Conner Kent. Our world's Superboy.

It was the last act in a crisis that shook the world. So many dead. So many lost forever.

And when I got the news --

I'M *SORRY,* SUPERMAN. YOUR POWERS ARE *GONE.* COMPLETELY.

BUT WE WON'T *REST* UNTIL WE FIND A WAY TO RESTORE THEM. YOU HAVE MY *WORD* ON THAT.

OF COURSE. WON'T REST...

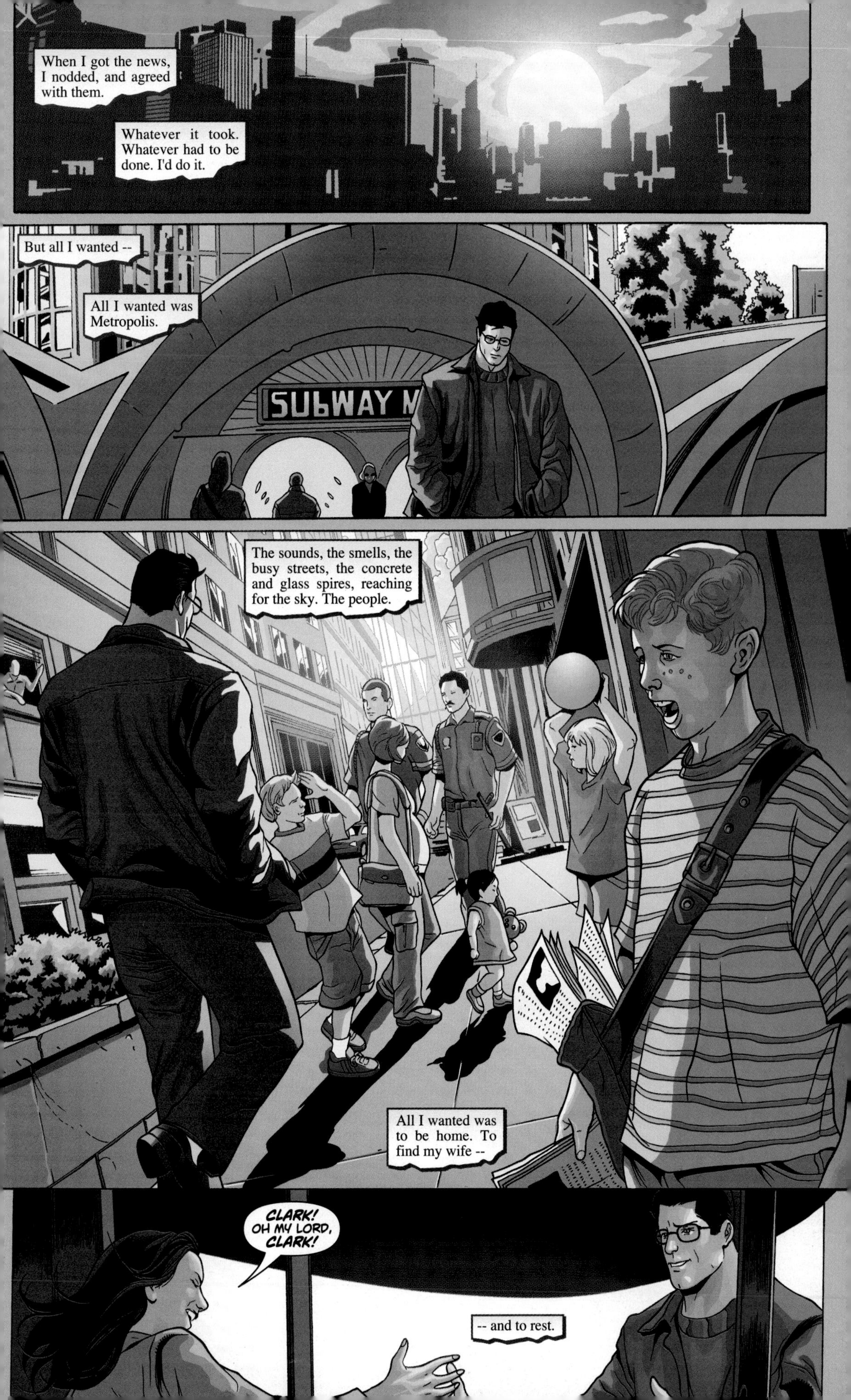
When I got the news, I nodded, and agreed with them.
Whatever it took. Whatever had to be done. I'd do it.
But all I wanted --
All I wanted was Metropolis.
SUBWAY
The sounds, the smells, the busy streets, the concrete and glass spires, reaching for the sky. The people.
All I wanted was to be home. To find my wife --
CLARK! OH MY LORD, CLARK!
-- and to rest.

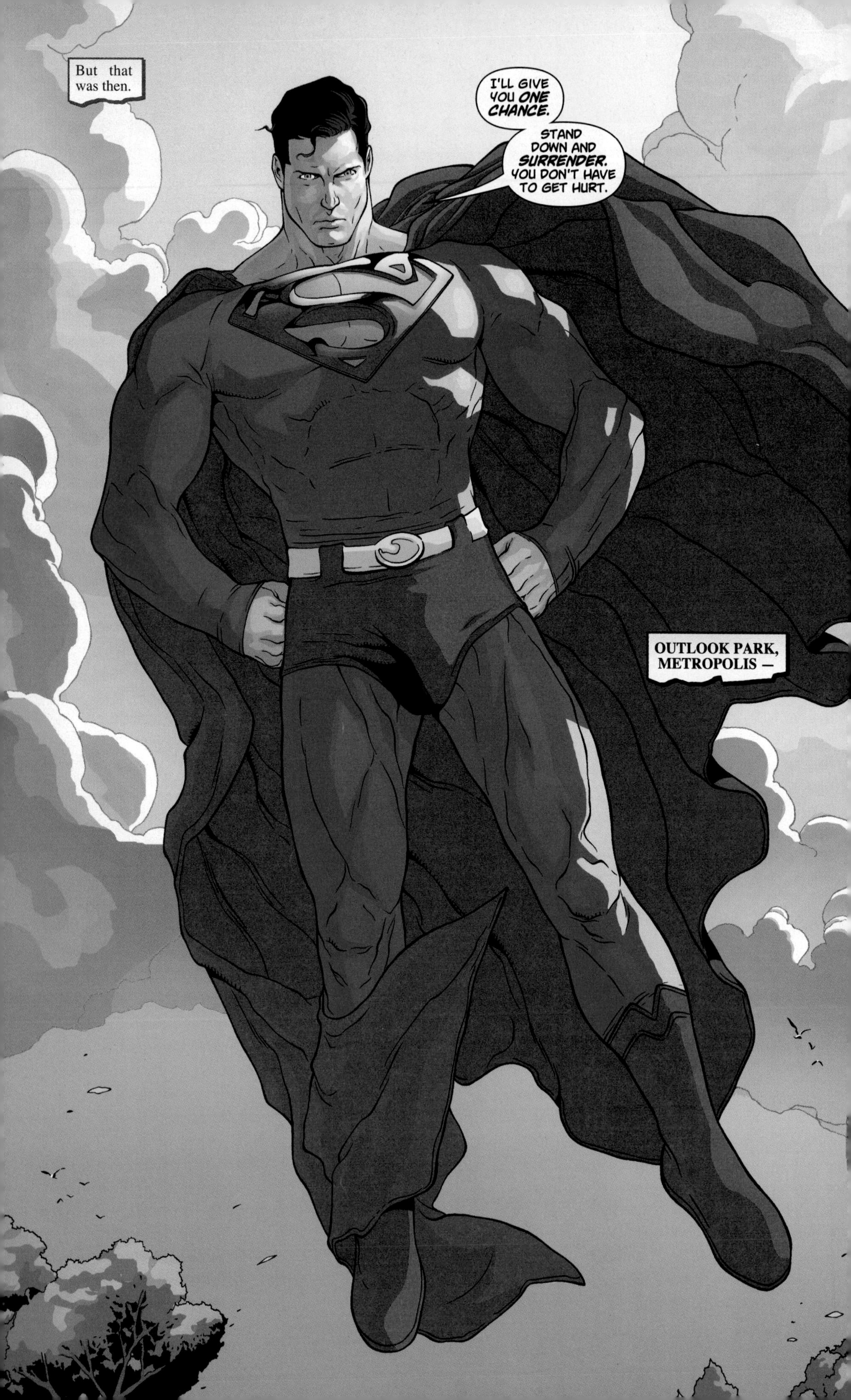

But that was then.
I'LL GIVE YOU ONE CHANCE.
STAND DOWN AND SURRENDER. YOU DON'T HAVE TO GET HURT.
OUTLOOK PARK, METROPOLIS —

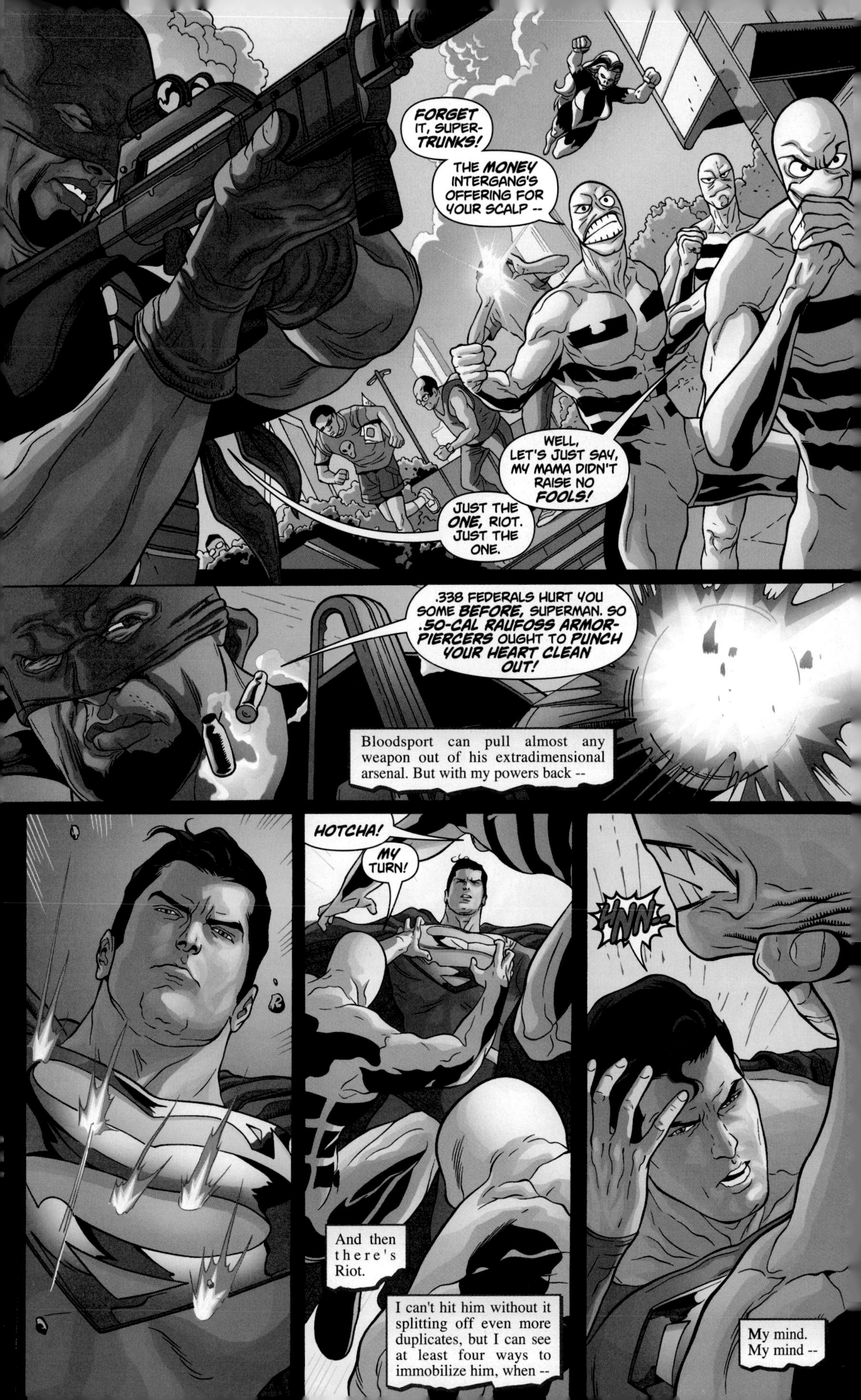
FORGET IT, SUPER-TRUNKS!
THE MONEY INTERGANG'S OFFERING FOR YOUR SCALP --
WELL, LET'S JUST SAY, MY MAMA DIDN'T RAISE NO FOOLS!
JUST THE ONE, RIOT. JUST THE ONE.
.338 FEDERALS HURT YOU SOME BEFORE, SUPERMAN. SO .50-CAL RAUFOSS ARMOR-PIERCERS OUGHT TO PUNCH YOUR HEART CLEAN OUT!
Bloodsport can pull almost any weapon out of his extradimensional arsenal. But with my powers back --
HOTCHA!
MY TURN!
And then there's Riot.
I can't hit him without it splitting off even more duplicates, but I can see at least four ways to immobilize him, when --
HNN--
My mind. My mind --

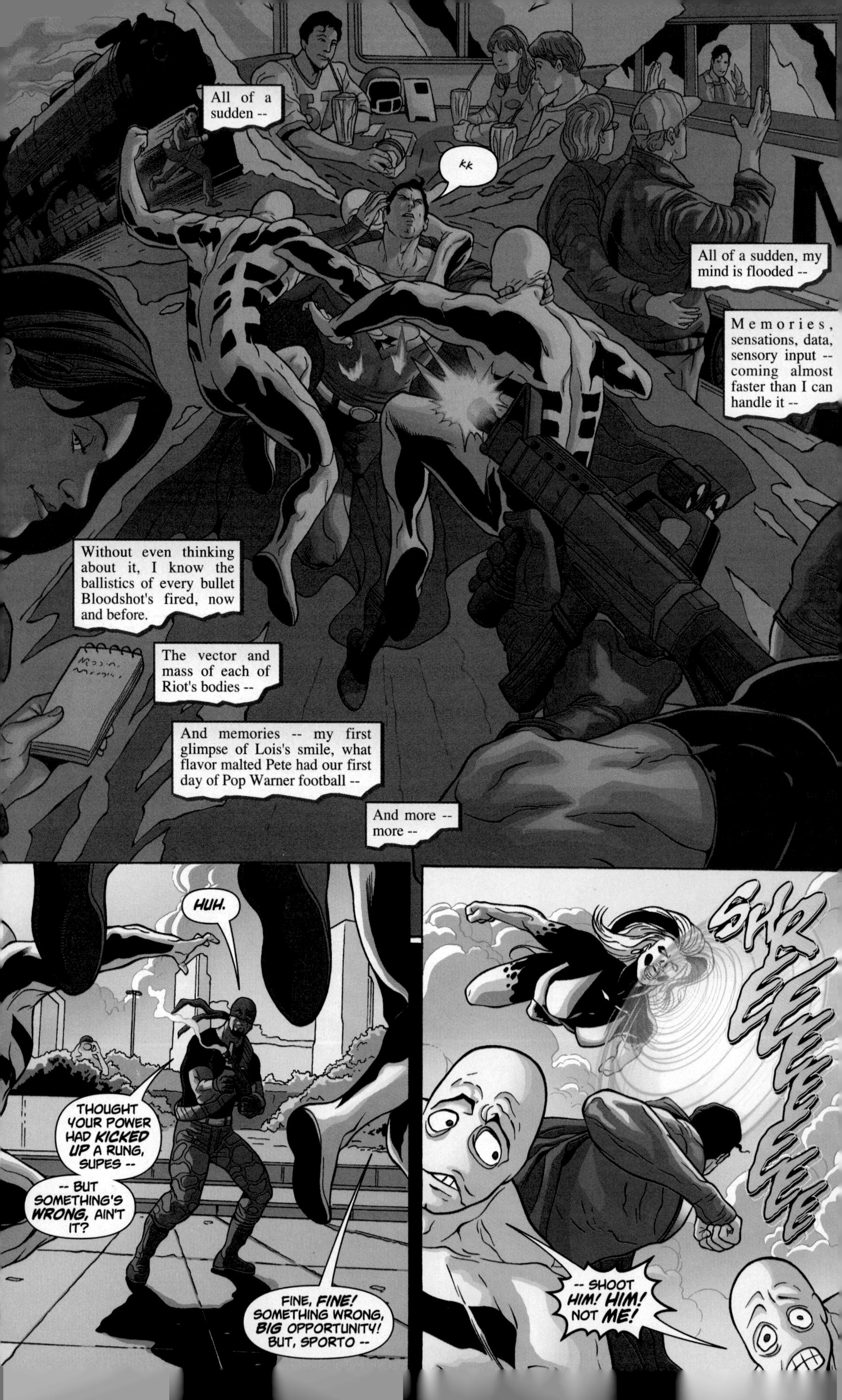
All of a sudden --
KK
All of a sudden, my mind is flooded --
Memories, sensations, data, sensory input -- coming almost faster than I can handle it --
Without even thinking about it, I know the ballistics of every bullet Bloodshot's fired, now and before.
The vector and mass of each of Riot's bodies --
And memories -- my first glimpse of Lois's smile, what flavor malted Pete had our first day of Pop Warner football --
And more -- more --
HUH.
THOUGHT YOUR POWER HAD KICKED UP A RUNG, SUPES --
-- BUT SOMETHING'S WRONG, AIN'T IT?
FINE, FINE! SOMETHING WRONG, BIG OPPORTUNITY! BUT, SPORTO --
SHREEEEEEE
-- SHOOT HIM! HIM! NOT ME!

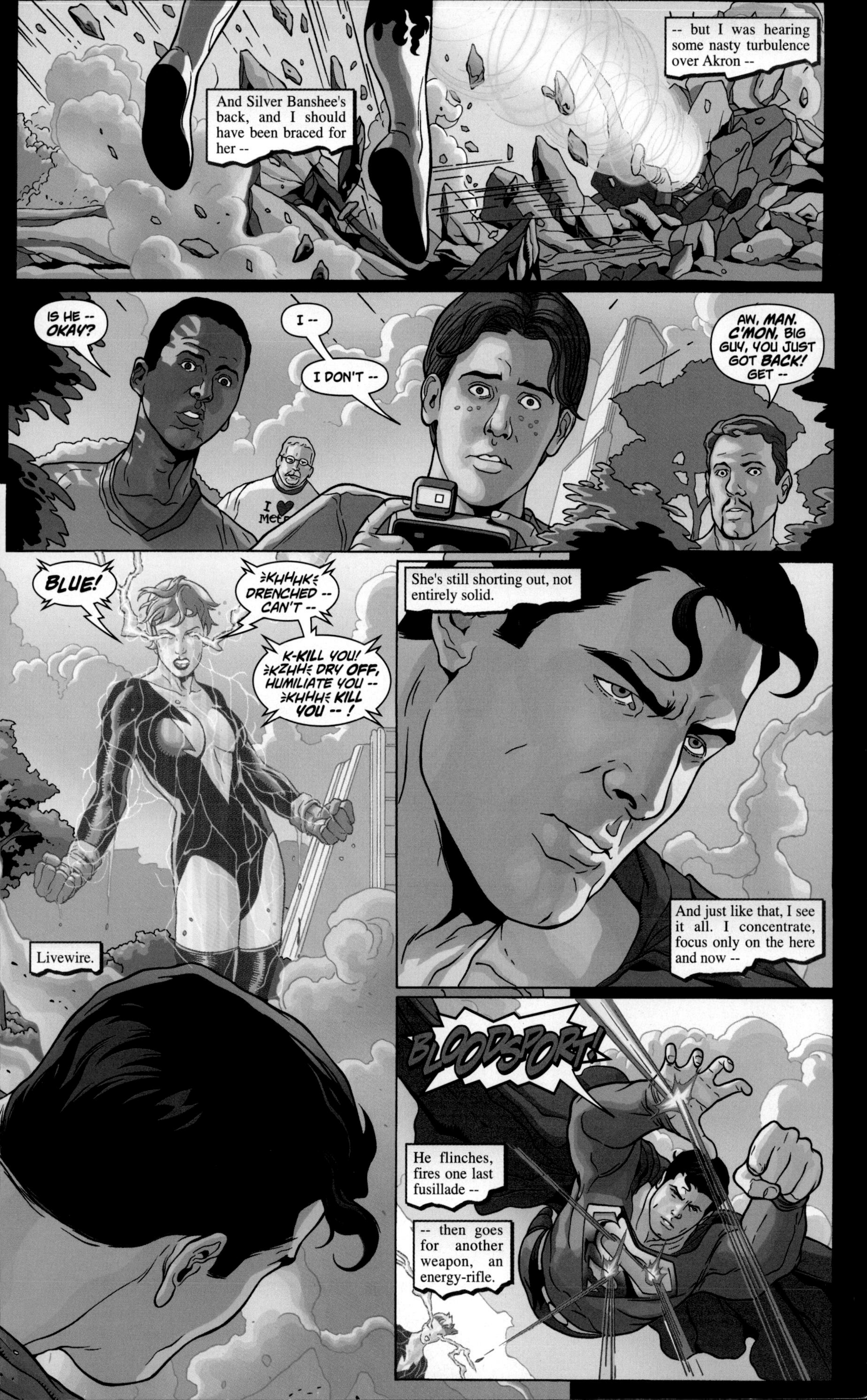
And Silver Banshee's back, and I should have been braced for her --
-- but I was hearing some nasty turbulence over Akron --
IS HE -- OKAY?
I --
I DON'T --
AW, MAN. C'MON, BIG GUY, YOU JUST GOT BACK! GET --
BLUE!
KHHHK DRENCHED -- CAN'T --
K-KILL YOU! KZHH DRY OFF, HUMILIATE YOU -- KHHH KILL YOU -- !
Livewire.
She's still shorting out, not entirely solid.
And just like that, I see it all. I concentrate, focus only on the here and now --
BLOODSPORT!
He flinches, fires one last fusillade --
-- then goes for another weapon, an energy-rifle.

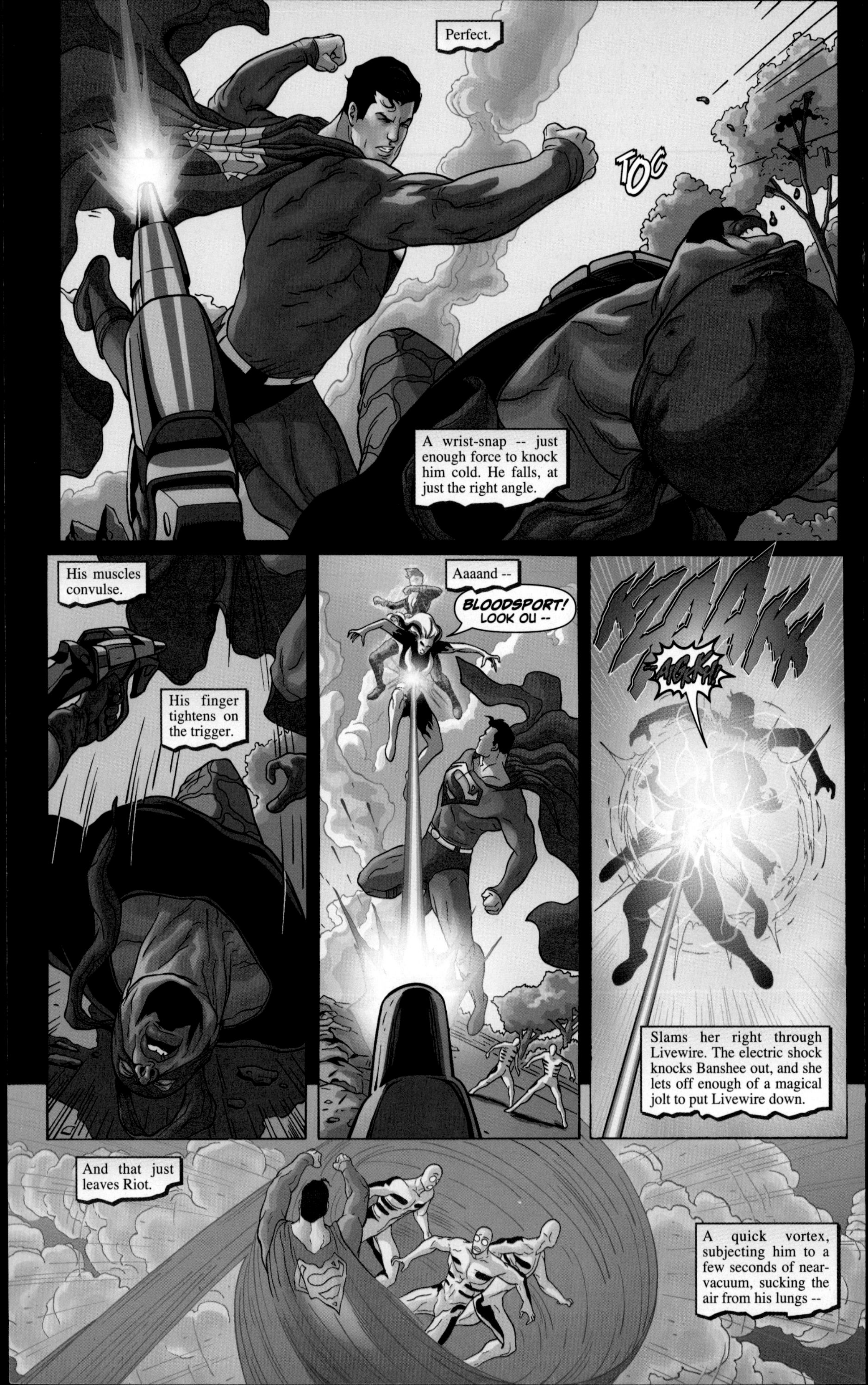

Perfect.
TOC
A wrist-snap -- just enough force to knock him cold. He falls, at just the right angle.
His muscles convulse.
His finger tightens on the trigger.
Aaaand --
BLOODSPORT! LOOK OU --
KZAAK
-AIGKH!
Slams her right through Livewire. The electric shock knocks Banshee out, and she lets off enough of a magical jolt to put Livewire down.
And that just leaves Riot.
A quick vortex, subjecting him to a few seconds of near-vacuum, sucking the air from his lungs --

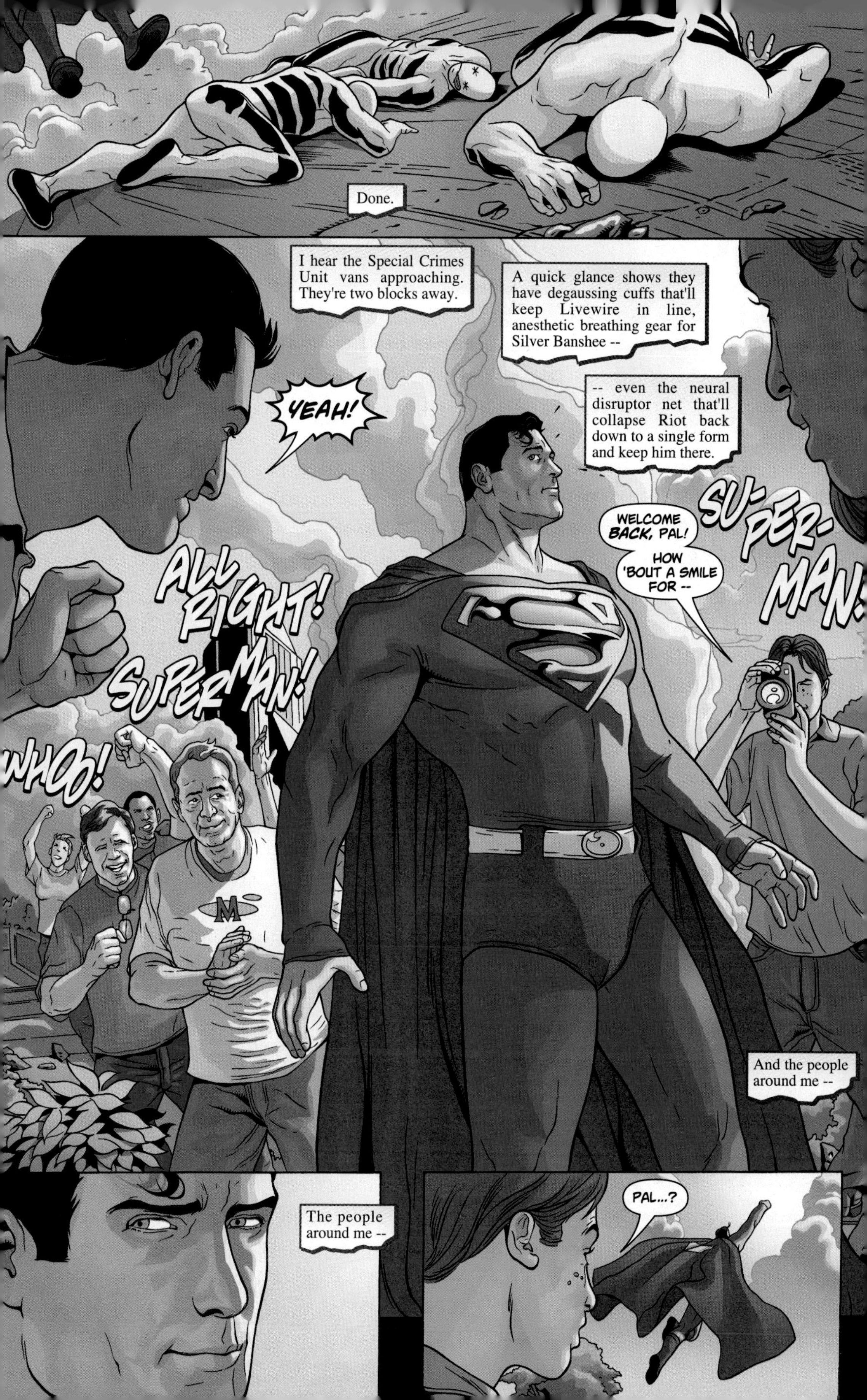
Done.
I hear the Special Crimes Unit vans approaching. They're two blocks away.
A quick glance shows they have degaussing cuffs that'll keep Livewire in line, anesthetic breathing gear for Silver Banshee --
-- even the neural disruptor net that'll collapse Riot back down to a single form and keep him there.
YEAH!
SU-PER-MAN!
WELCOME BACK, PAL!
HOW 'BOUT A SMILE FOR --
ALL RIGHT!
SUPERMAN!
WHOO!
And the people around me --
The people around me --
PAL...?

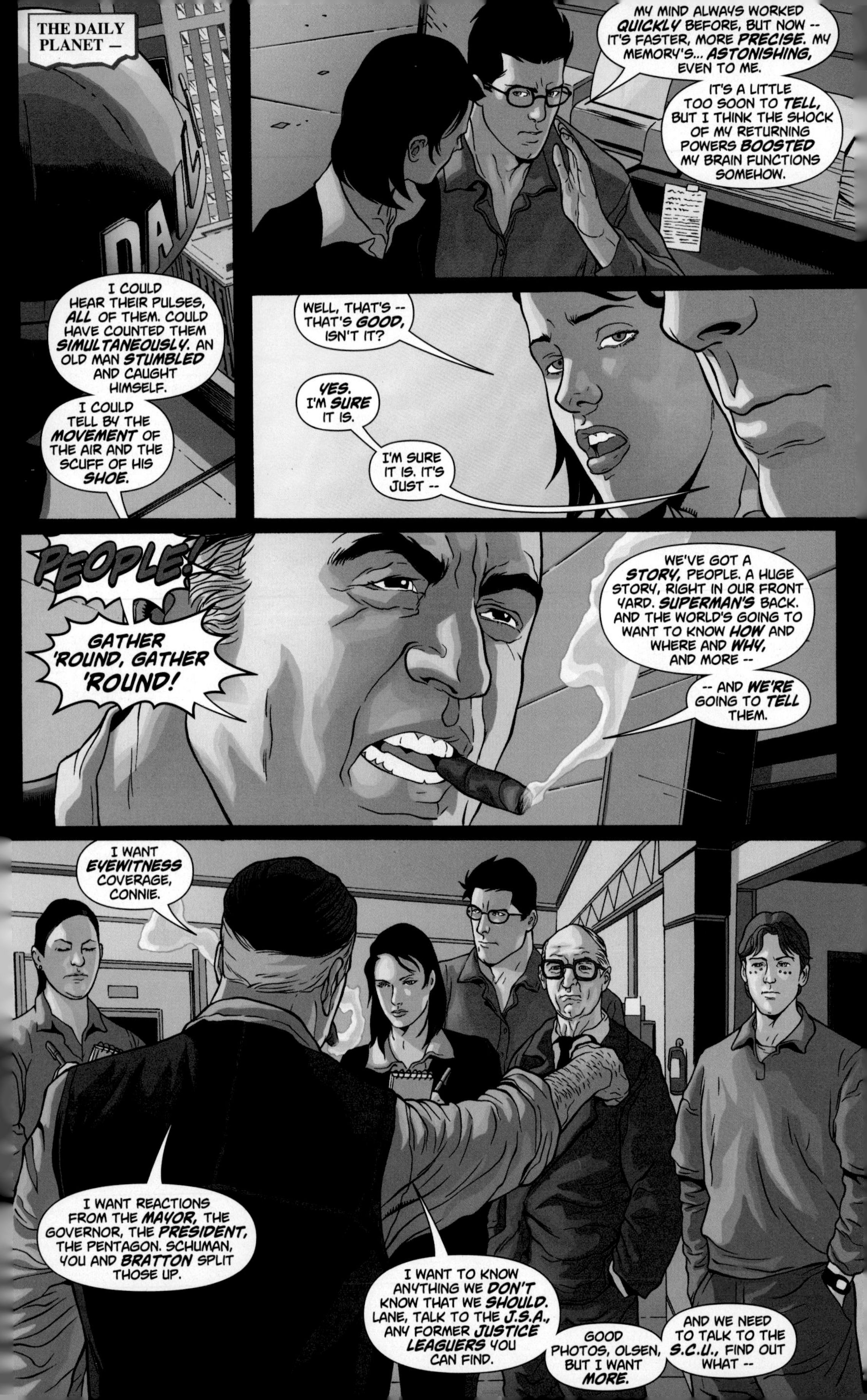
THE DAILY PLANET —
MY MIND ALWAYS WORKED QUICKLY BEFORE, BUT NOW -- IT'S FASTER, MORE PRECISE. MY MEMORY'S... ASTONISHING, EVEN TO ME.
IT'S A LITTLE TOO SOON TO TELL, BUT I THINK THE SHOCK OF MY RETURNING POWERS BOOSTED MY BRAIN FUNCTIONS SOMEHOW.
I COULD HEAR THEIR PULSES, ALL OF THEM. COULD HAVE COUNTED THEM SIMULTANEOUSLY. AN OLD MAN STUMBLED AND CAUGHT HIMSELF.
I COULD TELL BY THE MOVEMENT OF THE AIR AND THE SCUFF OF HIS SHOE.
WELL, THAT'S -- THAT'S GOOD, ISN'T IT?
YES. I'M SURE IT IS.
I'M SURE IT IS. IT'S JUST --
PEOPLE!
GATHER 'ROUND, GATHER 'ROUND!
WE'VE GOT A STORY, PEOPLE. A HUGE STORY, RIGHT IN OUR FRONT YARD. SUPERMAN'S BACK. AND THE WORLD'S GOING TO WANT TO KNOW HOW AND WHERE AND WHY, AND MORE --
-- AND WE'RE GOING TO TELL THEM.
I WANT EYEWITNESS COVERAGE, CONNIE.
I WANT REACTIONS FROM THE MAYOR, THE GOVERNOR, THE PRESIDENT, THE PENTAGON. SCHUMAN, YOU AND BRATTON SPLIT THOSE UP.
I WANT TO KNOW ANYTHING WE DON'T KNOW THAT WE SHOULD. LANE, TALK TO THE J.S.A., ANY FORMER JUSTICE LEAGUERS YOU CAN FIND.
GOOD PHOTOS, OLSEN, BUT I WANT MORE.
AND WE NEED TO TALK TO THE S.C.U., FIND OUT WHAT --

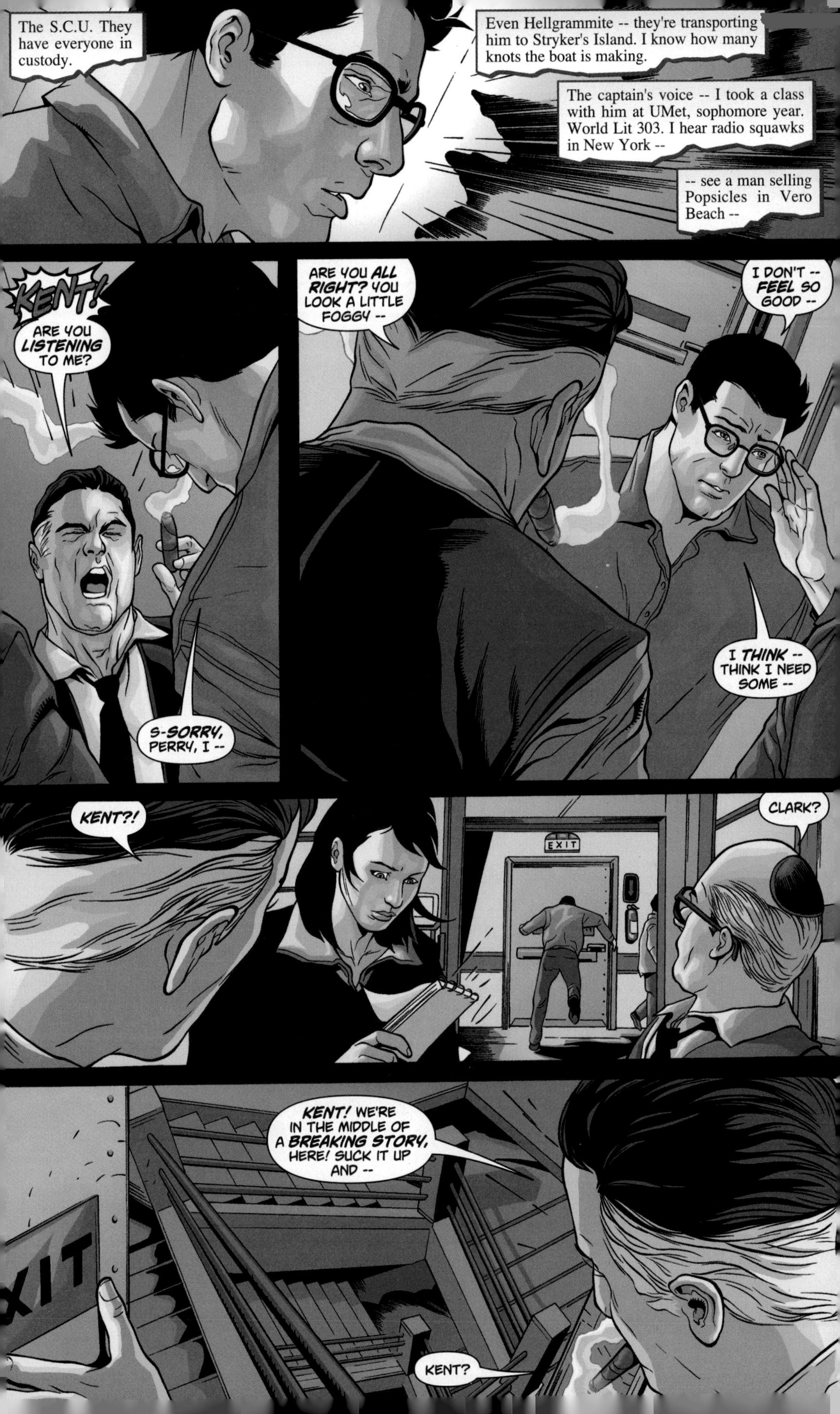
The S.C.U. They have everyone in custody.
Even Hellgrammite -- they're transporting him to Stryker's Island. I know how many knots the boat is making.
The captain's voice -- I took a class with him at UMet, sophomore year. World Lit 303. I hear radio squawks in New York --
-- see a man selling Popsicles in Vero Beach --
KENT!
ARE YOU LISTENING TO ME?
S-SORRY, PERRY, I --
ARE YOU ALL RIGHT? YOU LOOK A LITTLE FOGGY --
I DON'T -- FEEL SO GOOD --
I THINK -- THINK I NEED SOME --
KENT?!
CLARK?
EXIT
KENT! WE'RE IN THE MIDDLE OF A BREAKING STORY, HERE! SUCK IT UP AND --
EXIT
KENT?

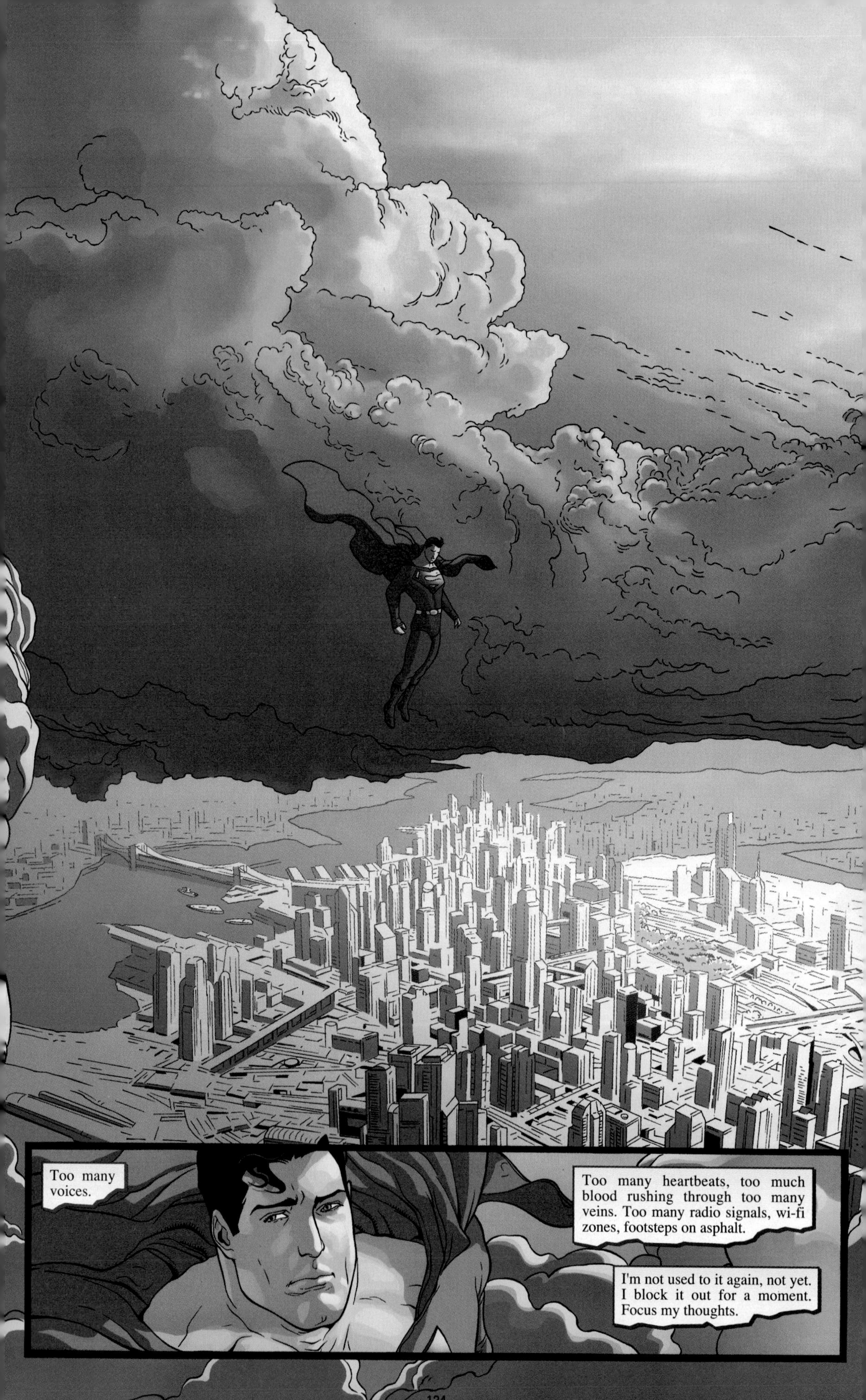

Too many voices.
Too many heartbeats, too much blood rushing through too many veins. Too many radio signals, wi-fi zones, footsteps on asphalt.
I'm not used to it again, not yet. I block it out for a moment. Focus my thoughts.

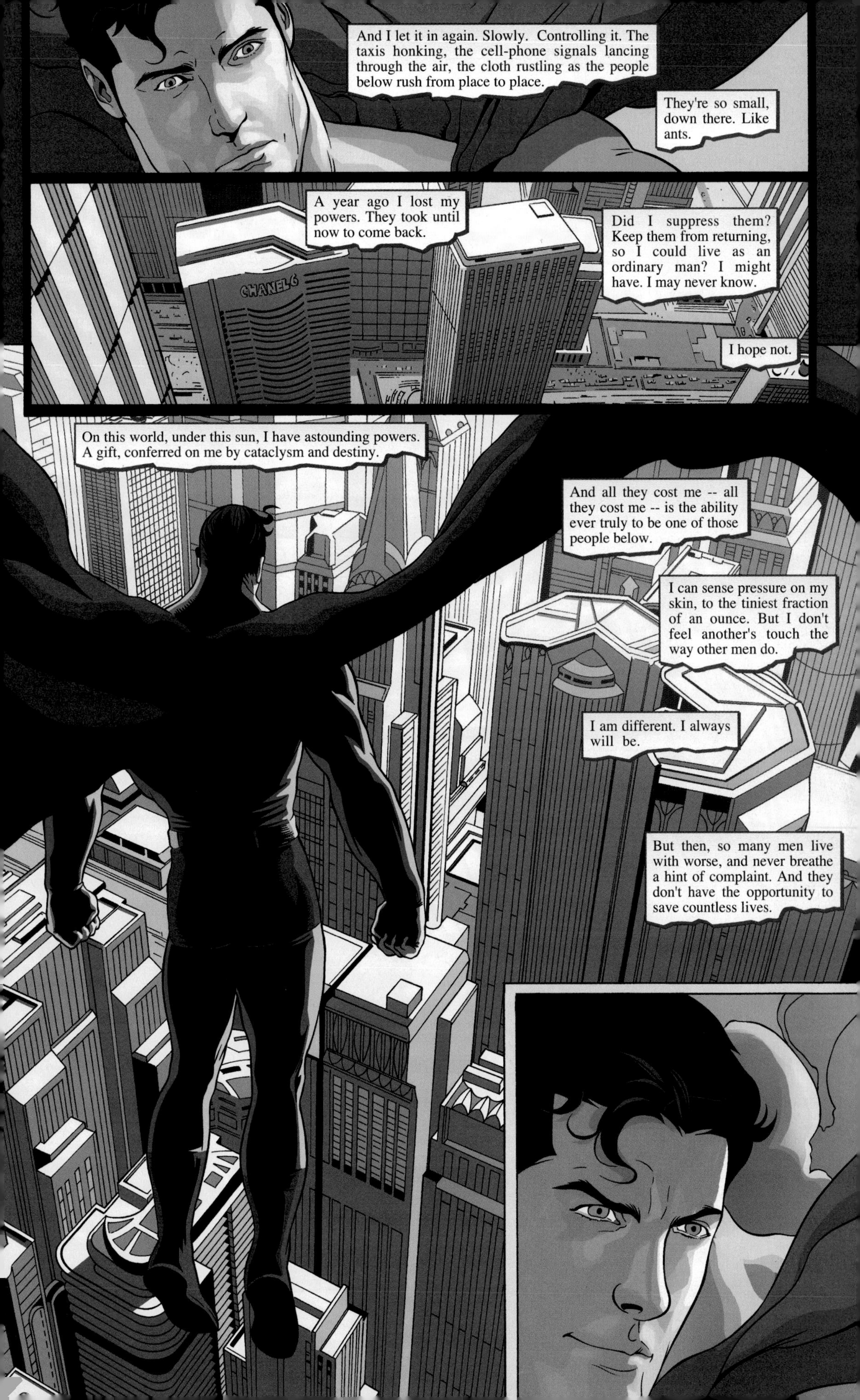
And I let it in again. Slowly. Controlling it. The taxis honking, the cell-phone signals lancing through the air, the cloth rustling as the people below rush from place to place.
They're so small, down there. Like ants.
A year ago I lost my powers. They took until now to come back.
Did I suppress them? Keep them from returning, so I could live as an ordinary man? I might have. I may never know.
I hope not.
CHANEL 6
On this world, under this sun, I have astounding powers. A gift, conferred on me by cataclysm and destiny.
And all they cost me -- all they cost me -- is the ability ever truly to be one of those people below.
I can sense pressure on my skin, to the tiniest fraction of an ounce. But I don't feel another's touch the way other men do.
I am different. I always will be.
But then, so many men live with worse, and never breathe a hint of complaint. And they don't have the opportunity to save countless lives.

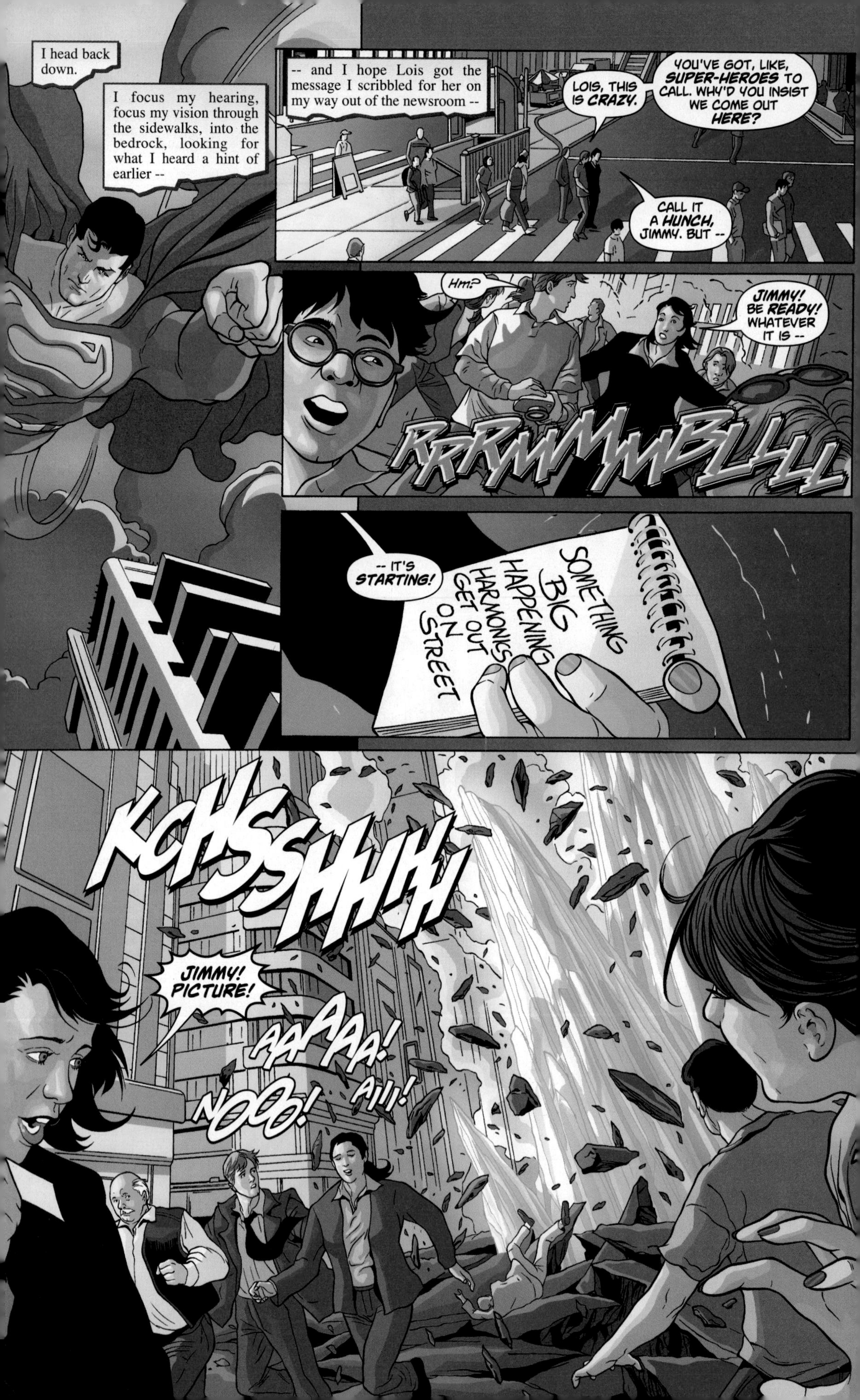

I head back down.
I focus my hearing, focus my vision through the sidewalks, into the bedrock, looking for what I heard a hint of earlier --
-- and I hope Lois got the message I scribbled for her on my way out of the newsroom --
LOIS, THIS IS CRAZY.
YOU'VE GOT, LIKE, SUPER-HEROES TO CALL. WHY'D YOU INSIST WE COME OUT HERE?
CALL IT A HUNCH, JIMMY. BUT --
Hm?
JIMMY! BE READY! WHATEVER IT IS --
RRRMMMMBLLLL
-- IT'S STARTING!
SOMETHING BIG HAPPENING HARMONIKS GET OUT ON STREET
KCHSSHHHH
JIMMY! PICTURE!
AAAAAA!
AIII!
NOOOO!

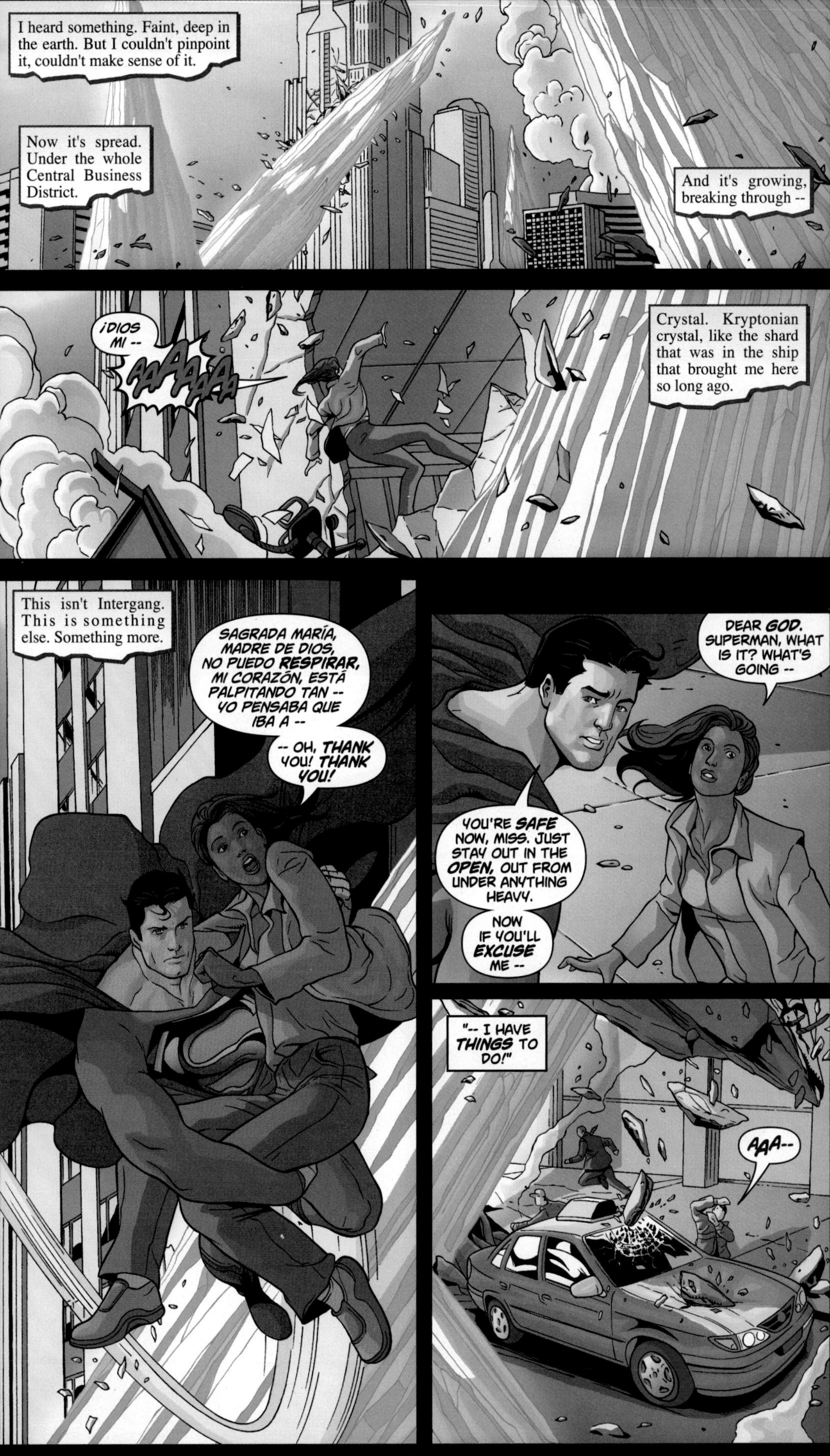
I heard something. Faint, deep in the earth. But I couldn't pinpoint it, couldn't make sense of it.
Now it's spread. Under the whole Central Business District.
And it's growing, breaking through --
¡DIOS MI --
AAAAAA
Crystal. Kryptonian crystal, like the shard that was in the ship that brought me here so long ago.
This isn't Intergang. This is something else. Something more.
SAGRADA MARÍA, MADRE DE DIOS, NO PUEDO RESPIRAR, MI CORAZÓN, ESTÁ PALPITANDO TAN -- YO PENSABA QUE IBA A --
-- OH, THANK YOU! THANK YOU!
DEAR GOD. SUPERMAN, WHAT IS IT? WHAT'S GOING --
YOU'RE SAFE NOW, MISS. JUST STAY OUT IN THE OPEN, OUT FROM UNDER ANYTHING HEAVY.
NOW IF YOU'LL EXCUSE ME --
"-- I HAVE THINGS TO DO!"
AAA--

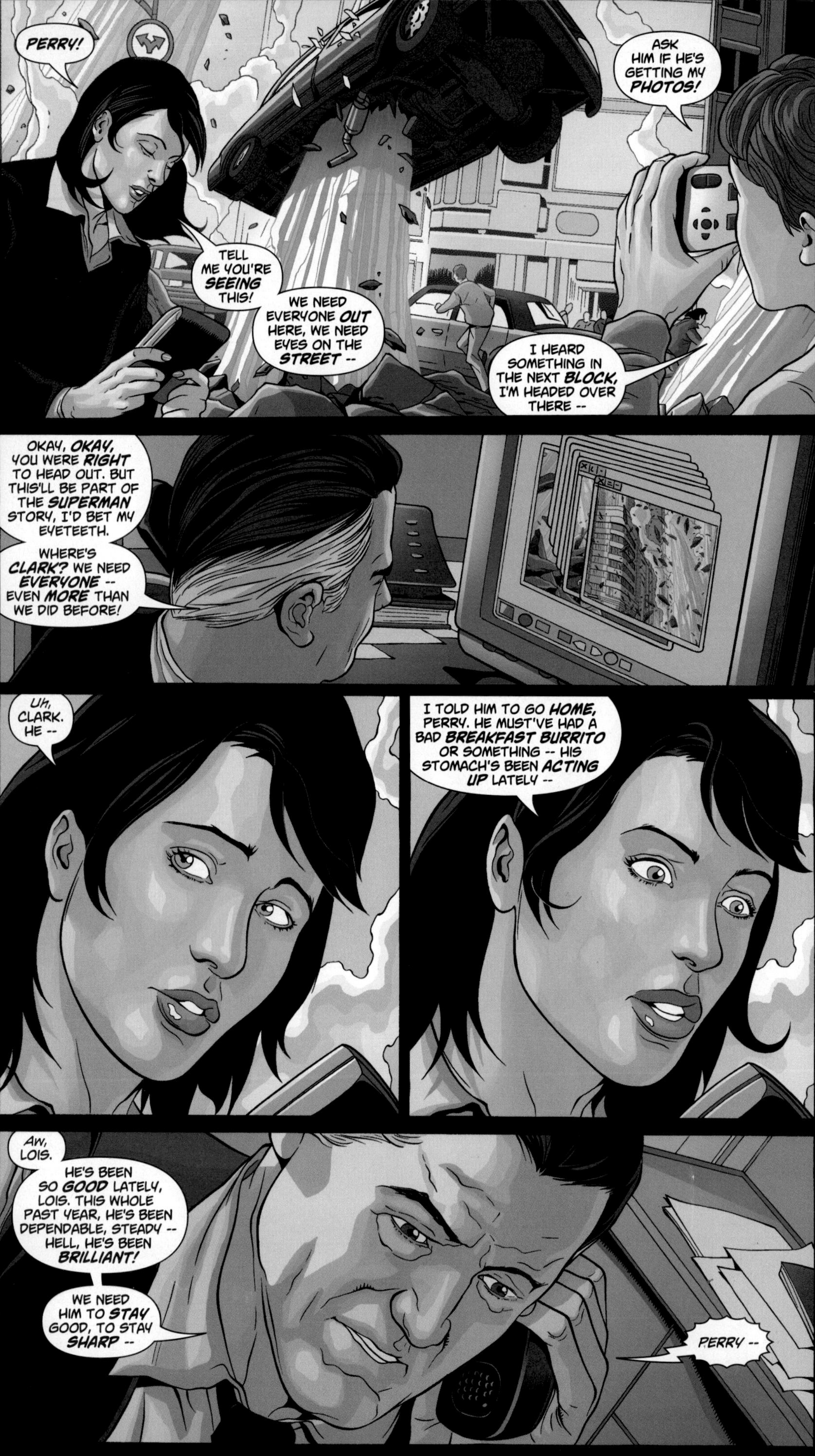
PERRY!
ASK HIM IF HE'S GETTING MY PHOTOS!
TELL ME YOU'RE SEEING THIS!
WE NEED EVERYONE OUT HERE, WE NEED EYES ON THE STREET --
I HEARD SOMETHING IN THE NEXT BLOCK, I'M HEADED OVER THERE --
OKAY, OKAY, YOU WERE RIGHT TO HEAD OUT. BUT THIS'LL BE PART OF THE SUPERMAN STORY, I'D BET MY EYETEETH.
WHERE'S CLARK? WE NEED EVERYONE -- EVEN MORE THAN WE DID BEFORE!
Uh, CLARK. HE --
I TOLD HIM TO GO HOME, PERRY. HE MUST'VE HAD A BAD BREAKFAST BURRITO OR SOMETHING -- HIS STOMACH'S BEEN ACTING UP LATELY --
AW, LOIS.
HE'S BEEN SO GOOD LATELY, LOIS. THIS WHOLE PAST YEAR, HE'S BEEN DEPENDABLE, STEADY -- HELL, HE'S BEEN BRILLIANT!
WE NEED HIM TO STAY GOOD, TO STAY SHARP --
PERRY --

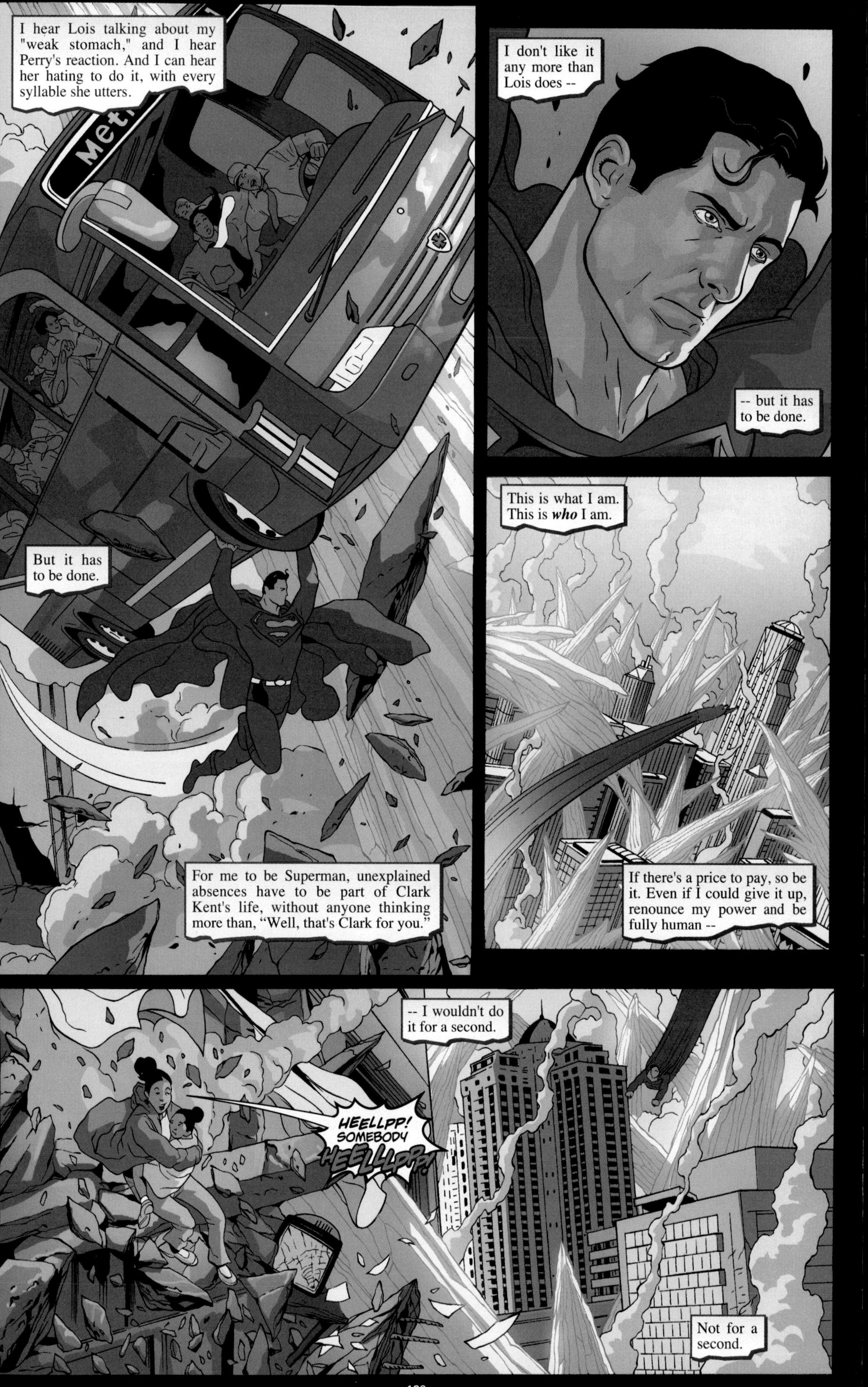
I hear Lois talking about my "weak stomach," and I hear Perry's reaction. And I can hear her hating to do it, with every syllable she utters.
But it has to be done.
For me to be Superman, unexplained absences have to be part of Clark Kent's life, without anyone thinking more than, "Well, that's Clark for you."
I don't like it any more than Lois does --
-- but it has to be done.
This is what I am. This is *who* I am.
If there's a price to pay, so be it. Even if I could give it up, renounce my power and be fully human --
-- I wouldn't do it for a second.
HEELLPP! SOMEBODY HEELLLPP!
Not for a second.

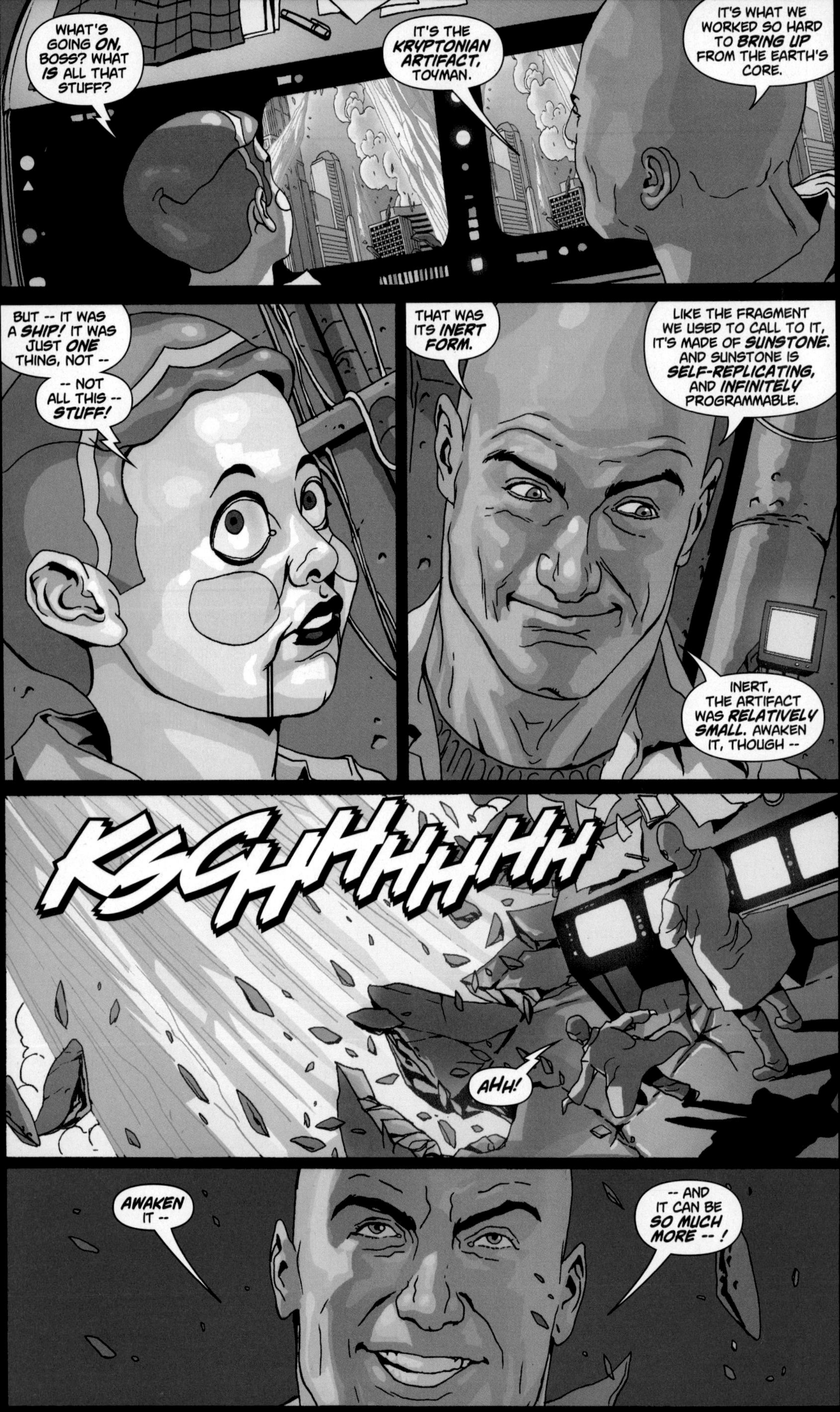
WHAT'S GOING ON, BOSS? WHAT IS ALL THAT STUFF?
IT'S THE KRYPTONIAN ARTIFACT, TOYMAN.
IT'S WHAT WE WORKED SO HARD TO BRING UP FROM THE EARTH'S CORE.
BUT -- IT WAS A SHIP! IT WAS JUST ONE THING, NOT --
-- NOT ALL THIS -- STUFF!
THAT WAS ITS INERT FORM.
LIKE THE FRAGMENT WE USED TO CALL TO IT, IT'S MADE OF SUNSTONE. AND SUNSTONE IS SELF-REPLICATING, AND INFINITELY PROGRAMMABLE.
INERT, THE ARTIFACT WAS RELATIVELY SMALL. AWAKEN IT, THOUGH --
KSCHHHHHHH
AHH!
AWAKEN IT --
-- AND IT CAN BE SO MUCH MORE -- !

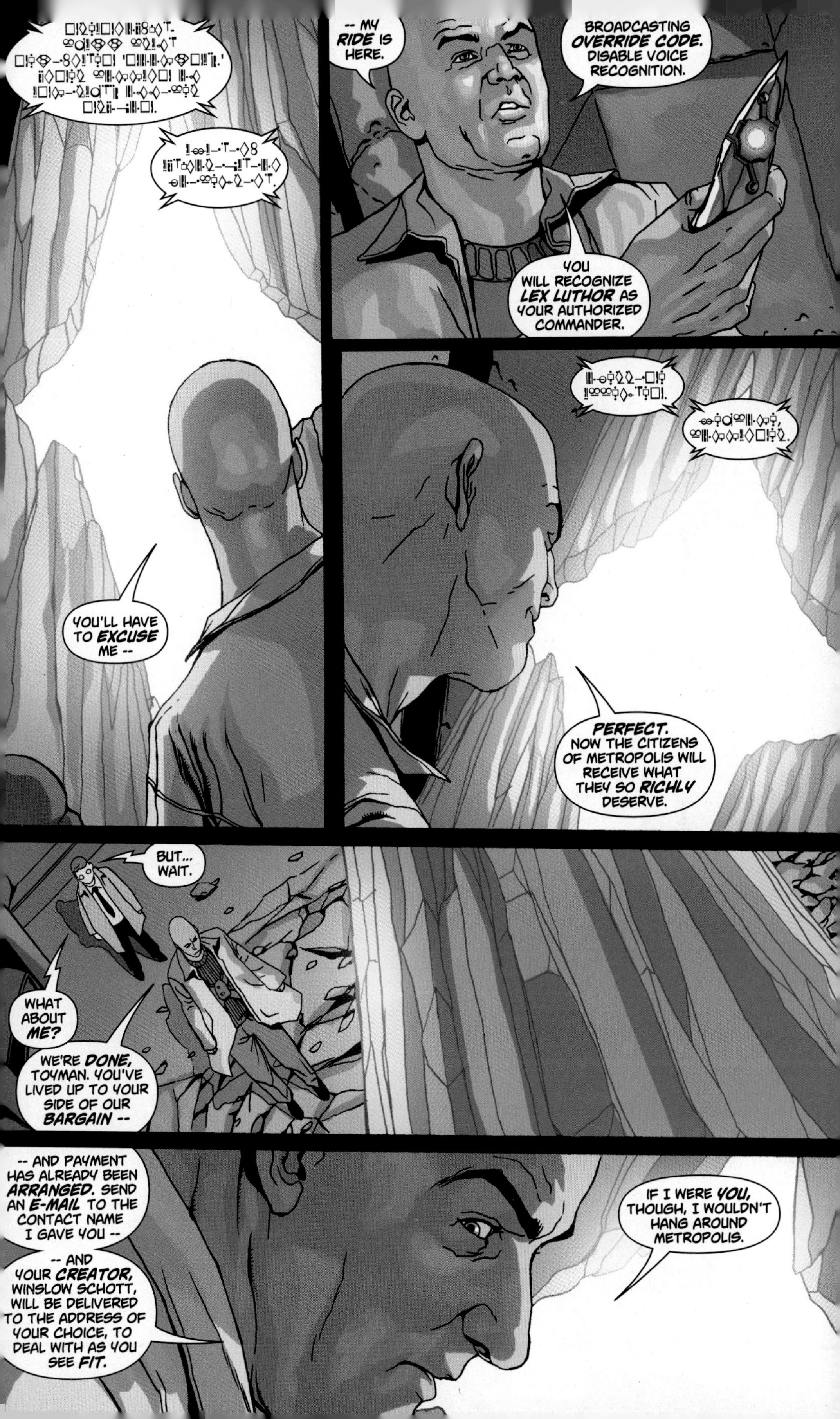
YOU'LL HAVE TO EXCUSE ME --
-- MY RIDE IS HERE.
BROADCASTING OVERRIDE CODE. DISABLE VOICE RECOGNITION.
YOU WILL RECOGNIZE LEX LUTHOR AS YOUR AUTHORIZED COMMANDER.
PERFECT. NOW THE CITIZENS OF METROPOLIS WILL RECEIVE WHAT THEY SO RICHLY DESERVE.
BUT... WAIT.
WHAT ABOUT ME?
WE'RE DONE, TOYMAN. YOU'VE LIVED UP TO YOUR SIDE OF OUR BARGAIN --
-- AND PAYMENT HAS ALREADY BEEN ARRANGED. SEND AN E-MAIL TO THE CONTACT NAME I GAVE YOU --
-- AND YOUR CREATOR, WINSLOW SCHOTT, WILL BE DELIVERED TO THE ADDRESS OF YOUR CHOICE, TO DEAL WITH AS YOU SEE FIT.
IF I WERE YOU, THOUGH, I WOULDN'T HANG AROUND METROPOLIS.

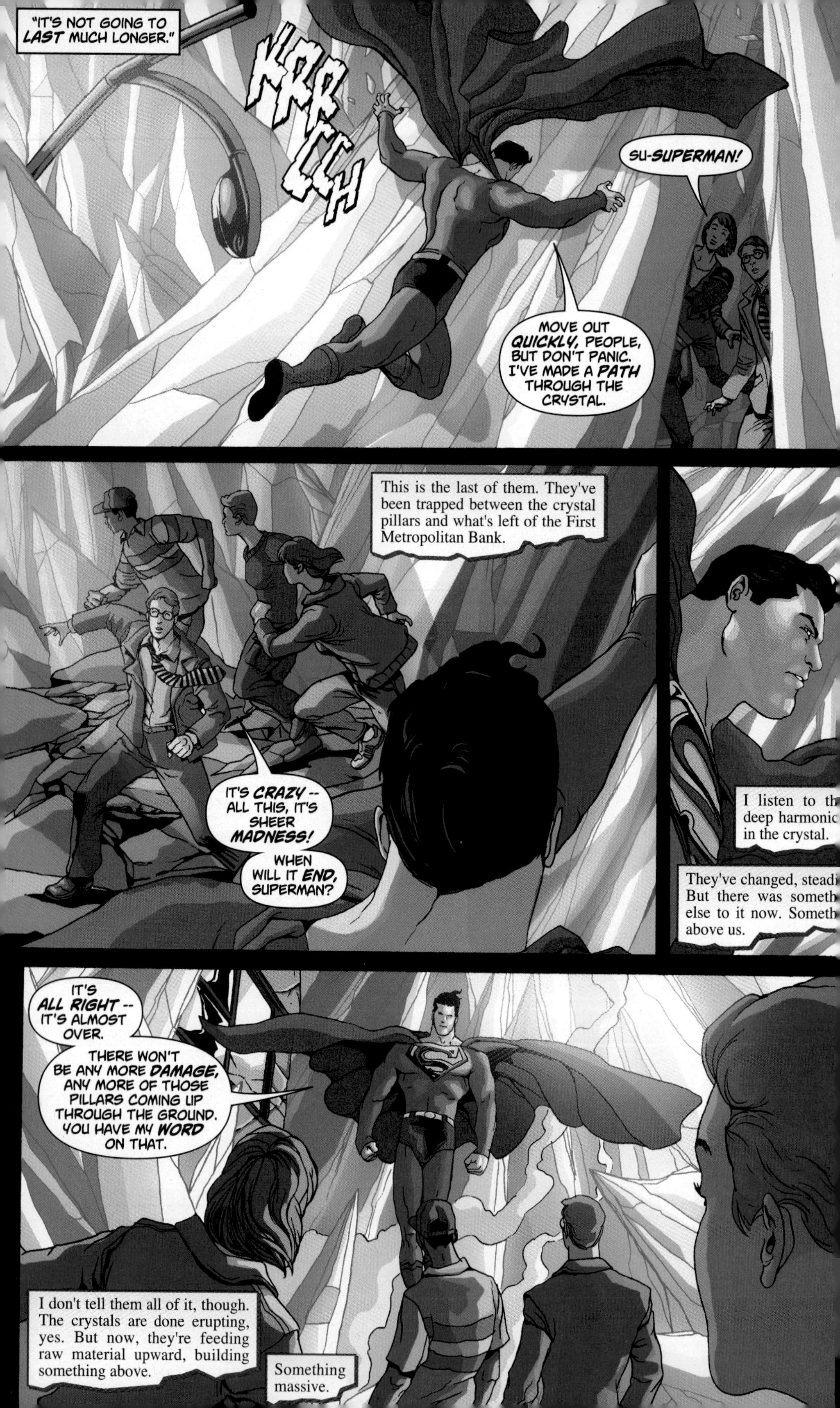

"IT'S NOT GOING TO LAST MUCH LONGER."
KRRCCH
SU-SUPERMAN!
MOVE OUT QUICKLY, PEOPLE, BUT DON'T PANIC. I'VE MADE A PATH THROUGH THE CRYSTAL.
This is the last of them. They've been trapped between the crystal pillars and what's left of the First Metropolitan Bank.
IT'S CRAZY -- ALL THIS, IT'S SHEER MADNESS!
WHEN WILL IT END, SUPERMAN?
I listen to th deep harmonic in the crystal.
They've changed, steadi But there was someth else to it now. Someth above us.
IT'S ALL RIGHT -- IT'S ALMOST OVER.
THERE WON'T BE ANY MORE DAMAGE, ANY MORE OF THOSE PILLARS COMING UP THROUGH THE GROUND. YOU HAVE MY WORD ON THAT.
I don't tell them all of it, though. The crystals are done erupting, yes. But now, they're feeding raw material upward, building something above.
Something massive.

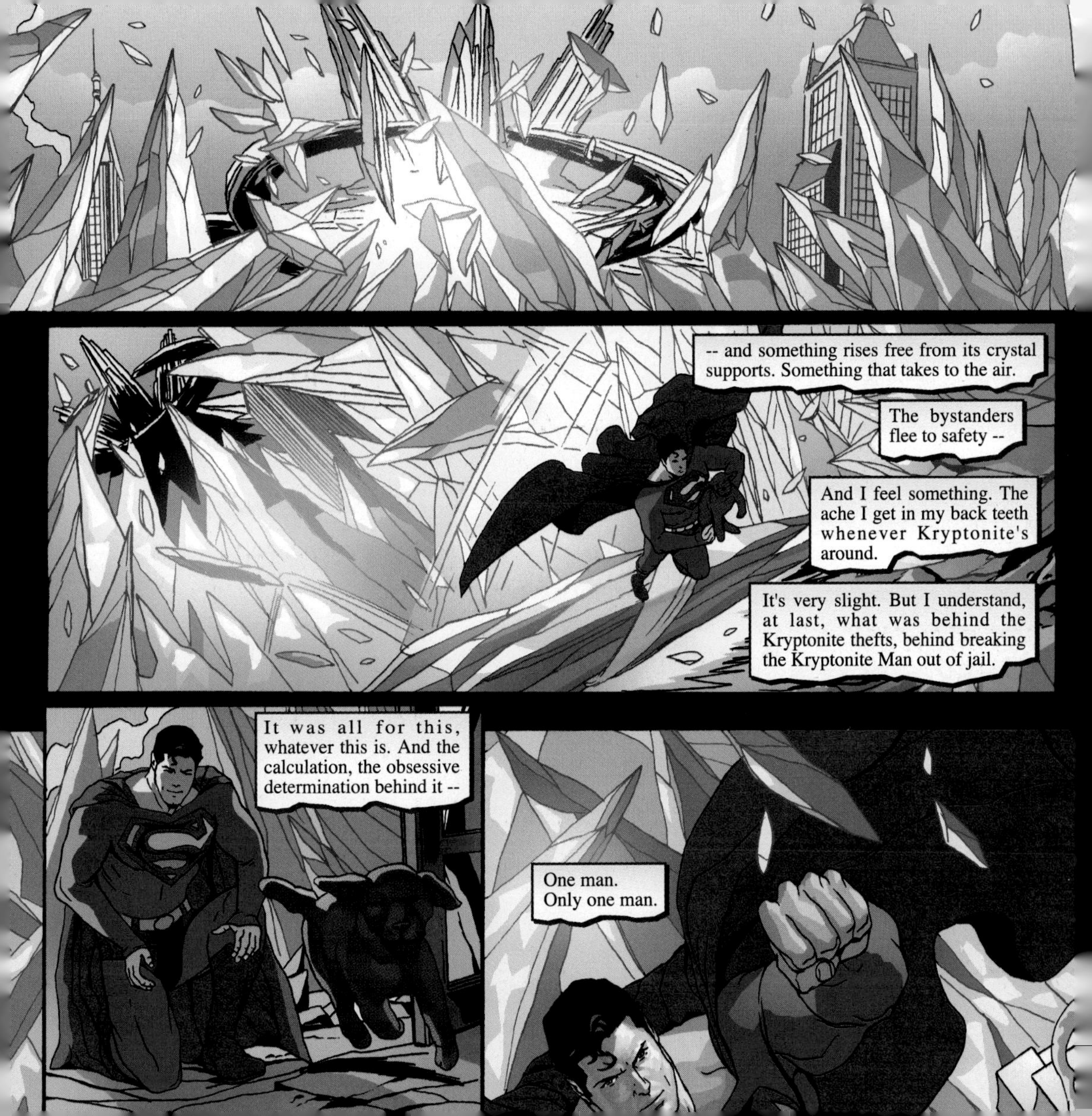
-- and something rises free from its crystal supports. Something that takes to the air.
The bystanders flee to safety --
And I feel something. The ache I get in my back teeth whenever Kryptonite's around.
It's very slight. But I understand, at last, what was behind the Kryptonite thefts, behind breaking the Kryptonite Man out of jail.
It was all for this, whatever this is. And the calculation, the obsessive determination behind it --
One man.
Only one man.

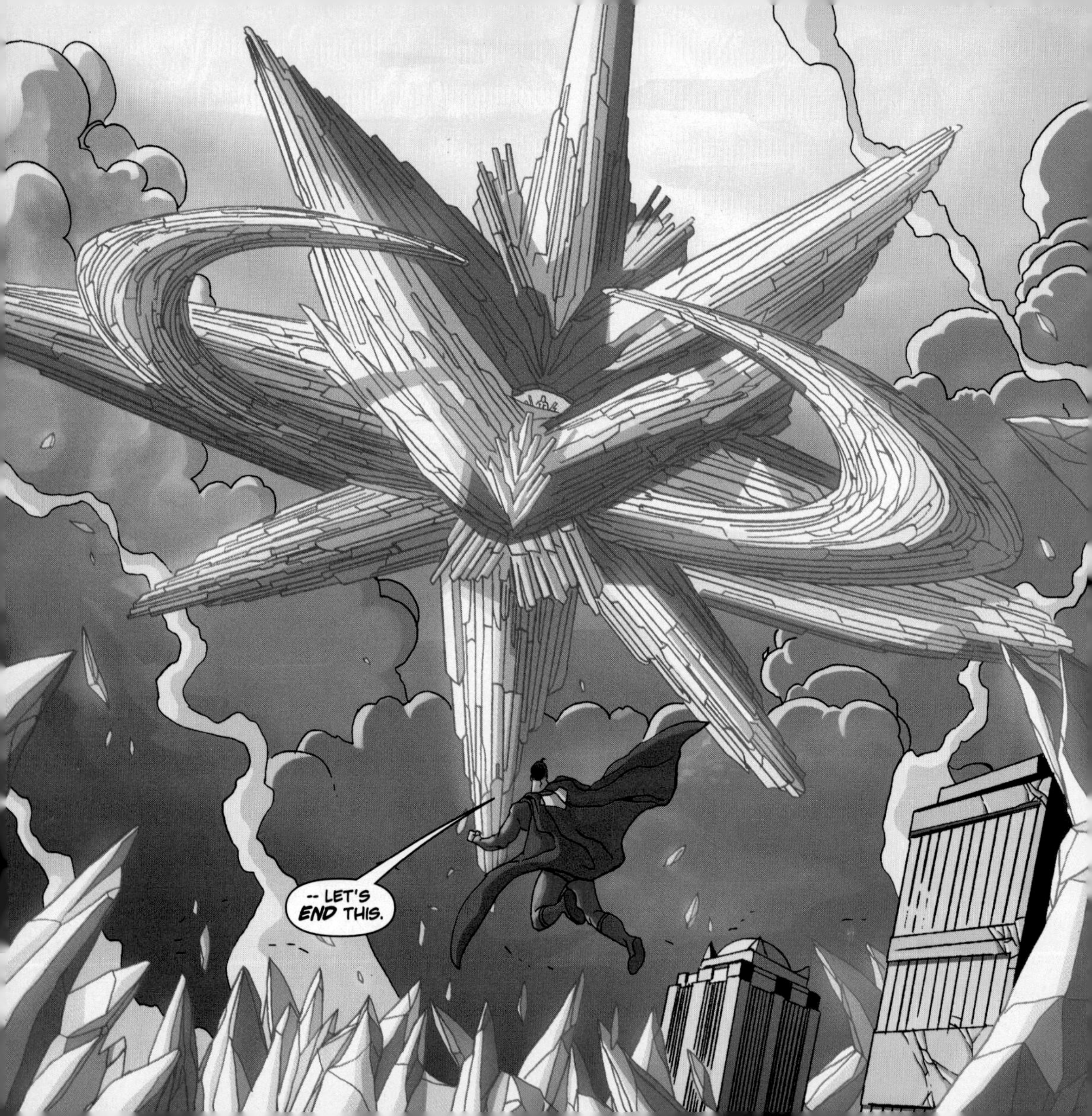
-- LET'S END THIS.

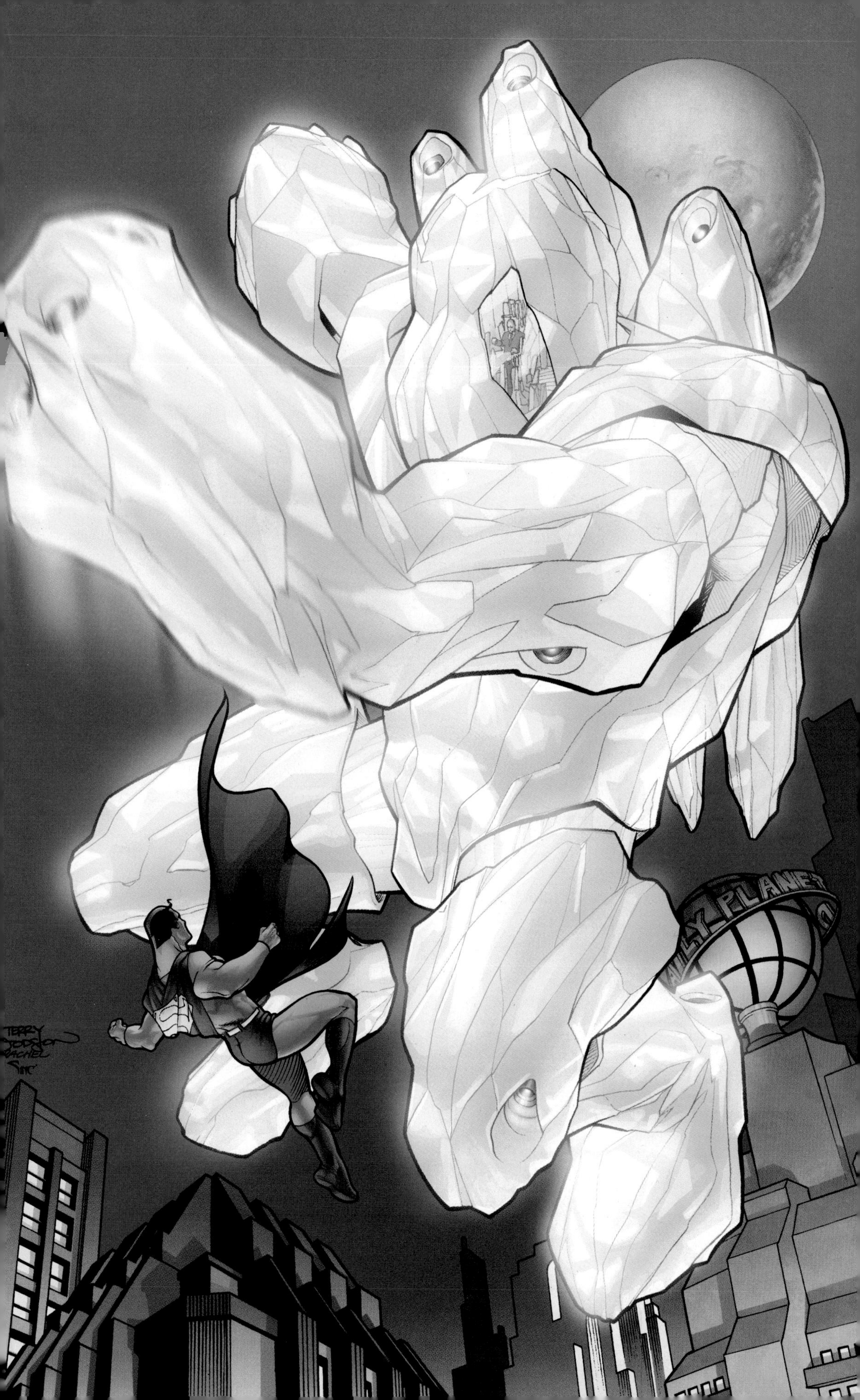
TERRY

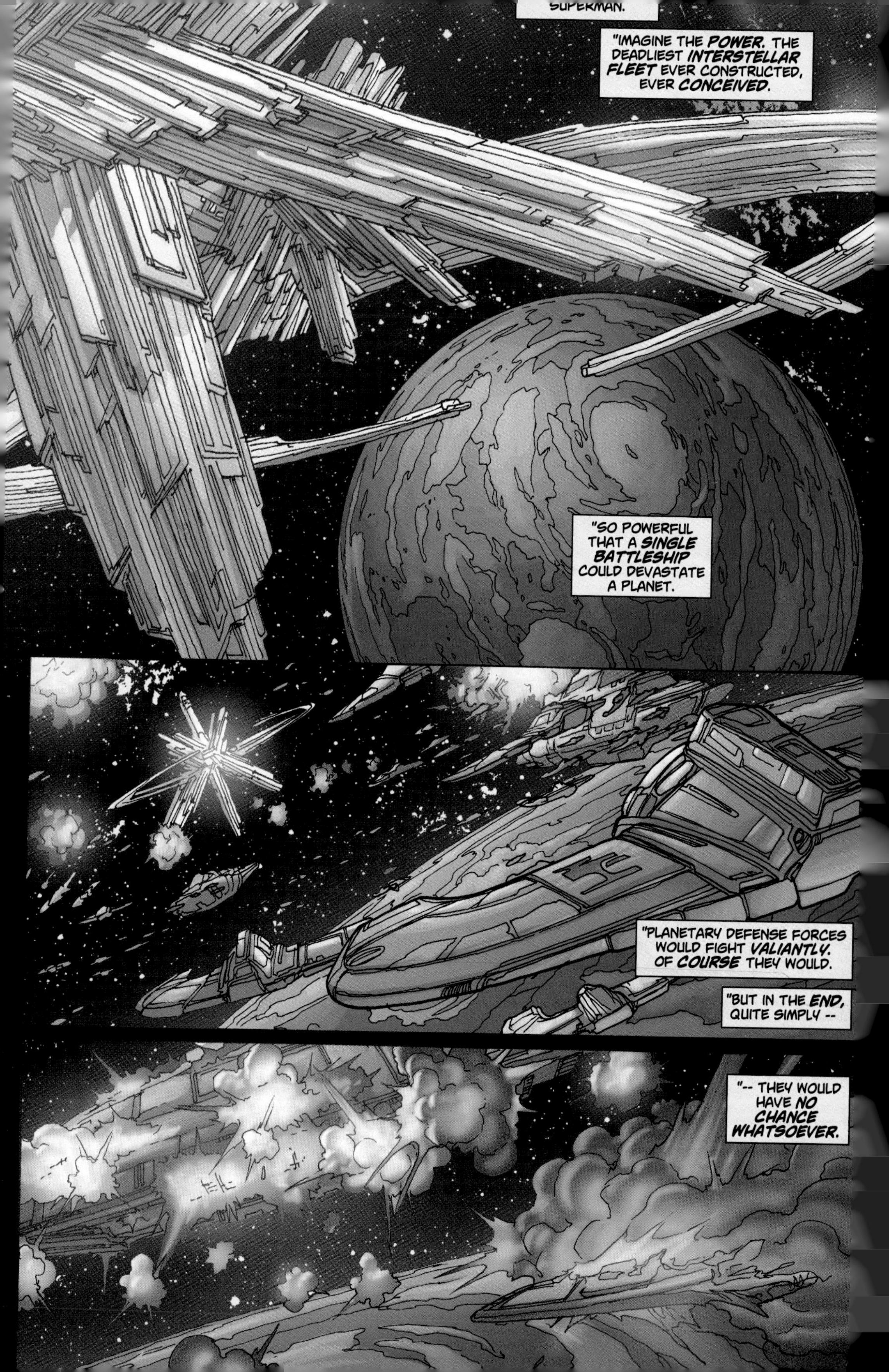
SUPERMAN.
"IMAGINE THE POWER. THE DEADLIEST INTERSTELLAR FLEET EVER CONSTRUCTED, EVER CONCEIVED.
"SO POWERFUL THAT A SINGLE BATTLESHIP COULD DEVASTATE A PLANET.
"PLANETARY DEFENSE FORCES WOULD FIGHT VALIANTLY. OF COURSE THEY WOULD.
"BUT IN THE END, QUITE SIMPLY --
"-- THEY WOULD HAVE NO CHANCE WHATSOEVER.

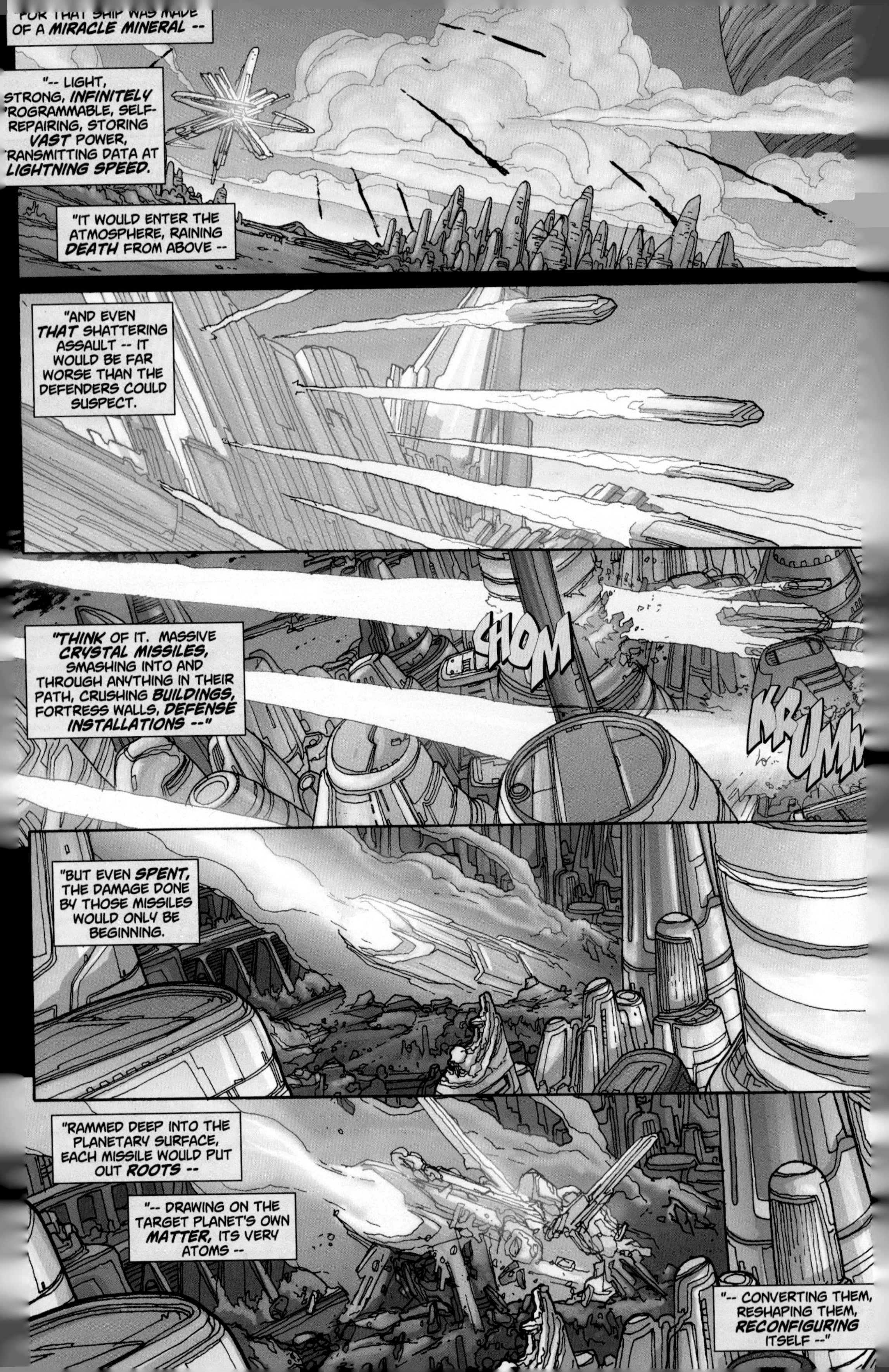
FOR THAT SHIP WAS MADE OF A MIRACLE MINERAL --
"-- LIGHT, STRONG, INFINITELY PROGRAMMABLE, SELF-REPAIRING, STORING VAST POWER, TRANSMITTING DATA AT LIGHTNING SPEED.
"IT WOULD ENTER THE ATMOSPHERE, RAINING DEATH FROM ABOVE --
"AND EVEN THAT SHATTERING ASSAULT -- IT WOULD BE FAR WORSE THAN THE DEFENDERS COULD SUSPECT.
"THINK OF IT. MASSIVE CRYSTAL MISSILES, SMASHING INTO AND THROUGH ANYTHING IN THEIR PATH, CRUSHING BUILDINGS, FORTRESS WALLS, DEFENSE INSTALLATIONS --"
SHOM
KRUMM
"BUT EVEN SPENT, THE DAMAGE DONE BY THOSE MISSILES WOULD ONLY BE BEGINNING.
"RAMMED DEEP INTO THE PLANETARY SURFACE, EACH MISSILE WOULD PUT OUT ROOTS --
"-- DRAWING ON THE TARGET PLANET'S OWN MATTER, ITS VERY ATOMS --
"-- CONVERTING THEM, RESHAPING THEM, RECONFIGURING ITSELF --"

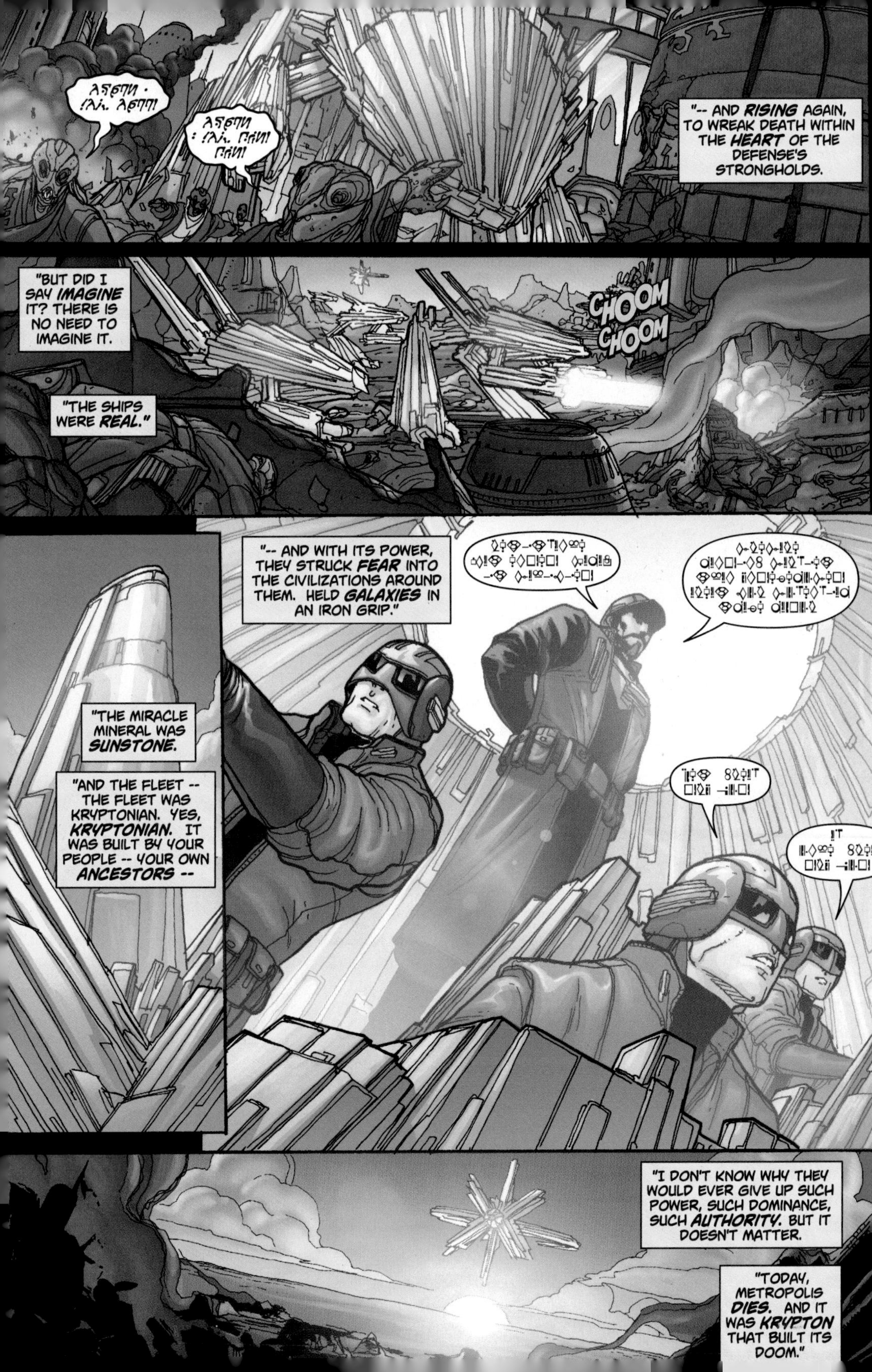
"-- AND RISING AGAIN, TO WREAK DEATH WITHIN THE HEART OF THE DEFENSE'S STRONGHOLDS.
"BUT DID I SAY IMAGINE IT? THERE IS NO NEED TO IMAGINE IT.
CHOOM CHOOM
"THE SHIPS WERE REAL."
"-- AND WITH ITS POWER, THEY STRUCK FEAR INTO THE CIVILIZATIONS AROUND THEM. HELD GALAXIES IN AN IRON GRIP."
"THE MIRACLE MINERAL WAS SUNSTONE.
"AND THE FLEET -- THE FLEET WAS KRYPTONIAN. YES, KRYPTONIAN. IT WAS BUILT BY YOUR PEOPLE -- YOUR OWN ANCESTORS --
"I DON'T KNOW WHY THEY WOULD EVER GIVE UP SUCH POWER, SUCH DOMINANCE, SUCH AUTHORITY. BUT IT DOESN'T MATTER.
"TODAY, METROPOLIS DIES. AND IT WAS KRYPTON THAT BUILT ITS DOOM."

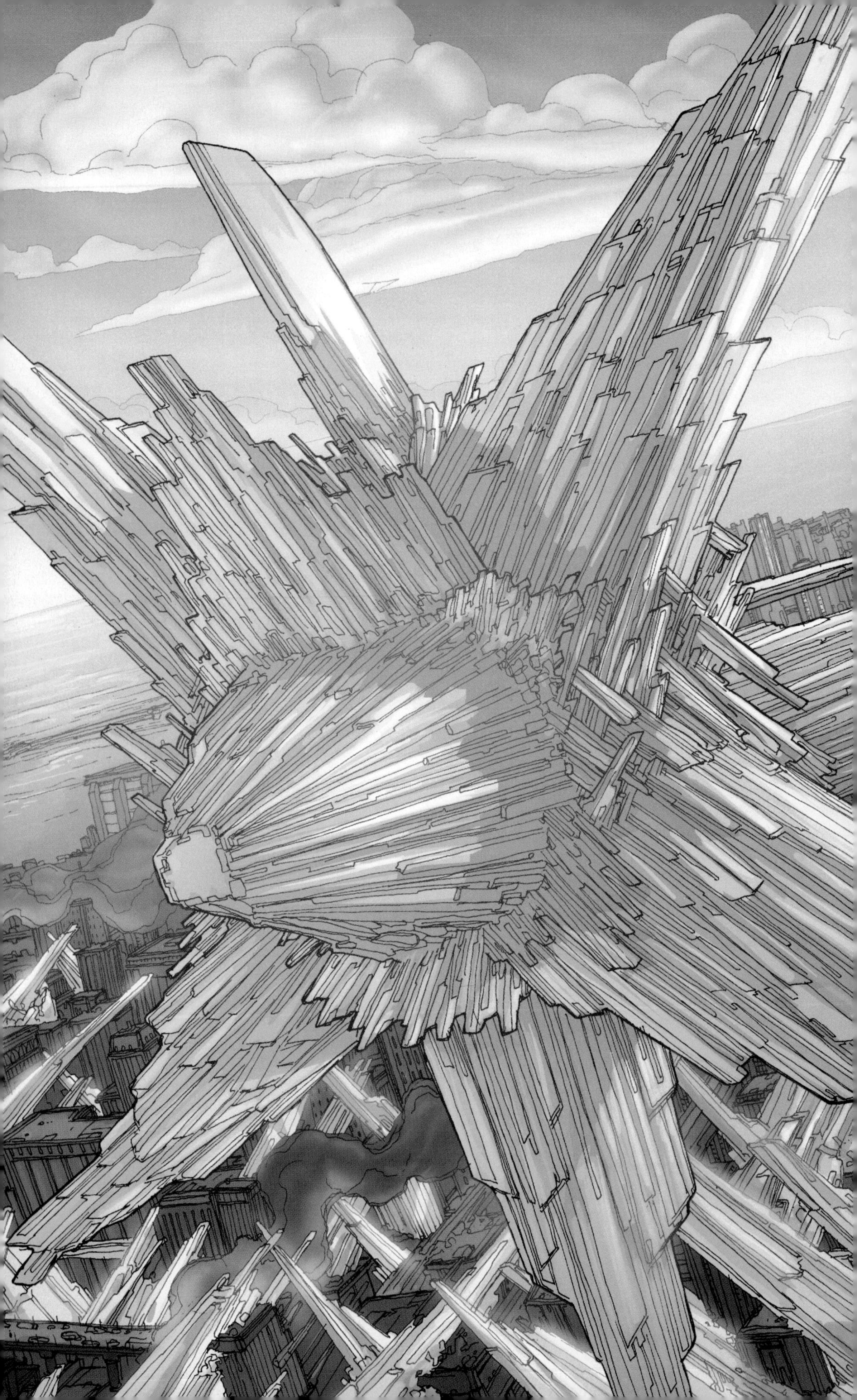

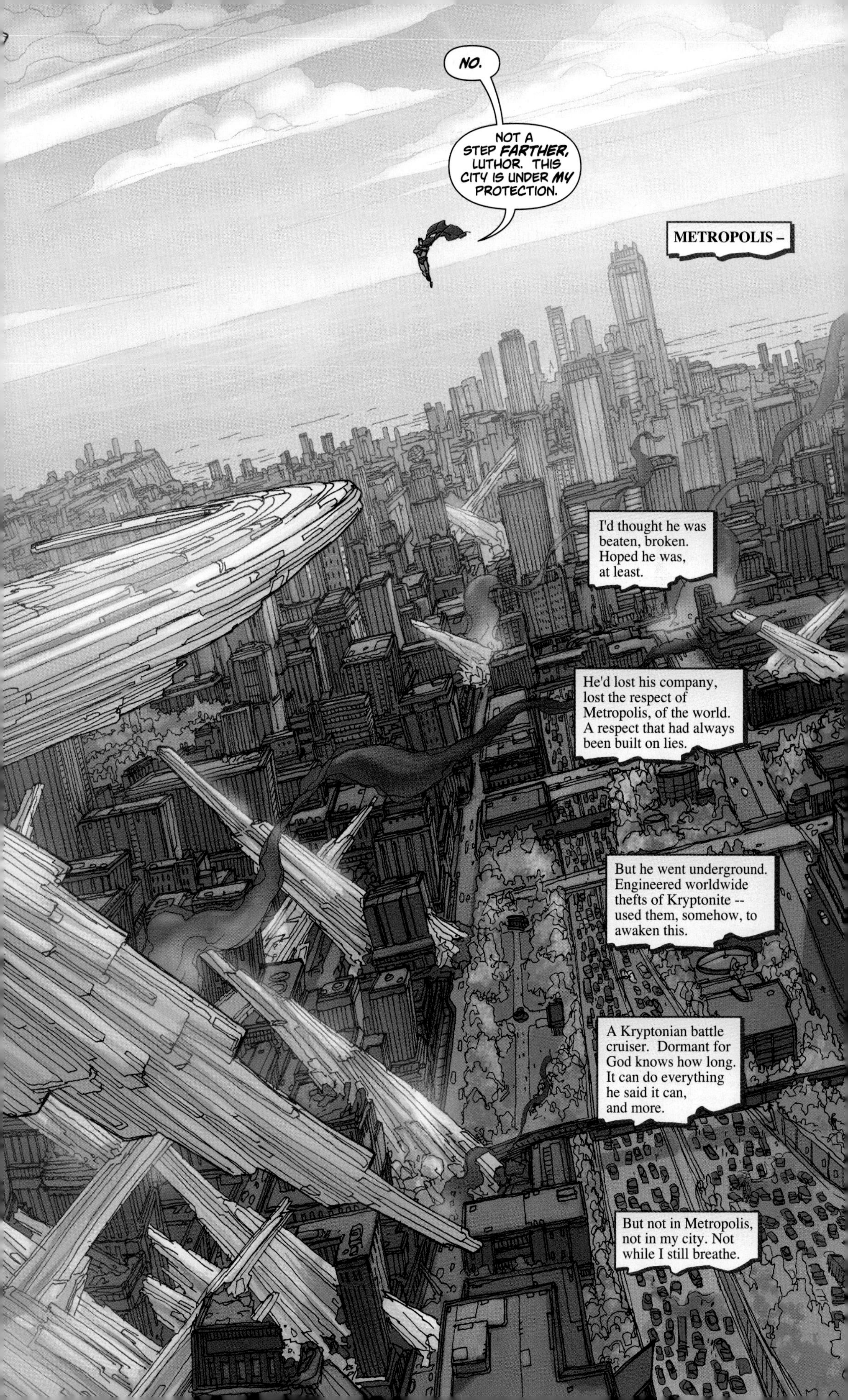
NO.
NOT A STEP FARTHER, LUTHOR. THIS CITY IS UNDER MY PROTECTION.
METROPOLIS –
I'd thought he was beaten, broken. Hoped he was, at least.
He'd lost his company, lost the respect of Metropolis, of the world. A respect that had always been built on lies.
But he went underground. Engineered worldwide thefts of Kryptonite -- used them, somehow, to awaken this.
A Kryptonian battle cruiser. Dormant for God knows how long. It can do everything he said it can, and more.
But not in Metropolis, not in my city. Not while I still breathe.

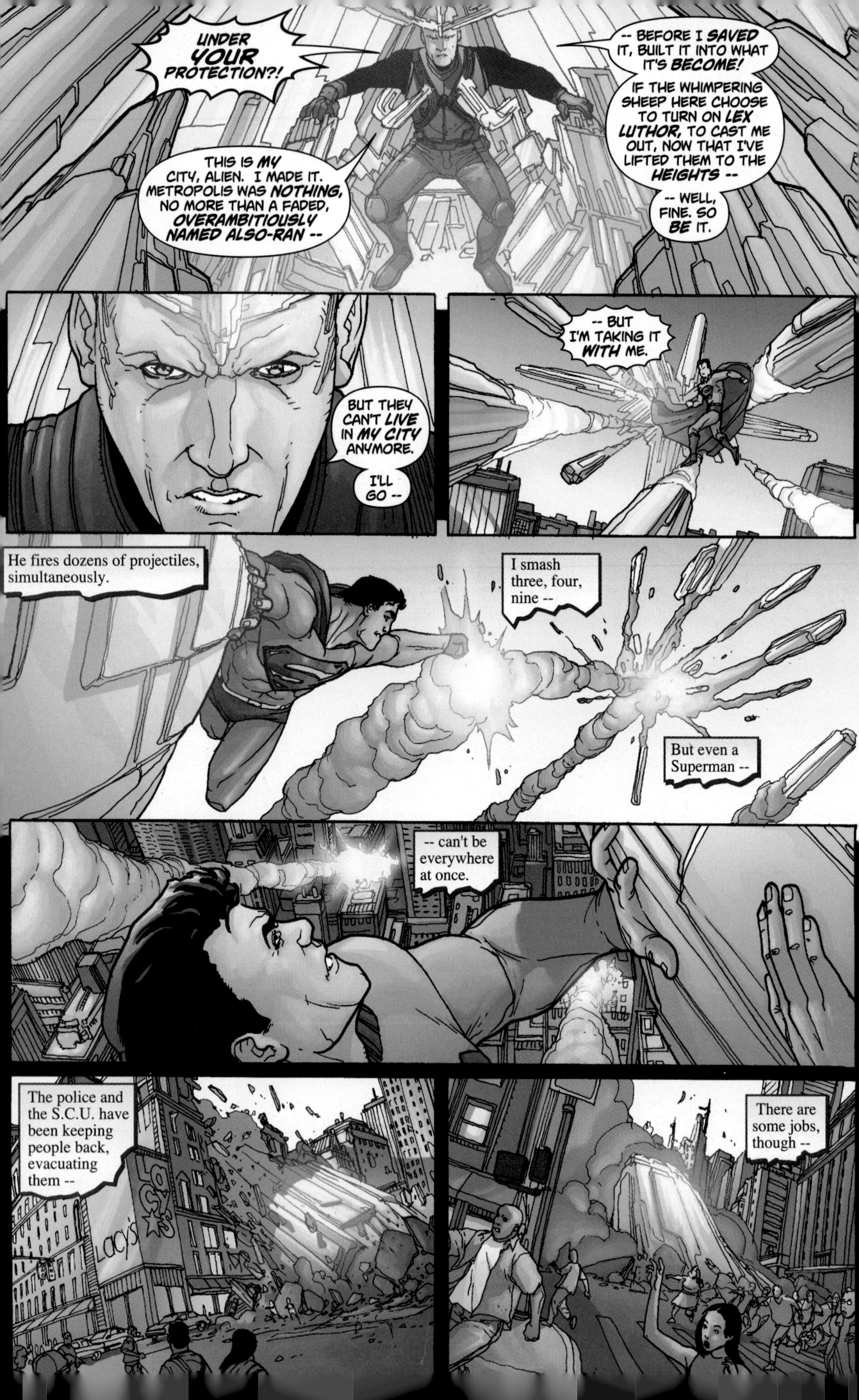
UNDER YOUR PROTECTION?!
THIS IS MY CITY, ALIEN. I MADE IT. METROPOLIS WAS NOTHING, NO MORE THAN A FADED, OVERAMBITIOUSLY NAMED ALSO-RAN --
-- BEFORE I SAVED IT, BUILT IT INTO WHAT IT'S BECOME!
IF THE WHIMPERING SHEEP HERE CHOOSE TO TURN ON LEX LUTHOR, TO CAST ME OUT, NOW THAT I'VE LIFTED THEM TO THE HEIGHTS --
-- WELL, FINE. SO BE IT.
BUT THEY CAN'T LIVE IN MY CITY ANYMORE.
I'LL GO --
-- BUT I'M TAKING IT WITH ME.
He fires dozens of projectiles, simultaneously.
I smash three, four, nine --
But even a Superman --
-- can't be everywhere at once.
The police and the S.C.U. have been keeping people back, evacuating them --
LACY'S
There are some jobs, though --

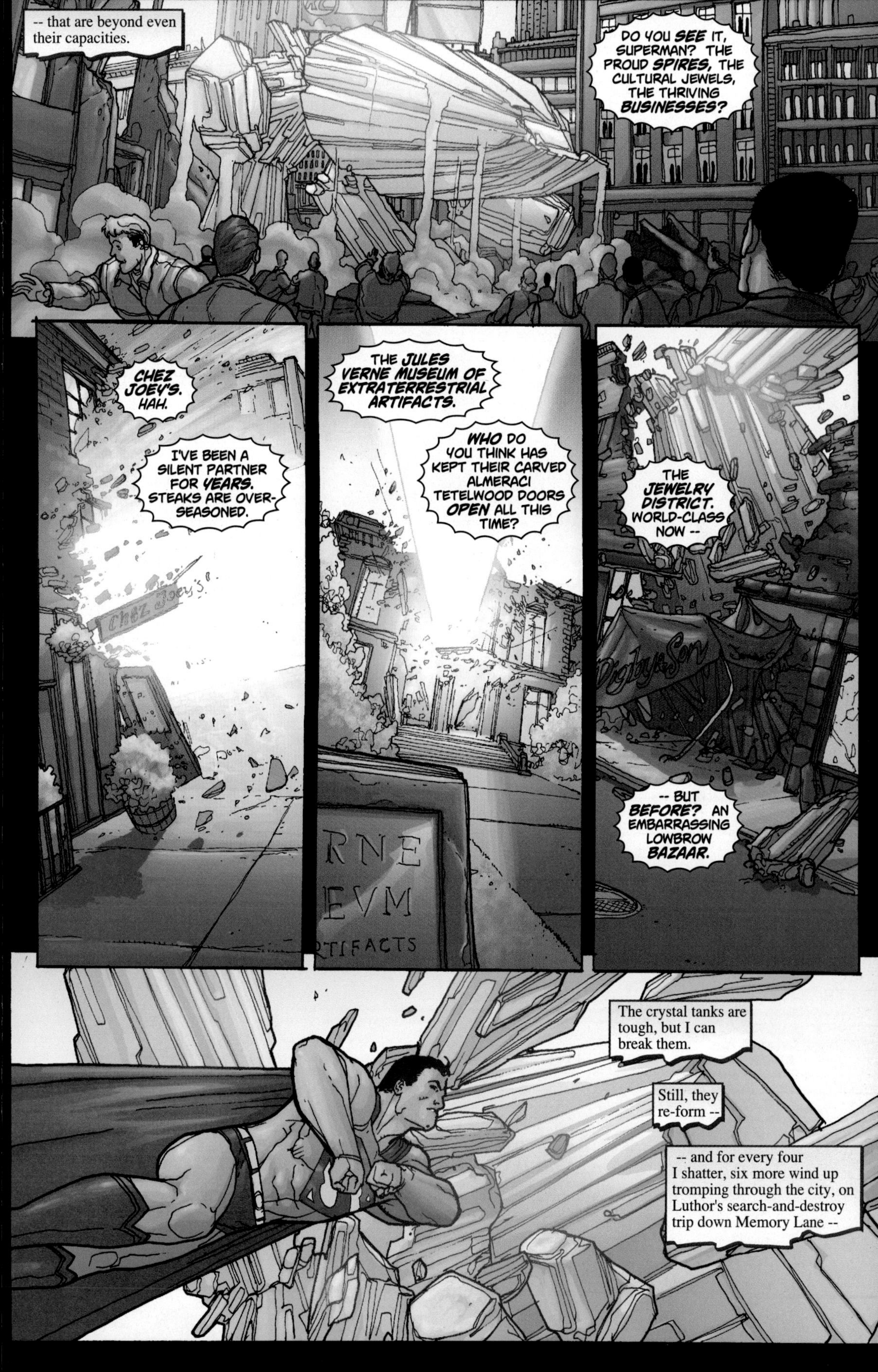

-- that are beyond even their capacities.
DO YOU SEE IT, SUPERMAN? THE PROUD SPIRES, THE CULTURAL JEWELS, THE THRIVING BUSINESSES?
CHEZ JOEY'S. HAH.
I'VE BEEN A SILENT PARTNER FOR YEARS. STEAKS ARE OVER-SEASONED.
Chez Joey's
THE JULES VERNE MUSEUM OF EXTRATERRESTRIAL ARTIFACTS.
WHO DO YOU THINK HAS KEPT THEIR CARVED ALMERACI TETELWOOD DOORS OPEN ALL THIS TIME?
RNE
EVM
TIFACTS
THE JEWELRY DISTRICT. WORLD-CLASS NOW --
-- BUT BEFORE? AN EMBARRASSING LOWBROW BAZAAR.
The crystal tanks are tough, but I can break them.
Still, they re-form --
-- and for every four I shatter, six more wind up tromping through the city, on Luthor's search-and-destroy trip down Memory Lane --

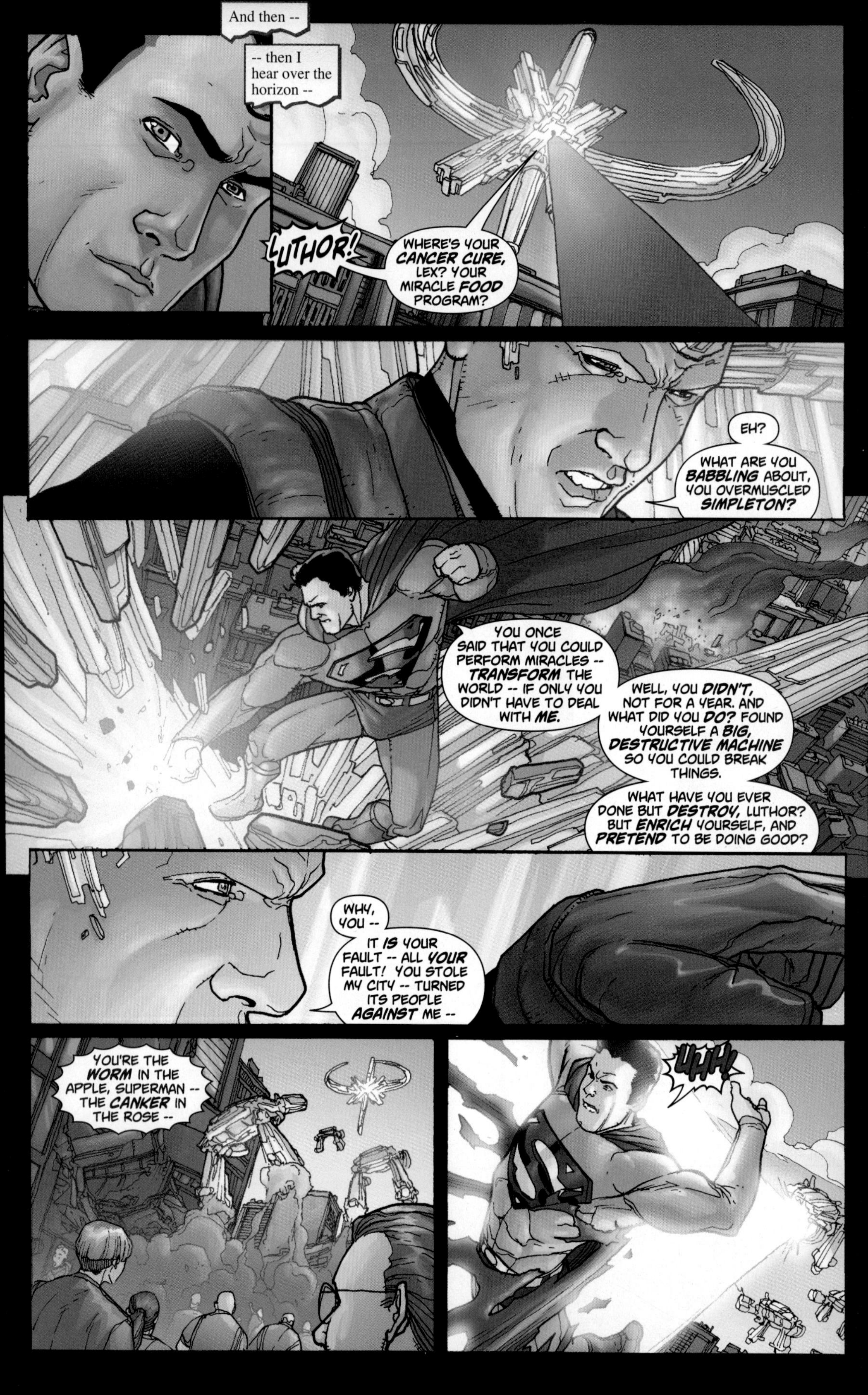

And then --
-- then I hear over the horizon --
LUTHOR!
WHERE'S YOUR CANCER CURE, LEX? YOUR MIRACLE FOOD PROGRAM?
EH?
WHAT ARE YOU BABBLING ABOUT, YOU OVERMUSCLED SIMPLETON?
YOU ONCE SAID THAT YOU COULD PERFORM MIRACLES -- TRANSFORM THE WORLD -- IF ONLY YOU DIDN'T HAVE TO DEAL WITH ME.
WELL, YOU DIDN'T, NOT FOR A YEAR. AND WHAT DID YOU DO? FOUND YOURSELF A BIG, DESTRUCTIVE MACHINE SO YOU COULD BREAK THINGS.
WHAT HAVE YOU EVER DONE BUT DESTROY, LUTHOR? BUT ENRICH YOURSELF, AND PRETEND TO BE DOING GOOD?
WHY, YOU --
IT IS YOUR FAULT -- ALL YOUR FAULT! YOU STOLE MY CITY -- TURNED ITS PEOPLE AGAINST ME --
YOU'RE THE WORM IN THE APPLE, SUPERMAN -- THE CANKER IN THE ROSE --
UHH!

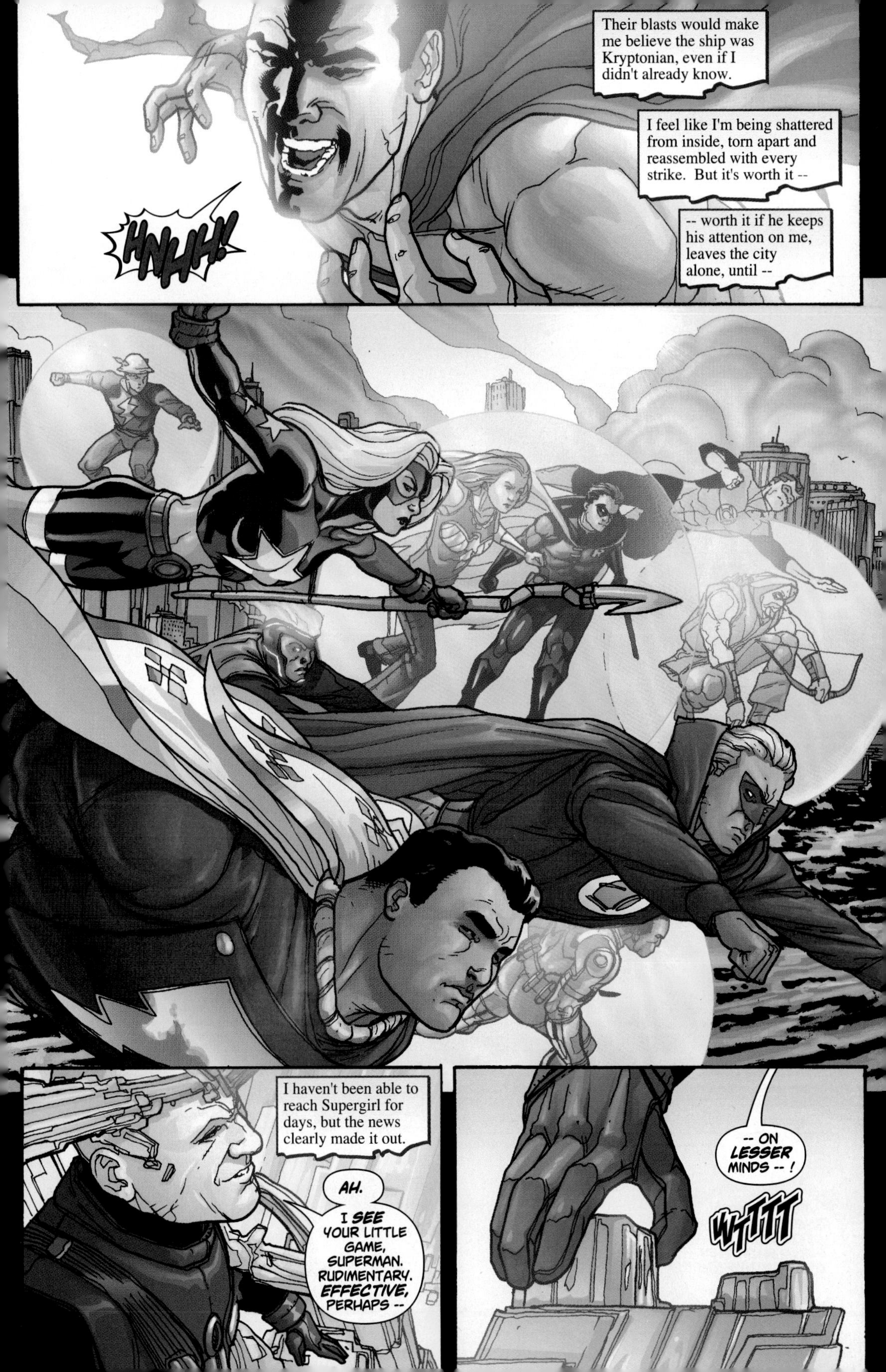
Their blasts would make me believe the ship was Kryptonian, even if I didn't already know.
I feel like I'm being shattered from inside, torn apart and reassembled with every strike. But it's worth it --
-- worth it if he keeps his attention on me, leaves the city alone, until --
HNUH!
I haven't been able to reach Supergirl for days, but the news clearly made it out.
AH.
I SEE YOUR LITTLE GAME, SUPERMAN. RUDIMENTARY. EFFECTIVE, PERHAPS --
-- ON LESSER MINDS -- !
WTTTT

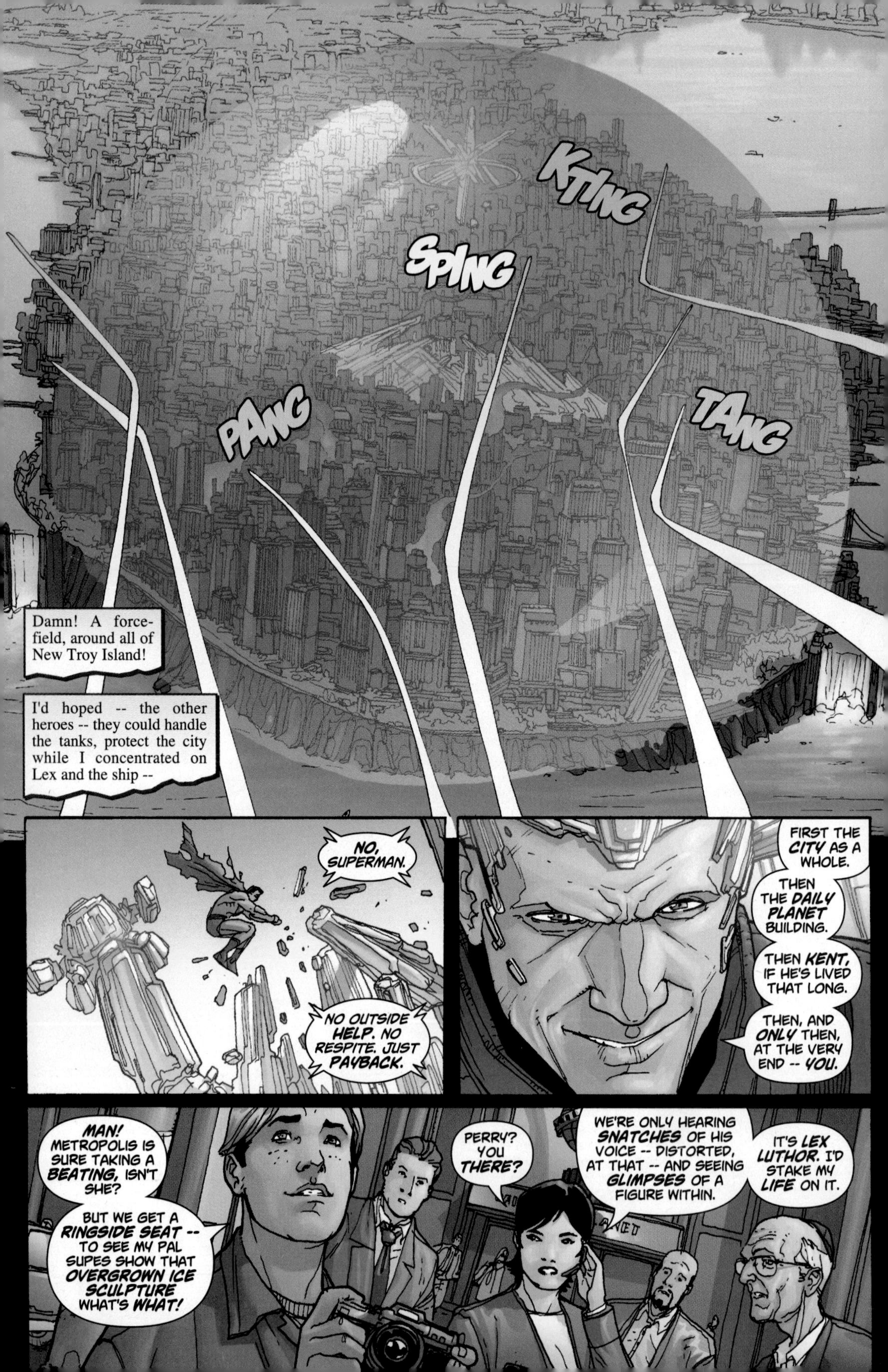
KTING
SPING
PANG
TANG
Damn! A force-field, around all of New Troy Island!
I'd hoped -- the other heroes -- they could handle the tanks, protect the city while I concentrated on Lex and the ship --
NO, SUPERMAN.
NO OUTSIDE HELP. NO RESPITE. JUST PAYBACK.
FIRST THE CITY AS A WHOLE.
THEN THE DAILY PLANET BUILDING.
THEN KENT, IF HE'S LIVED THAT LONG.
THEN, AND ONLY THEN, AT THE VERY END -- YOU.
MAN! METROPOLIS IS SURE TAKING A BEATING, ISN'T SHE?
BUT WE GET A RINGSIDE SEAT -- TO SEE MY PAL SUPES SHOW THAT OVERGROWN ICE SCULPTURE WHAT'S WHAT!
PERRY? YOU THERE?
WE'RE ONLY HEARING SNATCHES OF HIS VOICE -- DISTORTED, AT THAT -- AND SEEING GLIMPSES OF A FIGURE WITHIN.
IT'S LEX LUTHOR. I'D STAKE MY LIFE ON IT.

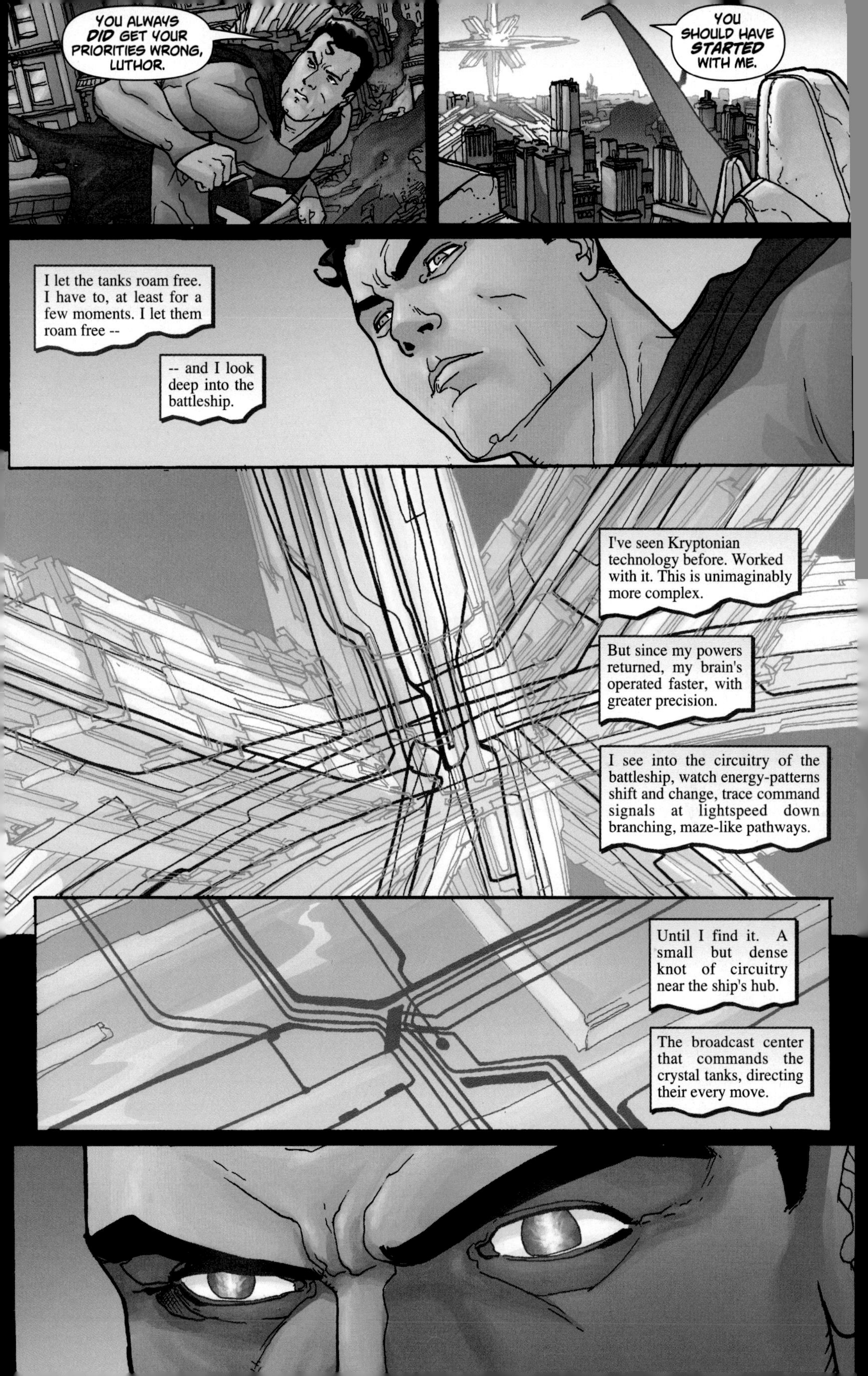
YOU ALWAYS DID GET YOUR PRIORITIES WRONG, LUTHOR.
YOU SHOULD HAVE STARTED WITH ME.
I let the tanks roam free. I have to, at least for a few moments. I let them roam free --
-- and I look deep into the battleship.
I've seen Kryptonian technology before. Worked with it. This is unimaginably more complex.
But since my powers returned, my brain's operated faster, with greater precision.
I see into the circuitry of the battleship, watch energy-patterns shift and change, trace command signals at lightspeed down branching, maze-like pathways.
Until I find it. A small but dense knot of circuitry near the ship's hub.
The broadcast center that commands the crystal tanks, directing their every move.

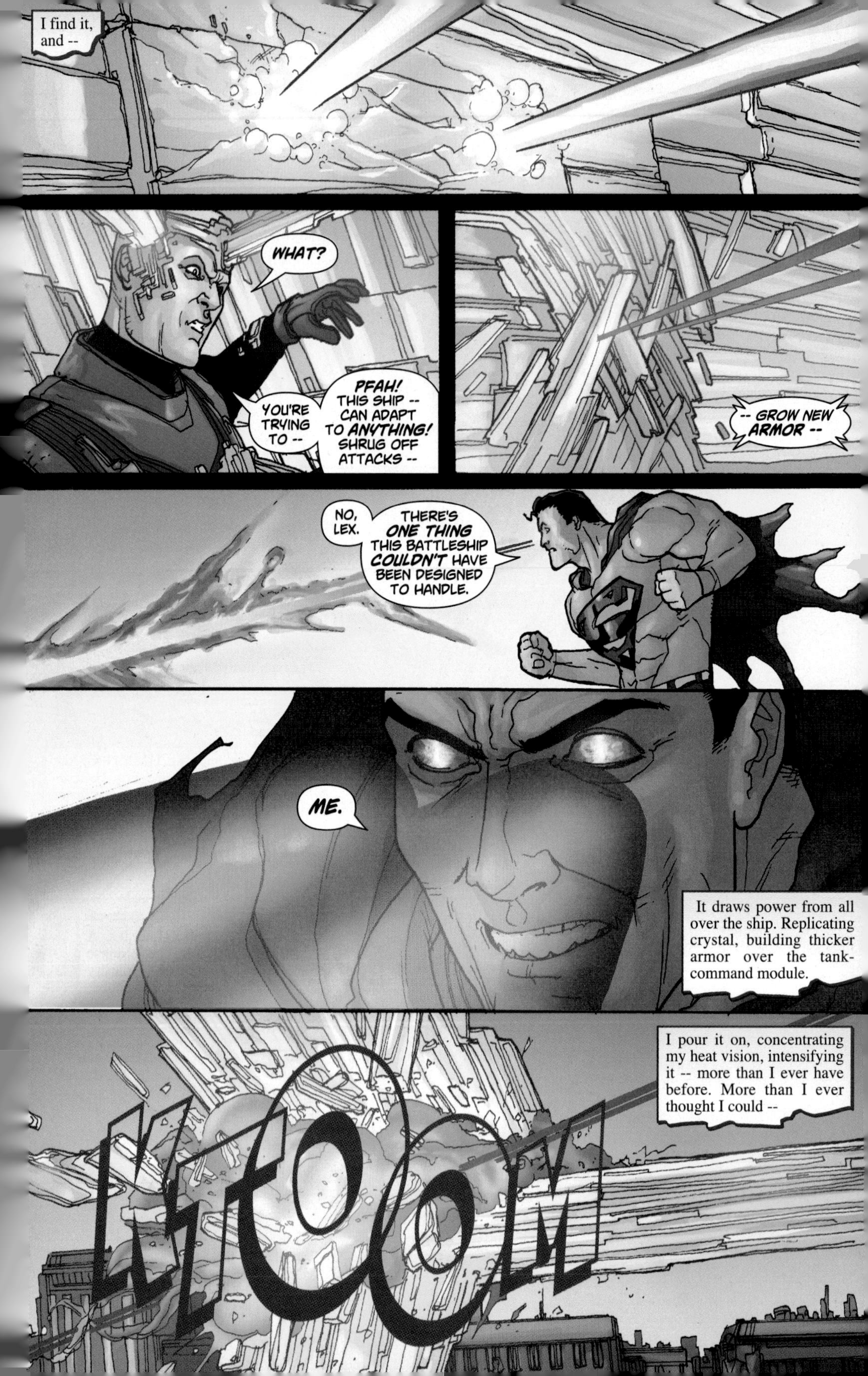
I find it, and --
WHAT?
YOU'RE TRYING TO --
PFAH! THIS SHIP -- CAN ADAPT TO ANYTHING! SHRUG OFF ATTACKS --
-- GROW NEW ARMOR --
NO, LEX.
THERE'S ONE THING THIS BATTLESHIP COULDN'T HAVE BEEN DESIGNED TO HANDLE.
ME.
It draws power from all over the ship. Replicating crystal, building thicker armor over the tank-command module.
I pour it on, concentrating my heat vision, intensifying it -- more than I ever have before. More than I ever thought I could --
KTCOOM

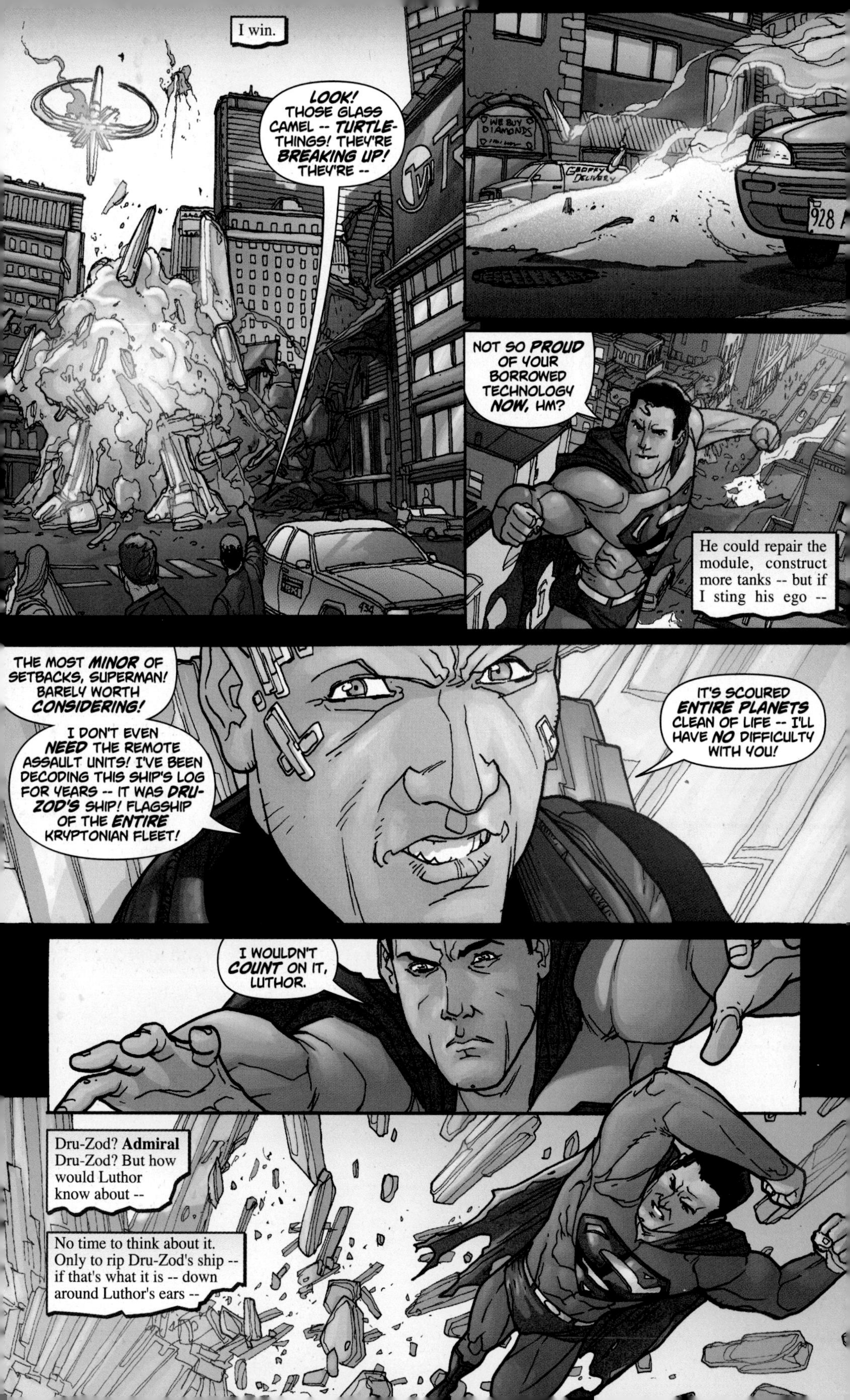
I win.
LOOK! THOSE GLASS CAMEL -- TURTLE-THINGS! THEY'RE BREAKING UP! THEY'RE --
NOT SO PROUD OF YOUR BORROWED TECHNOLOGY NOW, HM?
He could repair the module, construct more tanks -- but if I sting his ego --
THE MOST MINOR OF SETBACKS, SUPERMAN! BARELY WORTH CONSIDERING!
I DON'T EVEN NEED THE REMOTE ASSAULT UNITS! I'VE BEEN DECODING THIS SHIP'S LOG FOR YEARS -- IT WAS DRU-ZOD'S SHIP! FLAGSHIP OF THE ENTIRE KRYPTONIAN FLEET!
IT'S SCOURED ENTIRE PLANETS CLEAN OF LIFE -- I'LL HAVE NO DIFFICULTY WITH YOU!
I WOULDN'T COUNT ON IT, LUTHOR.
Dru-Zod? Admiral Dru-Zod? But how would Luthor know about --
No time to think about it. Only to rip Dru-Zod's ship -- if that's what it is -- down around Luthor's ears --

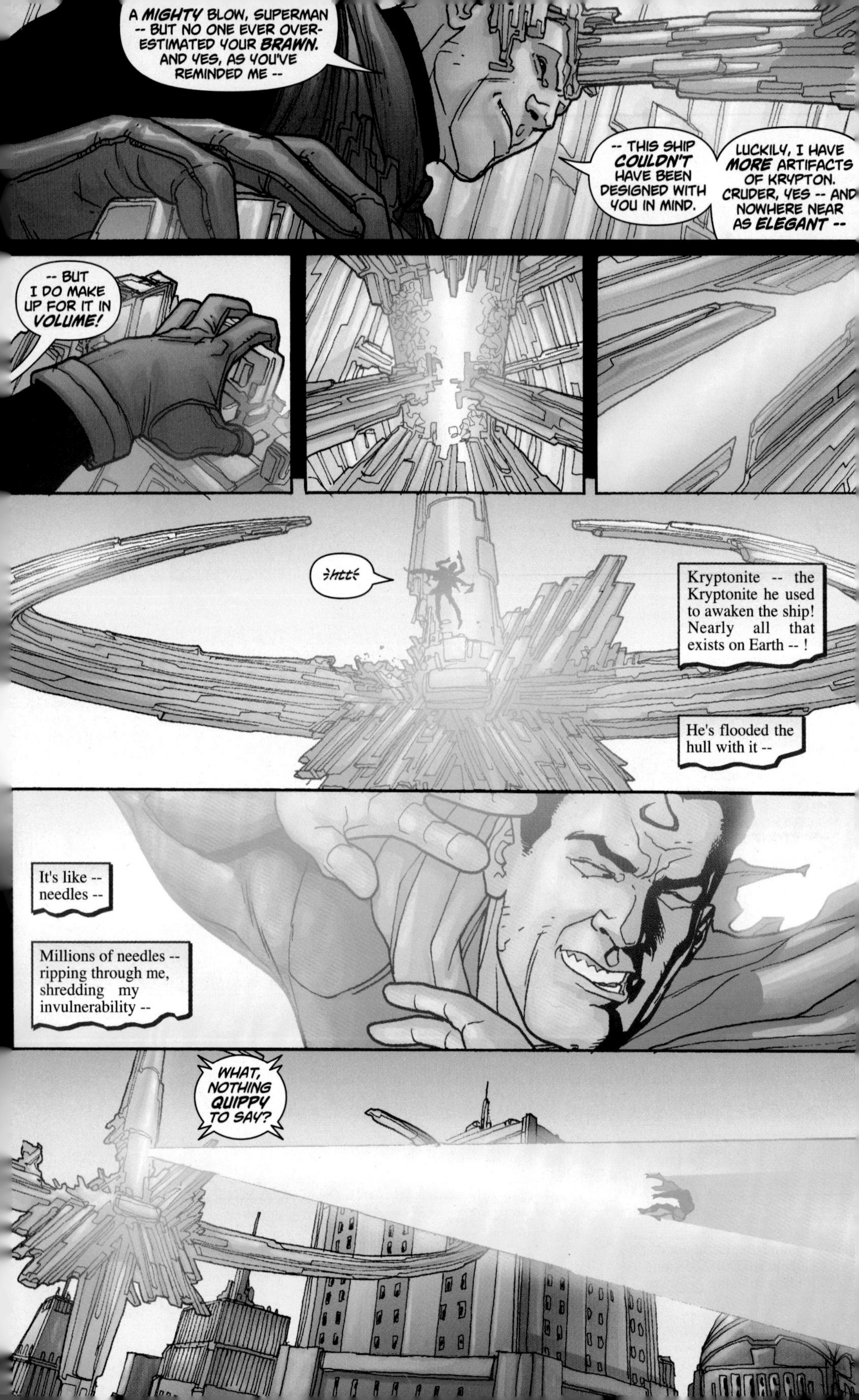
A MIGHTY BLOW, SUPERMAN -- BUT NO ONE EVER OVER-ESTIMATED YOUR BRAWN. AND YES, AS YOU'VE REMINDED ME --
-- THIS SHIP COULDN'T HAVE BEEN DESIGNED WITH YOU IN MIND.
LUCKILY, I HAVE MORE ARTIFACTS OF KRYPTON. CRUDER, YES -- AND NOWHERE NEAR AS ELEGANT --
-- BUT I DO MAKE UP FOR IT IN VOLUME!
HTT
Kryptonite -- the Kryptonite he used to awaken the ship! Nearly all that exists on Earth -- !
He's flooded the hull with it --
It's like -- needles --
Millions of needles -- ripping through me, shredding my invulnerability --
WHAT, NOTHING QUIPPY TO SAY?

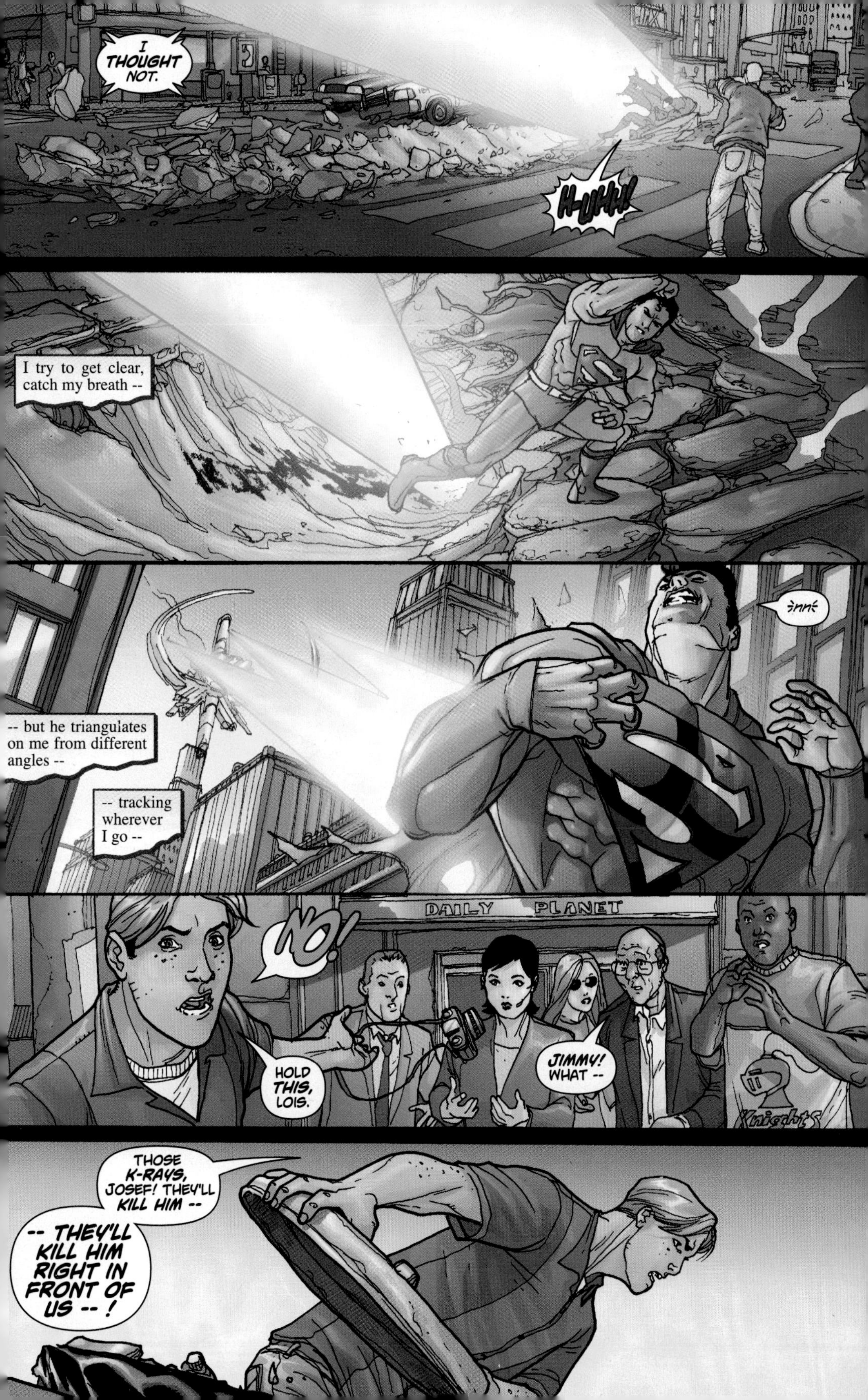

I THOUGHT NOT.
H-UHH!
I try to get clear, catch my breath --
-- but he triangulates on me from different angles --
-- tracking wherever I go --
nnn
DAILY PLANET
NO!
HOLD THIS, LOIS.
JIMMY! WHAT --
Knights
THOSE K-RAYS, JOSEF! THEY'LL KILL HIM --
-- THEY'LL KILL HIM RIGHT IN FRONT OF US -- !

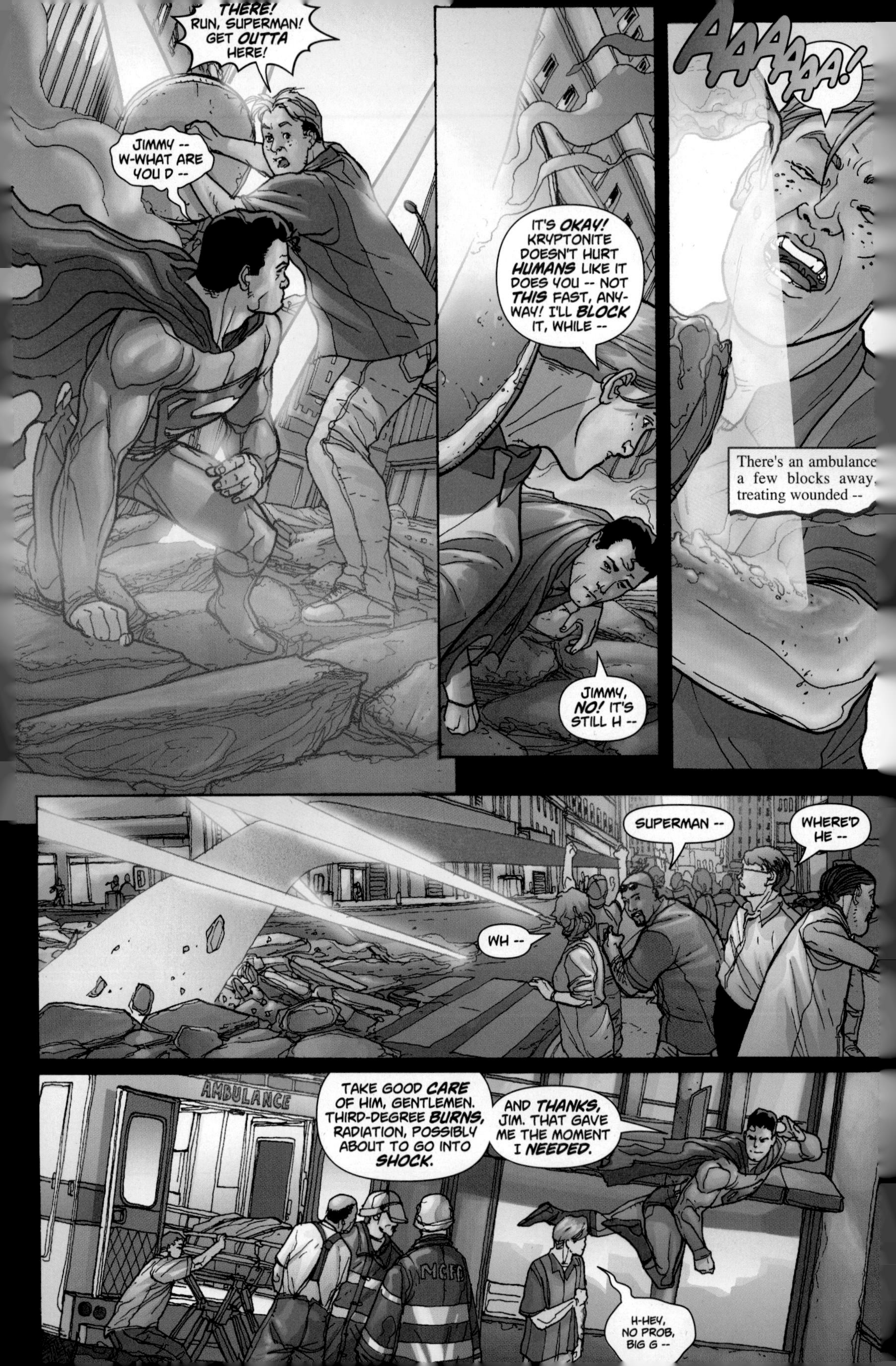
THERE! RUN, SUPERMAN! GET OUTTA HERE!
JIMMY -- W-WHAT ARE YOU D --
IT'S OKAY! KRYPTONITE DOESN'T HURT HUMANS LIKE IT DOES YOU -- NOT THIS FAST, ANYWAY! I'LL BLOCK IT, WHILE --
JIMMY, NO! IT'S STILL H --
AAAAAA!
There's an ambulance a few blocks away, treating wounded --
SUPERMAN --
WHERE'D HE --
WH --
AMBULANCE
TAKE GOOD CARE OF HIM, GENTLEMEN. THIRD-DEGREE BURNS, RADIATION, POSSIBLY ABOUT TO GO INTO SHOCK.
AND THANKS, JIM. THAT GAVE ME THE MOMENT I NEEDED.
H-HEY, NO PROB, BIG G --
MCFD

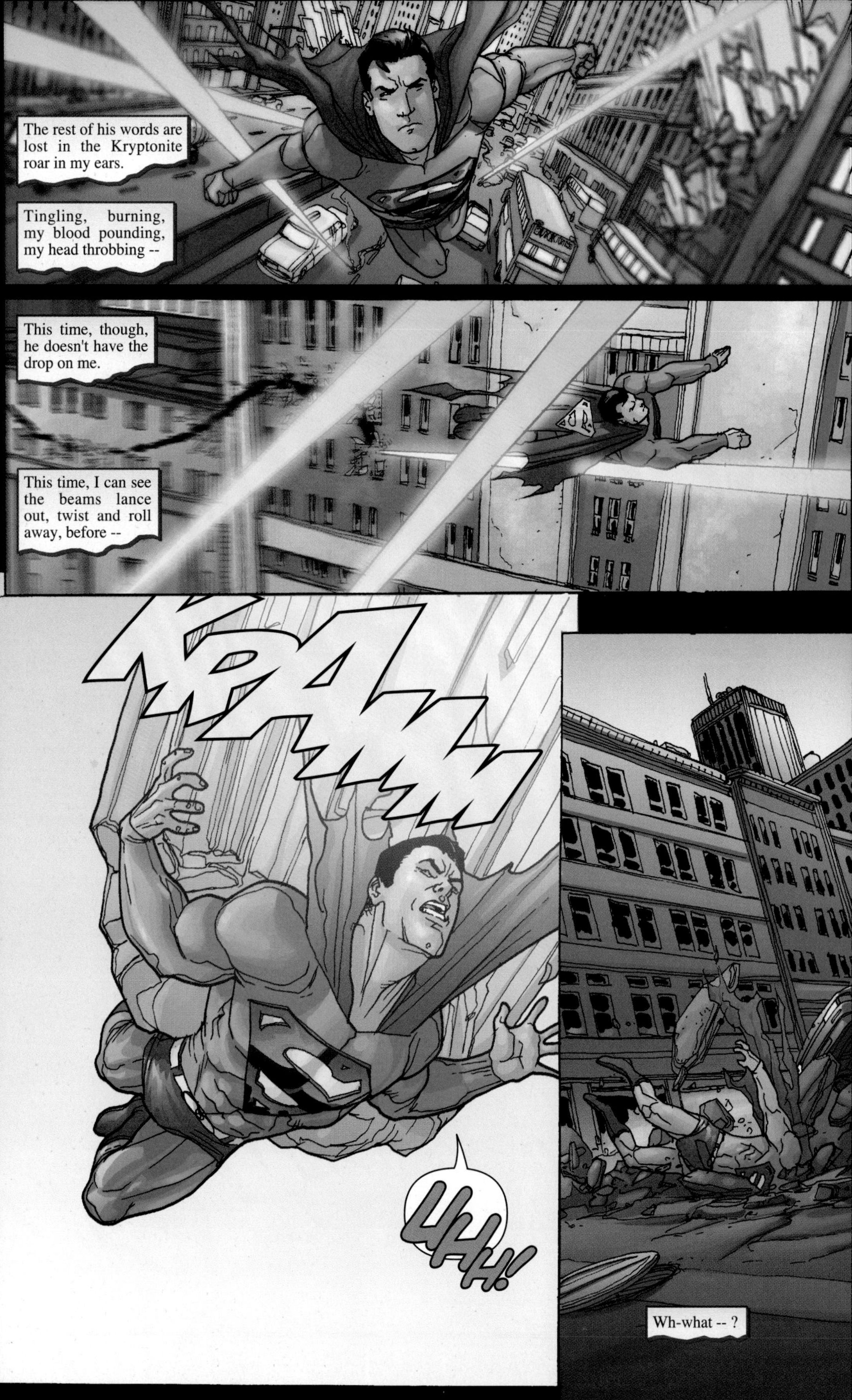

The rest of his words are lost in the Kryptonite roar in my ears.
Tingling, burning, my blood pounding, my head throbbing --
This time, though, he doesn't have the drop on me.
This time, I can see the beams lance out, twist and roll away, before --
KRAAM
UHH!
Wh-what -- ?

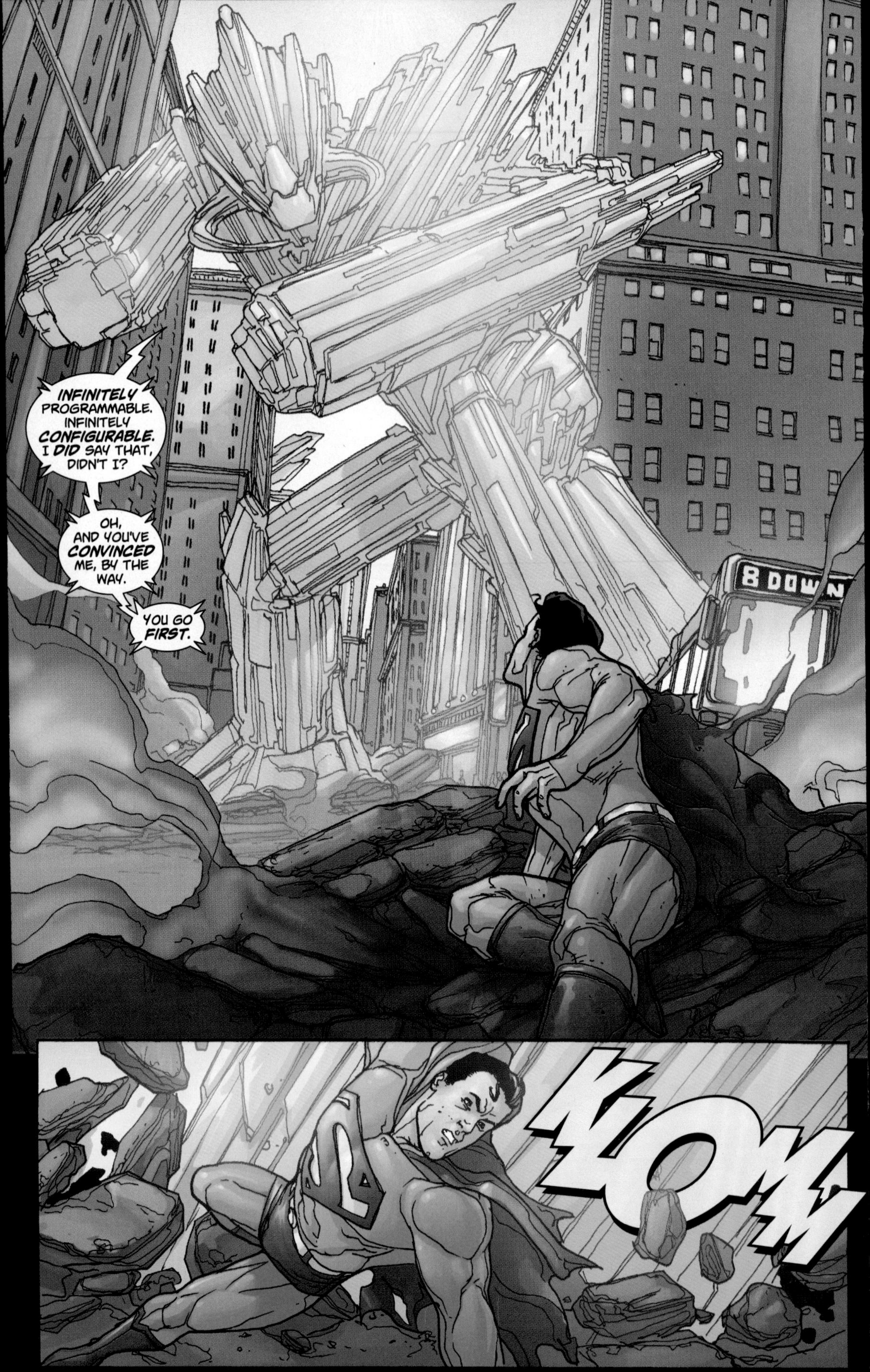
INFINITELY PROGRAMMABLE. INFINITELY CONFIGURABLE. I DID SAY THAT, DIDN'T I?
OH, AND YOU'VE CONVINCED ME, BY THE WAY.
YOU GO FIRST.
8 DOWN
KLOM

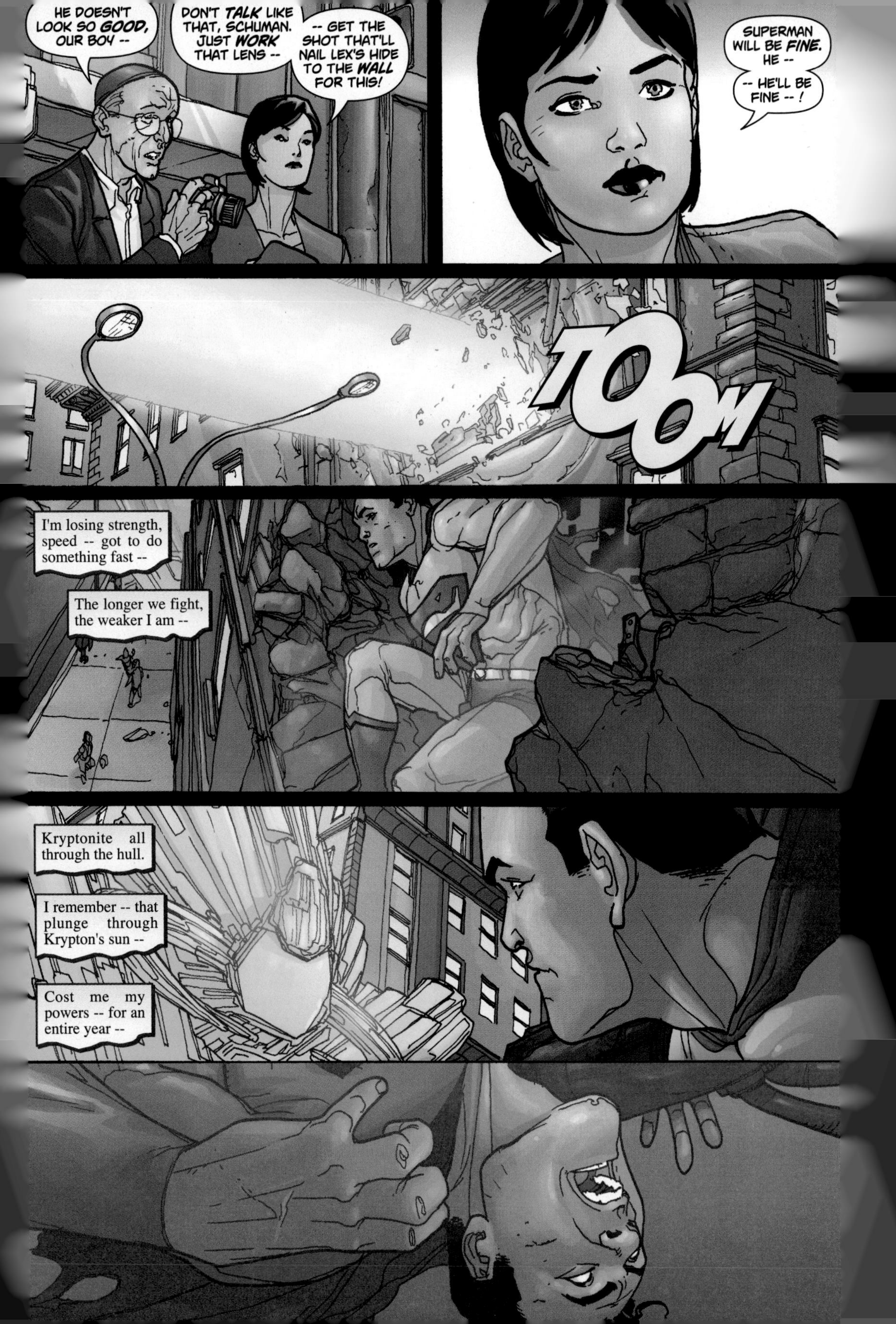
HE DOESN'T LOOK SO GOOD, OUR BOY --
DON'T TALK LIKE THAT, SCHUMAN. JUST WORK THAT LENS --
-- GET THE SHOT THAT'LL NAIL LEX'S HIDE TO THE WALL FOR THIS!
SUPERMAN WILL BE FINE. HE --
-- HE'LL BE FINE -- !
TOOOM
I'm losing strength, speed -- got to do something fast --
The longer we fight, the weaker I am --
Kryptonite all through the hull.
I remember -- that plunge through Krypton's sun --
Cost me my powers -- for an entire year --

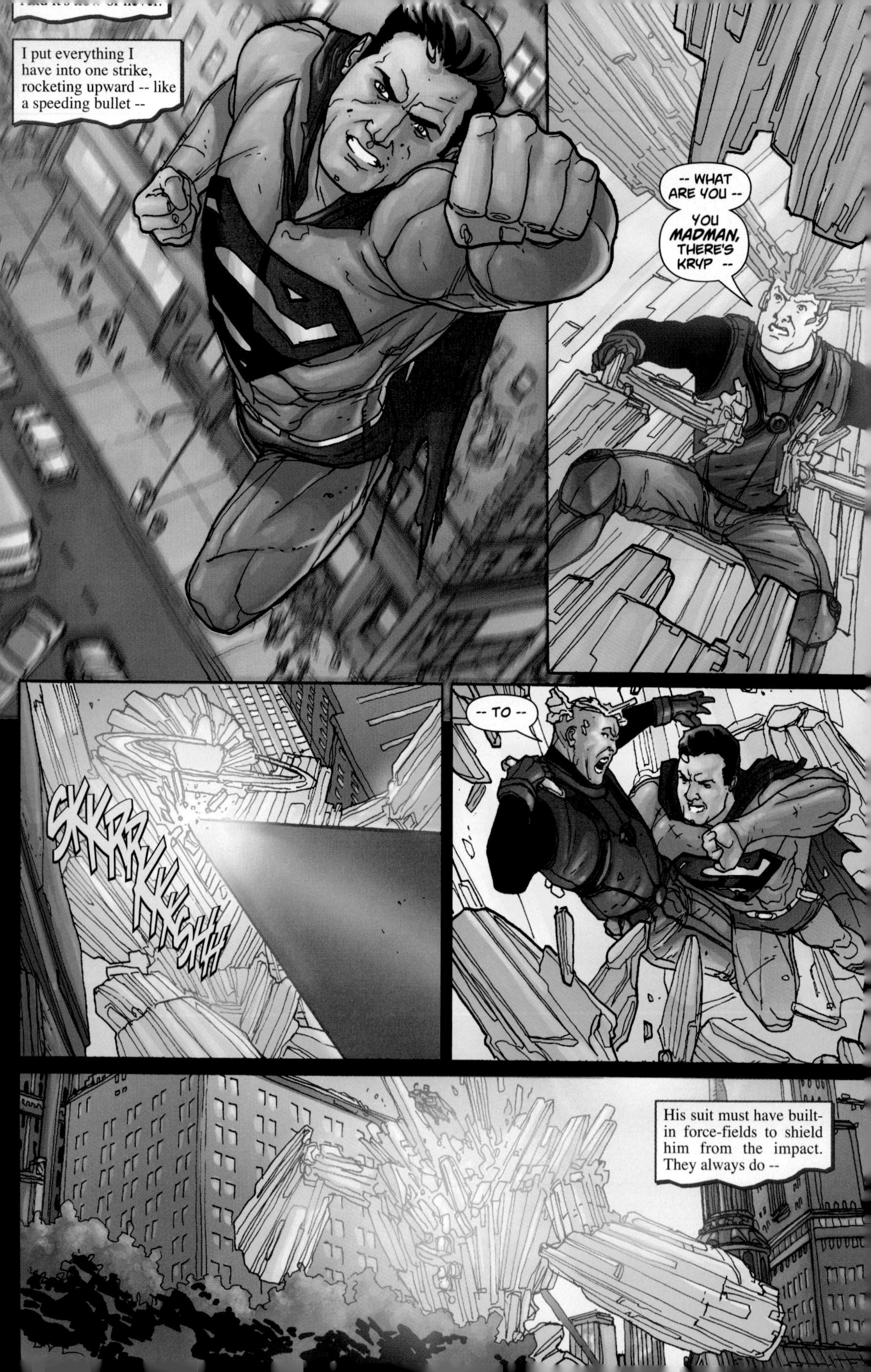
I put everything I have into one strike, rocketing upward -- like a speeding bullet --
-- WHAT ARE YOU --
YOU MADMAN, THERE'S KRYP --
-- TO --
His suit must have built-in force-fields to shield him from the impact. They always do --

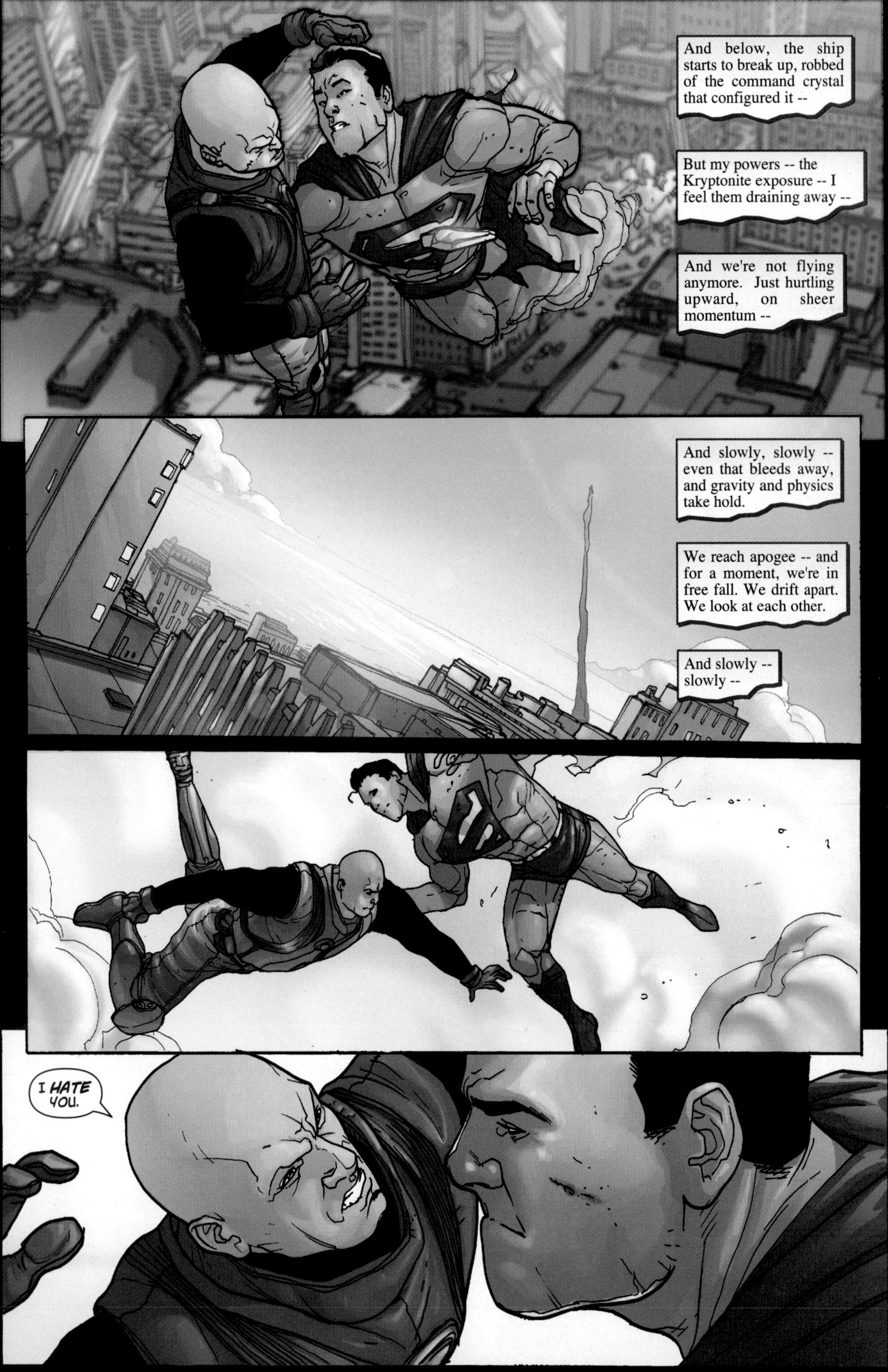

And below, the ship starts to break up, robbed of the command crystal that configured it --
But my powers -- the Kryptonite exposure -- I feel them draining away --
And we're not flying anymore. Just hurtling upward, on sheer momentum --
And slowly, slowly -- even that bleeds away, and gravity and physics take hold.
We reach apogee -- and for a moment, we're in free fall. We drift apart. We look at each other.
And slowly -- slowly --
I HATE YOU.

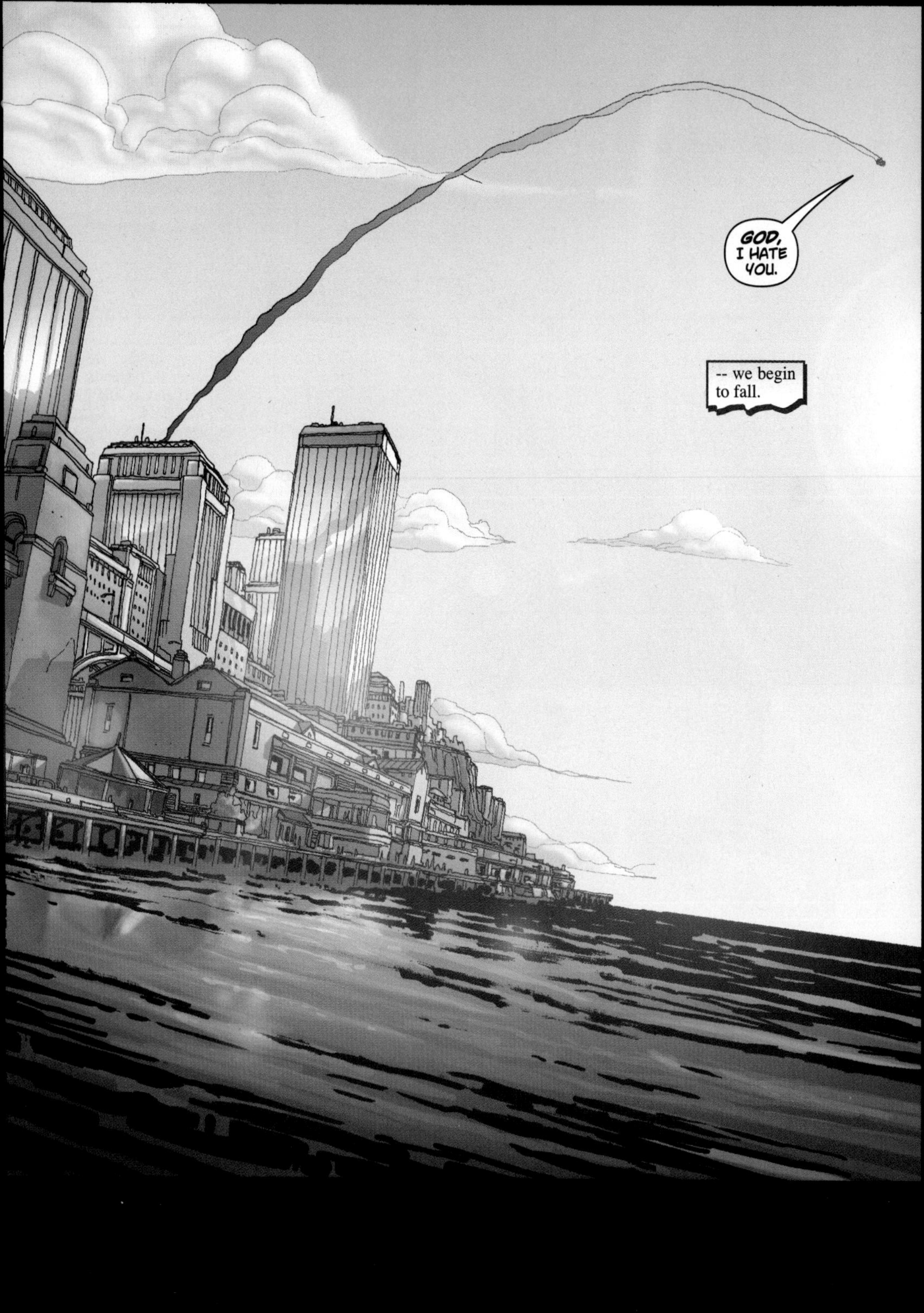
GOD, I HATE YOU.
-- we begin to fall.

Art by: Pete Woods

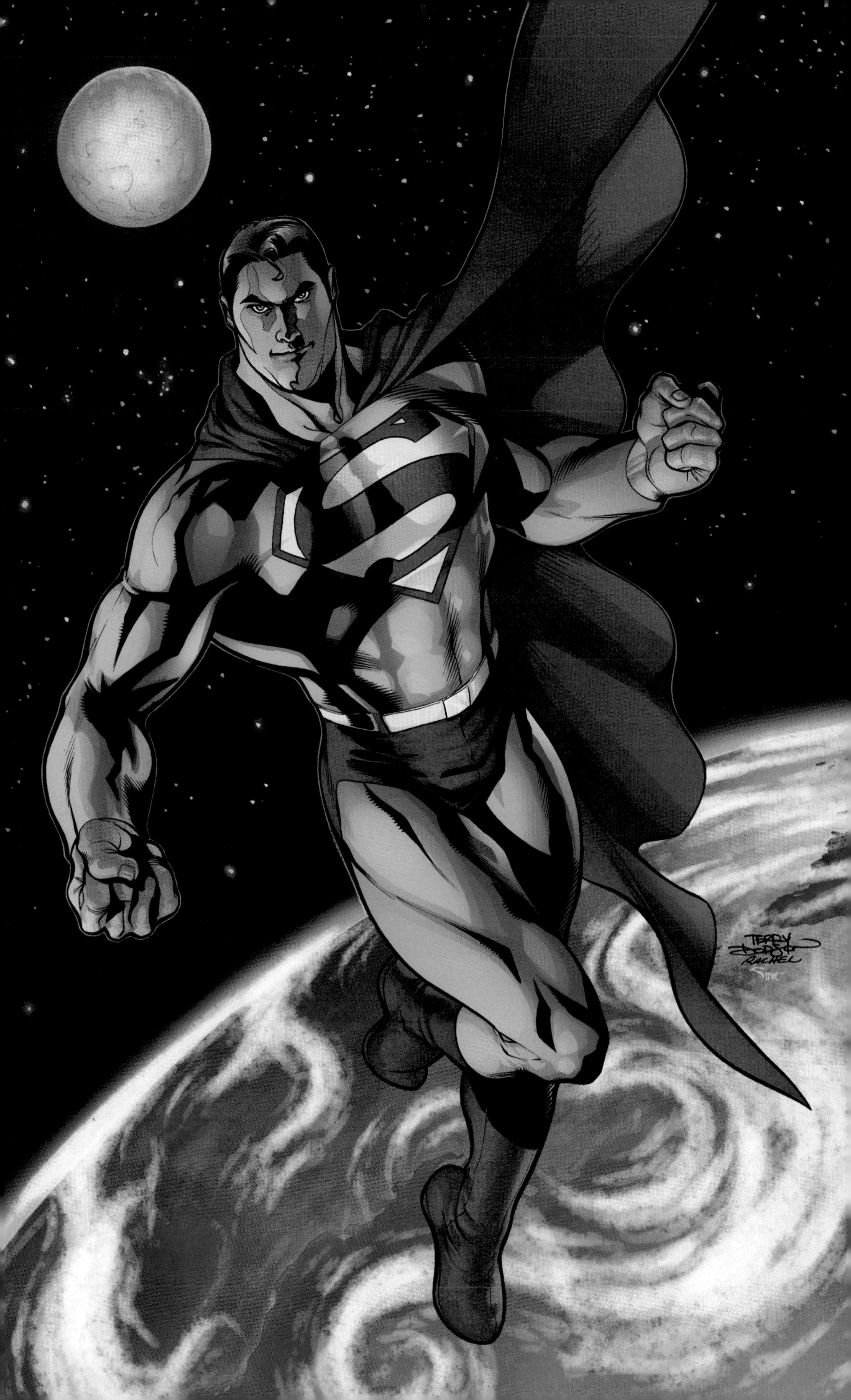

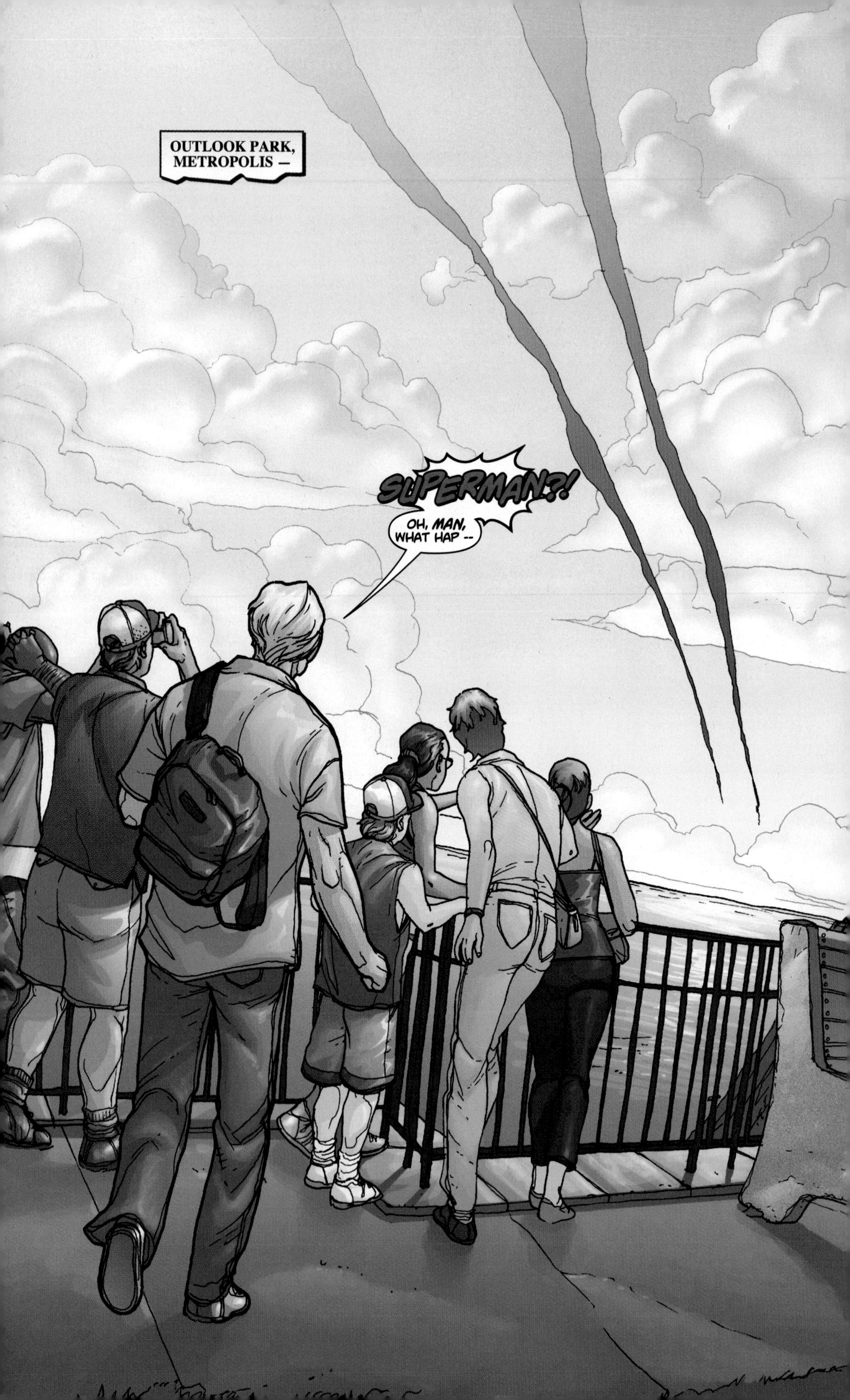
OUTLOOK PARK, METROPOLIS —
SUPERMAN?!
OH, MAN, WHAT HAP --

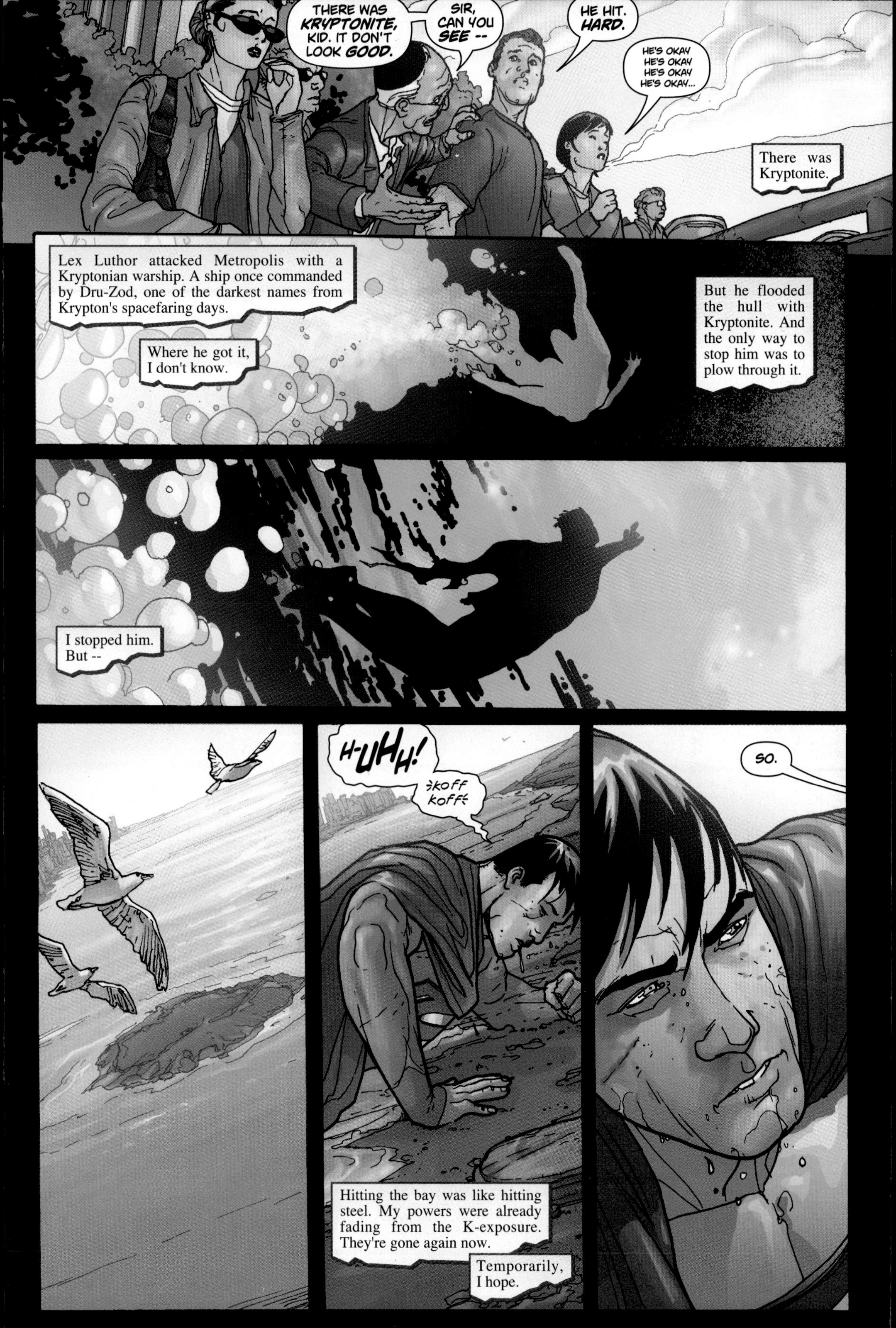
THERE WAS KRYPTONITE, KID. IT DON'T LOOK GOOD.
SIR, CAN YOU SEE --
HE HIT. HARD.
HE'S OKAY HE'S OKAY HE'S OKAY HE'S OKAY...
There was Kryptonite.
Lex Luthor attacked Metropolis with a Kryptonian warship. A ship once commanded by Dru-Zod, one of the darkest names from Krypton's spacefaring days.
Where he got it, I don't know.
But he flooded the hull with Kryptonite. And the only way to stop him was to plow through it.
I stopped him. But --
H-UHH!
KOFF KOFF
Hitting the bay was like hitting steel. My powers were already fading from the K-exposure. They're gone again now.
Temporarily, I hope.
SO.

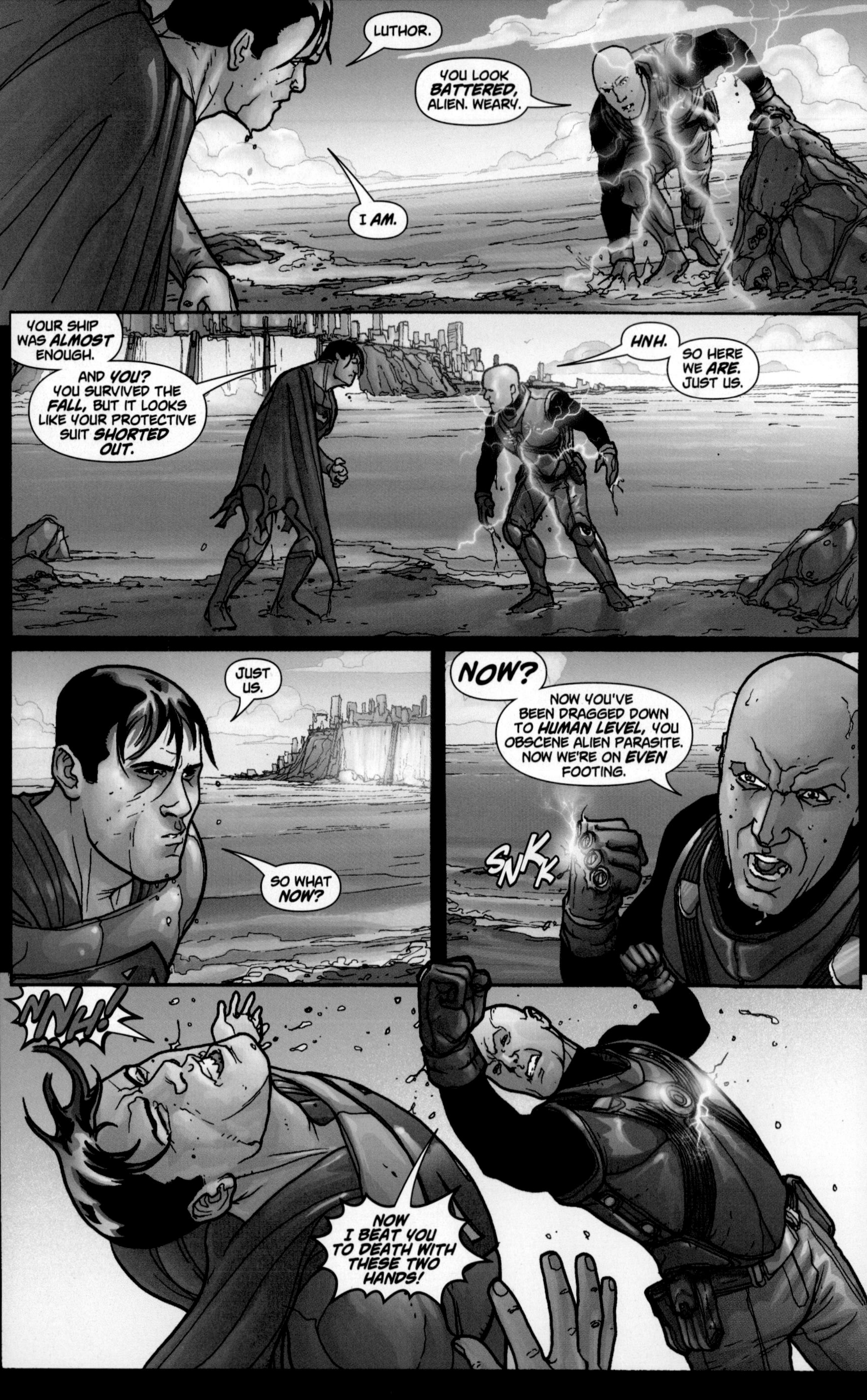
LUTHOR.
YOU LOOK BATTERED, ALIEN. WEARY.
I AM.
YOUR SHIP WAS ALMOST ENOUGH.
AND YOU? YOU SURVIVED THE FALL, BUT IT LOOKS LIKE YOUR PROTECTIVE SUIT SHORTED OUT.
HNH.
SO HERE WE ARE. JUST US.
JUST US.
SO WHAT NOW?
NOW?
NOW YOU'VE BEEN DRAGGED DOWN TO HUMAN LEVEL, YOU OBSCENE ALIEN PARASITE. NOW WE'RE ON EVEN FOOTING.
SNKK
NNH!
NOW I BEAT YOU TO DEATH WITH THESE TWO HANDS!

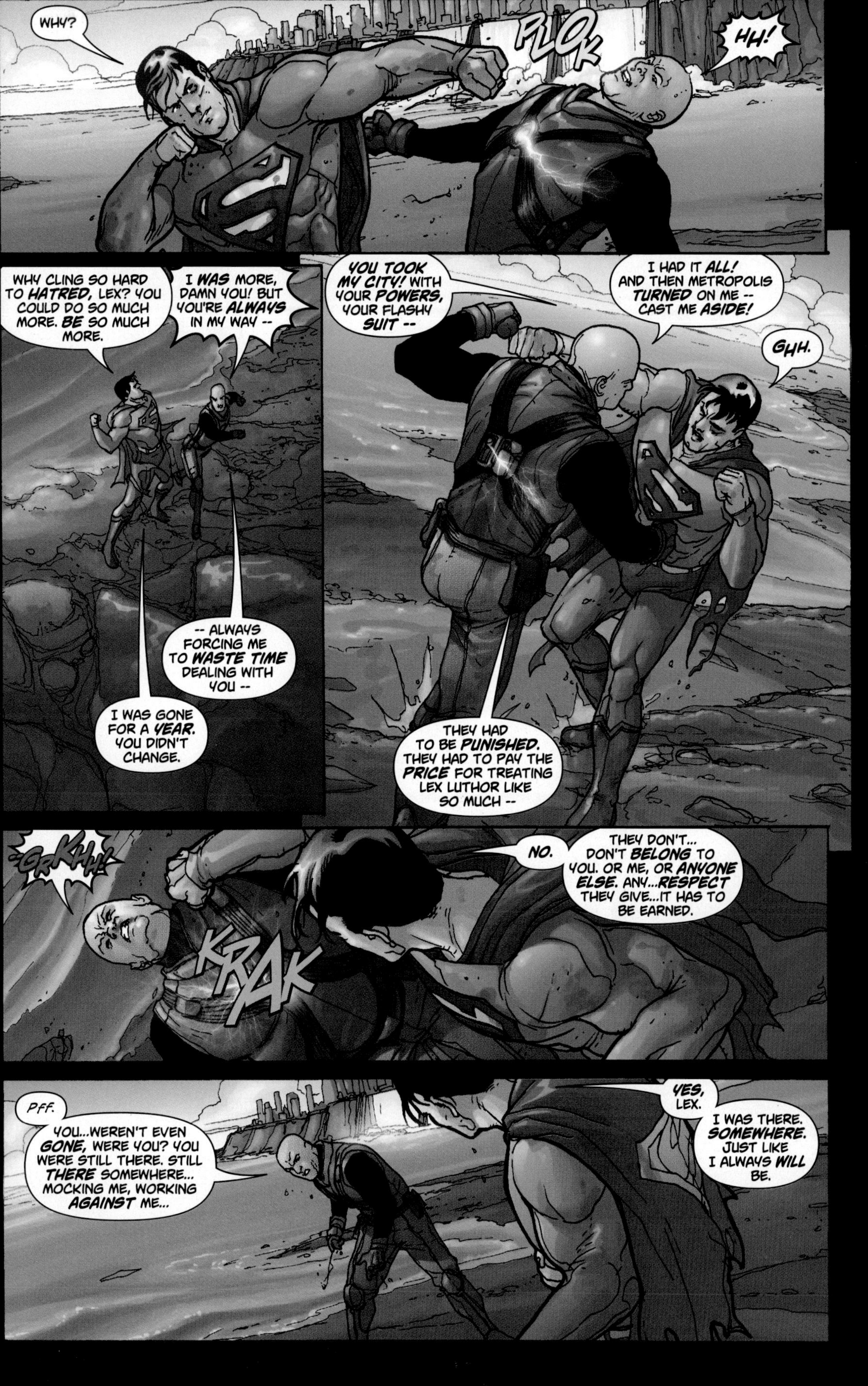
WHY?
FLOK
HH!
WHY CLING SO HARD TO HATRED, LEX? YOU COULD DO SO MUCH MORE. BE SO MUCH MORE.
I WAS MORE, DAMN YOU! BUT YOU'RE ALWAYS IN MY WAY --
-- ALWAYS FORCING ME TO WASTE TIME DEALING WITH YOU --
I WAS GONE FOR A YEAR. YOU DIDN'T CHANGE.
YOU TOOK MY CITY! WITH YOUR POWERS, YOUR FLASHY SUIT --
I HAD IT ALL! AND THEN METROPOLIS TURNED ON ME -- CAST ME ASIDE!
GHH.
THEY HAD TO BE PUNISHED. THEY HAD TO PAY THE PRICE FOR TREATING LEX LUTHOR LIKE SO MUCH --
GRKHH!
KRAK
NO.
THEY DON'T... DON'T BELONG TO YOU. OR ME, OR ANYONE ELSE. ANY...RESPECT THEY GIVE...IT HAS TO BE EARNED.
PFF.
YOU...WEREN'T EVEN GONE, WERE YOU? YOU WERE STILL THERE. STILL THERE SOMEWHERE... MOCKING ME, WORKING AGAINST ME...
YES, LEX.
I WAS THERE. SOMEWHERE. JUST LIKE I ALWAYS WILL BE.

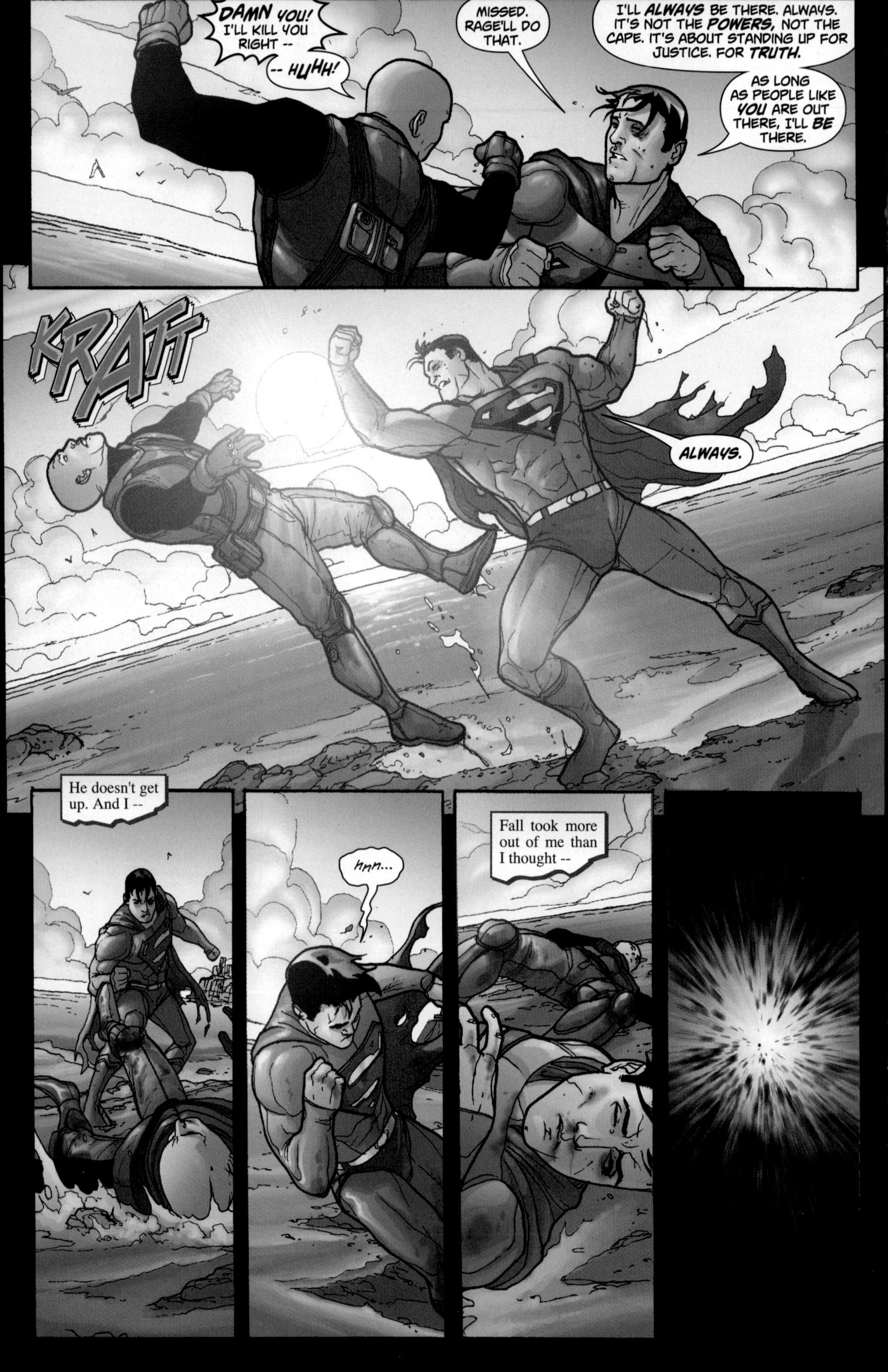
DAMN YOU! I'LL KILL YOU RIGHT --
-- HUHH!
MISSED. RAGE'LL DO THAT.
I'LL ALWAYS BE THERE. ALWAYS. IT'S NOT THE POWERS, NOT THE CAPE. IT'S ABOUT STANDING UP FOR JUSTICE. FOR TRUTH.
AS LONG AS PEOPLE LIKE YOU ARE OUT THERE, I'LL BE THERE.
KRAFF
ALWAYS.
He doesn't get up. And I --
hnn...
Fall took more out of me than I thought --

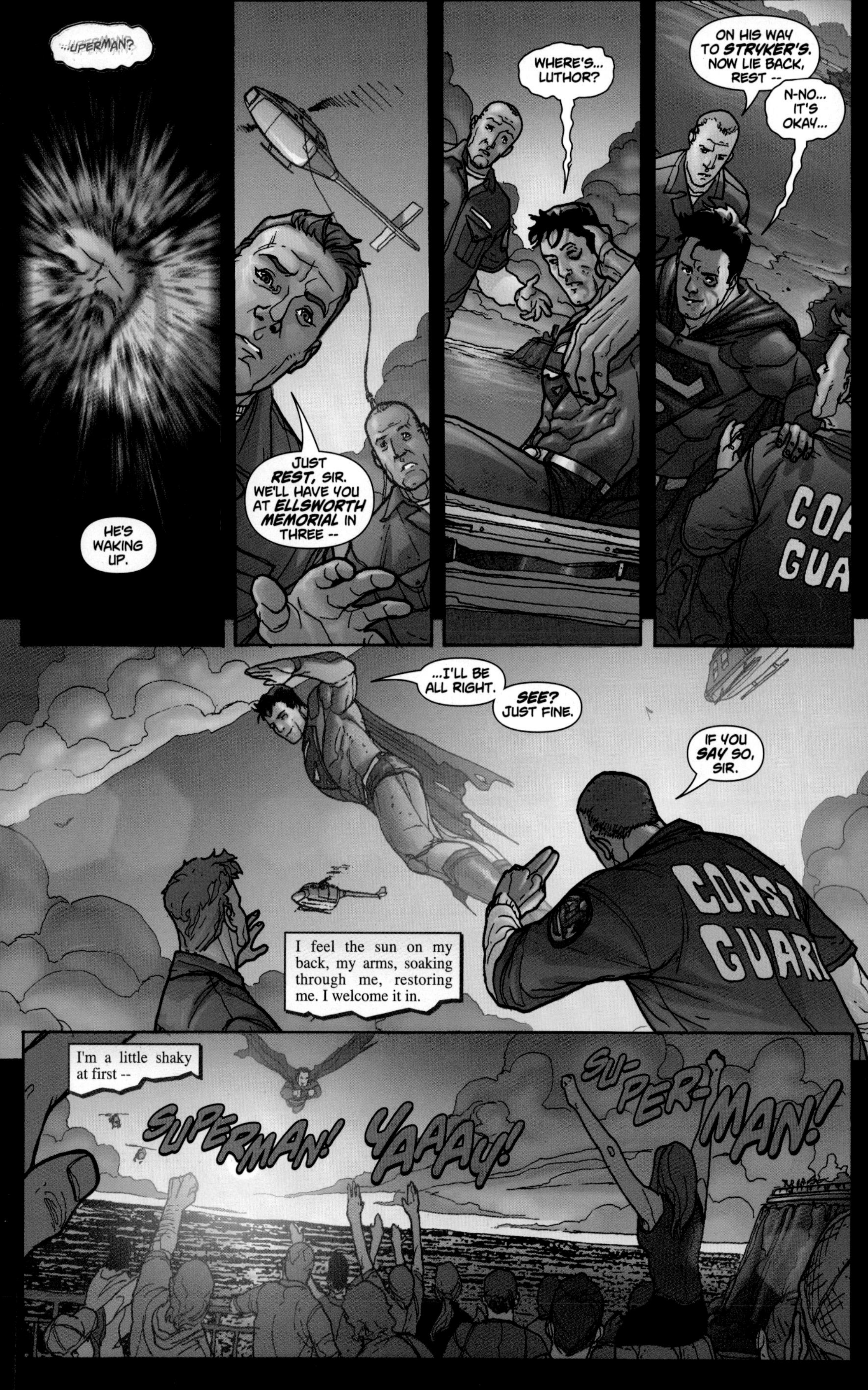
...UPERMAN?
HE'S WAKING UP.
JUST REST, SIR. WE'LL HAVE YOU AT ELLSWORTH MEMORIAL IN THREE --
WHERE'S... LUTHOR?
ON HIS WAY TO STRYKER'S. NOW LIE BACK, REST --
N-NO... IT'S OKAY...
COA GUA
...I'LL BE ALL RIGHT. SEE? JUST FINE.
IF YOU SAY SO, SIR.
COAST GUARD
I feel the sun on my back, my arms, soaking through me, restoring me. I welcome it in.
I'm a little shaky at first --
SUPERMAN! YAAAY!
SU-PER-MAN!

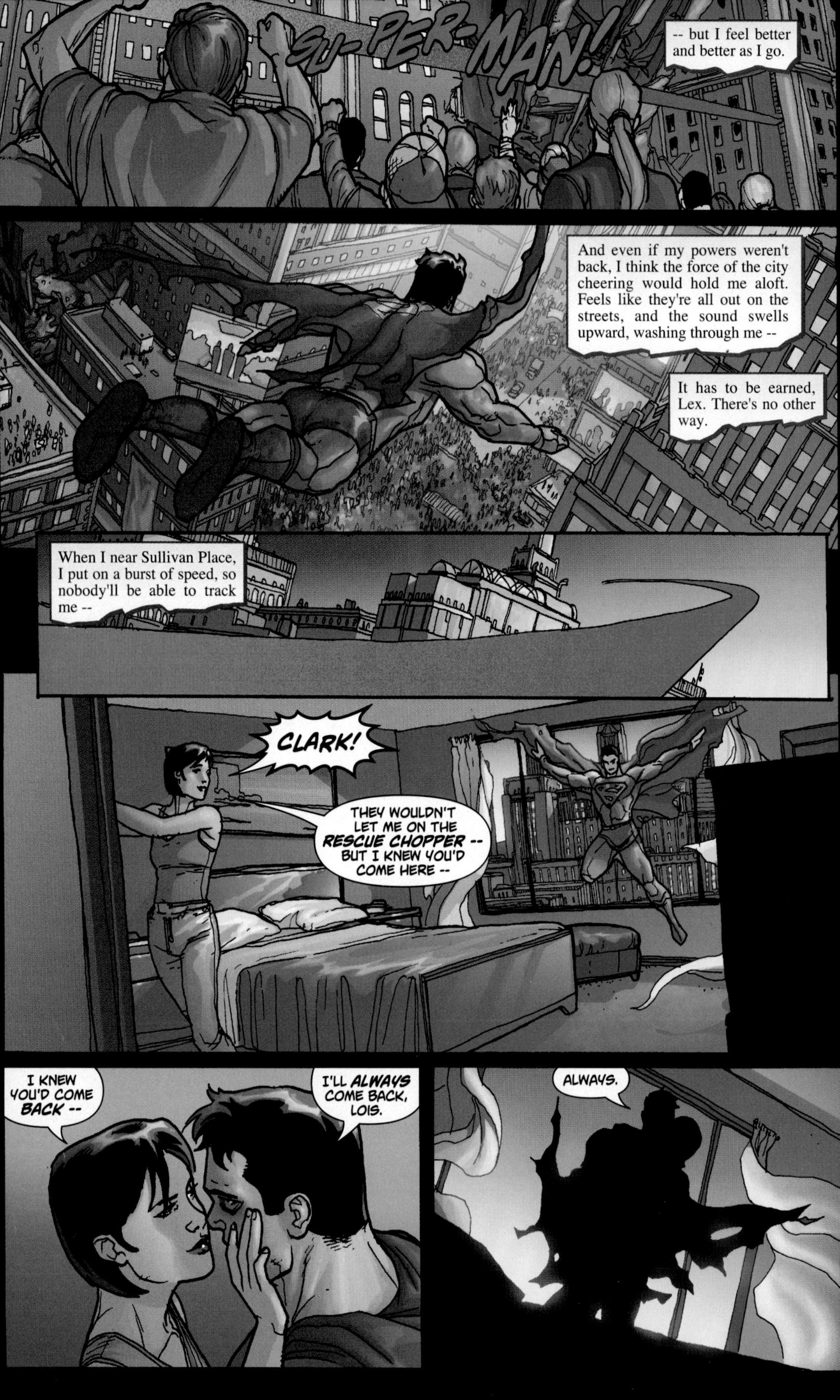
SU-PER-MAN!
-- but I feel better and better as I go.
And even if my powers weren't back, I think the force of the city cheering would hold me aloft. Feels like they're all out on the streets, and the sound swells upward, washing through me --
It has to be earned, Lex. There's no other way.
When I near Sullivan Place, I put on a burst of speed, so nobody'll be able to track me --
CLARK!
THEY WOULDN'T LET ME ON THE RESCUE CHOPPER -- BUT I KNEW YOU'D COME HERE --
I KNEW YOU'D COME BACK --
I'LL ALWAYS COME BACK, LOIS.
ALWAYS.

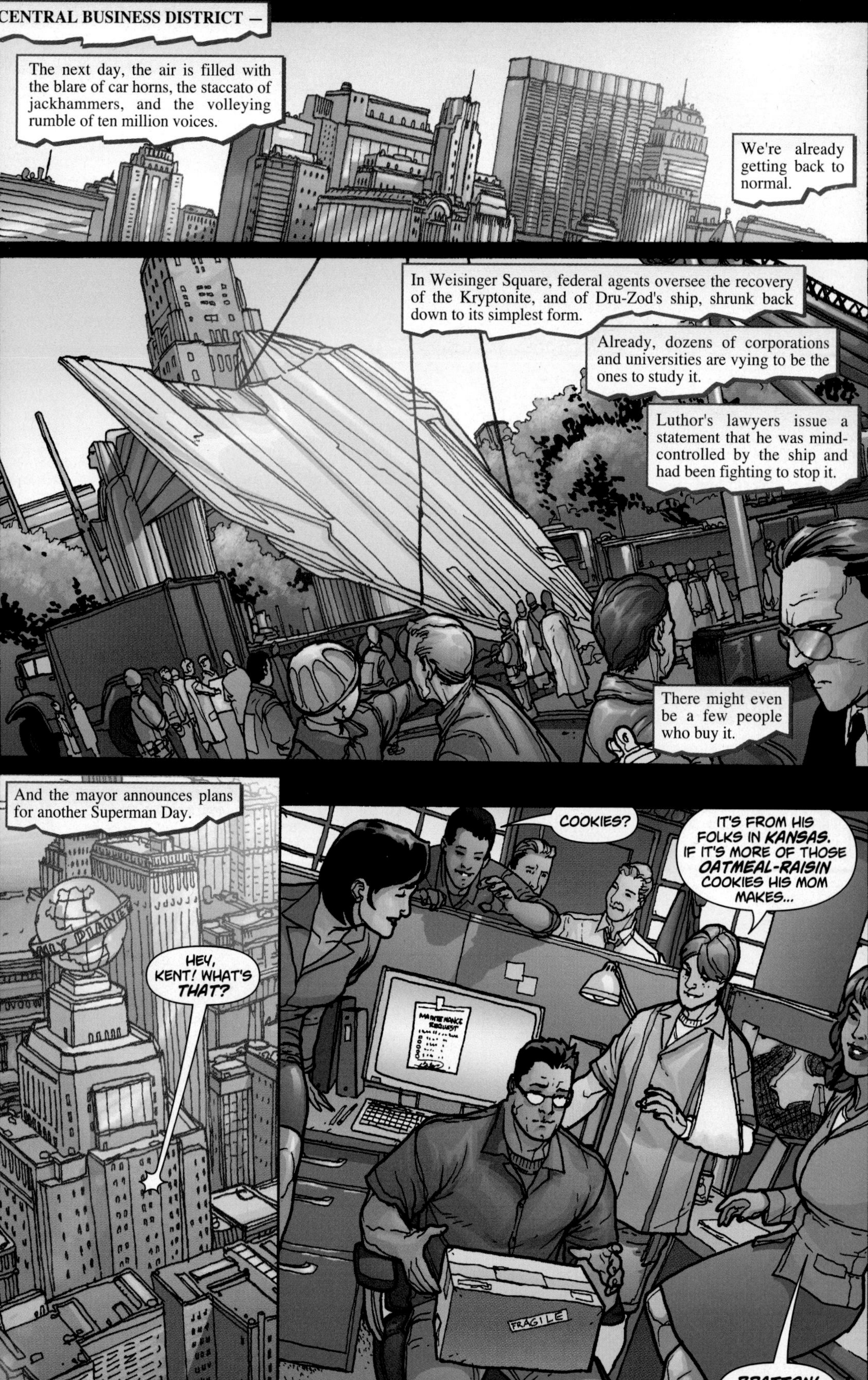
CENTRAL BUSINESS DISTRICT –
The next day, the air is filled with the blare of car horns, the staccato of jackhammers, and the volleying rumble of ten million voices.
We're already getting back to normal.
In Weisinger Square, federal agents oversee the recovery of the Kryptonite, and of Dru-Zod's ship, shrunk back down to its simplest form.
Already, dozens of corporations and universities are vying to be the ones to study it.
Luthor's lawyers issue a statement that he was mind-controlled by the ship and had been fighting to stop it.
There might even be a few people who buy it.
And the mayor announces plans for another Superman Day.
HEY, KENT! WHAT'S THAT?
COOKIES?
IT'S FROM HIS FOLKS IN KANSAS. IF IT'S MORE OF THOSE OATMEAL-RAISIN COOKIES HIS MOM MAKES...
BRATTON! KENT'S GOT COOKIES!
FRAGILE

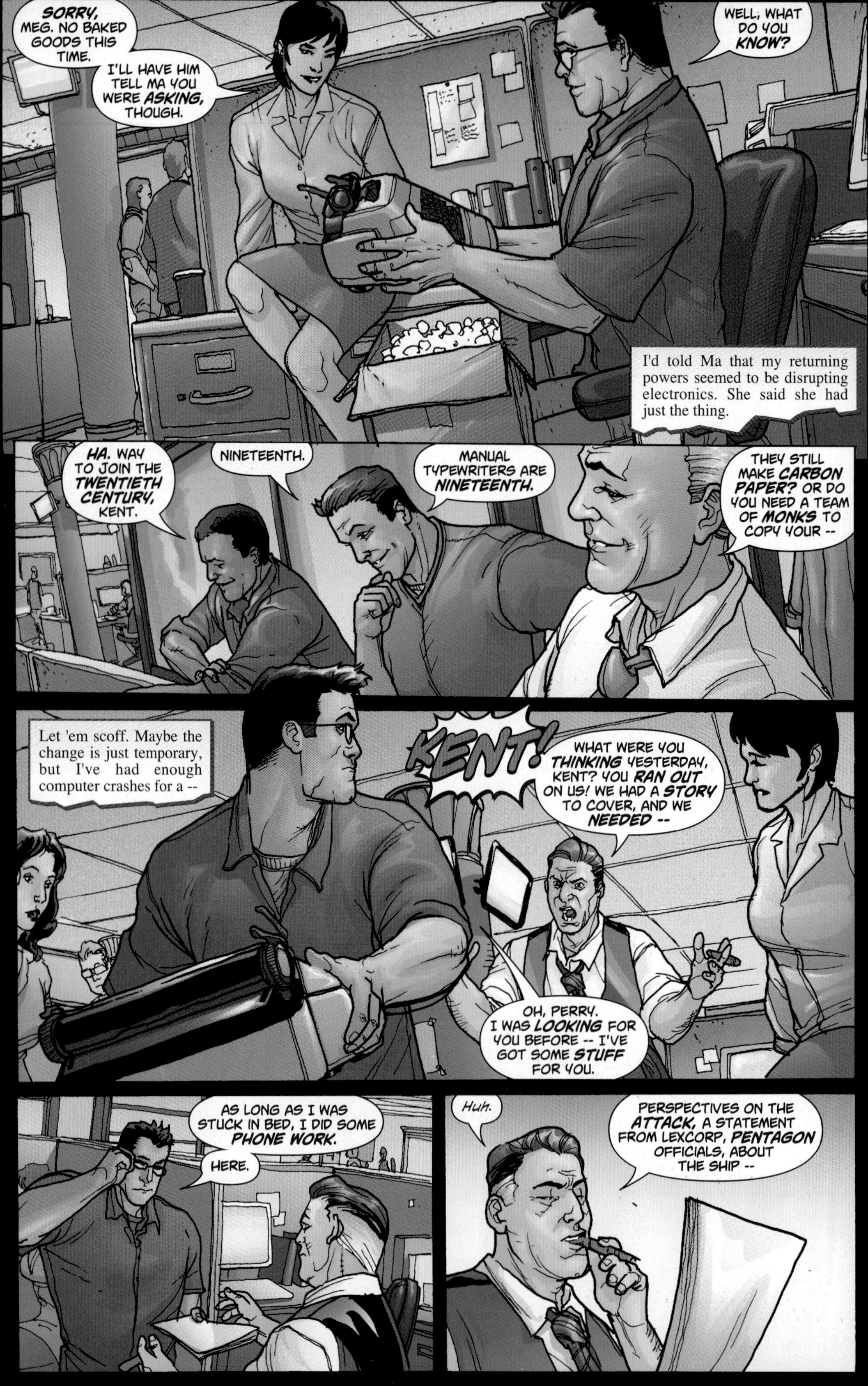
SORRY, MEG. NO BAKED GOODS THIS TIME.
I'LL HAVE HIM TELL MA YOU WERE ASKING, THOUGH.
WELL, WHAT DO YOU KNOW?
I'd told Ma that my returning powers seemed to be disrupting electronics. She said she had just the thing.
HA. WAY TO JOIN THE TWENTIETH CENTURY, KENT.
NINETEENTH.
MANUAL TYPEWRITERS ARE NINETEENTH.
THEY STILL MAKE CARBON PAPER? OR DO YOU NEED A TEAM OF MONKS TO COPY YOUR --
Let 'em scoff. Maybe the change is just temporary, but I've had enough computer crashes for a --
KENT!
WHAT WERE YOU THINKING YESTERDAY, KENT? YOU RAN OUT ON US! WE HAD A STORY TO COVER, AND WE NEEDED --
OH, PERRY. I WAS LOOKING FOR YOU BEFORE -- I'VE GOT SOME STUFF FOR YOU.
AS LONG AS I WAS STUCK IN BED, I DID SOME PHONE WORK.
HERE.
Huh.
PERSPECTIVES ON THE ATTACK, A STATEMENT FROM LEXCORP, PENTAGON OFFICIALS, ABOUT THE SHIP --

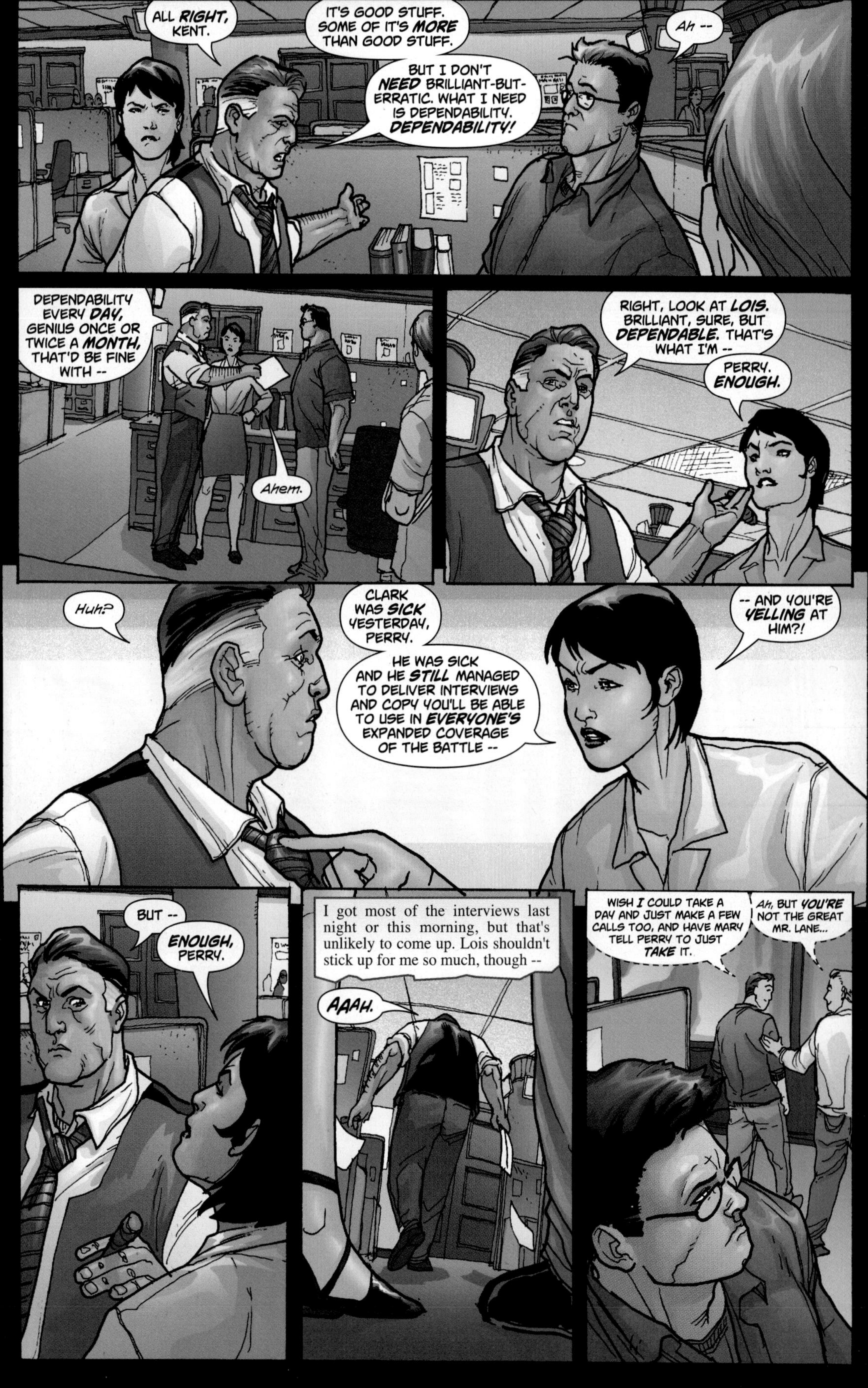
ALL RIGHT, KENT.
IT'S GOOD STUFF. SOME OF IT'S MORE THAN GOOD STUFF.
BUT I DON'T NEED BRILLIANT-BUT-ERRATIC. WHAT I NEED IS DEPENDABILITY. DEPENDABILITY!
Ah --
DEPENDABILITY EVERY DAY, GENIUS ONCE OR TWICE A MONTH, THAT'D BE FINE WITH --
Ahem.
RIGHT, LOOK AT LOIS. BRILLIANT, SURE, BUT DEPENDABLE. THAT'S WHAT I'M --
PERRY. ENOUGH.
Huh?
CLARK WAS SICK YESTERDAY, PERRY.
HE WAS SICK AND HE STILL MANAGED TO DELIVER INTERVIEWS AND COPY YOU'LL BE ABLE TO USE IN EVERYONE'S EXPANDED COVERAGE OF THE BATTLE --
-- AND YOU'RE YELLING AT HIM?!
BUT --
ENOUGH, PERRY.
I got most of the interviews last night or this morning, but that's unlikely to come up. Lois shouldn't stick up for me so much, though --
AAAH.
WISH I COULD TAKE A DAY AND JUST MAKE A FEW CALLS TOO, AND HAVE MARY TELL PERRY TO JUST TAKE IT.
Ah, BUT YOU'RE NOT THE GREAT MR. LANE...

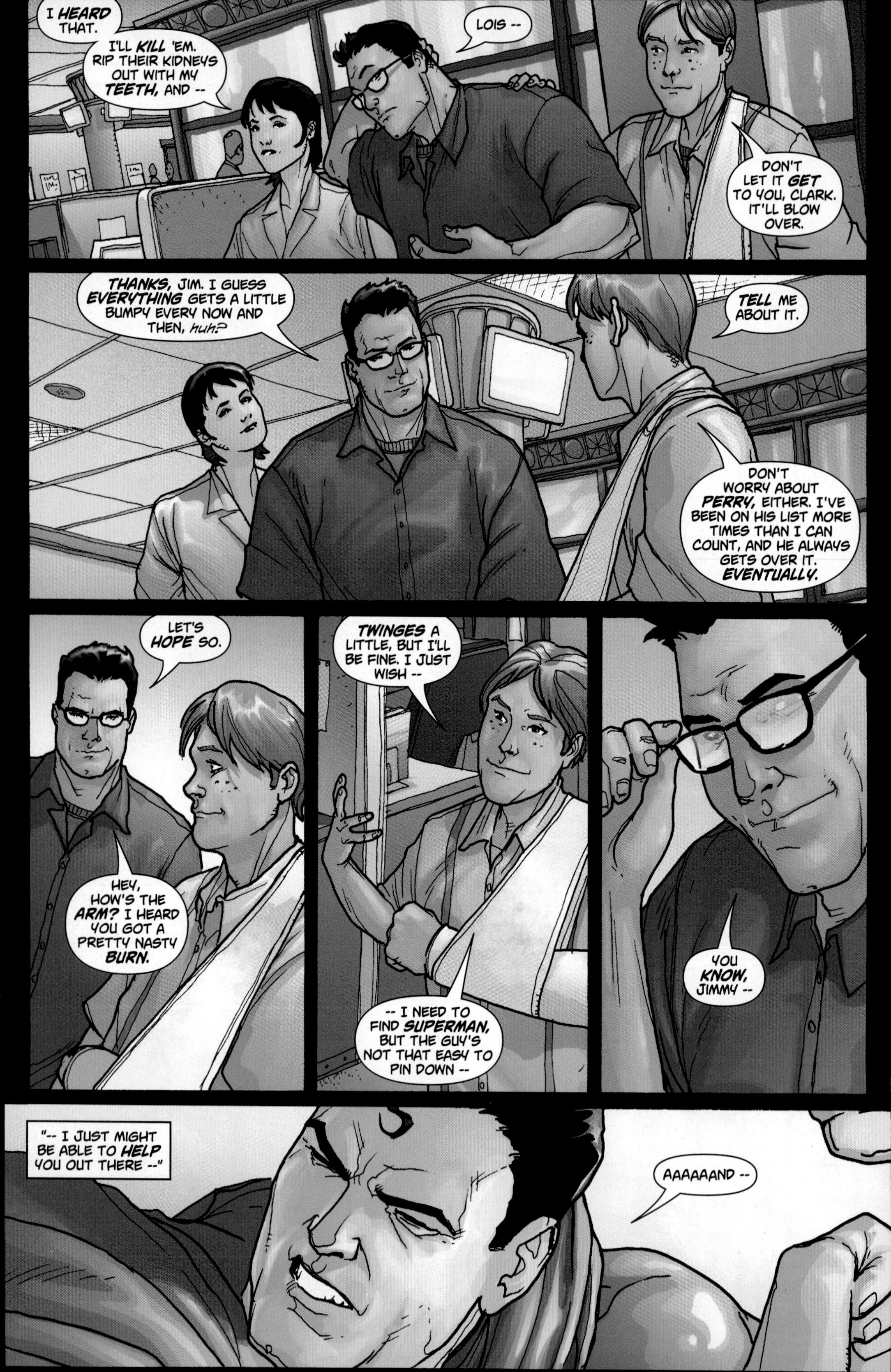
I HEARD THAT.
I'LL KILL 'EM. RIP THEIR KIDNEYS OUT WITH MY TEETH, AND --
LOIS --
DON'T LET IT GET TO YOU, CLARK. IT'LL BLOW OVER.
THANKS, JIM. I GUESS EVERYTHING GETS A LITTLE BUMPY EVERY NOW AND THEN, huh?
TELL ME ABOUT IT.
DON'T WORRY ABOUT PERRY, EITHER. I'VE BEEN ON HIS LIST MORE TIMES THAN I CAN COUNT, AND HE ALWAYS GETS OVER IT. EVENTUALLY.
LET'S HOPE SO.
HEY, HOW'S THE ARM? I HEARD YOU GOT A PRETTY NASTY BURN.
TWINGES A LITTLE, BUT I'LL BE FINE. I JUST WISH --
-- I NEED TO FIND SUPERMAN, BUT THE GUY'S NOT THAT EASY TO PIN DOWN --
YOU KNOW, JIMMY --
"-- I JUST MIGHT BE ABLE TO HELP YOU OUT THERE --"
AAAAAAND --

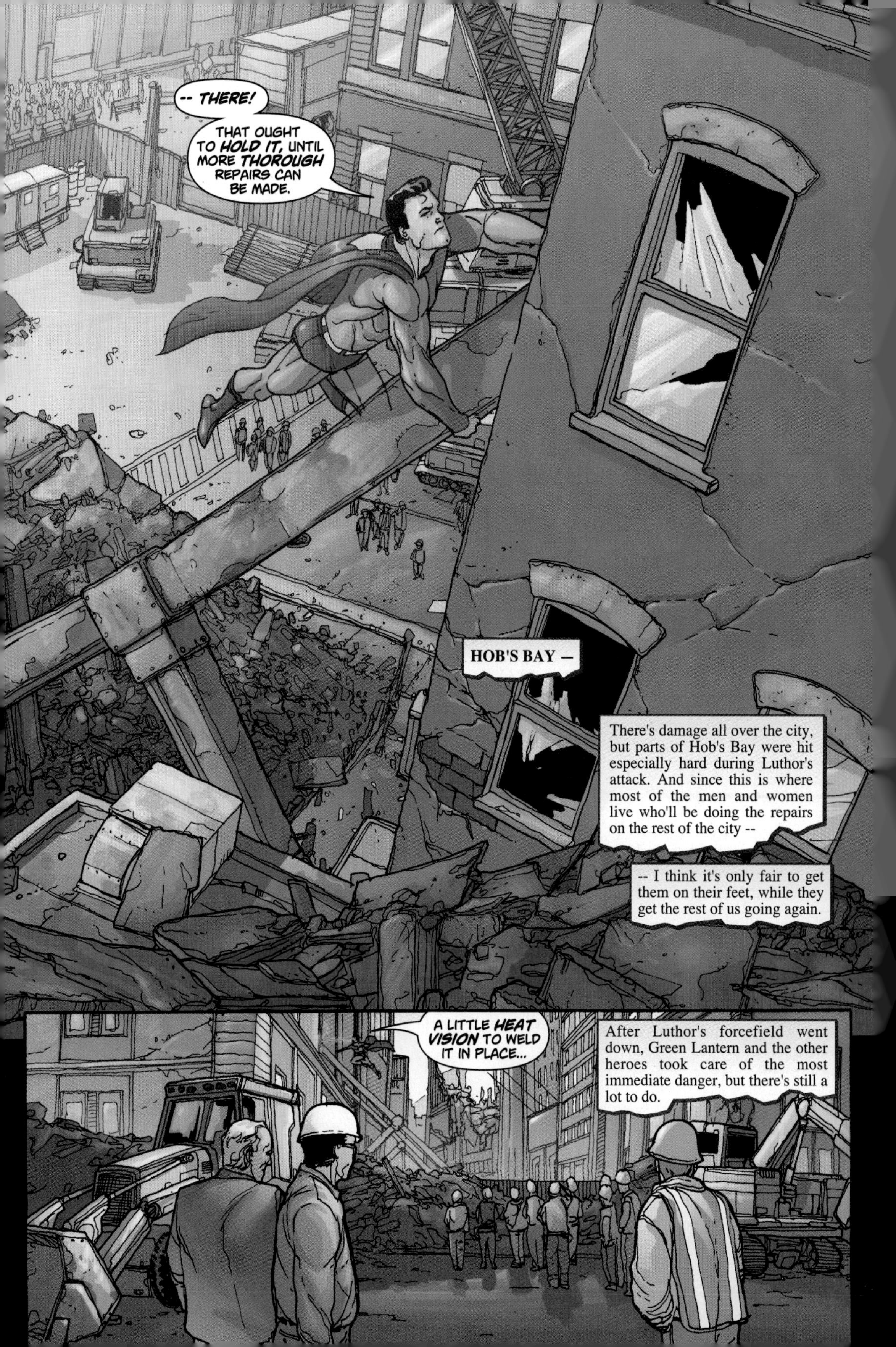
-- THERE!
THAT OUGHT TO HOLD IT, UNTIL MORE THOROUGH REPAIRS CAN BE MADE.
HOB'S BAY —
There's damage all over the city, but parts of Hob's Bay were hit especially hard during Luthor's attack. And since this is where most of the men and women live who'll be doing the repairs on the rest of the city --
-- I think it's only fair to get them on their feet, while they get the rest of us going again.
A LITTLE HEAT VISION TO WELD IT IN PLACE...
After Luthor's forcefield went down, Green Lantern and the other heroes took care of the most immediate danger, but there's still a lot to do.

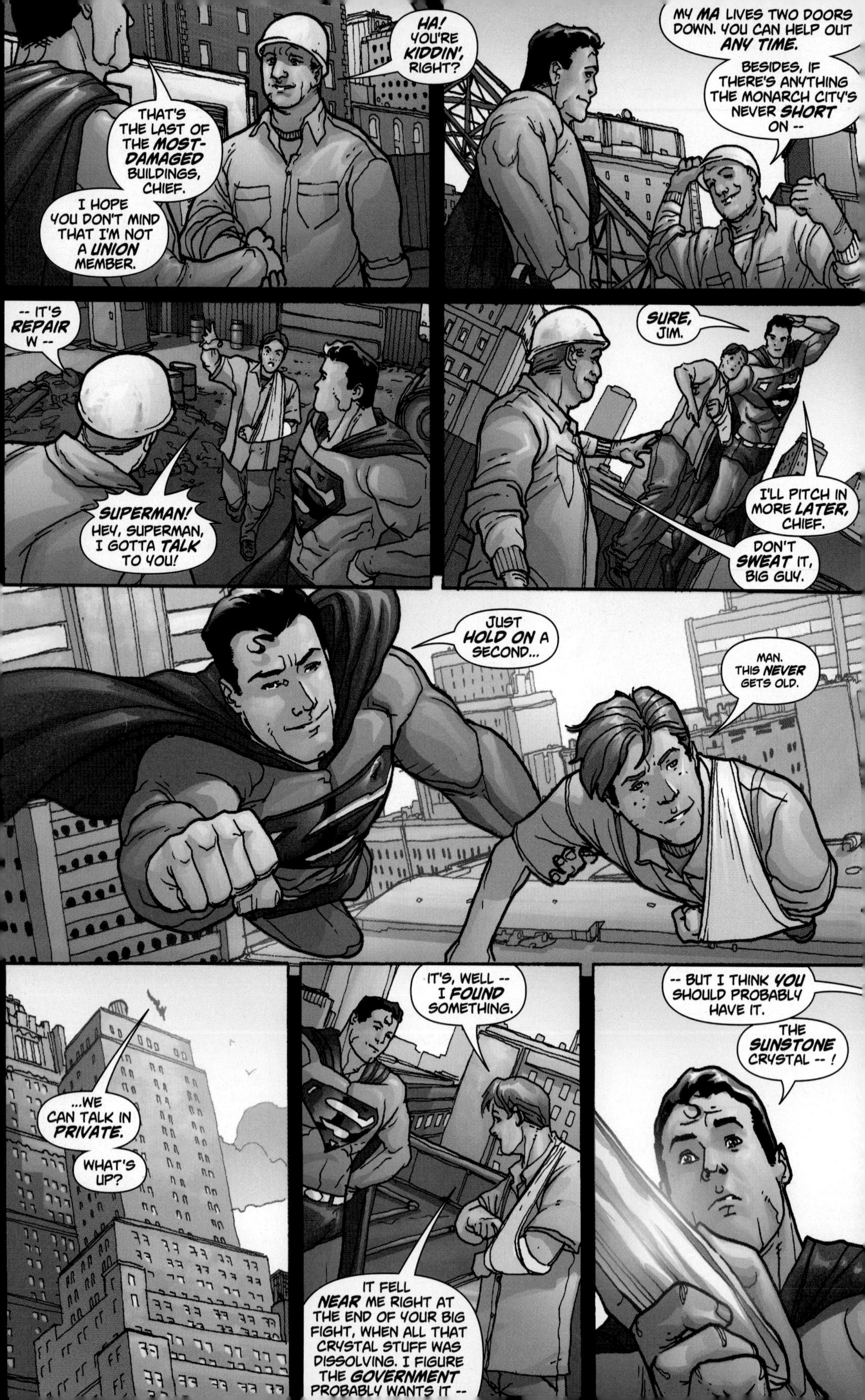
THAT'S THE LAST OF THE MOST-DAMAGED BUILDINGS, CHIEF.
I HOPE YOU DON'T MIND THAT I'M NOT A UNION MEMBER.
HA! YOU'RE KIDDIN', RIGHT?
MY MA LIVES TWO DOORS DOWN. YOU CAN HELP OUT ANY TIME.
BESIDES, IF THERE'S ANYTHING THE MONARCH CITY'S NEVER SHORT ON --
-- IT'S REPAIR W --
SUPERMAN! HEY, SUPERMAN, I GOTTA TALK TO YOU!
SURE, JIM.
I'LL PITCH IN MORE LATER, CHIEF.
DON'T SWEAT IT, BIG GUY.
JUST HOLD ON A SECOND...
MAN. THIS NEVER GETS OLD.
...WE CAN TALK IN PRIVATE.
WHAT'S UP?
IT'S, WELL -- I FOUND SOMETHING.
IT FELL NEAR ME RIGHT AT THE END OF YOUR BIG FIGHT, WHEN ALL THAT CRYSTAL STUFF WAS DISSOLVING. I FIGURE THE GOVERNMENT PROBABLY WANTS IT --
-- BUT I THINK YOU SHOULD PROBABLY HAVE IT.
THE SUNSTONE CRYSTAL -- !

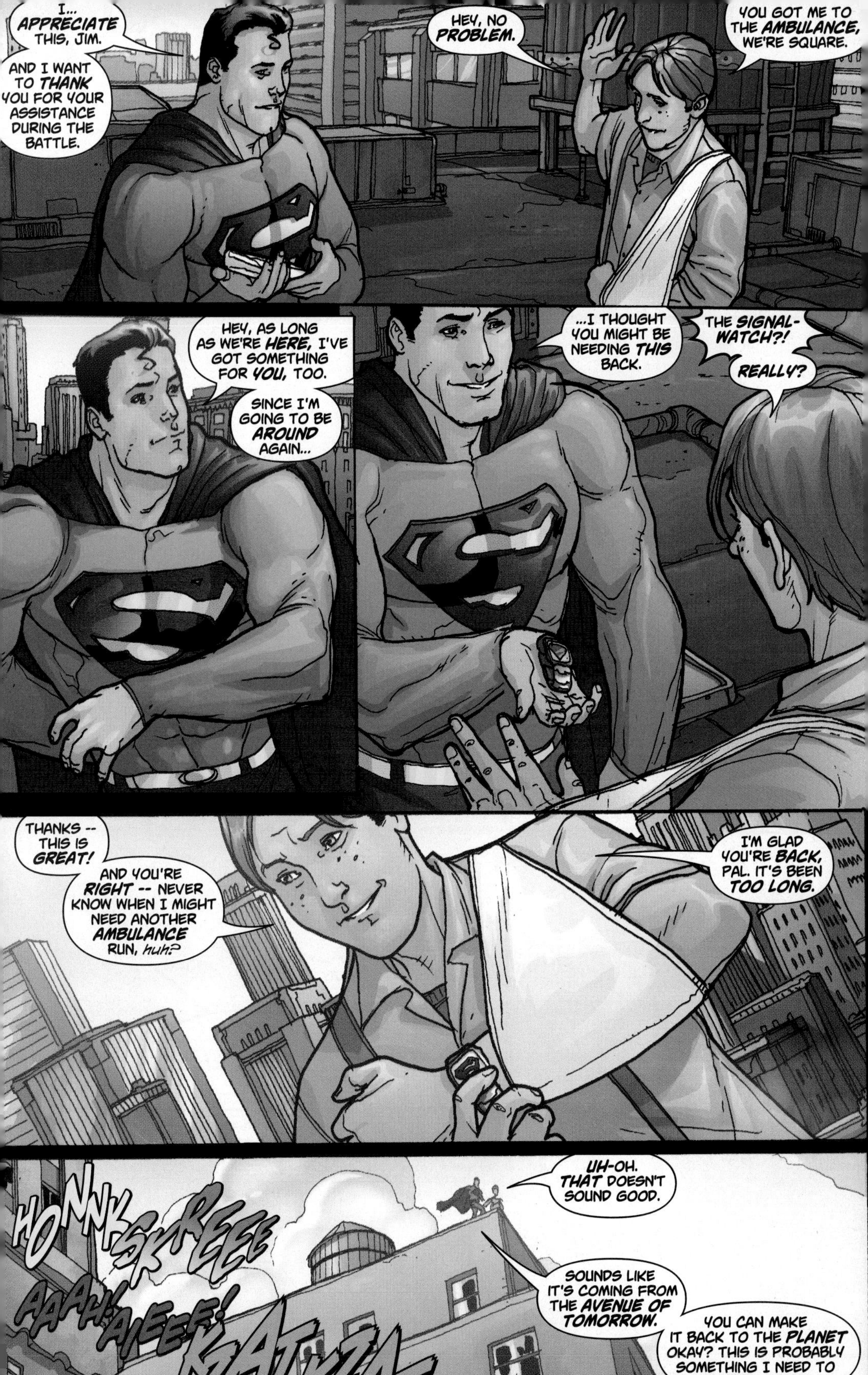
I... APPRECIATE THIS, JIM.
AND I WANT TO THANK YOU FOR YOUR ASSISTANCE DURING THE BATTLE.
HEY, NO PROBLEM.
YOU GOT ME TO THE AMBULANCE, WE'RE SQUARE.
HEY, AS LONG AS WE'RE HERE, I'VE GOT SOMETHING FOR YOU, TOO.
SINCE I'M GOING TO BE AROUND AGAIN...
...I THOUGHT YOU MIGHT BE NEEDING THIS BACK.
THE SIGNAL-WATCH?!
REALLY?
THANKS -- THIS IS GREAT!
AND YOU'RE RIGHT -- NEVER KNOW WHEN I MIGHT NEED ANOTHER AMBULANCE RUN, huh?
I'M GLAD YOU'RE BACK, PAL. IT'S BEEN TOO LONG.
HONNNK
SKREEE
UH-OH. THAT DOESN'T SOUND GOOD.
SOUNDS LIKE IT'S COMING FROM THE AVENUE OF TOMORROW.
YOU CAN MAKE IT BACK TO THE PLANET OKAY? THIS IS PROBABLY SOMETHING I NEED TO CHECK INTO.

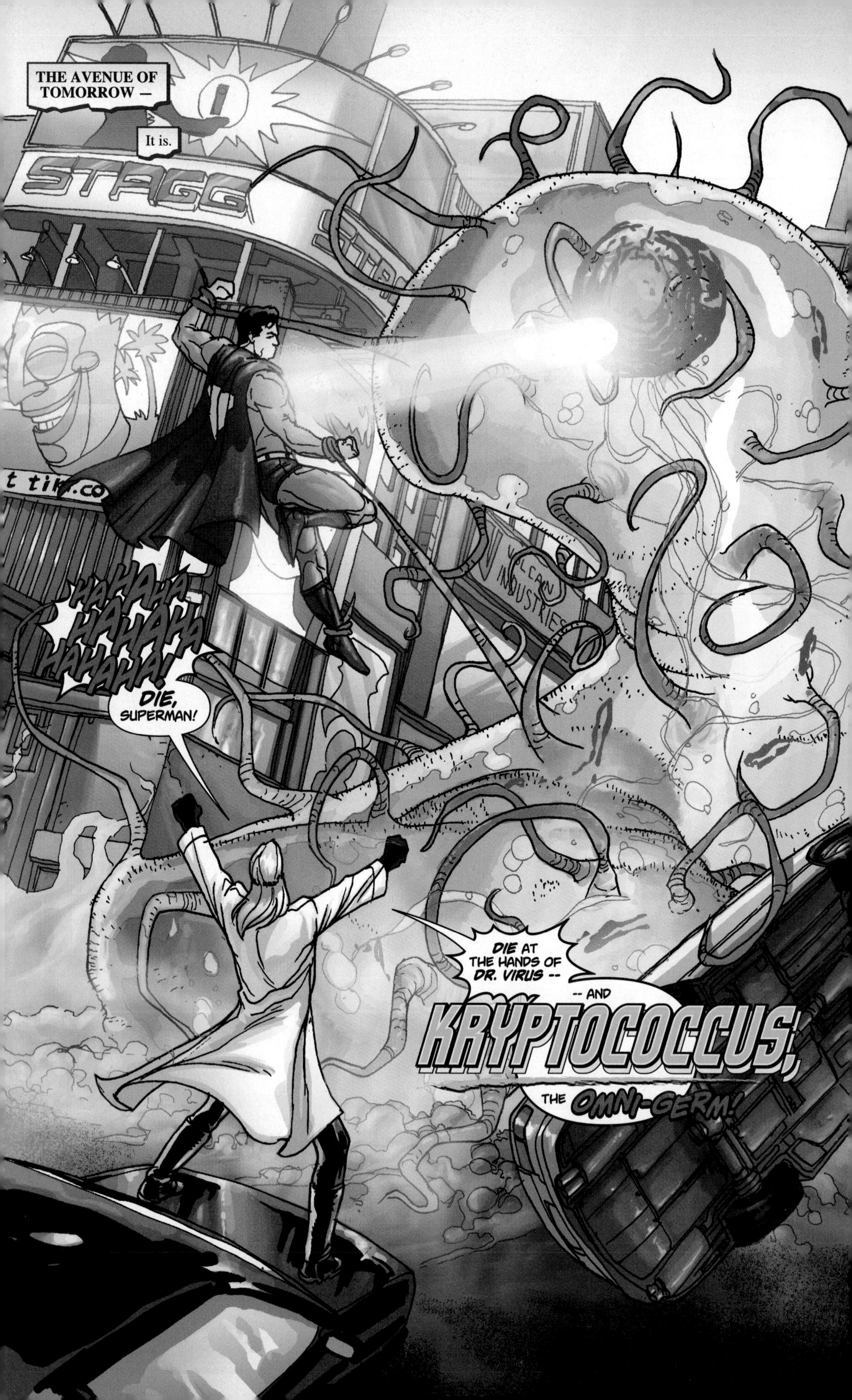
THE AVENUE OF TOMORROW —
It is.
STAGG
VULCAN INDUSTRIES
HAHAHA HAHAHA HAHAHA!
DIE, SUPERMAN!
DIE AT THE HANDS OF DR. VIRUS --
-- AND KRYPTOCOCCUS,
THE OMNI-GERM!

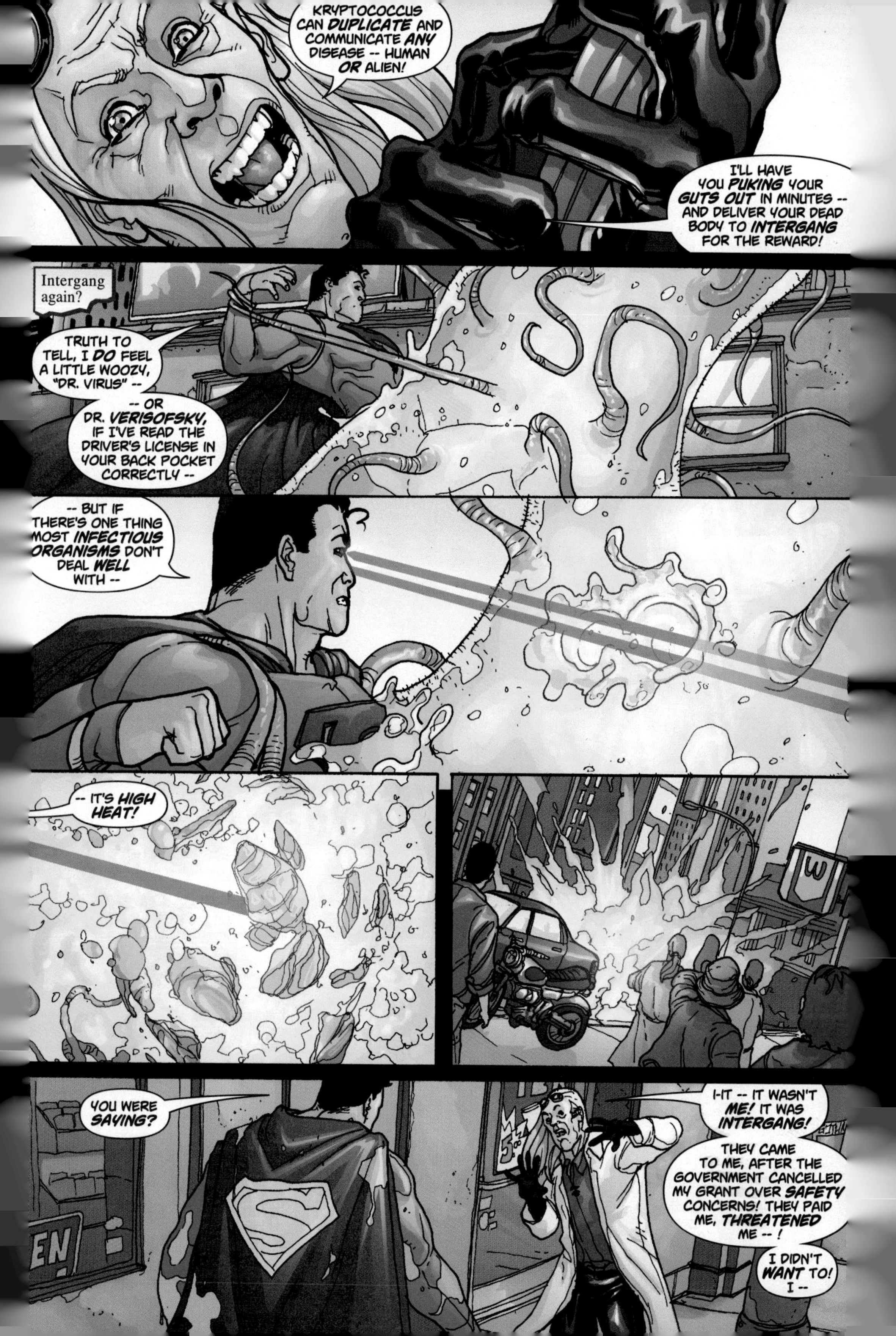
KRYPTOCOCCUS CAN DUPLICATE AND COMMUNICATE ANY DISEASE -- HUMAN OR ALIEN!
I'LL HAVE YOU PUKING YOUR GUTS OUT IN MINUTES -- AND DELIVER YOUR DEAD BODY TO INTERGANG FOR THE REWARD!
Intergang again?
TRUTH TO TELL, I DO FEEL A LITTLE WOOZY, "DR. VIRUS" --
-- OR DR. VERISOFSKY, IF I'VE READ THE DRIVER'S LICENSE IN YOUR BACK POCKET CORRECTLY --
-- BUT IF THERE'S ONE THING MOST INFECTIOUS ORGANISMS DON'T DEAL WELL WITH --
-- IT'S HIGH HEAT!
W
YOU WERE SAYING?
I-IT -- IT WASN'T ME! IT WAS INTERGANG!
THEY CAME TO ME, AFTER THE GOVERNMENT CANCELLED MY GRANT OVER SAFETY CONCERNS! THEY PAID ME, THREATENED ME -- !
I DIDN'T WANT TO! I --
EN

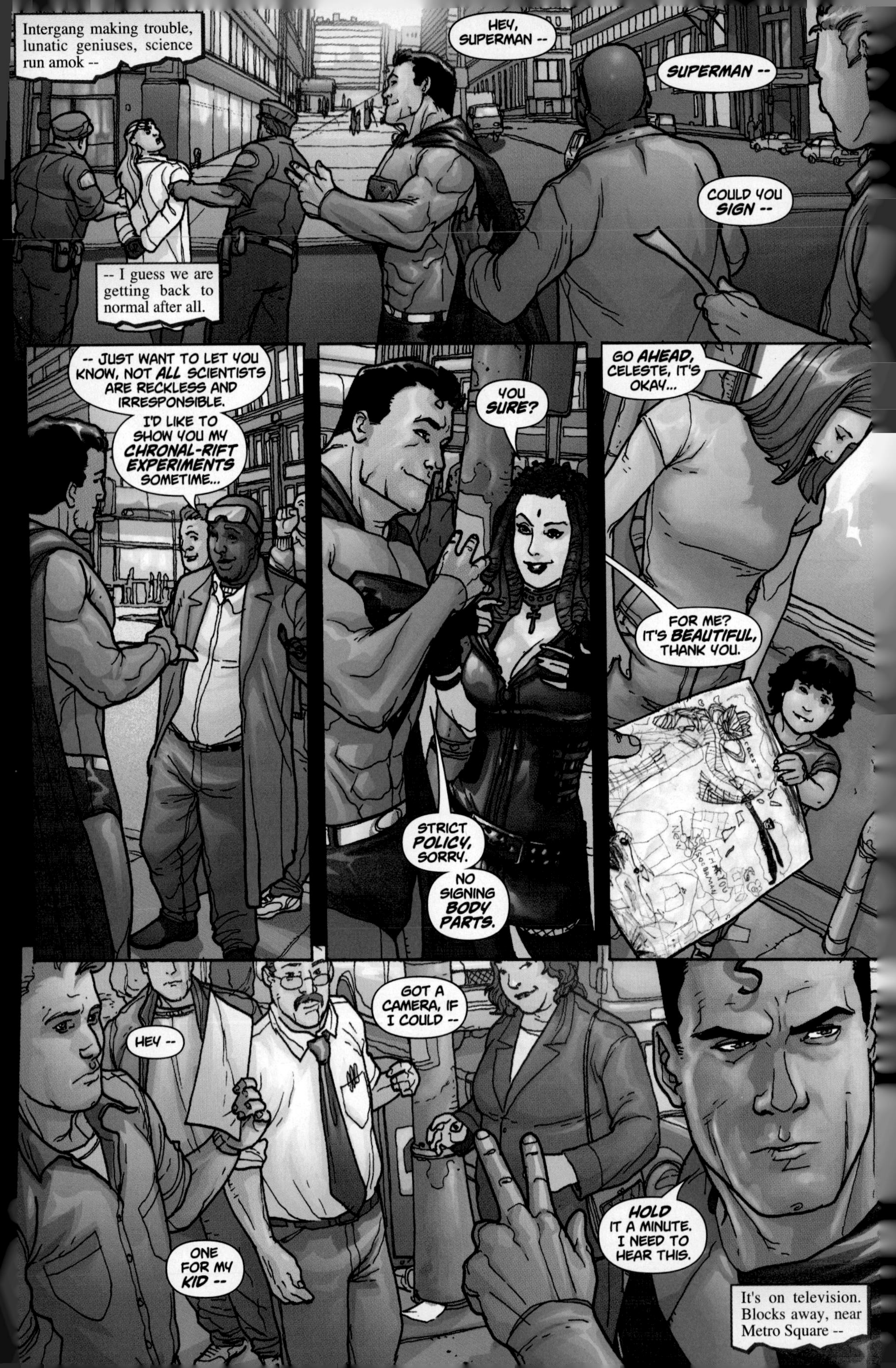
Intergang making trouble, lunatic geniuses, science run amok --
HEY, SUPERMAN --
SUPERMAN --
COULD YOU SIGN --
-- I guess we are getting back to normal after all.
-- JUST WANT TO LET YOU KNOW, NOT ALL SCIENTISTS ARE RECKLESS AND IRRESPONSIBLE.
I'D LIKE TO SHOW YOU MY CHRONAL-RIFT EXPERIMENTS SOMETIME...
YOU SURE?
STRICT POLICY, SORRY.
NO SIGNING BODY PARTS.
GO AHEAD, CELESTE, IT'S OKAY...
FOR ME? IT'S BEAUTIFUL, THANK YOU.
HEY --
GOT A CAMERA, IF I COULD --
ONE FOR MY KID --
HOLD IT A MINUTE. I NEED TO HEAR THIS.
It's on television. Blocks away, near Metro Square --

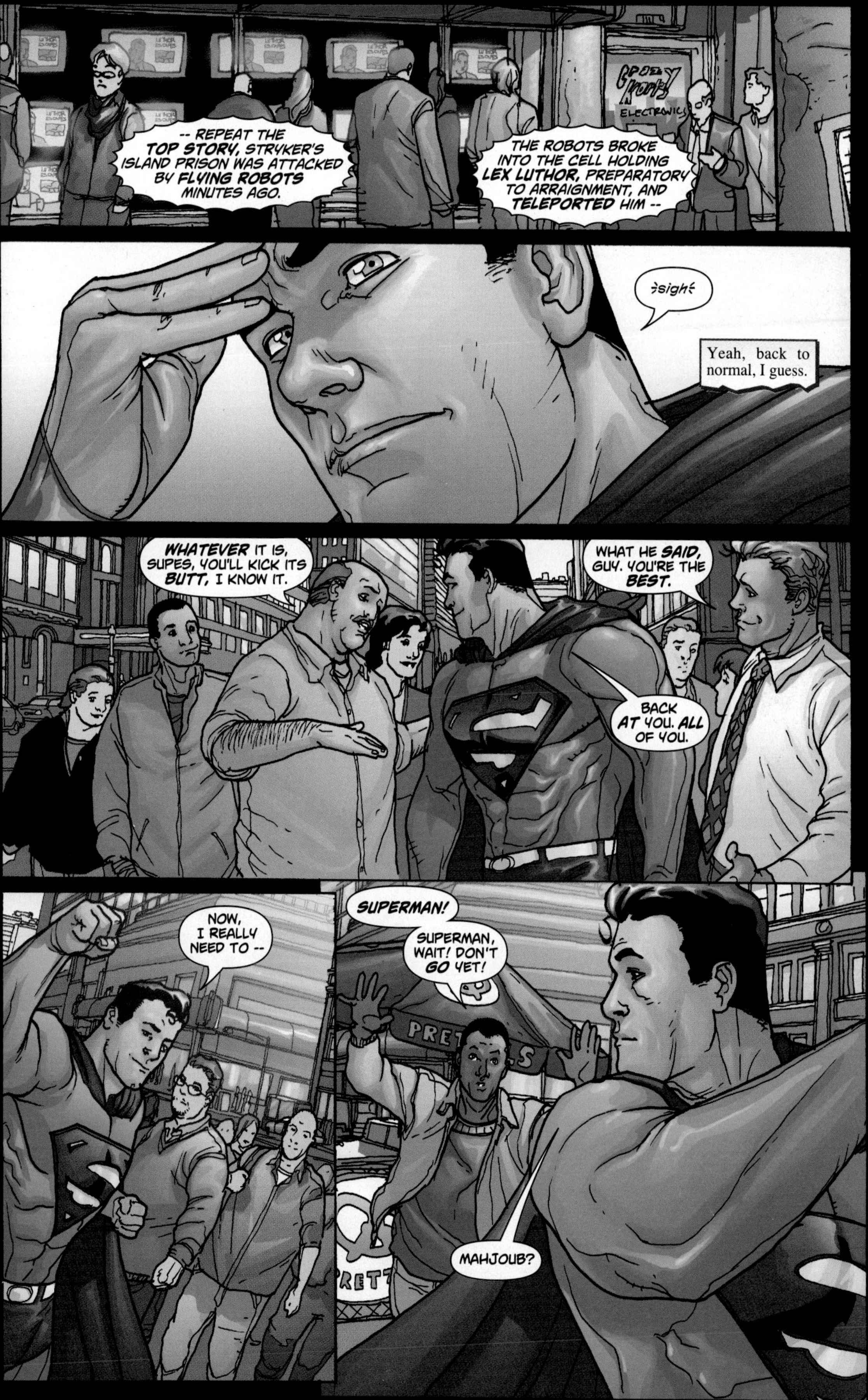
-- REPEAT THE TOP STORY, STRYKER'S ISLAND PRISON WAS ATTACKED BY FLYING ROBOTS MINUTES AGO.
THE ROBOTS BROKE INTO THE CELL HOLDING LEX LUTHOR, PREPARATORY TO ARRAIGNMENT, AND TELEPORTED HIM --
ELECTRONICS
sigh
Yeah, back to normal, I guess.
WHATEVER IT IS, SUPES, YOU'LL KICK ITS BUTT, I KNOW IT.
WHAT HE SAID, GUY. YOU'RE THE BEST.
BACK AT YOU. ALL OF YOU.
NOW, I REALLY NEED TO --
SUPERMAN!
SUPERMAN, WAIT! DON'T GO YET!
MAHJOUB?

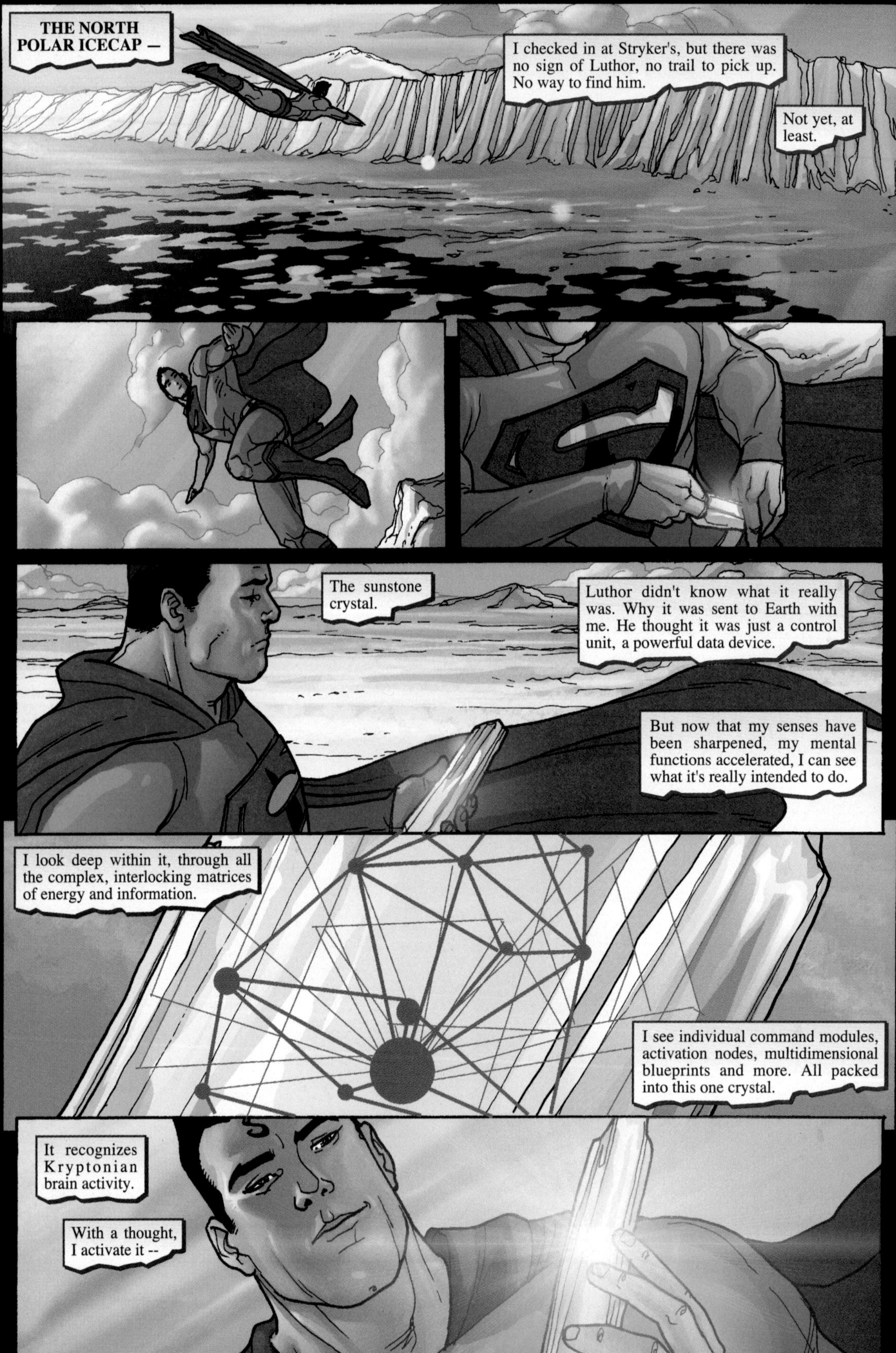

THE NORTH POLAR ICECAP —
I checked in at Stryker's, but there was no sign of Luthor, no trail to pick up. No way to find him.
Not yet, at least.
The sunstone crystal.
Luthor didn't know what it really was. Why it was sent to Earth with me. He thought it was just a control unit, a powerful data device.
But now that my senses have been sharpened, my mental functions accelerated, I can see what it's really intended to do.
I look deep within it, through all the complex, interlocking matrices of energy and information.
I see individual command modules, activation nodes, multidimensional blueprints and more. All packed into this one crystal.
It recognizes Kryptonian brain activity.
With a thought, I activate it --

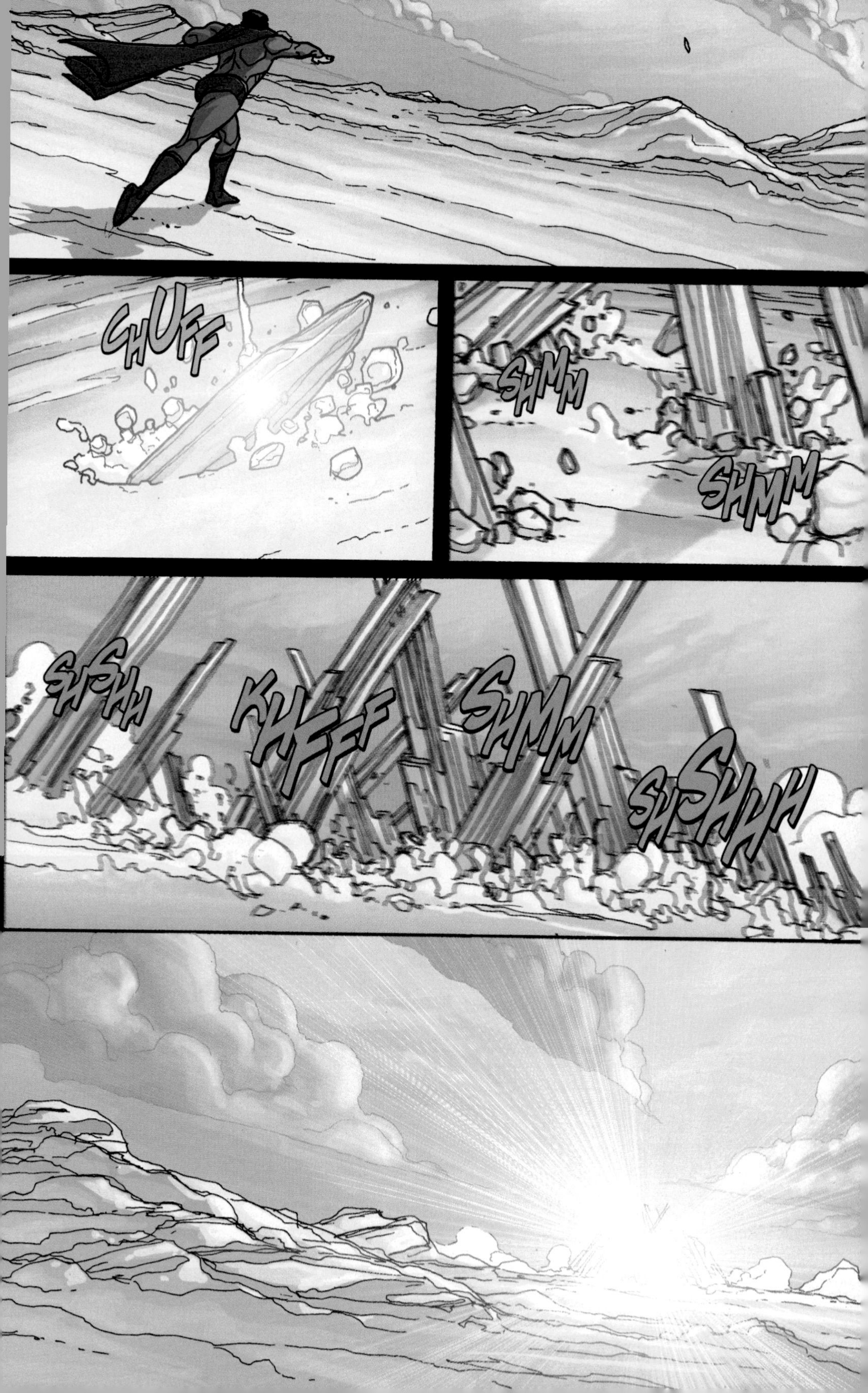
CHUFF
SHMM
SHMM
SUSHH
KHFFF
SHMM
SUSHHH

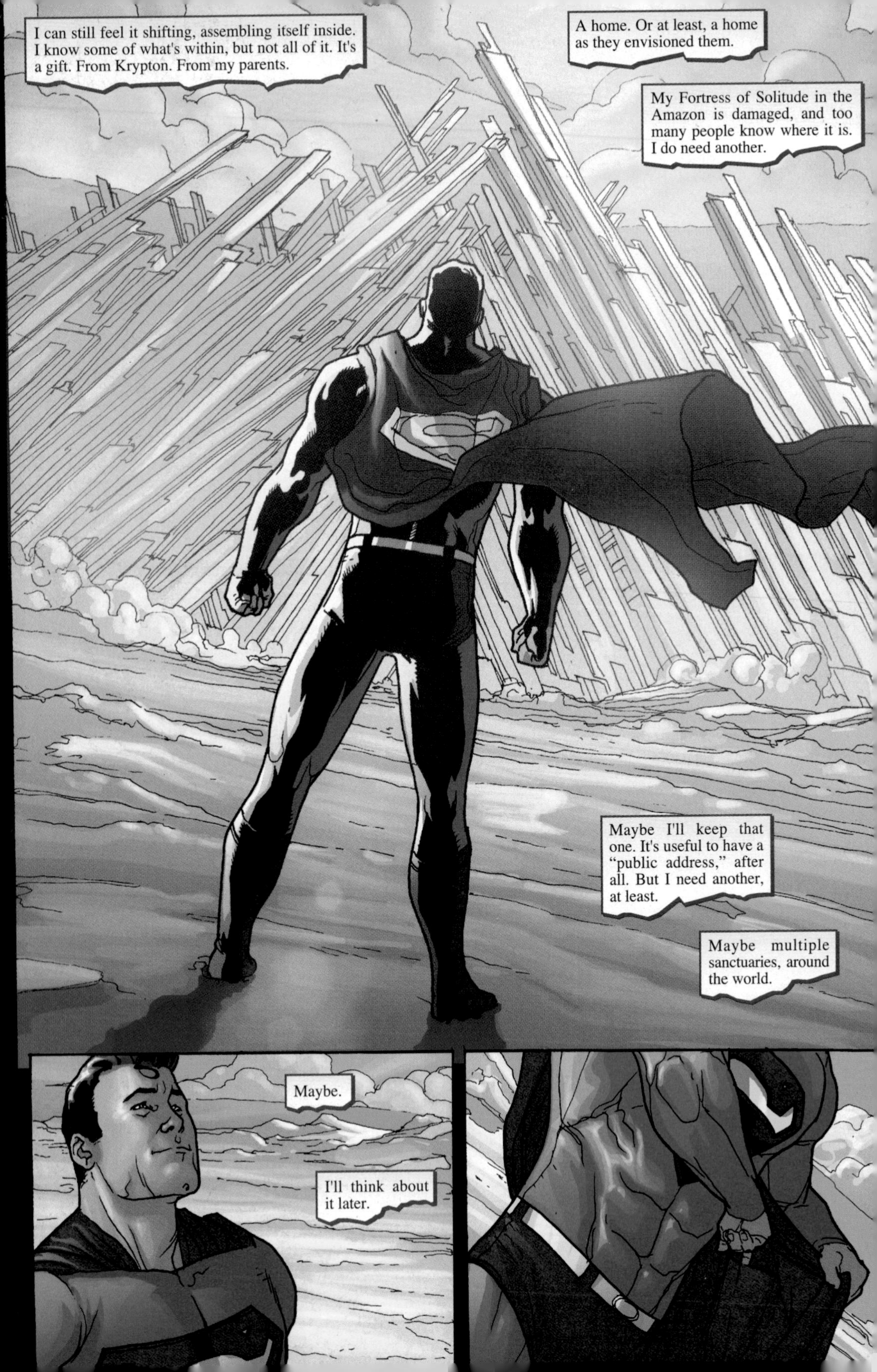

I can still feel it shifting, assembling itself inside. I know some of what's within, but not all of it. It's a gift. From Krypton. From my parents.
A home. Or at least, a home as they envisioned them.
My Fortress of Solitude in the Amazon is damaged, and too many people know where it is. I do need another.
Maybe I'll keep that one. It's useful to have a "public address," after all. But I need another, at least.
Maybe multiple sanctuaries, around the world.
Maybe.
I'll think about it later.

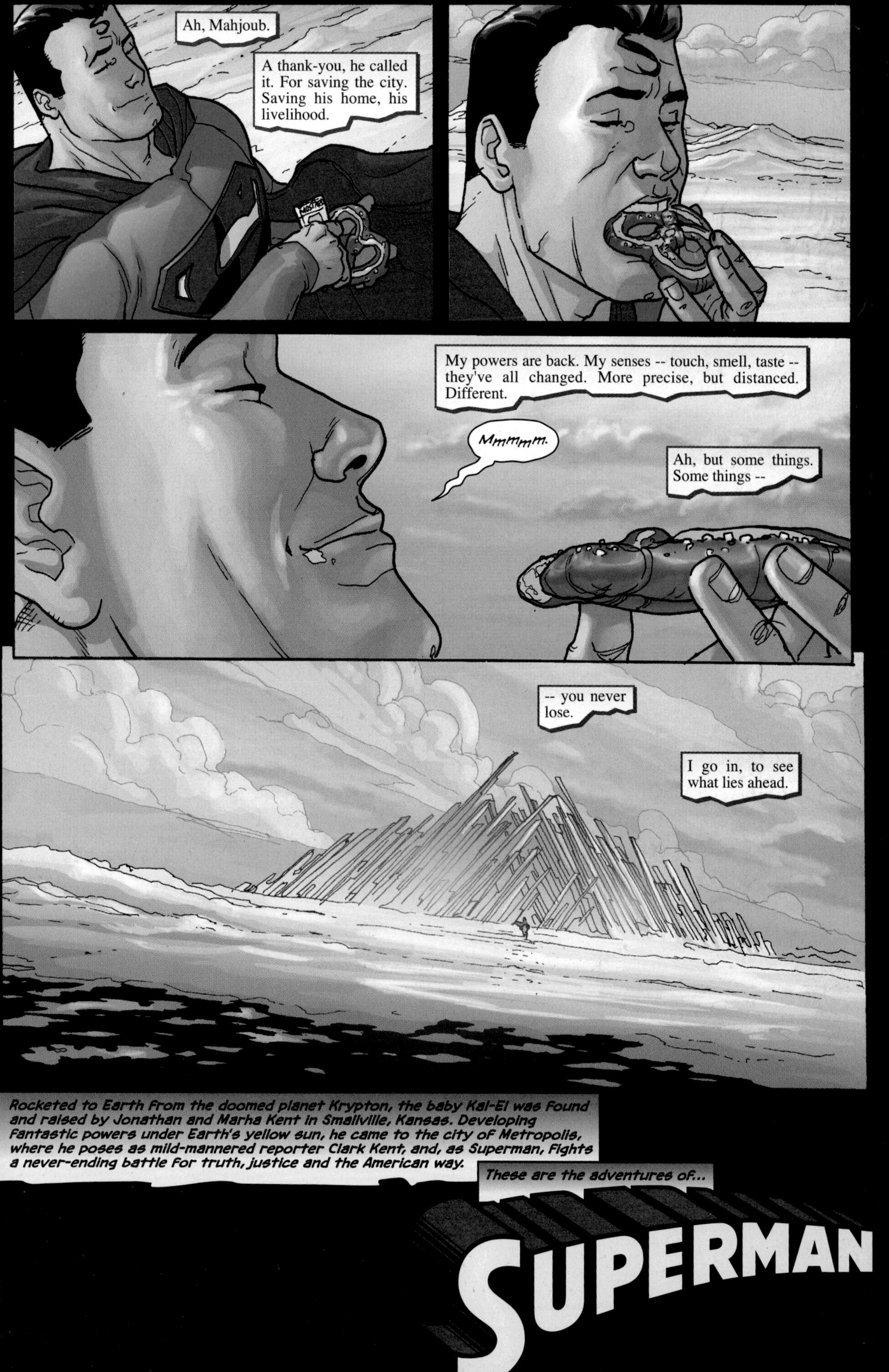
Ah, Mahjoub.
A thank-you, he called it. For saving the city. Saving his home, his livelihood.
My powers are back. My senses -- touch, smell, taste -- they've all changed. More precise, but distanced. Different.
Mmmmm.
Ah, but some things. Some things --
-- you never lose.
I go in, to see what lies ahead.
Rocketed to Earth from the doomed planet Krypton, the baby Kal-El was found and raised by Jonathan and Marha Kent in Smallville, Kansas. Developing fantastic powers under Earth's yellow sun, he came to the city of Metropolis, where he poses as mild-mannered reporter Clark Kent, and, as Superman, fights a never-ending battle for truth, justice and the American way.
These are the adventures of...
SUPERMAN

Art by: Pete Woods

MAN

: FOR TOMORROW VOLUME 1

Brian Azzarello, Jim Lee and **Scott Williams** tell the epic tale of a cataclysmic event that strikes the Earth, affecting millions – including those closest to the Man of Steel.

DC
BRIAN AZZARELLO JIM LEE SCOTT WILLIAMS
SUPERMAN
FOR TOMORROW
VOLUME ONE

"A BIG HERO NEEDS A BIG STORY, AND THIS TEAM DOESN'T DISAPPOINT."
— THE WASHINGTON POST

SUPERMAN: THE MAN OF STEEL VOLUME 1

DC
JOHN BYRNE DICK GIORDANO
SUPERMAN
THE MAN OF STEEL

JOHN BYRNE
DICK GIORDANO

SUPERMAN FOR ALL SEASONS

DC
Superman
For All Seasons
Jeph Loeb
Tim Sale
with Bjarne Hansen

JEPH LOEB
TIM SALE

THE DEATH OF SUPERMAN

THE BEST-SELLING GRAPHIC NOVEL OF ALL TIME!
THE DEATH OF
SUPERMAN
Dan JURGENS
Jerry ORDWAY
Louise SIMONSON
Roger STERN
Jon BOGDANOVE
Tom GRUMMETT
Jackson GUICE
Brett BREEDING
Rick BURCHETT
Doug HAZLEWOOD
Dennis JANKE
Denis RODIER
DC

DAN JURGENS
JERRY ORDWAY
JACKSON GUICE

SEARCH THE GRAPHIC NOVELS SECTION OF
www.DCCOMICS.com
FOR ART AND INFORMATION ON ALL OF OUR BOOKS!

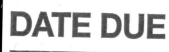

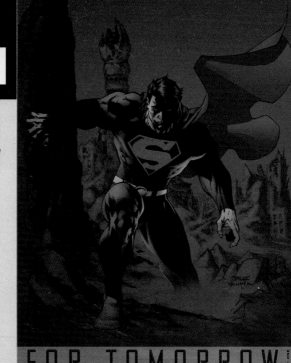

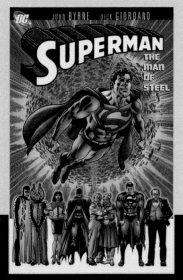

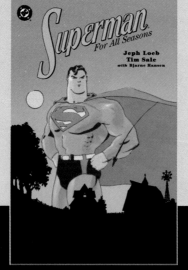

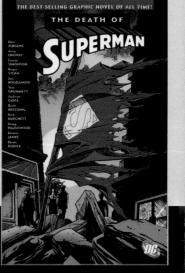